# FINNISH DIASPORA II:
## United States

*Edited by* Michael G. Karni

Papers of the FINN FORUM conference,
held in Toronto, Ontario, Canada,
November 1 - 3, 1979.

1981
The Multicultural History Society of Ontario
Toronto

The Multicultural History Society of Ontario is grateful to the
Ontario Ministry of Culture and Recreation for its continuing support. We also wish to thank the Multiculturalism Directorate, Office of the Secretary of State for its generous assistance in the
preparation of the manuscript.

Finnish Diaspora

ISBN 0-919045-08-1 (set)
ISBN 0-919045-10-3 (Volume 2)

The Multicultural History Society of Ontario
43 Queen's Park Crescent East
Toronto, Ontario M5S 2C3

# Contents

# Preface

The two volumes on the Finnish Diaspora are a result of an extraordinary conference that took place in Toronto, Canada in November 1979. The Multicultural History Society of Ontario drew Finnish scholars from throughout the world to present papers on Finnish migration and about the life of the ethnic group, especially in North America, but everywhere it had dispersed throughout the world.

North American Finns from every walk of life, of every political shading and from major settlements as far apart as Fairbanks, Alaska, Lake Worth, Florida, or Fitchburg, Massachussetts attended. Papers delivered and discussed by participants did not try to veil the significance and persistence of historic cleavages in the community between socialists and churchgoers, between temperance advocates and free-thinkers. Differences of attitude, and even the shadow of conflict among Finnish Americans, Finnish Canadians, and Finns about the Finnish Diaspora and the best methods and agenda for studying it also appeared. The audience for each session in most instances over 200 strong, reflected all their differences of opinion as well.

For all this, the conference proved a celebration of wholeness as well. Finns in Australia, South America, South Africa, the U.S. and Canada had survived the ordeal of immigration, had profited from acculturation, survived their own factiousness, had created a healthy culture of their own, neither slavish to the changing vogues of the Finland they had left nor lost in the melting pot blandness of the countries to which they had emigrated.

During the four days of meetings, the same audience that sat rapt while an amateur trouper of the old Finnish American theatre regaled them with anecdotes of the stage, listened attentively and critically to papers heavy with demographic and sociological jargon. When a historian offered a careful and scholarly account of a recent episode in Finnish migration history, members of the audience who had taken part in the events challenged and corrected some of his points. When papers were read on Finnish group survival in far-off continents, or about Finnish leadership in the cause of social justice in North America, the tiniest glimmer of smug cultural chauvinism drew together the scholars from Finland and Finnish North Americans. This volume, the continuing research engendered by the meetings, the general guide to Finnish migration archival sources that will emerge from the symposium, the transfer to the Archives of Ontario of the valuable Finnish Canadian Historical Society archives collection and the creation of a finding aid for it as well as the pride of participation of all those who attended are signals of the conference's success. The Finnish people have enabled the Multicultural History Society of Ontario to carry out its mandate to encourage serious ethnic research, to preserve the historical record of all ethnic groups, and to bring the lore and knowledge of the past of which the community is the repository into alliance with the methodology of modern historical scholarship.

Robert F. Harney

# Introduction

As the essays published in these two volumes clearly show, Finn Forum '79 was a success. The quality and quantity of presentations bespeak a growing number of younger scholars in Canada, Finland and the United States with an interest in the movement of Finns to all parts of the world during the last century. The study of Finnish migration has been enjoying a steady growth for the past ten years. Begun originally in Ohio during the Depression by Professor John I. Kolehmainen, and continued intermittently by scholars such as Professor A. William Hoglund, the late 1960s saw the beginning of an important upsurge in the formal study of Finns on the move.

A conference called "The Finnish Experience in the Western Great Lakes Region: New Perspectives" was held in the spring of 1974 at the University of Minnesota, Duluth, and indirectly sponsored by University of Minnesota's Immigration History Research Centre the IHRC. Several scholars from Turku University in Finland were present and made presentations. To make the conference clearly international, the Migration Institute of the city of Turku offered to publish the proceedings jointly with the IHRC. The volume of proceedings appeared in 1975 with the same title as the conference. The Duluth conference was followed by a similar undertaking at Lakehead University, Thunder Bay, in the spring of 1975. The proceedings, titled *The Finnish Experience*, were published in 1976 as a special issue of *Lakehead University Review*. In the summer of 1976, during the Finnish bicentennial celebration in Hancock, Michigan, a smaller conference was held after which a group of scholars gathered and voted to begin publishing *Finnish Americana.* Since then, three annual issues have appeared. When the essays published after the Duluth and Thunder Bay conferences are compared with the two volumes of *The Finnish Diaspora,* one can quickly see how Finn Forum '79 in Toronto supersedes all previous attempts at exploring Finnish migration to different parts of the world. Sponsored by the Multicultural History Society of Ontario, and held at the Ontario Institute for Studies in Education, Finn Forum '79 was more complete and the papers on a higher level of quality than any conference thus far held. Subject areas which the Duluth conference had to overlook for lack of anyone to investigate them are treated here. Two papers treating Finnish women, for example, appear beside others such as those on Laestadian groups in North America, on temperance, and on the rich dramatic traditions in Canada and the United States. Papers on Matti Kurikka and his experiences at Sointula, on the Canadian cooperative movement, on the study of "Finglish," on the early life of Finns in Toronto, and even on Finnish settlements in Saskatchewan detail for the first time some of the activities under taken by Finns in Canada. In addition, fifteen papers by Finnish scholars and students show us what has been going on in Finland with the materials gathered and microfilmed in North America. Finally, papers on Finnish migration to Sweden, Australia, Africa and South America have done away once and for all with the provincialism of the previous conferences. Finn Forum '79 was, indeed, a truly international undertaking.

The success of Finn Forum '79, however, can only be understood in terms of the nearly fifty years of collecting efforts which have provided scholars with the sources necessary for their work. In North America the first agency to begin collecting Finnish American documents was the Finnish American Historical Archives of Suomi College, Hancock, Michigan. Begun in 1932, expanded and catalogued after the Second World War, Suomi's archives were for years the only place in North America where serious study of migrating Finns could be done. In the early 1960s and continuing into the 1970s, the Immigration History Research Center, University of Minnesota, began a successful attempt to gather those documents remaining uncollected in the United States. The IHRC also joined in a working agreement with Turku University to share by means of microfilm each other's documents, either in Finland or the United States. Also in the 1960s, Turku University began its collecting effort by sending teams of young scholars to North America to collect and microfilm immigration data. While these scholars sent some original documents back to Finland—newspapers, books, manuscript collections, periodicals—their real contribution was in the five hundred reels of microfilm they produced on trips to North America over a period of ten years. In 1974 the Migration Institute was established outside Turku University to coordinate the study of migration from Finland and to publish studies on the movement of Finns to all parts of the World. The Migration Institute also publishes a quarterly journal called *Siirtolaisuus/Migration* in Finnish, Swedish and English on the general topic of migration from Finland.

More recently, Canada has become active in the process of gathering records of migrants. In 1972 the Public Archives of Canada established the National Ethnic Archives Program to ensure the preservation of the cultural heritage of that third of the nation's population which is not French, British or Native. Among the collections in the program is one dealing with Canada's 60,000 Finns; this collection includes religious and labour documents as well as papers on individuals. The Public Archives also has a large collection of books and pamphlets reflecting the life of Finnish Canadians.

The Multicultural History Society of Ontario, sponsors of Finn Forum '79, has been in operation since 1976. Fulfilling a need for a special program to preserve and record the province's ethnic history, the Society aims to promote and advance studies on the history of all ethnocultural groups in Ontario, to collect and catalogue relevant materials—the written record, unpublished sources and oral history—to encourage the publication about groups in the province, and to publicize the contributions of all ethnic groups in Ontario. The Society also cooperates in the retrieval of documents from foreign countries and research centres outside the province. Exchanges have been arranged, for example, with the Emigration History Research Center of Turku University and the Migration Institute of Finland as well as with the IHRC of the University of Minnesota. Finally the Society publishes a biannual bulletin called *Polyphony*, designed to make known the work of the Society and simultaneously point out the richness of ethnic life in the province of Ontario.

The Multicultural History Society of Ontario led off a long series of planned ethnic conferences with Finn Forum '79, and it is responsible for the publication of both volumes of *The Finnish Diaspora*. The weekend of November 1-3, 1979 was exciting and fulfilling as scholars from three nations gathered in Toronto to ponder the fate of modern Finnish emigrants to all parts of the

world. To the Multicultural History Society of Ontario we owe
thanks for a successful and interesting conference, to Paula Groen-
berg of the Society, who guided us efficiently and cheerfully
through the conference and the editing of these proceedings. To
Diane Mew who edited the English and Finglish with patience and
skill. And to the scholars from Finland, who have vowed to hold
the next conference in the Old Country, we wish them luck and we
promise them good attendance from North America.

Dr. Michael G. Karni
New Brighton, Minnesota, 1980

FINLAND

SOURCES OF EMIGRANTS
BY PROVINCE
1893-1920

OULU
39,352

KUOPIO
10,367

VAASA
134,490

MIKKELI
5,409

TURKU-
PORI
41,775

HAME
9,892

VIIPURI
17,681

UUDENMAA
14,400

Helsinki

Hanko

0       75       150
Scale in Miles

Based on Passport Data of the Finnish Government

# The Finnish Immigrant Experience in the United States

## John Kolehmainen

The United States, as the poet Walt Whitman so aptly said, "is not merely a nation, but a teeming nation of nations." Englishmen, Frenchmen, Spaniards, Dutch, Swedes, Norwegians, and scores of other peoples, representing every race and religion, have responded to the wonderful words inscribed on the base of the Statue of Liberty: "Give me your tired, your poor, your huddled masses yearning to breathe free, the wretched refuse of your teeming shore. Send these, the homeless, the tempest-tost, to me! I lift my lamp beside the golden door."

Among this varied company seeking new homes in the Western Eldorado were some 380,000 folk from faraway northern Suomi or Finland. Although several hundred persons of Finnish origin had taken part in the notable colonial venture known to history as New Sweden, mass emigration from Finland did not begin until the year 1865, nearly half a century after the coming of the Swedes and the Norwegians. The Finns thus were among the more recent immigrants.

Three major questions will be raised in this paper. First, why did the emigrants leave Finland? Second, where did they settle in the United States? Third, what has been the character of Finnish immigrant life, and what contributions, if any, have they made to the life of their adopted and beloved America?

# Why Did They Leave Finland?

It is on this epic theme, woven out of strands of despair and hope, sorrow and joy, misgivings and courage, that the story of the American Finns, like that of every other immigrant group, begins. Years ago, a Finnish poet told the story in charming brevity:

> I left because I felt
>> The home clearing too confining.
> I left because the home threshold
>> Rose too high.
> I left because bread
>> Always scarce, was now no more.
> I expected good fortune out in the world,
>> Since it did not roost under my home roof.
> I left to assure
>> A more secure old age,
> To provide a loving mother
>> With a happier twilight.
> I left, nay, not a traitor
>> To my land and people many,
> I left, for kinfolk drew me,
>> Necessity compelled, need commanded.

Economic considerations, thus, prompted many Finns to leave their land of birth. "The heart pleaded No, but the stomach commanded Yes." Agriculture, especially in northern Finland, was handicapped by a "thin and barren" soil and by a short growing season: "The April wind can wipe the tender rye-shoots off the soil and an August frost freeze the sap in the half-ripe ears of summer corn."

The lot of the country's many tenant farmers was deplorable. Dismal, indeed, was Prince Kropotkin's pen portrait of the Finnish tenant farmer of the 1890s: "He gnaws at his hard-as-stone rye-flour cake which he bakes twice a year; he has with it a morsel of fearfully salted cod and a drink of skimmed milk. How dare I talk to him of American machines, when all that he can raise must be sold to pay rent and taxes?"

Even worse was the condition of the landless cottagers, the agricultural dayworkers and hired hands. Some of them counted as their solitary blessing the privacy of a crude hut that stood far back in the submarginal zone, usually at the foot of a barren hillside. It was, a poet recalled,

A tiny log dwelling, a cheerless cottage,
    A low hut beside the hill.
Supper waits on the table:
    Black bread, a piece of fish,
Potatoes in a gnarled wooden bowl.
    Salt water, a pitcher of skimmed milk,
These were the delicacies.

The spectre of famine hung low over all these people. Memories of the horrible years from 1862 to 1868 were still fresh in many minds. From harrowing personal experience, many a Finn could say:

I remember, though a child,
    When frost stole the harvest.
We suffered hunger then,
    There was no food to be blest.
Mother cried until her death,
    Father sank, sorrowed,
Tears streaked his furrowed cheeks,
    As bread in vain we begged and borrowed.

The introduction in 1878 of compulsory military service, in addition, drove many peaceloving young men to America. Youth everywhere "had passports ready in their pockets, prepared to leave the country at a moment's notice." The russification policies of Russia in the years following 1899 intensified discontent in the small grand duchy and added hundreds and thousands to the lists of prospective emigrants.

There were, of course, many other factors contributing to the rise and spread of the America Fever, but perhaps the aforementioned will suffice. It was difficult to resist going to the new world, whatever the reason. Steamship companies and their resourceful agents filled the air with enticing appeals. In endless letters from America, too, came not only encouraging summons, but tickets and money. Frequently, indeed,

A letter came, a steamship ticket,
A bitter cup of coffee drunk in parting.
The emigrant left,
The home wept.

The Finnish emigrants were ordinary people, largely rural folk from the northern provinces of Vaasa and Oulu, with fine dreams and strong arms and a generous supply of common sense.

4    *J. Kolehmainen*

In varying degree, perhaps, they shared the national traits so vividly set down by the Finnish writer Zachris Topelius:

> The Finns are marked by their hardened, patient, passive strength; resignation; perseverance allied to a certain obstinacy; a slow contemplative way of thinking; an unwillingness to become angry, but a tendency, when anger has been aroused, to indulge in unmeasured wrath; coolness in deadly peril, but caution afterwards; an inclination for waiting, deferring, living for the day, interrupted sometimes by unseasonable haste; adherence to the old and well-known, and aversion to everything new; attention to duty, a law-abiding habit of mind; love of liberty; hospitality; a predilection for religious meditation, revealing itself in true piety, which, however, is apt to have too much respect for the mere letter. It takes the Finn some time to thaw and become intimate, but his friendship, when won, is to be depended upon. He is often late, often stands in your way without noticing it; does not greet a greeting friend until he has passed him, keeps quiet when he had better speak, and sometimes speaks when he ought to keep quiet. He is one of the first soldiers in the world, but one of the last arithmeticians; sees gold at his feet, but cannot make up his mind to pick it up; remains poor when others become rich ... Lastly, we must not forget their love of tales, of proverbs, riddles, exercices of thought, and a disposition for satire which mercilessly ridicules their own follies and those of others.

An English traveller saw the Finns leaving the seaport of Hanko, bound for America. "Any land," he said, "would be enriched by their patient endurance, industry, and resource."

"Not tar, not pitch, not Kauhava knives, nor birchbark knapsacks nor birchbark shoes, were Finland's gift to America, but—people!"

They came to America, not to frolic and play, but to work and live.

> I was born a Finn,
> I had to leave my childhood home.
> In search of work, in order to live,
> To a foreign land I had to roam.

# Where Are the American Finns?

In what regions of the United States did they settle? What factors determined the pattern of their settlement? These are the questions that concern us here. When a traveller observes that the American obstetrician prudently has added the word "Synnytyksiä" to his signpost, and the dentist the word "Hammaslääkäri," he knows he is in Finnish country. Sometimes it is the community's picturesque place name that reveals the presence of the Finns: Kalevala, Lönnrot, and Salo in Minnesota, Kaleva, Nisula, and Tapiola in Michigan, Oulu and Wäinö in Wisconsin, Pelto and Savo in the Dakotas. Such unmistakable evidence of Finnish settlement, however, is likely to be encountered in only a few regions: Michigan's Upper Peninsula, northern Minnesota, portions of Massachusetts, New York, Ohio, Wisconsin, California, Oregon, and Washington.

The heavy settlement of Finns in the northern regions of America naturally has invited speculation. Many have seen in it the play of geographical forces; in their opinion the "indispensable concomitants" of Finnish settlement have been "cold, snow, boulder-strewn areas, lakes typical of a glaciated terrain." Yet other factors also persuaded the immigrants to set up their households north of the Mason Dixon Line. Who, for example, could resist the shrewd land agent's description of Upper Michigan as a veritable Eden that counted among its varied blessings "a beautiful nature, healthful atmosphere, many lakes rich with fish, streams and rapids"; a domain eternally safe from "cyclones, snowslides, hail storms, floods, famines . . . and poisonous snakes." Then again, opportunities for employment, to which we will refer later, were largely concentrated in the northern states.

Yet the Finnish immigrant was, as an Upper Michigan newspaper correctly appraised in 1878, "as curious as Columbus." There was a vast world beyond the familiar settlements to explore, if not conquer. Long before the gold rush of the late 1890s, adventure-seeking Finns were trekking the wide expanses of Alaska. Far in the opposite direction, immigrants, falling victim to the magic of magnolia, established settlements in Creole, Mississippi; Port Richey, Florida; Galveston, Texas; and elsewhere. Deeper yet in the South, bold immigrants launched agricultural colonies in Cuba and Argentina.

Infrequently the northerners reported satisfactory adjustment to novel southern conditions. One of them, for example, wrote from

Denny, Mississippi, in 1906: "Winter had begun to harass me in Canada, so I bid it an eternal farewell." In the land of perpetual summer he confidently hoped to create "a paradise better than that of Adam." Yet for the most part the earlier Finnish settlements in the South failed to thrive. Many of them, duplicating the fate of an Argentine colony, fell before the unceasing onslaughts of "mosquitoes, heat, and droves of grasshoppers." They, like the first Finnish settlement along the Delaware River more than three centuries earlier, were destined to perish, leaving little evidence of their courageous, if short, history.

The immigrants' first need was, of course, employment. "We immigrants," confessed a Hancock, Michigan, journal, "came to America penniless." Inevitably their first thoughts were of "work, good wages, and savings." Newcomers quickly realized that "work, irrespective of its type, was necessary and had to be obtained first of all. What kind of work was secondary."

The Finnish immigrants, like many others, were well suited to the demands of heavy manual labour. They were, in the words of one of their number, "healthy, stiff-necked, endowed with the strength of a bear and the endurance of a mule." And most of them, duly instructed by emigrant guidebooks and anti-emigration tracts, sorrowfully realized that it was impossible—even in America —to "whittle gold with a wooden knife." "With sweated brow," was the dire prediction, "you must eat your bread."

The diversity of Finnish employment, while perhaps inevitable, was impressive. From Rockport, Quincy and Vinal Haven in New England to Rocklin, California, thousands of Finns laboriously took their bread from stone and sang the songs of the quarry workers:

> Stones, stones, crushers of stones—
> > Our work is hard, but there's zest in our
> > bones.
> There's no place here for an untrained mate,
> > With a sledge that's sixteen pounds in weight.
> And there's no soft shale, but the healthy crew
> > Just sing with a good tobacco chew.

Larger numbers yet toiled in the dark depths of coal mines in Nanty Glo, Pennsylvania; Clinton, Indiana; and Rock Springs, Wyoming; in the hot and wet iron mines in Ishpeming, Michigan, and Ely, Minnesota; in copper mines in Calumet, Michigan, and Butte, Montana; in silver mines in Utah, gold mines in California and the Black Hills. In America, the "mine's black mantle" covered thousands of Finns, a place where the rays of day never brought forth life. A black void it remained to many of them, where "a strong wind blew, like a powerful whirlwind that crashed, rumbled, whistled, and howled—as though all the underground spirits had rushed forth from their caves in attack."

Industrial establishments of every description recruited an endless stream of Finnish works—a chair factory in Gardner, Massachusetts; a textile mill in near-by Maynard; a wire mill in Waukegan, Illinois; a tin mill in Monessen, Pennsylvania; railroad shops in Brainerd, Minnesota.

Lumbering and logging, too, attracted hordes of immigrants. Was there, in truth, a camp from Maine to Louisiana, from Georgia to California, that did not have one or more Jussis from Finland, skilled axemen and silent, uncomplaining woodsmen, who on rare occasions might break out into song?

There is a happy timber lad,
Who in the morning wakes,
And to his work most cheerfully,
His keen-edged axe he takes.
In him there is no surly mind
Nor thoughts unworthy, no.
'Tis just his nature that is proud,
And cheeks so red they glow.

Other Finns found their calling in the hard and fickle fishing industry, supplying markets near and far with the cod of New England, the trout of Lake Superior, and the salmon of the Oregon country. On Lake Superior, for example, late fall and spring fishing meant "lashing gales, blizzards, bitter cold and sometimes sudden death and disaster." Foam-crested wreaths rose to mark the graves of Finnish fishermen lost at sea.

Many immigrants saw the opportunity of performing profitable middleman's functions in the rising Finnish communities, and established food stores, bakeries, clothing shops, and the like.

Finally, many Finns, responding to the call of the Finnish rural spirit, resumed the ancient and tranquil occupation of agriculture. Often it was the deficiencies in their industrial and mining employments that compelled the immigrants to return to the land: the danger of accidents in the mines; the spectre of silicosis in the quarries; the revolting conditions in the logging camps; the unsatisfactory conditions in the factories.

Sometimes the decision to seek security on the land came as the result of the assiduous efforts of aggressive realty companies and glib-tongue land agents. Often it was the driving force of economic depress, unemployment, and strikes.

Whatever the reason, nearly one-half of the Finnish immigrants sought refuge in forty-acre holdings wrought out of the winderness. In the words of a Finnish-American poet,

> What straying child of our mankind
> Has lost himself where the forest sighs
> And the wolfpack runs and cries?
> A Finn, no doubt, who wished to find
> A haven in the woods.

# What Have Been The Significant Character And Contributions Of The Finnish Immigrants?

Many years ago, a Finnish-American poet asked his fellow immigrants:

> Is bread life's only measure?
> A well-filled stomach the only treasure?
> Is all else, striving, sacrifice,
> Mere folly, not worth the price?

As if in answer, a church, a temperance society, a workingman's association, a cooperative store, stood in well-nigh every Finnish settlement. Each of them possessed "a holy and high ideal," mightier than "the power of gold." Each of them proclaimed a noble goal: the Kingdom of God; the overthrow of King Rum; justice for the wage earner; and the establishment of a Cooperative Commonwealth. "If there are no ideals," these characteristic immigrant institutions averred, "there is no real life, but only foam atop a wave's crest."

In his "Finnish-American Hymn," a noted immigrant musician urged his brethren to remain faithful to their Lutheran heritage, saying:

> This land, where fate has led me,
> This land is my land now.
> Its laws, customs, I shall observe,
> Its duties fulfill, I vow.
> But a solemn voice within me,

> Again and again saith,
> My soul will find security,
> Only in my Father's Faith.

Most of the immigrant churchgoers have heeded such counsel and stayed within the Lutheran fold. But whereas a single church held all old country Lutherans within its ample bosom, in the new world there emerged three major Lutheran bodies: the Suomi Synod, which before its merger with the Lutheran Church in America had its headquarters and its theological seminary and Junior College at Hancock, Michigan; the National Lutheran Church, which has merged with the Missouri Synod; and the Apostolic Lutheran Church, which had remained outside the American Lutheran movements. In addition, there have been a number of Lutheran congregations which have remained independent. A relatively small number of immigrants were won over by the Congregational, Methodist, Unitarian and Pentecostalist churches.

Temperance societies rose in response to a twofold need. First of all, they grew out of a concern that drunkenness and its allegedly related evils of gambling, dancing, smoking, and the like, threatened the very foundations of immigrant life. Yet there were other forces helping to create and to spread the temperance movement. The societies were called upon to carry on highly significant cultural and social functions. Through their modest insurance plans, they took some of the sting out of the unexpected shocks of accidents, illnesses and deaths. They sponsored dramatic and choral groups, bands and public speaking clubs. They maintained small libraries and reading rooms with well-thumbed books and newspapers. They tried to meet the recreational needs of the immigrants through folk games and dances, festivals and outings. Virtually all of the temperance societies have now disappeared; institutionally, the temperance crusade has come to an end. Yet there remains among the surviving immigrants a solid, unshakable devotion to temperance principles. Old crusaders live in memories and in hope. Days are spent in reliving a past, glorious battle, and in composing worthy epitaphs: "Temperance societies were not born to live forever. They rose to meet special needs, to guard the people in time of great danger, to encourage and educate them. And when the temperance societies pass away, they will do so in honor. They deserve to be remembered with pride, for they have given many good citizens to America."

The vision of social justice for industrial wage-earners found many followers among the Finnish immigrants. In the early 1900s, Socialist locals began to appear throughout immigrant America.

Using the weapons of education and peaceful persuasion, they devoted their energies to the creation of a "beautiful Bellamy Age." It was an appealing picture that one of their number painted:

> Let us make heaven here on earth,
> A bounty for those who work and dare.
> Let us make heaven here:
> A home, peace, and ample fare.
> Warm shirts for the children,
> Silver-stringed kanteles, many a book,
> Flowers underneath the window,
> A lovely birch in a secluded nook.
> Moments of rest
> Under the alder's greenest crest.

However, the dark clouds of industrial discord fell across the immigrant working class movement. In 1914 a militant Industrial Unionist movement challenged the Finnish Socialist Federation; in 1919-1920 it was the Communist intruder that divided the ranks of the working class. The dreams of a socialist commonwealth, of the One Big Union, and of proletarian revolution, have largely come to naught.

"Those Finns," wrote an American, "have consumer co-ops for everything from baby shoes to coffins." Impressive, indeed, was the variety of fields in which the Finnish immigrants experimented, for a time very successfully, with the Rochdale Principles. There were cooperative apartments and homes, bakeries, banks and credit unions, clothing stores, farms and dairies and creameries, fisheries, grocery stores, halls, insurance companies, mortuaries, newspapers, oil associations, restaurants and boarding-houses, steambaths and telephone associations. Many of the cooperatives, to be sure, remained small and unpretentious, like those once hidden in the remote recesses of northern Michigan, Wisconsin and Minnesota. But there were giants as well: the flourishing retail stores at Maynard and Fitchburg, Massachusetts; Waukegan, Illinois; and Cloquet, Minnesota; the impressive Central Cooperative Wholesale of Superior, Wisconsin; and the huge United Farmers Incorporated of Fitchburg. So important were the Finnish cooperatives in their heyday that an American writer felt moved to say, "Among the Finns, cooperation has evolved to the high plane of a culture, a mode of life ... around it the Finns move and find their being." As the immigrants passed into history, so too have most of the cooperatives they founded and sacrificed to maintain.

Finally, the Finnish immigrants in the United States had a flourishing press. Indeed, in the years since 1876, when the first Finnish-language newspaper appeared in the new world, there have been more than 350 immigrant newspapers and magazines. All of them, in one way or another, contributed to the fulfillment of the role of the foreign-language press in America, which was, in their own words: "To introduce the immigrants to the customs, political and social institutions of this country, and to make known to them the obligations of citizenship. To keep the immigrants in touch with the Old and the New Worlds."

Immigrant newspapers and periodicals were an inevitable and indispensable feature of Finnish life in America. As one newspaper so wisely said, the immigrant and his language press were inextricably bound together, the one unable to exist without the other. At this moment only four Finnish-language newspapers survive in the United States, two in the East (the Fitchburg, Massachusetts, Raivaaja, and the Brooklyn, New York, *New Yorkin Uutiset*), and two in the midwest (the Superior, Wisconsin, *Työmies-Eteenpäin*, and the New York Mills, Minnesota, *Amerikan Uutiset*).

These institutions—the churches, the temperance societies, the workingman's associations, the cooperatives, and the Finnish-language press—have made significant contributions to the life of the immigrants, and through them, to the life of America.

There have been, of course, other contributions, some of them made by specific individuals, like the Saarinens in architecture, Hannikainen and Nisonen in music, Wuorinen, Kalijärvi, Nikander and Kantonen in education. But more impressive is the contribution of a host of unnamed men and women who transformed the wilderness into prosperous farms, demonstrated the values of cooperative enterprise, gave others a touch of their idealism and shared their vision of a better America, educated themselves, and brought up new generations of Americans who look to Finland for their roots.

For, in the last analysis, the achievement of the Finns in America is a collective achievement. Not many distinguished names appear in the pages of Finnish-American history. Rather it is a moving story of humble, hard-working, honest people, who by patient toil and frugal living, found happiness in their—America.

# Finnish Immigrant Letter-Writers: Reporting from the United States to Finland, 1870s to World War I

*A. William Hoglund*

"Fate has created us into wanderers."
— *Vilma Nummela*[1]

Thousands of Finnish immigrant letter-writers roamed searching for jobs in the United States. Although their search inspired Finns to write poems, songs and stories about homeless wanderers and even a novel about tramps,[2] no one dealt with the theme more persistently than the letter-writers themselves. With limited opportunities for obtaining employment and land in Finland between the 1870s and World War One, the writers dreamed of material well-being in the United States. Consequently, their dream sent them wandering to work in obscure places such as Nemo in South Dakota and Nanty Glo in Pennsylvania as well as better-known communities such as Hancock in Michigan, Astoria in Oregon, and Fitchburg in Massachusetts. After reaching their destinations in the United States, these newcomers wrote confidently about job prospects and American experiences in their first letters to friends and relatives in Finland. Eventually the periodic occurrence of unemployment and other difficulties forced some writers, however, to modify their rosy accounts and even to return to their homeland. In contrast, other Finns remained in America often still writing letters about their almost constant search for better opportunities.

Within a decade after the main influx of immigrants began from Finland to the United States in the 1860s, the *Oulun Wiikko-*

*Sanomia* (Oulu Weekly News) was printing their letters. One such letter described its writer's new home since 1869—Minnesota—as the most ideal spot in the world, where workers could even earn $3.50 a day and no one need fear public officials or suffer from rigid class distinctions.[3] In 1876 the Oulu newspaper printed an equally appreciative but longer report by Alexander Leinonen who said that Finns without food or work at home could obtain them in America. If prosperity eluded anyone like the Michigan Finns who were complaining about low wages and economic exploitation, Leinonen explained that a worker had only himself to blame because one's own efforts determined material success.[4] These assessments were not shared, however, by a writer in Winona, Minnesota, who warned that no one should believe the glowing accounts and leave Finland. His letter stated that American Finns were suffering economic hardships and losing their religious commitments.[5] Its message underscored the impact of the prevailing depression in the United States that helped to limit the number of immigrants from Finland to about 3,000 during the 1870s. Nevertheless, these early letters whetted the interest of more Finns in coming to America.

The amount of letter-writing increased during the main period of emigration from Finland between the 1880s and World War One which brought upwards of 300,000 Finns to the United States. In 1894 alone, according to the *Uusi Suometar* (New Finn) of Helsinki, American Finns sent the bulk of the 479,470 overseas letters received in the provinces of Vaasa and Oulu.[6] Although possibly an average of ten to sixteen letters were sent per immigrant that year, the actual number was probably nearer and even below the lower figure.[7] In addition, the two provinces got 148,732 bundles of printed materials consisting of newspapers and other publications mainly from America. The *Uusi Suometar* concluded that almost as many newspapers printed in America as in Finland were read in Vaasa and Oulu.[8] This volume of newspapers and letters was an index of the high literacy rate among the American Finns which exceeded that of most other immigrant groups entering the United States.[9]

Nevertheless, the typical letter was an unpretentious composition, usually written on two to four sheets of poor quality paper. Sometimes the first sheet was embellished with a floral design and a printed verse expressing sentiments about friendship and love or assurances that the old homeland had not been forgotten in a strange new country. In 1914, for instance, Emmi Niemi of Fitchburg chose a letterhead proclaiming that, although circumstances forced a person to leave his land of birth, he returned like a migratory bird to its home.[10] Perhaps writers regarded such verses as adding literary flourishes to their letters which were often poorly written, ignored rules of spelling, punctuation and capitalization, and used "Finnicized" words from English such as *dollari* (dollar) and *kupai* (good-by). Using rather direct and simple declarative prose, moreover, the writers did not develop elaborate narratives.

Their failure to produce long accounts resulted partly from the lack of literary experience as well as leisure time for writing. Writers like Tilda Laaksonen of Ashtabula, Ohio, and Anna Mäki of Telluride, Colorado, apologized for their inability to express themselves better. Laaksonen said that, although she used a lot of words, her thoughts were unclearly stated, while Mäki said that it would be easier to say much more about her personal experiences in a conversation than a letter.[11] Another correspondent, John Pietilä, observed that it was difficult to write after working all day in a lumber camp in Hoquiam, Washington. Pietilä explained that a day's manual labour left him with little physical strength to use a pencil.[12] Many writers were also preoccupied with monotonous work routines and did not want to discuss the same activities repeatedly, saying merely that they were still employed in the same places as before and assuming that their readers would remember earlier details. All of these considerations therefore gave the letters a cryptic quality.

No regular schedule was ordinarily followed in writing letters for any great length of time. While some Finns felt obliged to write every month or so, particularly to a parent or spouse and to number their letters consecutively enabling their readers thereby to determine if any had been lost, other writers soon began to maintain contact more erratically after sending their first letters. They even let years elapse before writing again, as did Isak Kuusisto of Aberdeen, Washington. Apologizing for his failure to write in eight years after doing so during his first three years in America, Kuusisto wrote to his parents in September 1916, uncertain whether or not they were still alive. His reply to their answer was delayed until May 1917, because, as he explained, there had been no pencil available in the forest where he was employed.[13] It was common for other writers also to express regrets about their frequent failures to write promptly, giving such excuses as their own carelessness, lack of time, and life of "sin."[14] In 1896 another reason was given by Nikolai Lintula of Fall River, Massachusetts, who blamed his moving in search of work which presumably left him without a permanent address.[15] Both lost letters and slow mail deliveries, moreover, disrupted further the maintenance of any regular exchange of correspondence.

Because of the somewhat irregular pattern of corresponding, the typical letter was designed usually to serve different purposes all at once.[16] Invariably, a letter began and ended with profuse expressions of greetings and best wishes. It also commonly reported on its writer's health and mentioned sending money gifts, and less frequently, photographs. Besides reporting special news from time to time on such other matters as marriages, births, deaths and gossip, they gave advice sometimes on managing family affairs in Finland. Another purpose for writing was to answer inquiries from Finland seeking information about individuals, advice on whether or not to emigrate, and requests for money and steamship tickets. In one case, a writer's parents asked him to discuss his religious attachments, probably because of reports that America destroyed a person's faith.[17] On the other hand, letter writers asked questions themselves about family affairs such as the settlement of estates and the failure to write more frequently and to acknowledge receiving correspondence and money. Young writers were particularly curious about social affairs and courtships; for instance, August Aalto of California and Andrew Piipponen of South Dakota inquired about former girl friends.[18] Besides serving these various purposes, the letters also assessed the rightness of coming to America.

However, the main purpose to begin writing letters was to inform relatives and friends of a newcomer's safe arrival and reception in America. Often newcomers such as Johan W. Kuusisto began by recounting details of their trip. In 1902 Kuusisto marvelled at the different modes of transport bringing him by way of Copenhagen to England and then across the Atlantic Ocean to New York from whence he travelled to Cloquet, Minnesota. His main complaint was about the poor food served on shipboard in contrast to the incredibly good menu of breads and meats served daily at his boarding house in Cloquet. Although he had not yet secured employment which materialized later at a sawmill, there was no doubt in his mind about the prospect of getting a job.[19] Other travellers such as Ellen Länberg singled out such new experiences as eating oranges in Liverpool and her reception at New Haven, Connecticut, by a friend who wore "fine" silk clothes and her sister who helped her to secure employment as a domestic servant for $8 per month.[20] In 1960 still another newcomer, Anselmi Neva, wrote his first letter on the day that he began working as a trammer in a Michigan copper mine. Neva indicated that it was impossible to reimburse his family for expenses immediately because of the need to buy 14 dollars' worth of work clothes. Earning $1.25 per day on his new job and paying only $16 per month for board, he left the impression that the debt would soon be discharged.[21] By reporting such details about their arrival, reception and jobs, all of these writers suggested that their friends and relatives had no reason to worry about them. In addition, the writers wanted perhaps to allay any anxieties which they themselves might have felt.

The first letters also aften reassured the recipients homesickness had not overwhelmed their writers, who emphasized that even the lack of jobs did not make them yearn to return home. While Matti Knuuttila, who was without a job during his first three weeks in Ashtabula, denied feeling homesick, John Pietilä, who was employed by a lumber camp in Washington during a rainy season, did not want to return home. Pietilä emphasized that he would be happy even in a worse place and no longer remembered anything about Finland more than once a day on the average.[22] Other newcomers such as Isak Kuusisto were not lonely, associating with relatives and other countrymen in America. Six months after arriving to work with Finns in a lumber camp at Newberry, Michigan, Kuusisto confided that he already felt at home.[23] Another newcomer, Selma Walkama, was overwhelmed by her reception in Aberdeen, In 1914 her first letter happily reported that young fellows "treated" her by escorting her to theatres and Finnish halls and were willing to do so every night. Walkama's letter also observed that her escorts were more "high toned" than an acquaintance in Finland.[24] Still other newcomers, too, felt less homesick in communities with Finnish-speaking persons. The opportunity to consult with experienced fellow immigrants speaking their language made them more secure and contented in the new environment.

Unlike their relatively happy countrymen, however, some newcomers confessed to homesickness. The chances were that they had become isolated from their countrymen, like the domestic servant who complained about loneliness in Worcester, Massachusetts. After staying two months with relatives in that city, the servant became homesick in her employer's home where she was rarely to speak with Finns. The only source of social life, she reported, was a local Finnish temperance society which she reluctantly joined.[25] Another isolated immigrant wrote from the mining community of Neihart in Montana that the wilderness made him

lonely and inspired thoughts of Finland.[26] Even being with his
countrymen and sharing their activities, however, did not make
Manus Jokitalo content in Ironwood, Michigan. Expressing pleasure
at the opportunity to attend church, Jokitalo wanted to be with his
wife and family in Finland and concluded that it was better to live
in one's own homeland than elsewhere.[27] Besides longing to be
with their families and friends in Finland, writers also recalled
fondly social activities which had brought them together during
traditional holidays such as St. John's Day in June.

    Whether or not homesickness troubled them, many writers
had plans of returning to Finland eventually. Their expression of
intent was probably meant to reaffirm promises made to relatives
and friends before coming to America. Husbands such as John
Holma were notably reassuring to their wives. Working in Munis-
ing, Michigan, in 1911, Holma told his impatient wife that one had
to remain at least two years to earn enough money with which to
assist his family.[28] Unmarried newcomers such as Jalmari Ikala of
Ironwood similarly expected to stay only a short time, until they
had earned lots of money. Ignoring his parents' injunction not to
work underground in a mine where the pay was higher than on the
surface, Ikala explained that it would be nice to live in Finland
with a big pile of money from America.[29] Others reaffirmed similar
dreams of returning with money which they had shared before they
left Finland. Most writers could not set any definite timetable for
returning, however, because they usually lacked both money to buy
tickets for a speedy departure and time to evaluate fully their
American experiences.

    Generally, the new arrivals were impressed by their environ-
ment, tending to compare Finland unfavourably with America.
Writing from Roslyn, Washington, in 1905, a coal miner explained
why he thought America was better than Finland. He observed
that the United States was more advanced than Finland because
here a person was not limited to learning only from narrow-minded
pastors and officials.[30] In 1907 another newcomer in Fitchburg concluded that the two countries were different spiritually and materi-
ally. Although failing to have a job when he wrote his first letter,
he was sure that one could earn a livelihood more easily and gain
respect as a person in America.[31] These initial comparisons were
largely impressionistic since the writers had so little first-hand
experience of America. At the same time the writers were inclined
to assess their first experiences more positively because of negative
memories of their life in Finland.

    Their first comparisons focussed mainly on wages and material comforts in the two countries. If their friends and relatives did not understand the American system of money, writers began their comparisons often by equating the dollar with Finnish marks. Whatever their measure of comparison, they were persuaded that workers earned more money and could buy more goods in America. In 1902, for instance, Johan W. Kuusisto of Cloquet reported that one could readily earn a hired man's wages and need not pay much money for clothes. Furthermore, in his view, a person could buy all kinds of things at reasonable prices, making life pleasanter in America.[32] In 1905 August Jalo of Aberdeen agreed with him that a hired man was in a superior position in America, obtaining better food and living in a freer environment. Jalo meant that a worker no longer had to eat the skimpy meals provided by an arrogant and miserly employer as in Finland.[33] Similar points were made by Evert Lindroos, who was impressed that eggs were regularly served at his boarding house in Newport, New Hampshire, and that the food was better than in Finland; while Helmi Nyberg, a domestic servant in Fitchburg, reported that she ate at her employer's table better food than did gentlemen in Finland.[34] These initial comparisons reflected their writers' common experiences before coming to the United States. Coming from an agricultural economy with limited opportunities to earn money or to secure material comforts, the writers had no reason to doubt their first impressions if they found jobs quickly upon arrival.

These assessments of American opportunities were sooner or later deflated by discovering the inadequacy of wages and the lack of jobs during "bad times." Writers began talking more and more about low wages and job insecurity. Even in his first letter to his mother from Ashtabula in 1881, a worker reported the possibility of moving farther west to seek higher wages.[35] Others such as Viktor Nummela of Aberdeen had to move to new jobs because of periodic unemployment. While working at lumber mills between 1904 and 1911, Nummela reported three times that his job prospects were poor. In 1909, for instance, he blamed "hard times" for his latest bout with unemployment, and observed that many other men were also without work.[36] Other Finns similarly reported their recurring economic troubles, particularly during periods of seasonal unemployment and industrial strife as well as during economic depressions. If they could not cope with those difficulties, writers often moved in search of new jobs which meant reporting changes of address to correspondents in Finland. Besides confessing insecurity over their economic prospects, they were somewhat embarrassed because of their earlier boasts about material opportunities.

So their letters tried hard to explain why life was not always economically secure in America.

In particular, writers succumbed to the theory that presidential elections caused bad times and unemployment in the United States. After the depression of 1893 occurred during the administration of a Democratic president, the theory was repeated more widely than before. Recalling the crisis of 1893 which created widespread distress among their countrymen and frightened away prospective immigrants during the next six years, writers remained convinced that the theory was valid. In 1896 this conviction was expressed by a writer who blamed the reduction in jobs unloading ore boats at Ashtabula on the forthcoming election. Attributing the recent crisis to Democrats, moreover, the writer predicted that the election might produce bloodshed.[37] Subsequent elections, likewise, kept alive the fear that Democrats would bring bad times. In 1904, for instance, Viktor Nummela worried that, if the Democrats won, one would have to return to Finland or die from hunger in America.[38] Anticipating the electoral contest of 1912, Nummela still believed that bad times always began one year before an election.[39] The election of 1912 made Frans Erland of Nashwauk, Minnesota, equally apprehensive. Describing himself as one of thousands in a "tramp army" exploited by "capitalists" who forced them to move from place to place, Erland expressed uncertainty about job prospects pending the outcome of the election.[40] Although writers such as Erland also developed other explanations for the hardships of workers, the theory remained plausible until World War One, since unemployment problems kept recurring in election years.

Therefore, letter-writers began revising their initially confident expectations about opportunities to earn money in America. No matter how industrious and frugal he was, newcomers learned, a worker did not accumulate riches quickly. In 1890 a writer in Rockport, Massachusetts, confessed that it was not as easy as people thought in Finland to earn money in America. Even though practising extreme frugality, he said, his savings were modest because of low wages, high living costs, and part-time employment.[41] Vilma Nummela of Newport repeated the point that the opportunity to earn money was exaggerated, while Wäinö Lehto of Wolverine, Michigan, agreed, saying that "all that glittered was not gold."[42] Underscoring further their limited earnings, writers were apologetic about giving modest monetary gifts to relatives in Finland and delaying the repayment of debts. Thus August Lahti of Eldorado, Illinois, apologized for sending only $20 to his brother in 1912. After working seven years in the "land of gold," Lahti mused

that he had saved little money and did not know what his summertime prospects were for a job.[43] Writers said also that they kept
some cash reserves to pay for current needs such as work clothes
and to meet unexpected contingencies such as sickness or unemployment. Since life had so many uncertainties, one woman even
asked her father to send a promissory note for a gift of $100 in case
she might need it herself some day.[44] Besides sending small gifts
because of the lack of money, writers also indicated that they had
to adopt a modest lifestyle. In short, their message was clear that
one could not easily accumulate money though economic opportunities might be better than in Finland.

This sense of economic insecurity, furthermore, led writers to
regret their decision to leave Finland. Writers, who, like Urho
Koskinen, who had been determined to leave their homeland in
spite of family objections began to share these regrets. Working
every other day for $1.70 in New Castle, Pennsylvania, and earning
barely enough to pay for his board in 1911, Koskinen confessed
that the world had taught him to realize the heavy demands it
made on a person. Now he was ready to believe forever his father's
admonition that his parent had not compelled him to leave home
and that no one needed to earn his bread in America.[45] Viljam
Mäki of Biwabik, Minnesota, believed that life would have been
pleasanter for him in Finland than in the United States. But he also
reasoned that no matter where workers found themselves, life was
not pleasant because all had to work even if the weather was
bad.[46] Some deplored their lack of savings to pay for return tickets
to Finland. Describing the burdens of low pay and the inability of
workers to become millionaires in 1894, Isak Kangas hoped to
remain a bit longer and save enough to buy a ticket. Since no one
could get bread without labouring somewhere, he speculated that a
person could probably survive in Finland just as in America though
perhaps without enjoying as much good food. On the other hand,
he added, one at least would be home with relatives in the land of
one's birth.[47] Likewise, a worker in Chisholm, Minnesota, was
disillusioned and hoped to earn enough money to repay his debts
before returning to his parents. He confessed that life in America
was not as good as people imagined in Finland.[48]

If disappointed Finns managed to save money for tickets,
however, they were particularly inclined to return during periods
of unemployment and economic depressions. Also the chances of
anyone leaving were greatest if they had spent less than five years
in the United States. Twenty per cent or more of all Finns who
came to America probably returned to Finland.[49] At the same time

some Finns travelled back and forth between the two countries, for
ever trying to find the best opportunities.

On the other hand, the majority of immigrants remained,
struggling to find better jobs in America. After obtaining better
employment than their first jobs, Finns became less likely to leave.
Their decision to remain was also influenced by other considerations such as the lack of jobs in Finland or the pleasures of living in
America. Contented immigrants such as R. Oksa of Maynard, Massachusetts, refused to return home, saying that he was better off
than in Finland with his friends and pleasures in America. Oksa
observed further that he had fogotten his old home. It was terrible
to think of returning, he added, and could not understand why his
brother did not join him.[50] Others might have been tempted to
leave but remained as their fortunes improved. Reviewing his first
eight years in America in 1904, Sven Länberg told his parents that
he would have returned home if it had been impossible to leave his
first job in a Michigan iron mine. No one could long endure the
heavy labour or preserve his health in the mine, and only those
who were afraid to seek better jobs remained there. Becoming a
fisherman, learning to speak English, and acquiring American citizenship, he married a woman on the first of his four visits in
Finland.[51]

Although economic survival was difficult, others remained,
hoping to improve their position. After debating whether or not to
leave in 1910, one such worker in Eldorado, Illinois, decided to
stay at least for the time being to earn more money.[52] Others even
resolved to remain no matter how homesick they were and what
hardships faced them. Occasionally fantasizing that she had returned to Finland to escape her difficulties, Vilma Nummela explained that she forced herself to struggle for survival. Unable to
save money because of high living costs, she concluded, life was not
good anywhere for workers.[53] If newcomers like Nummela did not
give up their struggle—and most did not since they kept seeking
better jobs and eventually even becoming farmers—they also began
to raise families and to unite with each other in organizing
churches, temperance societies and labour organizations which prolonged their stay and made life more tolerable. So new organizational ties and family relationships further lessened their prospects
of leaving the United States.

Since economic uncertainty was most likely to send them
back home during their early years in America, the letter-writers
were usually cautious in advising friends and relatives to join them
from Finland. If newcomers such as Johan W. Kuusisto found

satisfying jobs and were contented, they became more inclined to encourage their correspondents to leave Finland. In 1902 Kuusisto advised one of his brothers to join him in Cloquet because a person could make a livelihood better in America than in Finland.[54] His brother Isak came but was more cautious in writing to another brother about joining them in 1905. Explaining that a healthy person could make a livelihood in America, he refused to offer any specific recommendation to his brother.[55] The second brother was more typical of the writers, realizing that is was impossible to guarantee jobs to anyone. Others were so discouraged that they warned others against emigrating like the newcomer in Fitchburg who advised his sister that no one should leave Finland. Deploring the lack of pleasures except in a saloon, he complained of loneliness, language difficulties and widespread economic distress which would intensify if Democrats won the presidential election of 1908.[56] Both he and the two Kuusisto brothers expressed the main types of advice. If conditions had been different under which they lived and worked, however, they probably might have revised their advice. In short, the writers were not agreed that it was wise to come to America at all times.

The tenor of advice to prospective immigrants reflected the economic experiences of the writers themselves. Since their letters discussed persistently changing job conditions, the writers gave advice logically based on an assessment of their own economic status. In other words, writers such as Antti Kangas of Ohio were not prepared to give the same kind of advice at all times. Because of the problems of finding jobs in 1882, Kangas discouraged anyone from leaving Finland until opportunities improved in the United States. In any event, the prospective immigrant had to make the decision himself realizing that it involved more than a short pleasant stroll into the woods. Remaining still cautious in a letter to a nephew in 1895, Kangas promised to send a ticket but warned the young man not to blame his benefactor in case prosperity eluded him.[57] Others, too, warned friends and relatives not to come during bad times. In 1907 Teodor Lehtinen of Proctor, Minnesota, did not think his brother should emigrate because of the prevailing low wages and the job scarcity as well as the economic uncertainty created by the impending presidential election.[58] Although offering the full range of possible advice, however, most letter-writers either qualified their counsel or left the decision to emigrate to their correspondents. Few, if any, wanted to be responsible for luring newcomers who might blame them for any failure to prosper.

Although leaving the decision to emigrate to their correspondents who had often asked for advice, however, letter-writers willingly counselled them about travel arrangements. In 1893, for instance, Henrik Mikkola of Ashtabula was unwilling to advise a friend on whether or not to come because of the economic difficulties and hard work. At the same time he gave extensive advice about travelling and particularly warned his friend not to bring Finnish-made shirts which would invite derision and to avoid a German steamship line which provided poor food for its passengers.[59] It was also common for writers like Mikkola to discuss coordinating one's departure with the best times for finding employment. In addition, the writers unintentionally provided continual advice by reporting about their own experiences.

During the heyday of this correspondence the editors of nationalist-minded newspapers in Finland printed some of the letters as warnings to persons who might want to go to America. Ever since the 1880s these editors, along with various public officials, rural landlords and clergymen had opposed emigration, arguing that it reduced the supply of farm labour, corrupted rural society and undermined the patriotic commitment of rural youth to military service.[60] Newspapers like the *Päivälehti* (Daily Journal) of Helsinki and the *Kaiku* (Echo) of Oulu published American letters usually portraying immigrant experiences with reservations. These letters spoke of the dangers of industrial accidents and the difficulties of obtaining employment.[61] Other letters deplored moral conditions in the mood expressed by a Michigan writer in the *Kaleva* of Oulu in 1904. His letter argued that, while America had greater material advantages than Finland, it lagged behind morally and caused Finns to drink and fight.[62] These newspapers also carried reports about disappointed Finns returning home as well as accounts of unemployment, economic crises and industrial accidents in the United States. Using such letters and reports to campaign against the exodus of emigrants, the editors of the *Kaiku* gloated with other critics that one could not pick the proverbial gold from the streets of America.[63]

In general, however, the campaign against emigration was ineffective. As early as 1887 the *Kaiku* described as futile the efforts of newspapers which printed the letters.[64] In 1909 the *Uusi Suometar* repeated the same point, conceding that agricultural education and other measures were needed to halt the departure of emigrants.[65] Despite the warnings of these newspapers and other opponents, Finns kept leaving between the early 1880s and World War One except during periods of unemploymen: and the onset of the depressions of 1893 and 1907 in the United States. In 1893 the number of Finns obtaining passports to emigrate was 9,117, and only 1,380 one year later, while the number of applicants fell almost two-thirds in the year after the start of the 1907 depression. The peak number of 23,152 was reached in 1902 when economic recovery in America coincided with political turmoil impelling unprecedented numbers of people to leave Finland.[66] Whatever the motives for leaving it was clear that the exodus correlated with economic conditions in the United States. Few were likely to emigrate if there was little prospect of obtaining jobs in America. On the other hand, most emigrants did so during good times in spite of their critics.

Although making some Finns undoubtedly apprehensive about bad times in America, the opponents of emigration lacked credibility among prospective emigrants. This lack was largely based on the social gap separating lower-class emigrants from their critics. Sharing the values of the land-owning gentry and representing the upper classes whose members were least likely to emigrate, the critics were contemptuous of the emigrants and their motives. The editors of newspapers like the *Kaiku* and *Uusi Suometar* portrayed emigrants as fickle, lazy, selfish, irresponsible persons deluded by animal desires for pleasure, adventure and wealth. Their appraisal described the emigrants, moreover, as lacking both patriotism and willingness to serve the fatherland. Besides deriding their motives and character, the critics insisted that proverty did not compel anyone to leave since there was enough land and work for everyone.[67] These reassurances misrepresented the social unrest spreading generally among the lower classes. Indeed, going to America was often an act of class defiance against the critics.

Unlike most of the critics who objected to emigration, a few upper-class representatives conceded that emigrants had justifiable reasons for leaving. In 1888 Alexandra Grippenberg, who was the daughter of a baron, visited in San Francisco and was amazed to discover that Finnish immigrants had an "unkind and indifferent attitude" toward their former homeland. Criticizing the Finnish gentry which feared the loss of agricultural workers, a local immigrant clergyman told her that there were two classes—the "gentlemen" and the "inferior people" in Finland. Members of the second group, he explained, could not escape its class as in America. Unless Finnish society improved its system of land distribution to aid the lower class, Grippenberg concluded that alienated rural workers would continue leaving for America.[68] Other social reformers agreed, but only token measures were developed to distribute land and ease tenant conditions before World War One.[69]

Thus, the new immigrants were more responsive to representatives of their class in America. Although occasionally exaggerating
and boasting about their experiences in America, immigrant letter-
writers did not lose their credibility. Since the writers had previous
contacts with their friends and relatives who might hold them
accountable for advice, they did not want to jeopardize their relationships. Instead they tempered their assessments of America and
did not bait their correspondents to come with promises which no
one could guarantee to fulfill. If their correspondents decided to
come, however, the writers welcomed them and even sent tickets.
Almost five-sixths of those entering the United States between 1907
and 1920 planned to join friends or relatives, while one-third arrived with prepaid tickets.[70] Besides the bonds of friendship and
family, most old and new immigrants shared common social origins. Upward of 90 per cent of all immigrants came from rural
areas, and over 50 per cent were mainly agricultural dependents
such as farm labourers and children of landowners and tenants, less
than 10 per cent were tenants and landowners. In addition, the rest
included artisans and general labourers, some of whom came in
growing numbers from urban communes.[71] Despite their differences about religion and other matters, however, the immigrants
shared a view that something was wrong with their society. In
short, prospective immigrants could relate best to their recently
arrived correspondents in America who were still likely to have a
strong sense of alienation from Finnish society.

Both the letter-writers in America and their correspondents
in Finland shared also a common migratory experience. Each
group came mainly from the most mobile sector of Finnish society
in which rural society had been increasing the ranks of the landless
classes. In contrast, the landowners decreased in relative importance so that by 1901 they represented less than one-fourth of the
heads of rural households.[72] When the growing number of dependents had no land or employment opportunities in rural areas, they
went to work in Finnish cities which could not absorb them easily.
So the migrants from more remote areas tended to emigrate to
America.[73] Both groups of migrants represented the most mobile
sector of society—the young unmarried adults. Of the group going
to America which initially included more men than women, 75 per
cent were unmarried and 69 per cent were between the ages of 16
and 30.[74] Whether or not the migrants went overseas, however,
they wanted in a sense to find jobs in America. Unable to travel to
America at the start of World War One, a group of young women
migrants who had already bought steamship tickets remained to

work at home, and as one of them recalled, she found her "America" working in Helsinki.[75] Her remark underscored the common aspirations of rural migrants seeking jobs at home and abroad. By sharing those aspirations which reinforced their common bonds of class, family and friendship, new rural migrants found even more believable letter-writers who had themselves gone through the process of deciding where to seek employment.

The letter-writers were members of a migratory class finding a homeland wherever economic opportunities lured them. If their land of birth did not provide opportunities, the migrants looked for them elsewhere. The ties of fatherland were not strong enough to keep them home. In 1890 Frans Nyman explained that necessity had compelled him to leave his native country because it did not offer those opportunities. After working first in St. Petersburg, Nyman travelled to work in a piano factory in Minneapolis where he said that happiness finally came to him.[76] Other immigrants did not find happiness quickly, so they kept searching for better opportunities in America, Canada or Finland. When the main era of immigration ended after World War One thousands of American Finns were still seeking better opportunities in the automobile factories of Detroit and the farm areas of northern Michigan, Wisconsin and Minnesota. Later the Great Depression of the 1930s sent hundreds of them to Soviet Karelia. It is not strange therefore that in more recent times thousands have retired to Florida. The spirit of the wanderer has still survived in them. In short, the America letters are a collective portrait of immigrants from Finland who began a life of wandering between the 1870s and World War One.

# Notes

1. Vilma Nummela to Milja Kreula, April 1, 1910, Satakunta America Letters (Institute of General History at the University of Turku, Finland), (microfilm at Immigration History Research Center, University of Minnesota), Reel 2, HIN: IX, no. 7.

2. A. William Hoglund, *Finnish Immigrants in America, 1880-1920* (Madison, 1960), pp. 33-35, 65.

3. *Oulun Wiikko-Sanomia* (Oulu, Finland), June 25, p. 1, and July 2, 1870, p. 1.

28    W. Hoglund

4. Ibid., July 8, pp. 1-2, and August 19, 1876, pp. 1-2. Reino Kero
identified the author of the series in his "Suomalaisten siirtolaisen
'vapaa Amerikka,'" Turun Yliopisto historian laitos yleinen historia,
*Eripainossarja*, no. 26 (Turku, 1975), p. 76.

5. *Oulun Wiikko-Sanomia*, June 7, 1873, p. 1.

6. *Uusi Suometar* (Helsinki), August 19, 1896, p. 2.

7. In 1900 Finns numbered 62,641 in the United States, including undoubtedly many of the 26,663 persons who received passports to
emigrate from Finland between 1895 and 1899. (Some emigrants travelled without passports.) If all of the passport applicants entered the
United States and were still living in the country in 1900, and if none
of the Finns residing in 1894 did not die or return to Finland before
1900, the maximum number of Finnish immigrants would have been
35,978 at the start of this period. If it is assumed that 85 per cent of
them were from Vaasa and Oulu and that all of the overseas letters
were from the United States, the average number of letters per Finn
was sixteen in 1894. But if all passport recipients did not come and
the maximum number was 45,000 of whom 38,000 were from the two
provinces in 1894, the average was twelve. (Prior to 1893 most immigrants came from those two provinces which provided two-thirds of
all Finns coming to the United States between 1893 and 1920.) Since
all of the letters were not from the United States, however, the
average probably was ten or less. On the other hand, all immigrants
did not write and therefore the number of letters per writer might
have been higher.

8. *Uusi Suometar*, August 19, 1896, p. 2.

9. Hoglund, *Finnish Immigrants in America*, p. 20.

10. Emmi Niemi to [family], December 11, 1914, Satakunta America
Letters, Reel 4, IKA: LXVII, no. 2.

11. Tilda Laaksonen to Kaarlo Lehtovuori, January 18, 1899, ibid., Reel
24, SAK: I, no. 7, and Anna Mäki to [cousin], June 10, 1912, ibid., Reel
13, LOIM: XVI, no. 3.

12. John Pietilä to [sister], September 9, 1911, ibid., Reel 2, HIN: XVII,
no. 9.

13. Isak Kuusisto to [parents], September 4, 1916 and May 17, 1917, ibid.,
HIN: III, nos. 20-21.

14. See, for example, Hilda Paananen to [sister's family], December 11,
1911, ibid., Reel 4, IKA: LXVIII, no. 4, and Jaakko Peltonen to [family],
December 7, 1903, Etelä-Pohjalinen Osakunta America Letters (University of Helsinki), (microfilm at Immigration History Research Center), Reel 12, no. 1494.

15. Nikolai Lintula to [parents], March 28, 1896, Etelä-Pohjalinen Osakunta America Letters, Reel 14, no. 2178/1.

16. The format of the letters is discussed in Marsha Penti-Vidutis, "The

America Letter: Immigrant Accounts of Life Overseas," *Finnish Americana*, 1:22-40 (1978).

17. _____ to Mary and Wili Wainio, June 10, 1911, Etelä-Pohjalainen Osakunta America Letters, Reel 5, no. 542/1.

18. August Aalto to Hilma Aerila, March 30, 1907, Varsinais-Suomi America Letters (microfilm at Immigration History Research Center), Reel 6, L-LA: VIII, no. 3, and Andrew Piipponen to Helly Piipponen, January 1, March 25 and September 17, 1911 (copies in writer's possession made from originals in private ownership).

19. Johan W. Kuusisto to Wilhelm Kuusisto, May 20, 1902, Satakunta America Letters, Reel 2, HIN: II, no. 1.

20. Ellen Länberg to Miina Länberg, June 17, 1904, ibid., Reel 15, MER: XXVIII, no. 1, and to [parents], *ca.* June or July and November 12, 1904, ibid., MER: XXVI, nos. 1-2.

21. Anselmi Neva to _____, July 6, 1906, ibid., MER: XLVI, no. 1.

22. John Pietilä to [sister], November 3, 1910, ibid., Reel 2, HIN: XVII, no. 4, and Matti Knuuttila to [cousin], June 16, 1913, Etelä-Pohjalainen Osakunta America Letters, Reel 13, no. 2068/1.

23. Isak Kuusisto to Wilho Kuusisto, November 21, 1905, Satakunta America Letters, Reel 2, HIN: III, no. 8.

24. Selma Walkama to Hilja Riihiaho, March 23, 1914, ibid., Reel 16, MER: CXXVI, no. 1.

25. _____ to [family], December 22, 1901 and February 28, 1902, Etelä-Pohjalainen Osakunta America Letters, Reel 13, nos. 2071/1-2.

26. _____ to Selma _____, October 15, 1905, ibid., Reel 13, no. 2039.

27. Manus Jokitalo to [family], March 3 and October 24, 1902, ibid., Reel 16, nos. 2373/1 and 8.

28. John Holma to Hulda Holma, March 20, 1911, Satakunta America Letters, Reel 7, JAM: LXI, no. 1.

29. Jalmari Ikala to Wilho Ikala, December 19, 1905, ibid., Reel 11, KOK: VIII, no. 1.

30. _____ to [family], October 4, 1905, Etelä-Pohjalainen Osakunta America Letters, Reel 9, no. 1166/1.

31. _____ Kamppila to [brother-in-law], January 22, 1907, ibid., Reel 5, no. 607/1.

32. Johan Kuusisto to Isak Kuusisto, June 2 and September 14, 1902, Satakunta America Letters, Reel 2, HIN: II, nos. 2 and 8.

33. August Jalo to Emil Kyläkreula, July 5, 1905, ibid., Reel 2, HIN: X, no. 1.

34. Evert Lindroos to [family], November 12, 1909, ibid., Reel 3, H:TI: VI, no. 1, and Helmi Nyberg to Sanda _____, October 28, 1909, ibid., Reel 2, HIN: XXVII, no. 1.

30    W. Hoglund

35. Antti ____ to [mother], December 4, 1881, Artturi Leinonen, *Atlanttia ja Amerikkaa katselemassa* (Porvoo, Finland, 1938), p. 130.

36. Viktor Nummela to Erland Heinilä, January 3, 1904, April 4, 1909, and January 6, 1911, Satakunta America Letters, Reel 12, LAP: I, nos. 9, 17, and 19.

37. ____ to [parents and relatives], September 16, 1896, Etelä-Pohjalainen Osakunta America Letters, Reel 10, no. 1289/1.

38. Viktor Nummela to Erland Heinilä, August 10, 1904, Satakunta America Letters, Reel 12, LAP: I, no. 12.

39. Viktor Nummela to Erland Heinilä, February 16, 1911, ibid., LAP: I, no. 22.

40. Frans Erland to Hilma Järvinen, September 18, 1912, Varsinais-Suomi America Letters, Reel 14, T-KV: VII, no. 4.

41. ____ to ____, November 8, 1890, Etelä-Pohjalainen Osakunta America Letters, Reel 13, no. 2042.

42. Vilma Nummela to Milja Kreula, March 30, 1907, Satakunta America Letters, Reel 2, HIN: IX, no. 6, and Wäinö J. Lehto to Julius Sarin Wirrat, July 27, 1903 (original in writer's possession).

43. August Lahti to [brother], December 14, 1912, Etelä-Pohjalainen Osakunta America Letters, Reel 12, no. 1486/3.

44. Elle ____ to [father], January 24, 1915, ibid., Reel 10, no. 1291/6.

45. Urho Koskinen to Frans ____, March 27, 1911, Satakunta America Letters Reel 13, LAV: III, no. 1.

46. Viljam to [brother and relatives], January 12, 1912, Etelä-Pohjalainen Osakunta America Letters, Reel 1, no. 71/13.

47. Isak Kangas to [brother-in-law], March 25, 1895, ibid., Reel 13, no. 1034/2.

48. ____ to ____, April 8, 1910, ibid., Reel 12, no. 1475/2.

49. Hoglund, *Finnish Immigrants in America*, pp. 8, 64. See also Reino Kero, "The Return of Emigrants from America to Finland," *Publications of the Institute of General History, University of Turku, Finland*, no. 4 (Turku, 1972).

50. R. Oksa to [brother], December 17, 1913, Satakunta America Letters, Reel 23, SIIK: LXXXIX, no. 6.

51. Sven Länberg to [parents, brothers and sister], February 7, 1904, ibid., Reel 15, MER: XXIX, no. 2.

52. Vihtori Myllymäki to Heikki Myllymäki, August 31, 1904, ibid., Reel 23, SIIK: LXXVIII, no. 2.

53. Vilma Nummela to Milja Kreula, April 1, 1910.

54. Johan Kuusisto to Iisakki Kuusisto, September 14, 1902.

55. Isak Kuusisto to Nestor Kuusisto, October 2, 1905, Satakunta America Letters, Reel 2, HIN: III, no. 7.

56. Juho ____ to [sister], July 12, 1907, Etelä-Pohjalainen Osakunta America Letters, Reel 5, no. 607/2.

57. Antti Kangas to Wilhem Kangas, March 16, 1882, and to Johan Kimari, March 30, 1895 (originals in writer's possession).

58. Teodor Lehtinen to [sister], December 23, 1907, Varsinais-Suomi America Letters, Reel 12, RYM: IX, no. 3.

59. Henrik Mikkola to G. Rooslin, April 8, 1893, Satakunta America Letters, Reel 15, MER: XX, no. 1.

60. A. William Hoglund, "No Land for Finns: Critics and Reformers View the Rural Exodus from Finland to America between the 1880's and World War I," *The Finnish Experience in the Western Great Lakes Region: New Perspectives*, ed. Michael G. Karni *et al.* (Vammala, Finland, 1975), pp. 36-40.

61. See, for example, *Kaiku* (Oulu), July 17, 1880, p. 3, and September 26, 1891, p. 1.

62. *Kaleva* (Oulu), October 6, 1905, pp. 2-3.

63. *Kaiku,* August 1, 1904, p. 3.

64. Ibid., April 20, 1887, p. 1.

65. *Uusi Suometar,* January 13, 1909, p. 2.

66. Walter F. Willcox, *International Migrations,* I: *Statistics* (New York, 1929), p. 776.

67. See, for example, *Uusi Suometar,* July 11, 1884, pp. 1-2; *Suomalainen* (Jyväskylä, Finland), May 16, 1900, pp. 1-2; *Kaleva,* May 8, 1900, p. 1, and *Kaiku,* March 17, 1899, p. 1.

68. Alexandra Grippenberg, *A Half Year in the New World: Miscellaneous Sketches of Travel in the United States (1888),* ed. Ernest J. Moyne (Newark, Del., 1954), pp. 160-65.

69. Hoglund, "No Land for Finns," pp. 43-44, 49-51.

70. Hoglund, *Finnish Immigrants in America,* p. 10, and Reino Kero, *Migration from Finland to North America in the Years between the United States Civil War and the First World War* (Vammala, 1974), p. 174.

71. Hoglund, *Finnish Immigrants in America,* p. 14, and Kero, *Migration from Finland,* p. 82.

72. Hoglund, *Finnish Immigrants in America,* pp. 5-6, and John Ilmari Kolehmainen, "Finland's Agrarian Structure and Overseas Migration," *Agricultural History,* 15:45-48 (January, 1941).

73. Hoglund, *Finnish Immigrants in America,* p. 7.

74. Ibid., pp. 80-81.

75. Interview with an elderly lady in Finland, July 1976.

76. Frans Johan Nyman to [mother and sister], November 13, 1890, Satakunta American Letters, Reel 1, EURA: I, no. 16.

# Finns and the Corporate Mining Environment of the Lake Superior Region

*Arnold R. Alanen*

Regarding the Finns, I have noticed, first, that when labor is needed they are bullheaded and troublesome; and second, that when work is scarce and labor plentiful that they are excellent workmen and tractable. I mean by this that they are a race that tries to take advantage of the companies at every opportunity, and one not to be trusted. Among the old Finns are many good, steady men, but the younger set, and especially those who have received a little education, are troublesome and agitators of the worst type.[1]

The above comment, made by a Mesabi Range mining superintendent to U.S. Immigration Commission investigators, typifies the situation of many Finns in the Lake Superior mining region during the early twentieth century. Applauded almost universally by mining company supervisors as being "good laborers, men who can stand the heavy work," and as being notable "for opening up new localities and for [having] the constitution to the stand hard physical labor," the Finns often were, in the same breath, con-

Research support for this paper was provided by grants from the College of Agricultural and Life Sciences, University of Wisconsin, Madison, and the Immigration History Research Center, University of Minnesota.

demned as "trouble breeders and a class not to be trusted," as being "troublesome and intractable, and given to radical agitation and labor disorder," and as possessing a pronounced tendency "to be rampagious when under the influence [of alcohol]."[2]

The Finnish experience in the Lake Superior region cannot be understood and assessed adequately unless the dichotomous interpretations noted above are given careful consideration and attention. Any historical evaluation of the region, in fact, must take account of the Finns, for immigrants from *Suomi* played a key role in shaping and forming the entire Lake Superior area environment. Not only did the Finns constitute the largest foreign-born contingent in many early twentieth century mining communities, but they also were unique in their willingness and ability to challenge the policies and dictates of a corporation-dominated economic system. This opposition emerged even though company-sponsored programs were developed which featured housing and community planning provisions, along with insurance and medical coverage, profit-sharing, and social-cultural activities for workers and their families. While corporate-sponsored benevolence was intended to foster harmony and productivity among employees in the Lake Superior mining region, many of the provisions ultimately were spurned by a sizable proportion of Finnish-American workers and residents.

Given these observations, the primary purposes of this paper are to describe and illustrate the salient features of the Lake Superior mining environment, and to present some of the major factors which contributed to the evolution of a Finnish community that, when compared to other immigrant groups in the region, dealt with the problems of industrial society in a unique and often controversial manner. The factors that will be discussed include the following: 1) the transition which occurred in the Finnish immigrant community when the basic conservative orientation of the nineteenth century group was augmented by the viewpoints of early twentieth century radicals; 2) the physical, social and governmental structure of the mining settlements which ranged from tightly controlled company enclaves where only limited Finnish organizational activities could occur, to relatively independent towns where the Finns were able to nurture and develop their labour-oriented movements; and 3) the attitudes and expressions of some company supervisors and mining community residents who, especially during the early 1900s, castigated the Finns for their behaviour and actions or stereotyped them in a pejorative manner.

# The Finns in the Region

When the first ten to twenty Finns arrived in the Copper Country of northern Michigan in 1864, mining activities had already been underway for two decades. By 1880, the number of Finns in Houghton and Keewenaw counties had probably reached some 1,500 persons, but this figure constituted a rather small component of the total population which by then approached almost 27,000 residents. As the six iron ore ranges of the region also began to be exploited for their mineral wealth, large numbers of Finns sought employment in these mining areas (Figure 1). The importance of Michigan, Minnesota and Wisconsin in Finnish-American settlement history is further borne out by the fact that in 1900, just over one-half of the nation's 62,650 foreign-born Finns lived in the three states. The Finns were especially concentrated in the Lake Superior region where, by 1920, they formed the largest foreign-born group in all major mining counties except Dickinson (Menominee Range) and Crow Wing (Cuyuna Range).[3]

Most nineteenth century Finnish immigrants came directly from a traditional folk society with its predominantly agrarian values and lifestyles. In addition, these immigrants "represented a decidely conservative, right wing as well as nationalistic element of the population."[4] With the dawning of a new century, however, an increasing number of recent emigrés who arrived in the new world had been schooled in the principles of socialism, or at least were ready to embrace its basic tenets. Not only had the Social Democratic Party been formed in Finland during the 1890s, but, as Kero and Ollila have suggested, many of the later immigrants were familiar with the dislocation problems caused by rural to urban migration and had been introduced to class-conscious idealism in their home country.[5] Several recent studies also have shed additional light upon the factors which contributed to the development of Finnish radicalism in America. It is not the intention of this paper to review these studies, except to note that the "highly structured company-corporate environment, complete with its well defined occupational hierarchy, inflexible working hours, established salary scales, regimentation, and hazardous working conditions," contributed significantly to the actions and attitudes of the Finns.[6] By 1912, socialism had been adopted as a way of life by more than 10 per cent of the Finns in America, and the movement gained strength in subsequent years.[7]

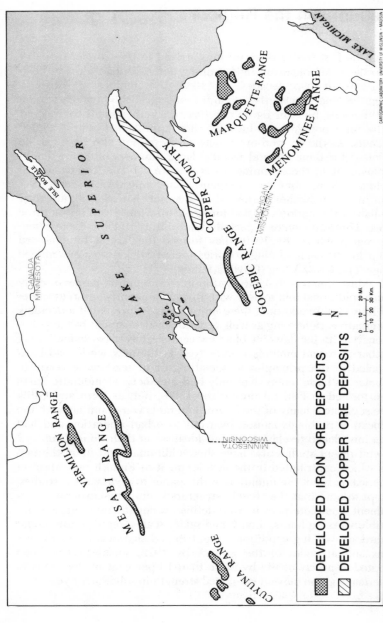

Figure 1. From the mid-1860s onward, Finns settled throughout the Lake Superior region and its seven ore producing ranges.

# The Corporate Environment

Though there were variations in theory and practice throughout the region, one ubiquitous theme was evident during the period of major Finnish settlement activity: corporate-sponsored paternalism. As a process whereby an authority treated those under its control in a "fatherly way," especially in regulating conduct and providing for human needs such as housing and community services, paternalism was already discernable once exploitation of Michigan's copper resources began in the 1840s. Thus, by the time the first Finns arrived in the mid-1860s, the stage was set for the development of what Jensen has termed a system of complete company domination.[8] The arrival of the Finns also coincided with the formation of the foremost corporate organization in the region: the Calumet and Hecla Mining Company. Under the initial direction of Alexander Agassiz, a stern, Swiss-born, Harvard-educated scientist, Calumet and Hecla provided its investors with a steady flow of dividends of many decades and sponsored numerous community and employee benefit programs in the area. Schools, libraries and an opera house were built; churches were subsidized; more than one thousand company houses were constructed; vice and sin were regulated; and employees were provided with insurance, relief and medical protection. Agassiz and his successors, however, demanded a *quid pro quo* for their seeming benevolence: the complete loyalty and allegiance of employees to company policies and practices. Nothing, in fact was opposed more strongly by the companies than efforts of employees to form labour unions and organizations. Following the unsuccessful strike of 1913-14, "paternalism with its evils of worker dependence and community domination" would even continue for another quarter century.[9]

Unlike endeavours in the copper mining areas, where steady investment by speculators from the eastern states provided capital for community development and planning endeavours, early iron ore mining ventures generally were very marginal. Communities such as Negaunee and Ishpeming, Michigan, simply grew without any conscious plan or forethought: "A hole in the ground, some houses around it for the miners to live in, presently town government, and a name—that is the story."[10] It was not until 1898 that a systematic program for community planning and employee welfare was even proposed for the iron ore mining ranges. Following a strike on the Marquette Range in 1895, W.G. Mather, president of the Cleveland-Cliffs Iron Mining Co., apparently recognized that labour problems were now more than just the discontent of a few "Huns, Poles, Slavs, and Finns."[11] He therefore spoke to his fellow executives and announced that the iron ore mining corporations of the Lake Superior region would have to adopt a program of planned community development and employee benefits.[12] During subsequent years, Cleveland-Cliffs, U.S. Steel and other large corporations proceeded to develop a few model communities, improve the appearance and sanitary conditions of existing settlements, and to introduce pension plans, safety programs and medical coverage for workers. This approach, termed "social welfare" rather than paternalism by the companies, supposedly emphasized the "cooperative" role of management in helping workers to improve their own condition.[13]

Whether termed paternalism or social welfare, the progams were based on the assumption that corporate benevolence would contribute to the stability, efficiency, health, morality and ultimately the productivity of the labour force. Whereas working and living conditions obviously improved with the implementation of benefit programs, many provisions were allocated on a selective basis only. The most attractive were reserved for essential and trustworthy employees, and some of the programs, such as stock subscription plans, were limited to the best-paid workers.[14] In addition, the mine owners and operators adopted an elitist attitude when dealing with their employees. Most programs were formulated in company boardrooms with virtually no input from the majority of employees and community residents. Thus, goal conflicts developed between the corporations and workers. Corporate motives were devoted almost entirely to the procurement of maximum profits, but many Finns and other mining labourers dreamed of "an industrially managed society where justice for the worker would prevail."[15] When the miners sought to organize or to question prevailing labour conditions, however, they were opposed on all fronts by the companies. Indeed, when the Oliver Iron Mining Company announced in 1918 that it was developing a "mutuality plan" for the airing of employee grievances, the corporation qualified its offer by stating that "soliciting membership for any organization while in the works or on the property of the community" would be sufficient cause for immediate dismissal.[16] It would not be until the early 1940s, following the passage of the National Labor Relations Act of 1935 (Wagner Act), that workers were free to join national labour organizations in the copper and iron ore producing areas.[17]

# The Mining Settlements[18]

To most outside observers, mining settlements in the Lake Superior region undoubtedly appeared similar both in form and function. As any resident understood, however, there was a distinctive settlement hierarchy, and the inter-community differences reflected the social and economic structure of the region.

Until the productive capacity of an area could be determined, the first settlements to emerge as part of any new mining venture were the camps. On the Mesabi Range the companies also built and managed boarding and sleeping camps adjacent to the permanent communities, but these enclaves were inhabited primarily by southern European males.[19] (Many single Finns lived in the Finnish *poikatalot* or boarding houses where conditions were much better than in the camps.) Life in the camps was spartan-like to say the least. "Hot bedding" often was the rule, with different workers on various shifts continuously occupying the bunks throughout the day and night. During the winter season, as reported by one worker, the bunkhouses were shut up tightly, the stove was fuelled intensively, and the men slept in very dirty underwear and came in at all hours of the night.[20]

The most common settlements in the region were the locations (*lokeeksi* in Finnish). Built on company-owned land, the locations generally were situated within walking distance of a mine site. Hundreds of locations emerged in the region, though three different forms predominated. The most primitive enclaves, the "unplotted squatters' locations," were characterized by their twisting streets and pathways, haphazard arrangements of houses and shacks, and almost complete lack of sanitary facilities. As described by one Mesabi Range observer, the squatters' locations displayed "ugly-looking houses, with dilapidated fences and outbuildings, and a general appearance of wretchedness that is comparable only to the slums of our great cities."[21] Though Finns generally did not reside in squatters' settlements, the Jordan location by Chisholm, Minnesota, and the Finn and Pool locations by Hibbing, Minnesota, had sizable numbers of Finnish inhabitants. In addition to the locations, some squatters constructed their homes on the fringes of existing settlements, or along paths and roadways (Figure 2).[22]

The most commonplace settlements in the Lake Superior region were the "company locations." Laid out by mining engineers in a monotonously similar grid pattern, these locations pro-

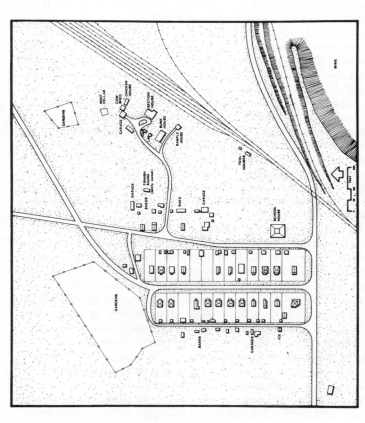

Figure 2.  Finns often were found in company locations similar to Myers, Minnesota, while smaller numbers were situated in squatters' enclaves that emerged along roads and pathways.

Source: Adapted from Oliver Iron Co. maps on file in the St. Louis County Historical Society (Duluth).

vided an expedient solution to the problem of providing housing for employees when new mines proved to have merchantable ore deposits (Figures 2-3). The first Finns in the general vicinity of the Michigan community of Calumet (*Kalma* as it sometimes was termed by early Finns) lived in company locations such as Swedetown, Rambaultown (*Ramboutown*) and Allouez (*Alue*).[23] In 1879 the *Amerikan Suomalainen Lehti* (American Finnish Journal) reported that the houses which Finns rented from the companies were small, squat and constructed of logs; but because the immigrants were from Tornio, Kemijoki and Finnmark—areas where the residents were claimed to be known for their habits of cleanliness— the interiors of the dwellings were as spotless and nice as any to be found in Finland. (It also was reported that one could immediately recognize the home of a Finnish family because of the two-piece shades that were used on the windows.) In some locations larger and more modern houses were built by the companies. Marked by their uniform design and colour, such housing concentrations eventually would proliferate throughout the region. On the Gogebic Range a landscape architect reported that the companies generally built rigid rows of standardized houses in an extremely monotonous manner, while another observer described similar locations on the Mesabi Range as standing "stark against an open and drear background of mine shafts, open pits, dumps, railroad tracks, and tree stumps and boulders." A young social worker depicted a company location inhabited by Finns in the vicinity of Mountain Iron, Minnesota, in somewhat kinder words, claiming it was "quite neat and liveable, although not especially attractive." Residents were allowed to build their own homes in some locations, but the land invariably was company-owned. Thus, the land leases of residents could be terminated abruptly if their conduct were deemed unacceptable by company officials; and on the Mesabi Range, location inhabitants faced the possibility of sudden removal to a new site whenever nearby open pit mining operatings were expanded.[24]

A third location type, though limited in number, was the "model location." These settlements were planned and built by the companies to attract and maintain skilled employees and supervisory personnel. Whereas the model locations often boasted of a community building and handsome schoolhouse, some were distinguished by their substantial housing and landscape design features. This was especially true of Montreal, Wisconsin, the premier example of model location planning in the region. Monroe, Minnesota, on the other hand, displayed a modern railway, good yards, and regular garbage collection, but still revealed, according to one observer, a "monotonous sameness of houses and rigid streets... where the ideas of beauty are coming in with efficiency but belatedly."[25]

Another group of enclaves in the region, also limited in number, were the company towns and model villages. Except for their larger size and greater array of services, these settlements were somewhat similar to the locations. The model villages were distinguished from the company towns in that the former were much more highly planned, and were considered by the companies as providing a utopian existence for essential employees and their families. While vice was strictly regulated in model villages such as Gwinn, Michigan, and Coleraine and Morgan Park, Minnesota, this only meant that "sin suburbs" flourished outside the boundaries.[26]

The final group of communities consisted of speculative developments. These settlements, of which there were hundreds, were plotted and sold by mining company executives and other speculators in an effort to capitalize upon the rapid growth of new extraction areas. During their formative years of development, all of these towns displayed the typical rawness of frontier mining communities. Ishpeming, Michigan, was described in 1874 as having buildings which were of "wood, mostly low, and set directly over what has been swamp, without drainings whatever, the water from the mines going into the main swamp"; whereas a reporter observing Nashwauk, Minnesota, as it emerged in 1903, stated that "a hole has been cut in the forest, the brush burnt away, and on the main street the stumps have been extracted."[27] About fifteen years later, Iron River, Michigan, was described in the following manner on the pages of *Red Cross Magazine:*

> Dust is blowing in the streets,—dust that washes off red. Off the paved street, wire-fenced yards defy the cattle and the chickens. Across the railroad, the Labour Hall of the Finns looms, dun, unpainted, giving little hint of the socialist plays which have taken the place of religion and a pastor in Finnish Iron River.[28]

The lack of sanitary provisions was a constant problem in these communities. Ten years after Hibbing had been carved out of the Minnesota wilderness, a local newspaper editor claimed "the stench which arises from some of the back alleys of our city is enough to kill a horse," while another account stated that "the drainage is poor and heaps of filth lie everywhere in the alleys and door yards and even in the public thoroughfares." In Eveleth,

Minnesota, a teacher staying in a Finnish-owned boarding house noted that the nearby sauna, "a high unpainted barn-like building with few windows," would emit, "especially on Saturday nights, a frequent stream of bath water draining out at the bottom and over the sidewalk into the gutter." Most of the immigrants also kept at least one cow in a backyard shed. Some companies provided free pasture on a community commons, but in many settlements the cattle often wandered throughout the towns. In northern Michigan it was claimed that during the nighttime hours, cows would stamp on the sidewalks and "bellow discordant notes"; and in Hibbing it was reported that women were even afraid to go on the sidewalks because of the cows. "Frequently they [the cows] stand there for hours at a time," announced the Hibbing reporter in 1900, "chewing their cuds and sunning themselves and leaving the sidewalks in a dirty shape." It would not be until the second decade of the twentieth century that the villages and locations, especially those on the Mesabi Range, began to assume, and even exceed, the refinements and accoutrements of traditional American counmunities.[29]

The mining companies exercised noticeable control in some of these communities, but many of the speculative developments eventually demonstrated their own political independence. Several Finnish institutions also flourished in such communities. Whereas the companies might have been able to limit Finnish organizational activities to churches and temperance halls in the locations and company towns, it was in communities with speculative origins such as Hibbing and Virginia, Minnestota, and Mass, Michigan, that socialist halls and consumers' cooperatives proliferated.

# Corporate and Community Impressions of the Finns

Though united by a common national heritage, the Finns who settled in the Lake Superior mining region displayed a diversity of viewpoints, especially in the area of religion and politics. As mentioned earlier, this spectrum of beliefs and attitudes, formed by a complex blending of backgrounds and experiences on both sides of the Atlantic, resulted in a Finnish-American community that eventually was characterized by its schisms and disagreements. Non-Finnish residents of the mining communities were cognizant of these differences, although it was quite unlikely that many could fully comprehend the factors which shaped the attitudes and practices of the Finns. Thus, mining town residents often resorted to labels when describing their neighbours from *Suomi*. Depending upon the Finns' politics or proclivities toward alcohol, these labels included "White Finns", "Red Finns," "Black Finns," "Drunken Finns" "Swede Finns," and "Russian Finns." Mining company officials likewise had difficulty in understanding why many Finns chose to spurn their offers of corporate largesse. An assessment of these attitudes and impressions is necessary if the position and place of Finns in the social and economic hierarchy of the region are to be comprehended.

Apparently the Finns quickly acquired a reputation in the mining areas for their willingness to work hard, to put in long hours, and to face difficult and dangerous conditions. When Finns searched for new employment opportunities in the region and other areas of the United States, some would report on their experiences by sending letters to early newspapers such as the *Amerikan Suomalainen Lehti*, published in Calumet, Michigan. These letters often contained brief statements describing the attitudes of employers toward Finnish miners and labourers. "The present-day mining officials," reported a Finnish correspondent from Michigan's Delaware Location in 1881, "only want Finnish workers'; and a labourer on a railroad construction crew by Marquette, Michigan, stated that the foreman had a positive impression of Finns because of their generally steady work habits. Though working conditions were difficult and dangerous, the editor of the *Amerikan Suomalainen Lehti* reminded his readers that it was not necessary to go hungry in America if one were willing to seek out employment. "Poverty does not afflict those who have the desire to work," stated the editor, "and idleness is less evident here than in the home country."[30]

When considering the various ethnic and nationality groups which populated the Calumet area in 1879, a Finnish correspondent claimed that harmony prevailed among Finns and other people, although there was one noticeable exception: the Irish. When an Irishman threatened a Finn, the reporter reasoned, it was done out of envy because the Irish could never equal the Finns. Altercations between the Finns and Irish were quite common, primarily in the saloons and dance halls of Red Jacket, Michigan. The Finns were especially renowned for their use of knives in barroom brawls whenever they sought to "carve the necks of some Irishmen." To avoid such confrontations the Finns were admonished to leave strangers alone and to say nothing bad about them—even in Finnish. "The Irish are hot tempered and suspicious of everyone," a Finnish correspondent announced in 1880, "but even among them are many good men, especially if they are treated as men." By his very nature, the reporter continued, the Irishman "generally likes to look for a fight, but his mouth is more threatening than he is himself."[31]

Although some Finnish immigrants in the 1870s and 1880s were receiving attention for their drinking and fighting sprees, the majority of early emigrés tended to be conservative, family and rural-oriented, and concerned about maintaining their cultural, linguistic and religious identity within a foreign land. This latter group of Finns also commented on the behaviour of their compatriots, with some of the earliest accounts expressing disgust over what was perceived to be an excessive amount of drinking and brawling. Headlines similar to the one from northern Michigan entitled, "Puukot heiluneet Balticassa" ("Knives brandished in Baltic"), describing the exploits of persons such as "Viipurin Antti" ("Andrew from Viipuri"), were commonplace in Finnish-language newspapers throughout the region. Eventually, the strict opposition expressed by a portion of the Finnish-American community toward Demon Rum and its influences contributed to the development of almost three hundred Finnish temperance societies in America. Some labour militancy also was demonstrated as early as 1874 by Finnish trammers in the Copper Country and by Marquette Range iron ore miners in 1895, but these events were overshadowed by the strikes which occurred in the region during the twentieth century, especially in 1907, 1913-14 and 1916. Though specific issues might have varied from place to place, the underlying concern of the striking workers, in virtually every instance, was to modify their voiceless and powerless position with industrial society.[32]

The transition in the composition of the Finnish population obviously did not go unnoticed by mining officials and community leaders and residents. The Finns were caught up in the wave of anti-southern and eastern European immigrant hysteria that was evident in America during the years prior to World War One, but they were especially singled out for their radical activities in the mining areas. Whereas accounts in local English-language newspapers of the nineteenth century apparently gave a positive or neutral picture of the Finns (or more often failed to mention them at all), these portrayals began to change during the subsequent century.[33] A perusal of accounts from Hibbing and Duluth, Minnesota, and Houghton, Michigan, newspapers revealed that by the early

1900s, an increasing number of reports began to deal with the socialism, intoxication, insanity, altercations or violent deaths of Finns.[34]

When Finns fought in northern Minnesota, according to the *Duluth News Tribune*, they did not merely engage in combat as mortal beings, but reportedly battled "like Norse Gods"; and likewise, Finns did not simply make threats when inebriated, but would seek out the "gore of (their) fellow men." Altercations between Finns and other immigrant groups often were treated satirically and were accompanied by ethnic slurs. A Hibbing account, for example, reported on the exploits of a Finn who supposedly decided to "carve his companions just by way of amusement." When one of the other Finns interrupted the proceedings by brandishing a club, both were arrested. Each man received a $10 fine, the latter reportedly "for being too prominent with a club while the carving is going on—a Finnlander [sic] has no right to use a club in Hibbing, that precious implement of offense and defense is reserved for the right of the Irish only."[35] In a 1905 account, the *Hibbing Tribune* also reported:

> Italy and Finland have declared war. The first engagement occurred on the public highway near the Mahoning mine Monday afternoon. A squad of a dozen or so Italians met four or five Fins [sic] and an altercation was begun, then followed a fistic combat, and a Fin [sic] sought to even matters by smashing a Dago's face with a rock.[36]

A Mesabi Range teacher, writing in 1908, stated that only one-fifth of the residents in the vicinity of Eveleth, Minnesota, were "civilized folk"; of the remainder (i.e., the "uncivilized"), she claimed that the Finns and Austrians were in the majority. Several monographs, some published as late as the 1950s, also commented on the Finns in a less than positive manner. J.B. Martin, in his book on the history of northern Michigan, stated that while the Irish and Swedes might have fought one another, they shared one opinion in common: "that Finns were no bloody good."[37] In another publication, L.C. Reimann claimed Finns in mining towns were clannish and could be divided into two groups: Swedish Finns and Russian Finns. The former were reported to be sober, industrious and devoted to their church, but the Russian Finns, also termed "Drunken Finns," were described in the following manner:

They were savage in their lovemaking, their revenge and their loyalty to their own kind. They were violent in whatever they did. They drank hard, fought hard and often died hard. The average Russian Finn carried a small razor-sharp knife ... with a carved handle, in his belt or boot-top, for "social purposes." In a fight he used his knife viciously and furiously. He felt little remorse over his acts of violence and cared little about the results of his acts on himself. A jail sentence for a knifing merely whetted his appetite for revenge and he awaited impatiently the day of his release to wreak vengeance on his adversary.[38]

In a similar vein, H.N. Casson's book-length tirade, titled *The Romance of Steel*, claimed America's steel industry was being "pulled down" by unskilled immigrants. Hungarians, Slavs, Italians and Finns, Casson retorted, "have hands but no heads." According to Casson, their employment around expensive machinery contributed to a dangerous situation: "It is apt to kill the men and injure the machinery."[39]

When Finns and other immigrants were killed in mining accidents, their demise was spelled out regularly in a depressingly large number of accounts. Though there were hundreds of such local announcements, the following is typical of these graphic reports:

Samuel Esola, a Finn, 23 years of age, was accidentally killed at the Hartley mine near Chisholm, Tuesday. Esola was attempting to repair a steam shovel beam and while stooping under the chains of [the] crane one of his fellow employees accidentally touched the crane throttle and young Esola was caught between the chains. His life was crushed out in an instant before the machinery could be stopped. The head was badly cut and he had numerous bruises on his body.[40]

The *Hibbing Tribune*, in 1904, even claimed that when a Finn died on the Mesabi Range, a lack of "sympathy was painfully noticeable." The same account stated, however, that some Finns, such as a recently departed local saloonkeeper who had left his wife and six children in "easy financial circumstances," did display "the many virtues of this sturdy race." When another Hibbing entrepreneur and his family returned to Finland in 1905, it was stated that they would "live the balance of their lives on the neat little competency accumulated during the few years in which . . . [he] was engaged in the mercantile business in Hibbing." When unmarried labourers returned to Finland and some southern European countries, however, a *Hibbing Tribune* editorial boldly asked: "What of it? . . . These are not the people that make the pith and back bone of any town or country."[41]

The labour militancy of some Finns often led to company-fostered restrictions in the mining areas. In their reports on immigrants in copper and iron ore mining operations, the U.S. Immigration Commission listed more than twenty references to the perceived radicalism and socialistic tendencies of the Finns. Admitting that discrimination had been practised in employing Finns, the report stated that they were tolerated only because of their excellent reputation as labourers. Although exact figures have never been available for actual inspection, the companies made efforts to blacklist or deny employment to many Finns who joined or were suspected of supporting radical groups. Berman has stated that whereas Finns comprised 18 per cent of the Oliver Iron Mining Company's Mesabi Range work force before the 1907 strike, the figure had fallen to 8 per cent one year later. Total work force figures for the Oliver Company, as reported by Virtue, also revealed that the Finns were the only major nationality group to experience a decline in employee numbers (-754) from 1907 to 1908. Landis noted that as these former miners left for the cutover lands of the Lake Superior area to take up farming, "they changed the ethnic composition of the Range towns and created a feeling of animosity between companies and Finns." On the Marquette Range during the early twentieth century, the U.S. Immigration Commission stated that there had been a tendency to employ as few Finns as possible and to mix them with other nationality groups; and employers on the Menominee Range reportedly endeavoured to hire as few Finns as possible because "of the radical tendencies of the members of the race who are reputed to be much less tractable than any other race and who are the cause of constant discontent."[42]

In the locations and company towns, it was possible for the corporations to regulate activities or even to practise outright discrimination when dealing with various nationality groups. Efforts were made in the model village of Coleraine, for example, to attract what the Oliver Iron Mining Company termed the "best classes of people." Company selection procedures created a community profile that ensured persons born in America and Western Europe would predominate, while the number of Finns was appreciably smaller than in other Mesabi Range communities. In Gwinn, Michigan, the Cleveland-Cliffs Iron Mining Company did go so far as to instruct its town planner to provide "special Finnish bath houses" for residents, but also sought to segregate Finns, Italians and Poles since it was believed they could not coexist side by side within the same community.[43] During the 1913-14 Copper Country conflict, one critic reported in a national magazine that the strikers were nothing more than "cheap foreign labor of the more undesirable kind," and were foolishly seeking to trade the paternalistic benefits of housing and libraries for wage increases. Indeed, the *Engineering and Mining Journal* reported that some companies were considering "the proposed elimination of the Finns" by cancelling their land and home leases. Although this threat apparently was not carried out directly to any great extent (many Finns left voluntarily), a U.S. Department of Labor analyst observed some years later that in at least one Copper Country community, a company rental agent discriminated against "Russian Finns" because of their socialistic leanings and lack of company loyalty.[44]

# Finnish Responses

Early Finnish immigrants in the Copper Country apparently were quite satisfied with certain aspects of corporate paternalism such as housing and community services. While the company-built log structures rented to employees in some enclaves surrounding Calumet were viewed by the Finns as being rather small and arranged in a "helter skelter" pattern, the frame dwelling units in other locations were appreciated for their larger size, modern design and uniform colour (Figure 3). "Life here is clean and quiet," reported a miner from Allouez, Michigan, in 1881. "The way of existence is rural in nature, and the Finns always appear to be working around their homes."[45]

Since the first mining activities took place in an unsettled region, it was necessary for the companies to provide their workers with everything needed for human existence. These activities might have been justified in an earlier day, but they could not be condoned once the region reached maturity. The eventual militant actions of the Finns in responding to conditions throughout the

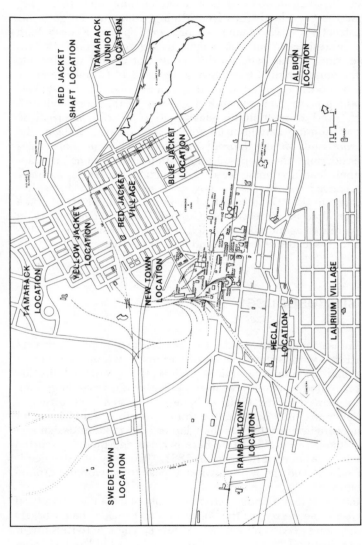

Figure 3.  Calumet, Michigan, one of the most important Finnish settlements in North America, included the villages of Red Jacket and Laurium and several surrounding locations.(Also see Figure 4).

Source:  Adapted from maps of the Calumet & Hecla Copper Company and Sanborn-Perris Fire Insurance maps.

mining region, despite the corporate-sponsored paternalism and welfare provisions that were offered, illustrated the unwillingness of the companies to modify their well-entrenched methods and procedures even throughout much of the 1900s.

Though early twentieth century Finnish socialists regularly stated that the mining companies were not scrupulous in their labour relation practices, some Finns were complaining about the actions of corporations and supervisors already in the 1800s. An 1879 account stated that miners at Quincy, Michigan, were not satisfied with their lot because of low wages and a contract system which offered little increased financial renumeration in spite of how hard one worked; and an Eveleth, Minnesota, miner reported in 1896 that wages were small on the Mesabi Range, "and if you bother the bosses only a little, then out you go immediately, and there is nothing more to do than search for another job."[46]

Whether conservative, radical or non-committal in their political viewpoints, there was one factor which constantly coloured the Finns' impressions of mining activities: the dangerous and unhealthy working conditions. Only a few miners could avoid illness or injury, commented the *Amerikan Suomalainen Lehti* in 1879, and most men lost their health within three years. When five deaths and four injuries occurred at Republic, Michigan, during a two-week span in 1880, a correspondent asked: "Is it no wonder then that Finns have had their fill of this terrible mine?" In the Copper Country the companies established employee-funded relief programs to assist the families of injured or deceased miners, but early Finnish immigrants deemed the payment ($25) insufficient, and formed the *Calumet'in Suomalainen Apu-yhtiö* (Calumet Finnish Relief Association) in 1878. One year later the organization had some two hundred members, including several Norwegians. The low-cost medical facilities offered by the companies often were touted as exemplary demonstrations of corporate largesse, but such provisions, of course, only treated the consequences of dangerous mining conditions and did not change or alleviate them. When one reporter for the *Industrialisti* visited the Calumet and Hecla hospital in northern Michigan, he equated it to a European army medical facility. The reporter claimed he was especially struck by the awful sight of old and young men going in and out in wheelchairs, with their legs crushed and hands and heads swathed in bandages.[47]

It generally was possible for Finnish groups to build churches and temperance halls in the locations and company towns, but less conservative Finns often found it difficult to establish cooperatives and all but impossible to develop labour organizations. In the area of Montreal, Wisconsin, for example, a Finnish labour organizer stated that the company was able to "dictate whom the boarding-house owner can keep as a boarder, [and] when meetings can be held.... The mines belong to the steel trust, the men are its, too— the whole town is in its care."[48] As mentioned earlier, it would be in the incorporated towns of speculative origin where Finnish radical movements could germinate and grow.

Unlike other American mining regions, the Lake Superior area landscape was dotted with only a few company stores. Nevertheless, some independent merchants charged excessive prices in communities where they held a commercial monopoly, and others denied credit to unemployed workers during periods of labour strife. To counteract these practices the Finns formed consumers' cooperatives in many mining towns and rural communities of the Lake Superior area. Between 1906 and 1917, a period which embraced the three major labour conflicts in the region, twenty-nine mining community cooperatives were organized by Finnish miners and their families, while eleven more developed prior to 1930. (Scores of others emerged in agricultural areas.) Several cooperatives, as at Virginia, Biwabik, Hibbing, and Gilbert, Minnesota, and Hancock and Mass, Michigan, developed when local merchants refused to serve striking workers. Finns outside the mining communities also provided moral and material support for their financially pressed, unemployed colleagues. A group of farmers associated with the Finnish cooperative at Brantwood, Wisconsin, for example, sent an entire carload of potatoes to the Copper Country during the 1913-14 strike. Likewise, the Finnish Socialist Federation, formed at Hibbing in 1906, could boast of eighteen locals and 630 members in Lake Superior mining towns by 1909; and these figures expanded to thirty locals and 1,440 members by 1914. Overall, Ollila has estimated that up to 20 to 25 per cent of all Finns in America during the early decades of the twentieth century might have been supporters of socialism.[49]

It must be emphasized that conservative Finns served notice that they did not condone the behaviour of their more radical counterparts. One year after the 1907 Mesabi Range strike, it was reported that 400 to 500 Finns had gathered in Hibbing to condemn "socialism and all its works ... at an exciting mass meeting"; while a lengthy resolution from the Marquette Range during the same year was headlined in a local newspaper as: "Socialism not Popular with Ishpeming Finns." Finnish church leaders also claimed that the nation's religious, social and political ideals were "being threatened by ultra-liberal propaganda."[50] The Finnish community in the Lake Superior region clearly was not a homogeneous unit, but was characterized by its diversity and differences of opinion and action.

Though it was a much quieter form of protest, a large number of Finns expressed their dissatisfaction with conditions in the mining areas (and, of course, revealed their undeniable land hunger) by moving out of the towns and establishing homesteads and farms throughout the Midwest. Beginning with the movement of Finns to agricultural enclaves in southern Minnesota during the 1860s, thousands of other immigrants later expanded their research for land to the much less productive soils of the cutover region. It is commonly noted that Finns who were blacklisted or denied employment in the mining areas often turned to agrarian pursuits, but it must be remembered that mobility and impermanence always characterized the total Finnish population in mining communities. Even as early as 1881 a newspaper correspondent from Calumet, Michigan, reported that during his two years of residence in the community, the Finnish population had increased noticeably; but most of his initial acquaintances had already left Calumet, and others were departing to pursue farming.[51] Also, of thirty-two Finns listed in the Hurley, Wisconsin, city directory for 1893, only two could still be found eight years later; this was the highest rate of non-persistence demonstrated by any of Hurley's European immigrant groups. Likewise, between 1889 and 1929 in the agricultural enclave at Oulu Township, Wisconsin, 65 per cent of 125 adult Finns for whom information was available had previously resided in at least one Lake Superior area mining community; in Owen, Wisconsin, for the 1911-1928 period, 78 per cent of 115 Finland-born adults had similar experiences.[52] As an 1897 account asked: "Why shouldn't the Finns, who in the homeland gained their bread with the assistance of a plow, also do the same thing at a larger scale in this country . . . ?" Thus, the clarion call for many Finns who fled the dangerous working conditions, fluctuating labour demands and contrasting life styles of the mining areas became: "Back to the land!—Mother Earth will provide for all of us."[53]

Unlike the situation which often prevailed in the mining areas, outside observers praised and applauded the Finns when they pursued agricultural endeavours.[54] One reporter, in 1916, noted that Finns chose not to remain in the mining towns, but were "found all over St. Louis Country (Minnesota) laboriously cleaning out the stumps and boulders of the cutover forest lands, redeeming the country for agriculture." Others claimed that Finns

"seem to thrive where the hardships are most severe"; and that
"stumps and lakes and stones, isolation and short growing season—
these do but woo them to the land." Geographer Derwent Whittlesey, writing for a Swedish journal in 1930, concluded that "time
proved that they [the Finns] alone could make a go of the refactory
farmland." After surveying agricultural endeavours in the area of
Oulu, a reporter for the *Wisconsin Agriculturist* stated that the
Finns might have been "self contained and somewhat apart from
the rest, " but they were superior in intelligence, physical strength,
patience and persistence. "They are the makers of history," concluded the reporter, "as it will be written of this new empire."[55]

# Conclusion

This paper has sought to provide an overview of the physical and
social environments which encompassed the Finnish community in
the Lake Superior mining region during the period from the mid-
1860s to the 1940s. Certain characteristics of the corporate mining
environment and its settlements were presented, attitudes toward
the Finns were discussed, and the responses of Finns to situations
they encountered were traced.

In the mining communities of the Lake Superior region the
Finns were noted for their willingness and ability to engage in
difficult labour, but they also were reputed to be hard drinkers and
pugnacious brawlers. There is no doubt that Finns did engage in
their share of rampagious activities, but it must be emphasized that
much of what was termed socially irresponsible behaviour during
this period was related to the nature of the mining area environment with its difficult and dangerous working conditions, strict
socio-economic hierarchy, predominance of men, and lack of services and facilities. The mining companies might have prided
themselves on their welfare provisions, but in reality many programs were selective since they often failed to address the unique
requirements of immigrants and single males. W.J. Bell, a mission-
ary/social worker who was active on the Mesabi Range during the
early twentieth century, noted that there was a complete lack of
anything to ameliorate the monotonous living conditions of workers
and their families. 'Bread, meat and beer, three times a day is
about all there is to the home life of many of the people of the
locations. They have no amusements—so they break out occasion-

ally in excesses." The saloon keeper, Bell sadly stated, often served as the immigrants' banker, ticket agent and sole friend.[56]

While over-indulgence was a concern to many, both within and outside the Finnish community, the activities of radical Finns during the early twentieth century were the subject of even greater attention. Paternalism and corporate welfare programs, therefore, not only sought to improve the morals of workers, but also endeavoured to mould their political and social values. A Menominee Range mining official, commenting on the entire foreign-born population of Caspian, Michigan, in 1919, stated that progress had to be made in making this "element a safe factor in the community, as such a community of foreign people, largely ignorant and without moral guidance or restraint, constitutes a real menace to the moral and industrial stability of the entire district."[57]

Corporate-sponsored paternalism and social welfare might have offered workers certain provisions ranging from libraries and insurance protection to indoor flush toilets and birth control instruction,[58] But these programs ultimately were demeaning to the very people they were intended to serve. While the companies claimed that everything necessary for human existence was offered in the mining towns, they failed to provide their employees with common justice or representation.[59] Services and amenities were exchanged for the individual and collective rights of employees, and contributed to the development of a regional economic-governmental system that was non-democratic both in concept and application.

During the 1960s and 1970s perceptive scholars have pointed out that no matter how benevolent paternalism appeared on the surface, such practices eventually led to frustration, bitterness and hostility.[60] It is important to note that the Finns, by their attitudes and actions, were already questioning these paternalistic practices more than seventy years ago. Whereas one normally thinks of radical activities when considering this period, the Finns also developed a viable institutional life of their own to counter the offerings of companies. Inis Weed contrasted the majority of community institutions in the Copper Country, all of which were dependent upon corporate good will—churches, baths, books, hospital, militia practice, sports and music—with the spirit of a local Finnish social centre and its hall, restaurant, daily paper and related social activities. "They [the Finns] planned the center and built it," related Weed, "[and] they love it." Undoubtedly the actions of many Finnish immigrants in questioning corporate policies and separating themselves from the mainstream of community life and activities appeared conspiratorial to their opponents, but in reality the Finns were doing nothing more than responding "to inhuman conditions in industrial America."[61] When viewed retrospectively, their efforts were not in vain.

# Notes

1. U.S. Immigration Commission, *Reports of the Immigration Commission: Immigrants in Industries*, Part 18. Senate Document No. 633, Serial 5677, 61st Cong., 2nd Session (Washington, D.C.: Government Printing Office, 1911), p. 341.

2. Ibid., p. 340; W.J. Lauck, "Iron Ore Mines on Mesabi and Vermilion Ranges," *Mining and Engineering World* 35 (Dec. 23, 1911), p. 1,270; and T.A. Rickard, "The Copper Mines of Lke Lake Superior" New York; *Engineering and Mining Journal*, 1905, p. 18.

3. M.E. Kaups, "The Finns in the Copper and Iron Ore Mines of the Western Great Lakes Region, 1864-1905: Some Preliminary Observations." In *The Finnish Experience in the Western Great Lakes Region: New Perspectives*, M.G. Karni, M.E. Kaups, and D.J. Ollila, Jr., eds. (Turku, Finland: Institute for Migration, 1975), pp. 56-60; and U.S. Department of Commerce, Bureau of the Census, *Population 1920*, Vol. 3 (Washington, D.C.: Government Printing Office, 1921).

4. D. Ollila, Jr., "The Finnish-American Church Organizations." In *Old Friends—Strong Ties*, V. Niitemaa, *et al.*, eds. (Turku, Finland: Institute for Migration, 1976), p. 146.

5. *Ibid.*, and R. Kero, "Roots of Finnish-American Left-Wing Radicalism." In *Publications of the Institute of General History*, No. 5. Turku, Finland: University of Turku (1975), pp. 45-55.

6. Kaups, "The Finns in the Copper and Iron Ore Mines," op. cit., pp. 55 & 57. For recent interpretations of Finnish labor movements in America see especially, C. Ross, *The Finn Factor in American Labor, Culture and Society* (New York Mills, Minn.: Parta Printers, Inc., 1977); A. Gedicks, "Ethnicity, Class Solidarity, and Labor Radicalism among Finnish Immigrants in Michigan Copper Country," *Politics & Society* 7 (No. 2, 1977), pp. 127-156; M.G. Karni, "The Founding of the Finnish Socialist Tradition and the Minnesota Strike of 1907"; and A.E. Puotinen, "Early Labor Organizations in the Copper Country." Both of the latter articles in *For the Common Good: Finnish Immigrants and the Radical Response to Industrial America*, M.G. Karni and D.J. Ollila, Jr., eds. (Superior, Wis.: Tyomies Society, 1977).

7.  D. Ollila, Jr., "From Socialism to Industrial Unionism (IWW): Social Factors in the Emergence of Left-Labor Radicalism among Finnish Workers on the Mesabi, 1911-19." In *The Finnish Experience in the Western Great Lakes Region: New Perspectives*, M.G. Karni, M.E. Kaups, and D.J. Ollila, Jr., eds. (Turku, Finland: Institute for Migration, 1975), p. 156.

8.  V.H. Jensen, *Heritage of Conflict: Labor Relations in the Nonferrous Metal Industries up to 1930* (Ithaca, N.Y.: Cornell University Press, 1950), p. 273.

9.  W.B. Gates, Jr., *Michigan Copper and Boston Dollars: An Economic History of the Michigan Copper Industry* (Cambridge, Mass.: Harvard University Press, 1951), p. 134.

10. J.B. Martin, *Call It North Country: The Story of Upper Michigan* (New York: Alfred A. Knopf, 1944), p. 120.

11. H.J. Brinks, "Marquette Iron Range Strike, 1895," *Michigan History* 50 (Dec. 1966), p. 305.

12. W.G. Mather, "Some Observations on the Principle of Benefit Funds and Their Place in the Lake Superior Iron Mining District," *Proceedings of the Lake Superior Mining Institute* 5 (1898), pp. 10-20.

13. W.H. Moulton, "The Sociological Side of the Mining Industry," *Proceedings of the Lake Superior Mining Institute* 14 (1909), pp. 97 and 98.

14. D. Brody, *Steelworkers in America: The Non-Union Era* (Cambridge, Mass.: Harvard University Press, 1960), p. 111.

15. Ollila, "From Socialism to Industrial Unionism," op. cit., p. 171.

16. "Oliver Iron Mining Co. Adopts Labor Co-operation Policy," *Engineering and Mining Journal* 105 (July 29, 1918), p. 1167.

17. P.F. Abrahams, *et al.*, "A Study of Labor Relations at Calumet Division of Calumet & Hecla" (M.S. Thesis, Houghton: Michigan Technological University, 1969), p. 42; and "A Bond of Interest," *Harlow's Wooden Man* (Marquette, Mich.) 14 (Fall 1978), p. 20.

18. The basic framework for the regional settlement hierarchy described in this paper is spelled out in A.R. Alanen, "The Planning of Company Communities in the Lake Superior Mining Region," *Journal of the American Planning Association* 45 (July 1979), pp. 260 and 261.

19. J. Syrjamaki, "Mesabi Communities: A Study of Their Development" (Ph.D. dissertation, New Haven, Conn.: Yale University, 1940), p. 113.

20. P. Hapgood, Copy of diary entry (Sept. 30, 1920), on file in Manuscript and Archives Division, Minnesota Historical Society (original deposited at Indiana University).

21. C.W. Pfeiffer, "From 'Bohunks' to Finns: The Scale of Life among the Ore Strippings of the Northwest," *Survey* 36 (April 1916),p. 11.

22. Syrjamaki, "Mesabi Communities," op. cit., pp. 236-38; and undated news clipping from the Hibbing (Minn.) Daily News (on file in the Hibbing Collection, St. Louis County Historical Society, Duluth).

23. Amerikan Suomalainen Lehti, July 11, 1879, p. 2. This issue also describes the use of Finnish spellings—i.e., Kalma, Ramboutown, and Alue—as substitutes for place names in northerm Michigan.

24. Ibid.; A.D. Taylor, Improvements Report on the Montreal Mining Company Properties in the Ironwood District, Michigan (Cleveland: Office of A.D. Taylor, 1921), p. 8; Syrjamaki, "Mesabi Communities," op. cit., p. 235; W. Fox Report (1926), in the W.J. Bell Papers, on file in Division of Archives and Manuscripts, Minnesota Historical Society; and N. Betten, "The Origins of Ethnic Radicalism in Northern Minnesota, 1900-1920," International Migration Review 4 (Spring 1970), p. 53.

25. Alanen, "The Planning of Company Communities," op. cit., p. 269; and Pfeiffer, "From 'Bohunks' to Finns," op. cit., p. 9.

26. D.L. Boese, John C. Greenway and the Opening of the Western Mesabi (Bovey, Minn.: Itasca Community College Foundation, 1975), p. 139; and Alanen, "The Planning of Company Communities," op. cit., p. 261.

27. Weekly Agitator (Ishpeming, Mich.), Sept. 5, 1874, p. 1; and Hibbing (Minn.) Tribune, June 12, 1903, p. 4.

28. F.R. Bellamy, "Bell of the Iron Range," Red Cross Magazine (Dec. 1919), p. 21.

29. Hibbing Tribune, April 7, 1904, p. 4; March 17, 1904, p. 1; and April 13, 1900, p. 1; P.C. Bullard, diary entry (1908) on file in Division of Archives and Manuscripts, Minnesota Historical Society; Portage Lake Mining Gazette (Houghton, Mich.), Nov. 9, 1876, p. 3; and C.A. Chambers, "Social Welfare Policies and Programs on the Minnesota Iron Range—1890-1930" (manuscript on file in the Immigration History Research Center, University of Minnesota, St. Paul, 1963), p. 14.

30. Amerikan Suomalainen Lehti, May 6, 1818, p. 3; July 23, 1880, p. 2; and Aug. 29, 1879, p. 2.

31. Ibid., Aug. 29, 1879, p. 2; and Aug. 20, 1880, p. 3. By the turn of the century these impressions apparently had changed, for the Finns now began to applaud the Irish for their festivals, social institutions and other efforts to maintain a viable cultural life and identity. Comment by J.I. Kolehmainen to the author, Nov. 3, 1979.

32. Päivälehti (Calumet, Mich.), July 25, 1913, p. 5; and Ross, The Finn Factor, op. cit., p. 173.

33. Many newspaper accounts were grossly exaggerated, and others were completely fictitious. The point must be made, however, that by publishing the accounts, no matter how biased or erroneous, the attitudes of editors, reporters, and residents were revealed.

34. During a five year period from 1874 through 1878, the *Portage Lake Mining Gazette* of Houghton contained only three accounts which referred to Finns in the Copper Country. Three decades later, the Finnish population had expanded from a small incipient community of some 1,000 persons to about 8,000 inhabitants; likewise, during one single year (1906), mention of Finns or Finnish groups increased to more than 200 listings in the *Daily Mining Gazette*. Of these accounts, about 55 percent addressed Finnish social, cultural, and economic activities such as Suomi College, temperence and church organizations, and the Finnish Mutual Insurance Company. The remainder reported on the altercations, violent deaths, court cases, drunkenness, or moral turpitude of Finns. (Only four accounts addressed their participation in socialist groups or strikes.) In the *Hibbing Tribune* during the early twentieth centure, however, the vast majority of reports mentioned the Finns in a negative or derogatory manner. The greater reportorial balance of the Michigan newspaper probably was due to several reasons, with some of the factors undoubtedly being: the fact that the initial development of the Mesabi Range and Finnish radicalism coincided during the late 1800s and early 1900s; there was a large number of single, footloose males on the raw Mesabi frontier; the devisive 1907 strike occurred in Minnesota during this period; and there was a lack of traditional, conservative Finnish organizations during the early years of mining activity on the Mesabi.

35. *Duluth News Tribune*, April 16, 1907, p. 12; and Dec. 14, 1906, p. 8; and *Hibbing Tribune*, July 29, 1899, p. 5.

36. *Ibid.*, Feb. 23, 1905, p. 3.

37. Bullard, 1906 diary, op. cit.; and Martin, *Call It North Country*, op. cit., p. 18.

38. L.C. Reimann, *Between the Iron and the Pine: A Biography of a Pioneer Family and a Pioneer Town* (Ann Arbor, Mich.: Edwards Brothers, Inc., 1951), p. 85.

39. H.N. Casson, *The Romance of Steel: The Story of a Thousand Millionaires* (New York: A.S. Barnes & Company, 1907), pp. 252 & 253.

40. *Hibbing Tribune*, Oct. 4, 1906, p. 1.

41. Ibid., March 31, 1904, p. 1; Aug. 30, 1906, p. 5; and Nov. 12, 1903, p. 4.

42. U.S. Immigration Commission, *Reports of the Immigration Commission*, op. cit., pp. 337, 395 and 398; H. Berman, "Education for Work and Labor Solidarity: The Immigrant Miners and Radicalism on the Mesabi Range" (manuscript in possession of Immigration History Research Center, University of Minnesota, St. Paul, 1963), pp. 43 and 44; G.O. Virtue, *The Minnesota Iron Ranges*, Bulletin of the Bureau of Labor, No. 84 (Washington, D.C.: Government Printing Office, 1909), pp. 345 and 346; and P.H. Landis, *Three Iron Mining Towns: A Study*

in Cultural Change (Ann Arbor, Mich.: Edwards Borthers, Inc., 1938). p. 110.

43.  Boese, John C. Greenway, op. cit., p. 109; and W.H. Manning, "Villages and Homes for Working Men," Western Architect 16 (Aug. 1910), pp. 85 and 87. Most mining communities in the region were not strictly limited to specific ethnic groups.

44.  P.B. McDonald, "The Michigan Copper Miners," Outlook 106 (Feb. 7, 1914), p 298; "The Proposed Elimination of the Finns," Engineering and Mining Journal 97 (May 2, 1914), p. 920; and L. Magnusson, Housing by Employers in the United States, U.S. Bureau of Labor Statistics Bulletin No. 263, Miscellaneous Series (Washington, D.C.: Government Printing Office, 1920), p. 38.

45.  Amerikan Suomalainen Lehti, Aug. 29, 1879, p. 1; July 11, 1879, p. 2; and Aug. 26, 1881, p. 2.

46.  Ibid., July 11, 1879, p. 2; and Kuparisaaren Sanomat (Hancock, Mich.), Jan. 31, 1896, p. 2.

47.  Amerikan Suomalainen Lehti, Aug. 29, 1879, p. 2; Dec. 3, 1880, p. 3; Aug. 8, 1879, p. 1; and Industrialisti (Duluth), April 11, 1918, p. 2.

48.  J.I. Kolehmainen and G.W. Hill, Haven in the Woods: The Story of the Finns in Wisconsin (Madison: State Historical Society of Wisconsin, 1951), pp. 119 and 120.

49.  A.R. Alanen, "The Development of Finnish Consumers' Cooperatives in Michigan, Minnesota, and Wisconsin, 1903-1973." In The Finnish Experience in the Western Great Lakes Region: New Perspectives, M.G. Karni, M.E. Kaups, and D.J. Ollila, eds. op. cit., pp. 110-117; Pelto ja Koti (Superior, Wis.) 3 (Jan. 1914), p. 21; Kolmannen Amerikan Suomalaisen Sosialistijärjestön edustajakokoukseen, Hancock, Aug. 23-30, 1909 (Fitchburg, Mass.: Raivajan Kirjapaino, 1909), pp. 26-29; Yhdysvaltain Suomalaisen Sosialistijärjestön neljännen edustajakouuksen pöytäkirja, Chicago, Nov. 22-Dec. 1, 1914 (Astoria, Ore.: Toveri Press, 1915), pp. 99-101; Ollila, "From Socialism to Industrial Unionism," op. cit., p. 157.

50.  Hibbing Tribune, Feb. 27, 1908, p. 1; Iron Ore (Ishpeming, Mich.), July 4, 1908, p. 1; and letter from J. Wargelin to W.J. Olcott (Jan. 6, 1921), on file in Oliver Iron Mining Co. Papers, Division of Archives and Manuscripts, Minnesota Historical Society.

51.  Amerikan Suomalainen Lehti, May 13, 1881, p. 3.

52.  Data for Hurley from forthcoming MS Thesis by M. Taylor (Madison: University of Wisconsin). Information on Oulu and Owen area Finns from S. Ilmonen, Amerikan Suomalaisten Historia, Vol. 3 (Hancock, Mich.: Suom.-Lut. Kustannusliikkeen Kirjapaino, 1926); Sunnyside Homemakers' Club, Historical Sketches of the Town of Oulu: Bayfield County, Wisconsin, 1880-1956 (Oulu, Wis.: The Club, 1956); records of the Oulu and Owen Lutheran Churches; and personal interviews conducted by the author and Dr. Michael Berry in 1974-75.

53. *Lännetär* (Astoria, Ore.), Jan. 14, 1897, p. 2; Kaups, "The Finns in the Copper and Iron Ore Mines," op. cit., p. 66; J.I. Kolehmainen, "Takaisiin maalle!—'Maaemoa se meidät kaikki elätää', " *Työväen Osuustoimintalehti* (Superior, Wis.), Feb. 2, 1946, p. 5.

54. Hoglund has made a similar observation. See A.W. Hoglund, "Flight from Industry: Finns and Farming in America," *Finnish-Americana* 1 (1978), pp. 14 and 15.

55. Pfeiffer, "From 'Bohunks' to Finns," op. cit., p. 13; L. Hodges, "Immigrant Life in the Ore Region of Northern Minnesota," *Survey* 28 (Sept. 7,1912), p. 709; W.J. Bell, untitled manuscript for speech (1927), on file in W.J. Bell Papers, Division of Archives and Manuscripts, Minnesota Historical Society; D. Whittlesey, "A Locality on a Stubborn Frontier at the Close of a Cycle of Occupance," *Geografiska Annaler* 12 (1930), p. 182; and "Our Most Thickly Populated Township," *Wisconsin Agriculturist* 39 (Feb. 1915), p. 8.

56. *Hibbing Daily Tribune*, Sept. 25, 1913, p. 1; and W.J. Bell, script for lecture (c. 1916), on file in W.J. Bell Papers, op. cit.

57. Letter from E.P. Lockhart and G.L. Woodworth to J.S. Wall (Nov. 20, 1919), on file in Oliver Iron Mining Company Papers, op. cit.

58. A. Murdoch, *Boom Copper: The Story of the First U.S. Mining Boom* (New York: Macmillan Company, 1943), p. 154

59. H.A. Atkinson, *The Church and Industrial Welfare: A Report on the Labor Troubles in Colorado and Michigan* (Prepared for the Federal Council of the Churches of Christ in America, 1914), p. 44.

60. See, for example, Brody, *Steelworkers in America*, op. cit.; J.A. Garraty, "The United States Steel Corporation Versus Labor: The Early Years," *Labor History* 1 (Winter 1960), pp. 3-38; M.A McLaurin, *Paternalism and Protest: Southern Cotton Mill Workers and Organized Labor: 1875-1905* (Westport, Conn.: Greenwood Publishing Corp., 1971); and L.F. Litwack, *Been in the Storm So Long: The Aftermath of Slavery* (New York: Alfred A. Knopf, 1979).

61. I. Weed, "The Reason Why the Copper Miners Struck," *Survey* 106 (Jan. 31, 1914), p. 251; and Ollila, "From Socialism to Industrial Unionism," op. cit., p. 170.

# Finns in Urban America: A View from Duluth

*Matti Kaups*

From the very beginning of Finnish immigration to the United States in the nineteenth century, urbanism was an integral component of the immigrant experience.[1] While for some the stay in cities and towns—including mining settlements—was a transitory phase before settling on land either as bona fide or part-time farmers, the majority preferred the amenities of city life on permanent bases. In 1920, 53.4 per cent of the total of 149,824 foreign-born Finns (hereafter Finns, unless indicated otherwise) in the United States resided in cities. Moreover, a large but undetermined number of the Finns classified by the United States census as rural population (46.6 per cent) actually lived in small mining towns which in their economic function and settlement characteristics were akin to urban places. And there was a tendency for the Finns to settle increasingly in medium and large-sized cities after the turn of the century. While in 1900, 12,089 Finns (19.3 per cent of the total Finnish population) resided in cities with 25,000 or more inhabitants, in 1920, the number of Finns in such cities had increased to 43,995 (29.4 per cent of the total Finnish population).[2] Data for specific cities well illustrate the general trend. During the twenty-year period, the Finnish population in Detroit increased from a total of 4 to 1,785; in New York the increase was from 3,733 to 10,240; and in Duluth, from 702 to 3,210 (see Table 1 and Map 1).

The quantitative growth on the Finnish immigrant urban frontier also had a definite geographical expression as the Finns settled in a

TABLE 1: Finnish Urban Population Centres (with 1,000 or more
Finns) in Cities of 25,000 or more Inhabitants in 1920

| Rank | 1920 | 1900 | Increase |
|---|---|---|---|
| 1. New York, NY | 10,240 | 3,733 | 6,507 |
| 2. Duluth, MN | 3,210 | 702 | 2,508 |
| 3. Fitchburg, MA | 2,823 | 963 | 1,860 |
| 4. Seattle, WA | 2,256 | 424 | 1,832 |
| 5. Worcester, MA | 2,175 | 1,143 | 1,032 |
| 6. San Francisco, CA | 1,810 | 935 | 875 |
| 7. Detroit, MI | 1,785 | 4 | 1,781 |
| 8. Chicago, IL | 1,577 | 416 | 1,161 |
| 9. Portland, OR | 1,394 | 98 | 1,296 |
| 10. Quincy, MA | 1,338 | n.d. | - |
| 11. Cleveland, OH | 1,122 | 79 | 1,043 |
| 12. Minneapolis, MN | 1,120 | 348 | 772 |
| 13. Butte, MT | 1,003 | 414 | 589 |

greater number of cities. The number of urban places with 25,000
or more inhabitants in which the Finns dwelled increased from 120
in 1900 to 246 in 1920. The percentage increase (263.9 per cent) of
Finns in these cities was nearly double the increase (139.2 per cent)
of Finns in the country as a whole during the time period. The
growth of the Finnish population in American cities derived primarily from three sources: through direct immigration from Finland,
through internal migration from mining towns and smaller urban
centres, and from Finnish rural communities in the United States.

With some notable exceptions,[3] students of Finnish immigrant life in the United States have, either because of personal
preferences, available data sources, or particular research priorities,
produced numerous pages on the history of how the immigrant
founded and maintained social, religious, and political institutions,
so that we have some knowledge of the vicissitudes of the temperance and labour movements, the Mesabi Range strike of 1907, the
conflicts between the "church" Finns and the "Socialist" Finns, the
involvement of the Finns in the Industrial Workers of the World
(IWW) movement, and of other perturbations of greater and lesser
significance.[4] That is all to the common good, and the authors
ought to be commended for examining these topics from an intra-
ethnic perspective. On the other hand, there has been an utter void
of studies concerning the urban ecology of the Finns, though there
are encouraging signs of recent research in that direction both in
Canada and the United States.[5] Needed are monographs that ex-

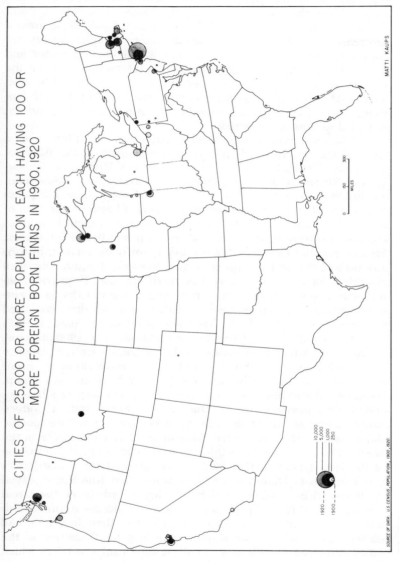

CITIES OF 25,000 OR MORE POPULATION EACH HAVING 100 OR MORE FOREIGN BORN FINNS IN 1900, 1920

MATTI KAUPS

SOURCE OF DATA: U.S CENSUS, POPULATION, 1900, 1920

MAP 1.

plore the Finnish immigrant life and institutions in North American cities from the perspective of transatlantic rural to urban migration, as the large majority of the Finns came from a rural, agrarian setting in Finland, and the transition of individuals from a predominantly folk society to that of a more complex society occurred in the process of urbanization in the United States and Canada.[6] Such undertakings regarding the interaction between the Finns and the changing urban environments require, of course, more than a casual acquaintance with the relevant Finnish-language sources, the extensive literature on American urban history, and local manuscript materials.

The most widely circulated portrayal of the Finns in the cities of the American Middle West is imbedded in the pages of such general histories as Armas K. E. Holmio's *Michiganin Suomalaisten Historia* (1967), and Hans R. Wasastjerna's *Minnesotan Suomalaisten Historia* (1957). Wasastjerna devotes some 150 pages to Duluth, most of which concerns the period between the turn of the century and the mid-1950s. The volume, which is said to contain "inadvertent inaccuracies," relies primarily on interviews, life histories and local histories compiled mostly by amateur historians in the 1950s at the request of the Minnesota Finnish-American Historical Society.[7] The book has merit, in that it provides an intra-ethnic perspective on how the Finns perceived the local Finnish immigrant community and the milieu in which they lived, and how Finns were thought to have perceived in the past. In that respect the comments relating to the period prior to 1900 are most illuminating. Although Wasastjerna does acknowledge the presence of Swedish Finns in Duluth, his qualitative description of the Finns is that of a sociologically and economically homogeneous group, composed almost entirely of males who held low paying jobs associated with sawmills, docks, construction work, grain elevators, road building and other subordinate tasks that required no specific skills. Some of the Finns were also employed as lumberjacks in the nearby forests during the winter months. The seasonal fluctuation of the local labour market may in part account for Wasastjerna's conclusion that "Duluth was a place where they [the Finns] stayed no longer than necessary before moving to whatever their real destinations were."[8] There was a slow development of Finnish immigrant voluntary associations, which after their founding, had exceedingly small memberships. According to Wasastjerna, the Finns perceived Duluth as a "small, insignificant town," in which "houses were built at random," a view that is contrary to antecedent events, as the city had been planned years earlier.[9] Moreover, the urban environment was viewed as overbearing and deterministic because the Finns "were compelled to live in miserable lodgings in the oldest part of town, and the morale of some suffered accordingly."[10]

Aside from employment, formal relations with the "outside world" and its institutions were few and seemingly limited to law enforcement agencies and the courts of law. Informal relations, on the other hand, took place under different circumstances: "For amusement, the Finns visited the numerous saloons, and the houses of joy, in which the various nationalities all met each other, and met in peace."[11] According to Wasastjerna, these activities constituted the only positive elements of an otherwise drab and impersonal American urban environment, in which the Finns allegedly occupied the lowest socio-economic strata, or according to contemporary parlance, the lowest rungs on the urban-escalator model.

The Finns had closer contacts with each other, however, within the confines of the Finnish immigrant community. Although the following vignette is probably more idealistic than reliable, it nonetheless alludes to the continuity of rural folkways in urban America: "On beautiful summer evenings, however, the Finns lived practically in the street, calling out from their doorsteps to passing friends, running out to see if their cows were still grazing along the shore meadows, and sometimes leading the cows down the street to greener pastures."[12] Had Wasastjerna contacted sources about the area he is referring to (St. Croix Avenue – Lake Superior shore on Minnesota Point), he would have discovered that sandy and boulder-strewn beaches, subject to periodic onslaught of waves, do not support shore meadows nor green pastures on which to graze cows. It is a diagnostic of Wasastjerna's general disregard for the non-Finnish language sources.

Indeed, his study raises a number of questions about the Finnish immigrant experience in American cities. Is Wasastjerna's model for the Finns in Duluth applicable to the different Finnish urban communities in America? Did the Finns in San Francisco, Portland, Detroit, Fitchburg, New York and elsewhere find themselves living in the "worst parts of town," and were the worst jobs likewise reserved for the Finns? Were the Finns always pushed into ghetto-like existence, assuming that to have been the case, and if so, was it a product of urban environment or did a measure of ethnicity bring it about? What were the demographic characteristics of the different Finnish communities? What were the consequences of the high degree of geographical mobility, as implied for Duluth, on the formation of voluntary associations? Did the immigrants remain in a "culture of poverty," or were there avenues of social and economic mobility available to them? Extensive research is needed before these and related questions can be answered adequately.

First of all, studies are needed that examine the Finnish communities in specific cities, that investigate the residential patterns, or how the Finns were accommodated within the general urban settlement fabric, that probe the matter of how the Finns interacted or collaborated with the different ethnic groups present, that examine the development of voluntary associations, that probe the degree of geographical and social mobility of the Finns, and investigate the involvement of the Finns in the market place and in the political arena—that is, the role of the Finnish entrepreneurs and the emergence of Finns in urban politics. There is a lack of studies along the lines of Oscar Handlin's *Boston's Immigrants* (1968), Humbert S. Nelli's *Italians in Chicago 1880-1930* (1970), Ulf Beijbom's *Swedes in Chicago* (1971), Stephan Ternstrom's *The Other Bostonians* (1973), and Kathleen Neils Conzen's *Immigrant Milwaukee 1836-1860* (1976), studies that analyse ethnic communities and relationships in urban settings.

Secondly, the anticipated studies of Finnish urban communities ought to have a degree of commonality of approach in terms of national perspective, so that they yield data for further comparative studies. The concept of population growth processes curve provides a framework for such undertakings.[13] The bell-shaped theoretical immigrant population growth processes curve consists of several distinct phases: introductory, growth, saturation and regression; it is of value in that it incorporates the variables of emigration-immigration (as they are merely opposite geographical events within a closed system of transatlantic migration), population mobility in the United States and Canada, and the internal labour market characteristics of cities or receiving areas in which the Finns settled (see Figure 1). Although empirical data suggest that, relative to different economic functions of cities or receiving areas, the Finnish immigrant communities experienced differential growth rates and variations in growth processes, the theoretical growth processes curve, nonetheless, provides a common denominator, a spectrum on which the life cycles of individual communities can be plotted for comparative analysis and the formulation of a general theory of Finnish immigrant life and institutions in urban United States and Canada.[14]

The beginnings of the introductory phase of the Finnish immigration to Duluth coincided with the expanding local labour market and the related population growth. The town's population increased from 294 in 1865 to 3,131 in 1870.[15] It was directly related to the construction of the Lake Superior and Mississippi railroad between Duluth and St. Paul in the years 1869-1870 (completed on August 1, 1870), the construction of the Northern Pacific railroad to the westward, the building of port facilities and the town itself. Duluth was in the process of becoming a significant northern transportation node through which populations and manufactured goods from the east entered the Middle West, and through which Middle Western grain was shipped to the eastern markets.[16] Opinions vary as to when Finns first arrived in Duluth. Salomon Ilmonen held that a few Finns were in Duluth already in the year 1868, but "they did not settle down in that unruly town."[17] Although no Finns are listed in the federal manuscript census of 1870, evidence suggests that a certain Johan Moilanen from Oulu had arrived as a permanent settler in the year 1869. Significantly, six out of the seven Finnish males who arrived in the city in the years 1869-1872 were by profession fishermen.[18] They were a part of the westward expanding commercial fisheries frontier on Lake Superior.[19]

The enlarged labour market associated with the transportation and urban frontiers at Duluth had failed to attract a large number of Finns to the city on a permanent basis for the time being. Yet Duluth was not a terra incognita to the hundreds of Finns who worked in the copper and iron ore mines in nearby northern Michigan.[20] On their journeys to the incipient Finnish agricultural communities located in central Minnesota, and in Midway and Thomson townships near Duluth (established in 1872-1873), the Finns made use of the most direct communication linkages, travelling on regularly scheduled steamships during the ice-free season on Lake Superior to Duluth, thence continuing on railroads to the south and westward. Evidently some of the Finns who had settled on land near Duluth found part-time employment in the city. It appears that none of the estimated 110 Finns who arrived directly from Finland in Duluth in the summer of 1873, for the purpose of working on the Northern Pacific railroad, but who decided against it, settled in the city.[21] According to the Minnesota State manuscript Census of 1875, there were a total of nine Finns in Duluth in the summer of that year.[22] The nationwide financial panic that lasted for some five years, from 1873 through 1878, rendered Duluth a negative receiving area for immigrants in general, as the city's economy slumped and its total population declined through out-migration. It is certain, however, that some of the Finnish fisherman remained in Duluth.[23] The introductory phase of the Finnish immigration to Duluth was characterized by a lack of Finnish social and religious organizations as well as business enterprises.

The initial growth phase of the Finnish immigrant population in Duluth, which commenced in the early 1880s and continued until the beginning years of the present century, was a corollary to the revitalization of Duluth's economy and development of the timber and iron ore resources of northeastern Minnesota. The expansion of sawmills, construction industry, wholesale trade, shipping and railroad facilities at Duluth brought about a greater demand for labour, albeit subject to notable seasonal fluctuation.[24] The city's total population increased from 3,487 in 1880, to 17,418 in 1885, and to 52,969 in 1900. The number of Finns increased from a mere 9 in 1880 to 415 in 1885.[25] At this time the Finnish population was composed primarily of males (76.4 per cent), of whom one-half were between twenty and thirty-four years of age (see Figure 2). Present were 51 Finnish family units and 238 "unattached" males, most of whom boarded with the families.[26] It is important to note, however, that it was not a stationary population, as the Finns experienced a remarkably high degree of geographical mobility. Duluth was one of the significant nodes in the hierarchy of places within the Finnish immigrant spatial-communication network in North America. By the 1880s, it was connected through a series of direct transportation linkages with most of the growing number of Finnish population centres as well as with Finland. Duluth had access to, and was accessible from, the mines and lumber camps of northern Michigan, Wisconsin and Minnesota, the Finnish agricultural communities in the Middle West, the mining towns of the Rocky Mountain states, the Pacific Northwest, and Canada. Through it hundreds of Finns journeyed westward, some of them to work on the construction camps on the Canadian Pacific railroad in the 1880s.[27] In 1895, 620 Finns were enumerated in Duluth, and five years later their number had increased to 702.[28]

Amid the geographical mobility of the Finns, there was, nevertheless, a measure of permanency, as several Finnish immigrant organizations and businesses were established in the city during the initial growth phase. Already by 1881, there were several Finnish boarding-houses on St. Croix Avenue on Minnesota Point, and on Rice's Point (see Map 2). A tailor (Johan Ranto) had located on Minnesota Point in 1884, and in the following year, Victor Lauri opened his "Suomalainen Salooni" on Lake Avenue on Minnesota

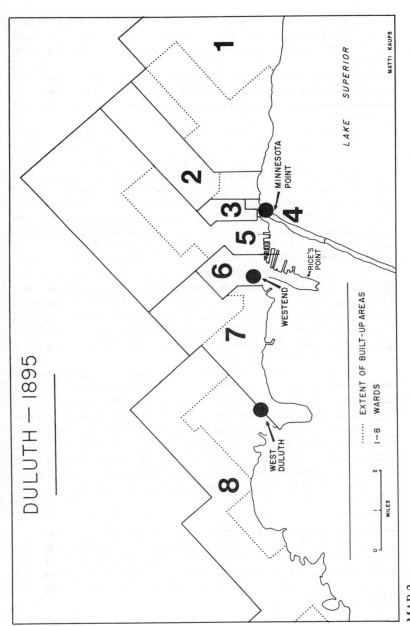

MAP 2.

Point which he claimed to be the nearest drinking place to the docks. He also sold passenger tickets to "all destinations" in Canada. In 1886, a stock company was organized in Duluth for the purpose of mining gold in nearby Carlton County. It was, of course, an abortive venture. By 1890, there had been added to the incipient Finnish immigrant entrepreneurial efforts, largely service-oriented in nature, a restaurant and a steamship agency that sold tickets for transatlantic travel to and from Finland.[29]

Apparently the earliest of the several Finnish immigrant organizations in Duluth was the Finnish Cultural Society (established in 1881). A library was maintained by the short-lived association. A "Finlander band" had been organized in the early 1880s and performed at Finnish as well as "Scandinavian" social functions. The *Toivon Tähti* temperance society was organized in 1886. The Duluth Finnish Evangelical Lutheran congregation has its origins in 1888, though religious services in the Finnish language had been conducted occasionally by Peter Raattamaa, Johan Takkinen, J. C. Nikander and William Williamson in the city some years earlier.[30]Also, the three separate retail and residential areas of the Finns in Duluth evolved into recognizable entities during the initial growth phase (see Map 2). Adverse political conditions in Finland, as well as the expansion of local economy in and about Duluth, contributed directly to a secondary intensification of the growth phase after the turn of the century. In 1905, there were a total of 2,131 Finns enumerated in Duluth.[31]

The saturation phase was reached during the second decade of the century and it continued until about the year 1930. A maximum of 3,210 Finns were enumerated in the city in 1920.[32] From a societal-cultural perspective, the saturation phase was an era characterized by a proliferation of Finnish immigrant organizations and other enterprises. It was the heyday of political debates, athletic clubs, theatrical groups, the church, the temperance society, and it witnessed the publication of most of the total of forty-three Finnish-language newspapers, periodicals and annuals published in the city during the years 1894-1976.[33] This burst of activity may be dubbed the era of ethnic flowering of the Finnish immigrant community in Duluth.

After 1930, the Finnish-born population, together with the immigrant-founded and maintained organizations, entered the fourth phase, what seemingly is the final regression phase. The number of foreign-born Finns in the city has declined to a total of 1,030 by 1960.[34]

In order to gain an understanding of the urban experience of the Finnish immigrants in the United States and Canada, each of the four stages of the growth processes curve ought to be scrutinized for the different communities studied. Moreover, the Finns should be placed in the perspective of their time of arrival, and that of other nationality groups (see Figure 1). What, then, was the likeness of the Finnish immigrant community in Duluth during the initial growth phase in the 1890s? In light of recent research, Wasastjerna's conception of it is untenable because the community was far more atomistic than homogeneous in character. It was diverse in its residential, occupational and marriage patterns, as well as in its age and sex structure. Moreover, the members of the community experienced a high degree of geographical mobility.

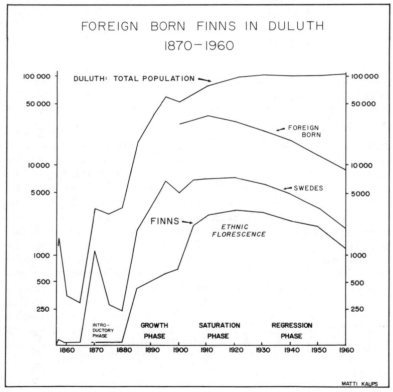

Figure 1.

The residential pattern of the Finns in Duluth in 1895 does not support the ghetto hypothesis—that is, that the Finns were geographically separated from other ethnic groups in the city.[35] Indexes of dissimilarity calculated for the ten leading nationality groups reveal a significant degree of dispersion for all of the populations, including the Finns, and confirms the absence of ethnic ghettos in the city.[36]

TABLE 2: Indexes of Dissimilarity, Duluth, 1895

| Country of Birth | 1895 |
|---|---|
| Canada | 14.4 |
| Denmark | 27.9 |
| England | 26.7 |
| Finland | 27.4 |
| Germany | 23.6 |
| Ireland | 27.0 |
| Norway | 21.1 |
| Russia | 25.9 |
| Scotland | 27.4 |
| Sweden | 15.5 |

The narrow, elongated shape of the city (measuring 23.2 miles along the northeast-southwest axis), the dispersal of places of employment, and the presence of multi-nucleated commercial districts, did not favour a high degree of spatial clustering of the various nationality groups. Most of the Finns (87.9 per cent) resided interspersed with other nationalities in three different parts of the city, in the Fourth, Sixth, Seventh and Eighth wards.[37] Even in the so-called worst part of town, in the Fourth Ward on Minnesota Point, where 35.3 per cent of the Finns resided, they accounted for only 7.6 per cent of the ward's foreign-born population. The Canadians, Swedes, Norwegians and Germans were present in greater numbers. The Finnish social and religious organizations, retail businesses, saloons and boarding-houses were located in the aforementioned wards at three nodes identified with circles on Map 2; in West Duluth, some five and a half miles from Minnesota Point; in West End, in the heart of Duluth's "Swede Town"; and on St. Croix and Lake avenues on Minnesota Point. These were the visible Finnish neighbourhoods in the city, because of the presence of Finnish businesses and organizations, and the fact that most of the Finns resided in and about these nodes, though they did not constitute the majority of the foreign-born population. There was, however, small-scale clustering of the Finns on city block level along St. Croix and Lake avenues on Minnesota Point. The scale of clustering was undoubtedly influenced by the relatively small size of the Finnish population present in the city, and its location reflected the occupations of the early arrivals and the geographical proximity to the steamship and railroad passenger terminals. Available data do not support Wasastjerna's contention that the Finns were "compelled" to live in the Fourth Ward on Minnesota Point, in the worst part of town, or that "the morale of some suffered accordingly." Rather, the location of the Finns on St. Croix Avenue had its beginnings with the arrival of Finnish fishermen in the city during the introductory growth phase, in the years 1869-1872. At this time, the lakeshore near the base of Minnesota Point was the centre of Duluth's fisheries and the section of town where most of the fishermen lived, whose residences and equipment sheds were occasionally intruded upon by autumnal, storm-swept waves.[38] With the growth of the Finnish population in the 1880s, Duluth's incipient "Finn Town" spread from St. Croix Avenue—sometimes referred to as "Finlander Avenue" in the local English-language press—to the adjacent St. Croix Alley and Lake Avenue.[39]

TABLE 3: Distribution of Finns by City Wards, Duluth, 1895

| Ward | Absolute Numbers | Per Cent | Per Cent of Total Foreign Born | Per Cent of Total Population |
|------|------------------|----------|-------------------------------|------------------------------|
| One | 23 | 3.7 | 1.4 | ° |
| Two | 15 | 2.4 | ° | ° |
| Three | 16 | 2.6 | ° | ° |
| Four | 219 | 35.3 | 7.6 | 3.3 |
| Five | 21 | 3.4 | ° | ° |
| Six | 106 | 17.1 | 2.4 | 1.3 |
| Seven | 103 | 16.6 | 2.5 | 1.2 |
| Eight | 117 | 18.9 | 3.3 | 1.6 |
| | 620 | 100 | | |

° Less than 1 per cent

The age and sex composition of the Finns in Duluth in 1895 (see Figure 2) conformed to the characteristics of Finnish immigration in general in that most of them (62.2 per cent) were between 20 and 34 years of age and male (61.1 per cent).[40] The

population was, however, less male-dominated than it had been ten
years earlier when the males accounted for 76.4 per cent. Moreover, the number of family units in which both of the partners
were born in Finland had increased from 51 in 1885 to 130 in
1895, while the total of "unattached" males had decreased from
238 to 155.[41] Nearly 80 per cent of the "unattached" males resided
with Finnish family units and in boarding-houses operated by the
Finns, a fact that reinforced the residential clustering of the Finns
in the city. It is important to note, however, that because of the
high degree of geographical mobility the Finns experienced, there
was but a small fraction of the 1885 population present in 1895. In
1895, out of the total of 330 household heads and "unattached"
males, 21 (6.4 per cent) had resided in the city's census enumera-
tion districts (wards) for ten or more years, while 24.9 per cent had
lived in the State of Minnesota for ten or more years (see Table 4).
The data thus reveal a high level of inter-city and inter-regional
mobility.

TABLE 4: Length of Residency of Male Household Heads and
Unattached Males in Duluth's Wards and in the State of
Minnesota, 1895

| Length of Residence | Duluth's Wards | | State of Minnesota | |
|---|---|---|---|---|
| | Absolute Numbers | Per Cent | Absolute Numbers | Per Cent |
| Less than 1 year | 67 | 20.3 | 21 | 6.4 |
| 1 - 5 years | 198 | 60.0 | 158 | 47.9 |
| 6 - 10 years | 48 | 14.5 | 92 | 27.9 |
| 11 - 15 years | 17 | 5.2 | 50 | 15.1 |
| 16 years and more | 0 | 0 | 9 | 2.7 |
| | 330 | 100 | 330 | 100 |

The high degree of inter-regional geographical mobility had
an adverse effect on the membership and programs of the immigrant social and religious organizations during the initial growth
phase. The geographical mobility of the Finns was, indeed, a function of the seasonal character of Duluth's labour market, and the
fact that the majority of the Finnish immigrants were unskilled
labourers, many of whom followed the seasonal rhythm of employment opportunities, moving in and out of cities, mining towns and
lumber and railroad camps. They were a part of the "floating
proletariat" in nineteenth-century America.[42]

TABLE 5: Occupation Structure of the Finns, Duluth, 1895

|  | Males | Per Cent | Females | Per Cent |
|---|---|---|---|---|
| Professionals | 2 | ° | | |
| Proprietors | 19 | 5.5 | 1 | 1.7 |
| Semi-Professionals | 1 | ° | | |
| Clerical and Sales | 7 | 2.0 | | |
| Skilled | 24 | 7.0 | 4 | 6.9 |
| Semi-Skilled and Service | 34 | 9.9 | 34 | 58.6 |
| Unskilled | 257 | 74.7 | 19 | 32.8 |
| | 344 | 100 | 58 | 100 |

° Less than 1 per cent

A salient characteristic of the occupational structure of the Finnish males in Duluth was the preponderance of unskilled workers. Out of the total of 344 employed males present in the city during the summer of 1895, 74.7 per cent were in that category. The convenient label "labourer," however, more aptly identifies an income group rather than a specific task, as the Finns worked in sawmills, construction, grain elevators, railroad yards and as dock-hands loading and unloading ships.[43] As a rule, the sawmills and shipping activity closed down during the five winter months, while the construction jobs were also reduced, so that a good number of the labourers left the city during the autumn months, only to return the next spring. And there was yet another movement during the summer months to harvest grain in the fields of the Dakotas.[44] The occupations of the remaining 25.3 per cent fell into the categories of professional (including a Lutheran minister), proprietors, semi-professional, clerical and sales, skilled, semi-skilled and service. The proprietor group was composed of innovators, of entrepreneurs who owned and operated four grocery stores, four saloons, three boarding-houses, a hotel, a shoestore, a boathouse and a contracting firm. In addition, a plumber operated his own service, as probably did some of the teamsters and the water-delivery men.[45]

In time, the number of Finnish entrepreneurs and professionals increased. They formed the elite and the residentially more stable component of the immigrant society who kept its organizations alive. Moreover, they joined Duluth's civic organizations and participated in local politics. Charles Kauppi, for example, was elected county commissioner in St. Louis County in 1896, a position he held altogether for sixteen years. The position of the Finnish entrepreneurs and professionals was eventually challenged by the arrival of a fresh wave of immigrants and the doctrine of socialism after the turn of the century. Out of the total of fifty-eight Finnish women who were formally employed, 58.6 per cent were in the semi-skilled and service category, working primarily as domestics in American families. It was the presence of domestics that gave the females a slight excess over the males in the 15-19 age group.[46] The unskilled category was composed primarily of laundresses and kitchen help. A boarding-house was operated by a Finnish woman, and one of the dressmakers apparently was a co-owner of a dress shop. However, a number of Finnish women were employed informally in that they helped to augment the families' income by taking care of boarders in their homes; 71 Finnish families had boarders in 1895.[47]

The ethnic composition of the Finnish community in Duluth was not homogeneous. It is a rather difficult task to determine the numerical strength of the Swede-Finns in Duluth because the state and federal censuses provide data only on the geographical origin of the foreign-born population. According to Akseli Järnefelt's estimate, there were some four hundred Swede-Finns in Duluth in 1899.[48] The estimate, which is unreasonably inflated, suggests that some 60 per cent of the Finns in the city were Swedish-speaking. According to more recent calculations by Carl Silfversten and Andres Myhrman, probably 25 per cent of the Finland-born population was made up of Swede-Finns.[49] Despite some attempts to cooperate with the Finnish-speaking population, the Swede-Finns established separate religious and social organizations which were located in the Sixth Ward, in West End. The Ebenezer Baptist congregation was organized in 1893, the Bethel Lutheran congregation in 1897, and the Ljusstralen Temperance Society in 1904.[50]

The ethnically mixed marriages introduced another aspect of diversity among the Finns in Duluth. In 46 (26.1 per cent) of the 176 married couples present in the city in 1895, one of the spouses was a non-Finn. The preference to marry out of one's own group was somewhat greater among the Finnish females than the Finnish males. Significantly, 63.1 per cent of the inter-ethnic marriages were to Swedes and Norwegians. It is probable that the inter-ethnic marriages, which reduced the immigrant group's solidarity, were a by-product of the geographical juxtaposition and the intermingling of the various nationality groups in residential areas of the city.[51] Yet another element of diversity was introduced by the growing number of the American-born offspring of the Finns. The 130 marriages in which both partners were Finnish had a total of

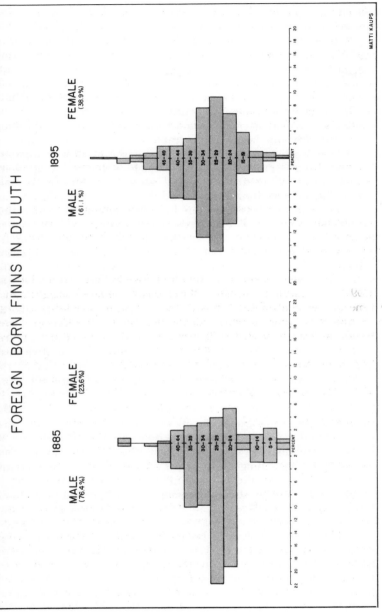

Figure 2.

251 children, of whom 42 were born in Finland, 1 in Norway, and 208 in the United States (the latter statistic is not included in the population pyramid in Figure 2). The point is that the growth of the bilingual second-generation Finns was well under way during the initial growth phase. At the same time that the immigrants organized voluntary associations and advocated the maintenance of ethnic cohesion, there was a parallel trend of potential ethnic conflict and erosion going on within the family structure, as the children, by attending public schools, were subject to enculturation into the American ethos at a more rapid rate than their parents.

Shortly after the turn of the century, the Finnish community in Duluth underwent profound changes—changes that were brought about by the arrival of a fresh wave of predominantly male immigrants directly from Finland and the spread of the doctrine of socialism. The socialists and their followers succeeded in invading and taking over several of the existing immigrant organizations in the city. For example, in 1902 the Messiah Lutheran Church's Nuija Youth Society was transformed into a labour organization called the Ystävät, or Friends, which two years later joined the American Finnish Labor League, and subsequently took over the *Suomalainen Kansanopisto ja Teologinen Seminaari*, or the Finnish Peoples' Institute and Theological Seminary, located at Smithville (Duluth), and renamed it in 1908 the *Työväen Opisto*, or Work People's College, with the result that religious studies were removed from the curriculum.[52] Also, a number of cooperative business ventures were established eventually. The activities of the socialist introduced a serious and irreconcilable split in the Finnish community to which the conservatives reacted strongly in time. In a broader perspective, the ideological stance and actions of the socialists, communists, and the IWW activists, constituted a tragedy of the Finnish immigrant experience in Duluth as well as elsewhere in America. They succeeded in capturing the imagination and in channelling the energies of the numerous immigrants down a diviant path of common good in a direction that was not in keeping with the mainstream of American thought and institutions, thereby rendering the American transition more cumbersome than it would have been otherwise.[53]

The time has come to broaden the scope of Finnish immigrant studies in Canada and the United States. While it seems desirable that the investigations of the internal structures and ideological stances of the various immigrant organizations be pursued, it is equally desirable to bring the Finnish experience into a broader American perspective. The relationships between the Finns and the different nationality groups should also be studied. Moreover, quantitative methods and procedures current in urban historical research ought to be applied to the study of Finns in American cities.[54] At the same time, conclusions reached in bygone days ought to be examined anew, both from intra as well as inter-ethnic perspectives. In addition to Wasastjerna's work, the following characterizations of the Finns in Duluth provide a point of departure. The Finnish observer, Akseli Järnefelt, commented in 1899: "Those who have traveled a great deal in Finnish communities in America, report the Finns of Duluth to be in such a wretched state of moral decay, the like of which is hardly to be found elsewhere. Those who have not yet fallen into moral decadence, and those who have mended their ways, move away from that town."[55] A year later, the editor of an American-English language newspaper published in Duluth described the Finns in far more positive terms: "The Finns are generally intelligent and patriotic.... They are hardy and industrious.... They make good citizens and an increase in their numbers will be welcomed."[56]

Järnefelt's assessment of the Finns was unduly harsh. Being a proponent of the temperance movement, he failed to comprehend that his countrymen's enjoyment of dancing, of musical performances, of visits to theatres, saloons and roller rinks, were in part manifestations of ongoing cultural change in which old folkways and social constraints were being modified and abandoned in favour of an urban lifestyle. The role of the saloons in the Finnish immigrant society remains to be studied. Aside from serving alcoholic beverages, they functioned as social clubs, and were frequented by temperate Finns as well. The saloons were places where the Finns met and visited with their friends, played cards and exchanged information in their native tongue about the availability of jobs. Some of the saloon keepers sold steamship and railroad tickets and were the bankers for their countrymen.[578]

# Notes

1. This article is a part of a more comprehensive study of the Finnish immigrant community in Duluth; the author is thankful to the Minnesota Finnish-American Historical Society for a financial grant. Also, he wishes to extend his appreciation to Professor Cotton Mather, Depart-

82    M. Kaups

ment of Geography, University of Minnesota, Minneapolis, for scholarly advice.

2. In 1920, 24.0 per cent of the Finns in the United States resided in cities with total populations of less than 25,000. U.S. Department of the Interior, Twelfth Census of the United States, *Population*, Part 1, (Washington: United States Census Office, 1901), pp. 796-801; U.S. Department of Commerce, Bureau of the Census, Fourteenth Census of the United States, *Population*, 1920, Vol. 2 (Washington: Government Printing Office, 1922), pp. 730, 760-67.

3. For example, see A. William Hoglund,*Finnish Immigrants in America, 1880-1920* (Madison, Wisc.,1960); John I. Kolehmainen and George W. Hill, *Haven in the Woods* (Madison, Wisc., 1951).

4. For articles and monographs, consult Olavi Koivukangas and Simo Toivonen, *Suomen Siirtolaisuuden ja Maassamuuton Bibliografia* (The Migration Institute, Turku, Finland, 1978).

5. See P. George Hummasti, "The Establishment of the Finnish Settlement in Astoria, Oregon: A Look at Community Development," *Finnish* Americana, Vol. 1 (1978), pp. 84-98; Varpu Lindstrom-Best, *The Finnish Immigrant Conmmunity of Toronto, 1887-1913* (Toronto, Ont., 1979).

6. Suomen Tilastollinen Päätoimisto, *Suomen Tilastollinen Vuosikirja* (Helsinki, 1922), p. 74; O.K. Kilpi, *Suomen Siirtolaisuus ja 19 Vuosisadan Kansantalous* (Taloustieteellisiä Tulkimuksia XXII, Helsinki, 1917), pp. 48-162; John Ilmari Kolehmainen, "Finland's Agrarian Structure and Overseas Migration", *Agricultural History*, Vol. 15, no. 1, (1941), pp. 44-48; Anna-Leena Toivonen, *Etelä-Pohjanmaan Valtameren Takainen Siirtolaisuus 1867-1930* (Historiallisia Tutkimuksia LXVI, Helsinki, 1963), pp. 46-47; Hoglund, *op. cit.*, p. 62.

7. W. J. Jokinen, "The Finns in Minnesota", *Siirtokansan Kalenteri 1960*, Vol. 43 (New York Mills, Minn., 1960), p. 39.

8. Hans R. Wasastjerna, *Minnesotan Suomalaisten Historia* (Duluth, Minn., 1957), p. 232.

9. Duluth City Planning Department, *Land Platting History, Duluth, Minnesota, 1856-1939* (Duluth, Minn., 1940), p. 3.

10. Wasastjerna, *op. cit.*, p. 233.

11. Ibid., p. 234.

12. Ibid.

13. See Sune Åkerman, "From Stockholm to San Francisco: The Development of the Historical Study of External Migrations", *Annales Acadamiae Regiae Scientiarum Upsaliensis*, Vol. 19 (1975), pp. 7-8.

14. On the use of the concept, see Matti Kaups, "Swedish Immigrants in Duluth, 1856-1870", in Nils Hasselmo, ed., *Perspectives on Swedish Immigration* (Chicago, Ill., 1978), pp. 166-98.

15. State of Minnesota, Census of 1865, Population Schedules; United States, Department of the Interior, Ninth Census, Population of the United States, Vol. 1 (Washington: Government Printing Office, 1872), p. 181.

16. Dwight E. Woodbridge and John S. Pardee, eds., *History of Duluth and St. Louis Country*, Vol. 1 (Chicago, Ill., 1910), pp. 108-9, 120; Walter Van Brunt, *Duluth and St. Louis County, Minnesota*, Vol. 1 (Chicago and New York, 1921), pp. 248, 255.

17. S. Ilmonen, *Amerikan Suomalaisten Historia*, Vol. 2 (Jyväskylä, 1923), p. 222.

18. Charles Kauppi, "Siirtokansamme Historia," *Päivälehti* (Duluth, Minn.), January 15, 1941, p. 3; Matti Kaups, "Europeans in Duluth: 1870," in Ryck Lydecker and Lawrence J. Sommer, eds., *Duluth, Sketches of the Past* (Duluth, Minn., 1976), pp. 70-81.

19. Matti Kaups, "North Shore Commercial Fishing, 1849-1870", *Minnesota History*, Vol. 46, no.2 (1978), pp. 57-58.

20. Matti E. Kaups, "The Finns in the Copper and Iron Ore Mines of the Western Great Lakes Region, 1864-1905: Some Preliminary Observations," in Michael G. Karni, Matti E. Kaups, Douglas J. Ollila, Jr., eds., *The Finnish Experience in the Western Great Lakes Region: New Perspectives* (Vammala, 1975), pp. 66-72.

21. *Duluth Minnesotian*, July 26, 1873, p.3.

22. State of Minnesota, Census of 1875, Population Schedules.

23. *Duluth Minnesotian – Herald*, January 27, 1877, p. 4; *Duluth Weekly Tribune*, February 27, 1880, p. 4.

24. Woodbridge and Pardee, *op. cit.*, pp. 150-51, 156-57, 165; Vol. 2, pp. 545-66; Van Brunt, *op. cit.*, pp. 254-55, 268-69, 286-89; Angnes M. Larson, *History of the White Pine Industry in Minnesota* (Minneapolis, Minn., 1949), pp. 250-59.

25. State of Minnesota, Census of 1885, Population Schedules; United States, Department of the Interior, Tenth Census, 1880, Population Schedules; U.S. Department of Commerce, Bureau of the Census, Fourteenth Census of the United States, *Population*, 1920, Vol. 1 (Washington: Government Printing Office, 1921), p. 84.

26. State of Minnesota, Census of 1885, Population Schedules.

27. *Amerikan Suomalainen Lehti* (Calumet, Mich.), July 18, 1879, p. 1; August 8, 1879, p. 2; July 9, 1880, p. 2; August 6, 1880, p. 2; April 28, 1882, p. 2; January 5, 1883, p. 1.; May 11, 1883, p. 2; May 16, 1884, p. 2; June 6, 1884, p. 3; *Uusi Kotimaa* (Minneapolis, Minn.), April 4, 1884, p. 2; July 11, 1884, p. 2; January 31, 1885, p. 3; Eugene V. Smalley, *History of the Northern Pacific Railroad* (New York, 1883), pp. 388-421; R.L. Polk and Company, *Duluth Directory, 1885-6* (St. Paul, Minn., 1885), pp. 23, 40-41, 54.

28. State of Minnesota, Census of 1895, Population Schedules; U.S. Department of the Interior, 1901, *op. cit.*, pp. 796-97.

29. *Uusi Kotimaa* (Minneapolis, Minn.), November 19, 1881, p. 2; May 9, 1884, p. 3; *Amerikan Suomalainen Lehti* (Calumet, Mich.), April 4, 1885, p. 4; June 5, 1885, p. 3; *Uusi Kotimaa* (New York Mills, Minn.), March 13, 1886, p. 3; May 17, 1890, p. 3.

30. S. Ilmonen, *Amerikan Suomalaisten Sivistyshistoria*, Vol. 1 (Hancock, Mich., 1930), p. 27; *Duluth Daily Tribune*, February 21, 1883, p. 4; July 31, 1883, p. 4; *Amerikan Suomalainen Lehti* (Red Jacket, Mich.), June 27, 1888, p. 3; *Uusi Kotimaa* (New York Mills, Minn.), January 3, 1885, p. 3; August 8, 1885, p. 3; August 22, 1885, p. 3; December 24, 1886, p. 3; April 28, 1887, p.3; W. Anttila "'Toiwon Tähti' r.-seura Duluthissa," *Raittius-Kalenteri wuodelle, 1902* (Hancock, Mich., 1901), pp. 124-27.

31. State of Minnesota, *Fifth Decennial Census* (St. Paul, Minn., 1905), p. 177.

32. U.S. Department of Commerce, 1922, *op. cit.*, p. 763.

33. John I. Kolehmainen, *The Finns in America. A Bibliographical Guide to Their History* (Hancock, Mich., 1947), pp. 75-97; Wasastjerna, *op. cit.*, pp. 240-382.

34. U.S. Department of Commerce, Bureau of the Census, *Census of Population: 1960*, Vol. 1, Part 25 (Washington: Government Printing Office, 1963), p. 254.

35. For a statement on immigrant ghettos, see Oscar Handlin, *The Uprooted: The Epic Story of the Great Migration That Made America* (Boston, 1951), pp. 144-69. On re-evaluation of the ghetto hypothesis, see David Ward, "The Emergence of Central Immigrant Ghettoes in American Cities: 1840-1920," *Annals of the Association of American Geographers*, Vol. 58, no. 2 (1968), pp. 343-59; Sam Bass Warner, Jr., and Colin B. Burke, "Cultural Change and the Ghetto," *Journal of Contemporary History*, Vol. 4, no. 3 (1969), pp. 173-87; Howard P. Chudacoff, "A New Look at Ethnic Neighborhoods: Residential Dispersion and the Concept of Visibility in a Medium Sized City," *Journal of American History*, Vol. 60, no. 1 (1973), pp. 76-93; Kathleen Neils Conzen, *Immigrant Milwaukee, 1836-1860: Accommodation and Community in a Frontier City* (Cambridge, Mass., 1976), pp. 3-7.

36. An index of O denotes lack of residential segregation. An index of 25 is generally considered the value below which segregation is almost totally absent. For comparative data, see, Chudacoff, *op. cit.*, pp. 78-79, Conzen, *op. cit.*, pp. 127-30, 269.

37. These and following figures and computations for 1895 are based on hand count of the 1895 Minnesota State manuscript census. The census was taken "as of June 1, 1895."

38. *Duluth Weekly Tribune*, October 22, 1880, p. 2; *Duluth Daily Tribune*, November 7, 1885, p. 4.

39. *Duluth Weekly Tribune*, June 18, 1880, p. 4.

40. The character of local labour markets and towns had an impact on the sex structure of populations. In the nearby Mesabi Range mining towns, 81.5 per cent of the Finnish population was composed of males in 1895. See, Kaups, 1975, *op. cit.*, pp. 72-73.

41. The data on conjugality is based on the State of Minnesota, Census of 1885 Population Schedules listing of "families numbered in order of visitation." Though most of the Finland-born men appear single or "unattached" in the manuscript census, they were not necessarily single, for some had families in Finland, or elsewhere in the United States.

42. Stephan Thernstrom, *Poverty and Progress: Social Mobility in a Nineteenth Century City* (Cambridge, Mass., 1964, pp. 84-90, 168, 197-99; Chudacoff, *op. cit.*, p. 83. See footnote 43 below.

43. State of Minnesota, Census of 1895, Population Schedules; *Amerikan Suomalainen Lehti* (Calumet, Mich.), September 15, 1882, p. 2; *Uusi Kotimaa* (Minneapolis, Minn.), February 15, 1884, p. 2; November 15, 1884, p. 2; April 10, 1886, p. 2; *Amerikan Suomalainen Lehti* (Red Jacket, Mich.), May 29, 1891, p. 2; Wasastjerna, *op. cit.*, p. 237; Hoglund, *op. cit.*, pp. 59-66.

44. *Duluth Evening Herald*, August 9, 1898, p. 5; Hoglund, *op. cit.*, p. 60.

45. R.L. Polk and Company, *Duluth Directory, 1895-96* (Duluth, Minn., 1895), p. 738; State of Minnesota, Census of 1895, Population Schedules; *Uusi Kotimaa* (New York Mills, Minn.), May 22, 1886, p. 2.

46. Because of a large labour market for domestics, Finnish women outnumbered men in some of the eastern cities. See Hoglund, *op. cit.*, p. 81. The same held for certain age groups of the Swedish immigrants in Chicago. See Ulf Beijbom, *Swedes in Chicago: a Demographic and Social Study of the 1846-1880 Immigration* (Stockholm, 1971), pp. 120-21.

47. The Finnish immigrant family and household, and the accommodation of boarders, is a fertile field for investigation. For a general statement regarding boarders, see John Modell and Tamera K. Hareven, "Urbanization and the Malleable Household: An Examination of Boarding and Lodging in American Families," *Journal of Marriage and the Family*, Vol. 35, no. 3 (1973), pp. 467-78.

48. Akseli Järnefelt, *Suomalaiset Amerikassa* (Helsinki, 1899), p. 255.

49. Carl J. Silfversten, *Finlandssvenskarna i Amerika* (Duluth, Minn., 1931), p. 81; Anders Myhrman, *Finlandssvenskar i Amerika* (Helsingfors, 1972), p. 18.

50. Silfversten, *op. cit.*, pp. 268-69; Myhrman, *op. cit.*, pp. 247-50; Anders M. Myhrman, "The Finland-Swedes in Duluth, Minnesota," *Swedish Pioneer Historical Quarterly*, Vol. 14, no. 1 (1963), p. 26.

51. Some of the inter-ethnic marriages may, of course, have been concluded elsewhere. The matter requires further research.

52. Wasastjerna, *op. cit.*, p. 247; Douglas J. Ollila, Jr., "The Work People's College: Immigrant Education For Adjustment and Solidarity," in Michael G. Karni and Douglas J. Ollila, Jr., eds, *For the Common Good* (Superior, Wisc., 1977), p. 102.

53. The theme will be analysed by the author in a forthcoming study of the Finnish immigrant community in Duluth.

54. In additions to the several works already cited, see Stephan Thernstrom and Richard Sennett, eds., *Nineteenth Century Cities: Essays in New Urban History* (New Haven, Conn., 1969); Stephan Thernstrom, *The Other Bostonians: Poverty and Progress in American Metropolis, 1880-1970* (Cambridge, Mass., 1973); Leo F. Schnore, *The Urban History: Quantitative Explorations by American Historians* (Princeton, N.J., 1975); Josef J. Barton, *Peasants and Strangers: Italians, Pumanians and Slovaks in an American City, 1890-1950* (Cambridge, Mass., 1975).

55. Järnefelt, *op. cit.*, p. 131.

56. *Duluth Evening Herald*, September 7, 1900, p. 10.

57. *Uusi Kotimaa* (New York Mills, Minn.), May 23, 1885, p. 3; *Amerikan Suomalainen Lehti* (Red Jacket, Mich.), May 29, 1891, p. 2; Myhrman, 1972, *op. cit.*, p. 246.

# The Life History of a Southeastern Massachusetts Finnish Cranberry Growing Community

*Marsha Penti*

In southeastern Massachusetts, in cranberry-producing Plymouth County,[1] there has been a Finnish community since the late nineteenth century. This community, centred in the towns of Carver, Middleborough and Wareham, was most vigorous in the 1910s, 1920s and 1930s. Throughout the rapid developmental period of the cranberry industry Finnish immigrants were vital as labourers, foremen and supervisors on the Yankee-owned bogs and then as diligent bog owners and growers in their own right. As we enter the 1980s third and even fourth generation Finnish families remain in the industry.

This paper will attempt to convey an understanding of the quality of life in the pre-World War Two years of the community which was defined both by its ethnicity and by its work on the bogs. I interviewed and recorded the informants, who are second generation Finns born in the community, in their homes. I have transcribed their narratives faithfully although I have been forced to choose excerpts from them. In respect for my informants I have changed their names and, to some extent, have avoided using specific locations. I am grateful for their help in sharing their observations with me. This paper tells of a history found, not in written words, but in the spoken works of the informants as conveyed through autobiographical experience stories, life experience narratives and labour reminiscences.

It has been impossible to discover the exact arrival date of

Finns in the area; but it occurred during the second half of the nineteenth century.[2] The Finns who settled in the community came from many parts of Finland. One man observed: "As far as I know they came from all over, just about all over Finland. It's not like up in Maine; there they're all *Savolaisia*. But around here they came from just about every part of Finland that I know of—the north, the south, Karjala." There were, nevertheless, quite a number of settlers from Karstula; for example, twelve of the thirty-two charter members of the West Wareham Finnish Congregational Church were born there.[3] Other Finns in the community were from Alajärvi, Brändo, Espoo, Helsinki, Ikaalinen, Jurva, Kivijärvi, Kärsämäki, Parkano, Pyhäjärvi, Saarijärvi, Soini, Tampere, Turku and Viitasaari. They were mostly poor men and women who came to America to better themselves. A man who became one of the richest Finnish growers is remembered in this way: "I heard him tell when he was across he was pretty hard up. He'd . . . eaten the tree bark. It sounds impossible, but I heard him say that."[5]

The vast majority of Finns came to the area via other American cities and towns. Some moved north off Cape Cod. Some came from the fishing centre of Gloucester (Massachusetts). Some left Worcester (Massachusetts) steel and wire mills because of failing health, seeking fresh air and outdoor work. Some moved south from New Hampshire and Maine. A few even came from the Midwest. A very few came directly from Finland, encouraged by relatives and friends who had settled in the area. Most apparently came beginning just before the turn of the century and continuing into the early thirties.

The majority of those who came during the Depression were single men. They came often from Massachusetts cities. Many lived in the various bog camps or they boarded in local boarding-houses or with local Finnish families. One informant has estimated that there were between twenty and twenty-five of these men at any one time in any one of the towns.[6] Another estimates there were about fifty.[7] Some came to work only seasonally; others stayed throughout the Depression and did not leave until World War Two when they were able to get other jobs. A few stayed permanently; and one man who stayed is now one of the largest Finnish growers in the area.

The cranberry industry did quite well in the Depression and since so much work was hand labour, it was possible for a man to get a job. "During the Depression there was no depression amongst the cranberry growers. . . . There was more profit in the cranberry business than there is today, much more."[8] The men did not earn much, but they survived. "Just enough to live, that's all they wanted anyhow. A place, a roof over their heads, and a place to live and most of them had nothing anyway and a lot of them had no place to go. They had a place to come here and make enough so that they could get their food and they had a shelter which didn't cost them anything."[9] Some of the men were a hard-drinking lot and their antics caused more than a little consternation among the permanently settled Finns. They were by all accounts a most colourful lot. To this day no one has forgotten Piru Erkki, Lihava Heikki and his pal Laiha Jussi, Hullu Kusti, or Iso Vihtori.

As previously noted, the area is inter-ethnic. The Nova Scotian immigrants integrated easily into town life; and the French Canadians were such a small group they were barely noticed. But the presence of the Finns and the Cape Verdeans was felt, even if not acknowledged. Although the Finns and their children experienced varying degrees of prejudice, they all agree that the Yankees felt themselves to be superior. The second generation still feels the undertones: "Oh yes, definitely there was all that feeling. To this day . . . I think occasionally you get an air. I don't like to confess it; but I think my friends, every once in a while it comes out if there is that Yankee blood there and there is this feeling of belittling a certain group or people or a kind of people."[10] One man described the situation: "If you were a foreigner, no matter if you were a Cape Verdean, Finn, or a French Canadian, you were a second-class citizen. . . . In Fitchburg, over there for example, . . . there were so many other foreigners it didn't make a difference. . . . But this was a Yankee town and they didn't like to have anyone living here that wasn't a descendant of the Mayflower."[11] Sometimes the discrimination was less than subtle.

> In this town I can remember as a kid growing up these Yankees. . . . Any job in town, a Yankee got it. Finns weren't even considered smart enough to be truck drivers. The Cape Verdeans were less than that. That's the attitude I was brought up in down here and I can remember back in the early thirties there was a bunch of us guys [Finns and French Canadians] . . . who wanted to join the fire department. . . . They were told that they didn't want any foreigners in the fire department. . . . That's the way this town was. It was a Yankee town. Everyone was a stupid foreigner. . . . These stupid foreigners were nothing. . . . Of course now in later years it's changed, but that's the way it used to be.[12]

The Cape Verdeans (*Purkiisit*) fared worse than the Finns. They were separate from other groups. "They knew where they belonged."[13]

> In our own little world of that time there were the Cape Verdeans. They had their own thing and their own work and their own place.... They knew where their place was. There was a segregation. It wasn't like the segregation down South; but they knew better than to push ahead from their own area, their own sections, because it just wasn't done.... They had their own little streets or their own little parts of town where they lived and most of them worked on the cranberry bogs and this is all they knew.... And they had their own clubs and dances and their own, well they didn't have their own church 'cause whites would go to the Catholic church too. But there was some segregation, definitely.[14]

The Finns and the Cape Verdeans got along well. As one man said: "Why shouldn't they get along? They were all doing the same damn crappy work."[15] The primary and almost exclusive contact between the groups was in bog work. Here the Finns felt they had a higher status, because they were regarded as better workers than the Cape Verdeans. There was no actual socializing between the groups although the Finns in one town attended dances at the small Cape Verdean Hall and both Finns and Cape Verdeans would attend the dances held occasionally in some screenhouses.

The Finns had little to do with the Nova Scotians, because they were primarily carpenters and rarely worked on the bogs. The French Canadians (*Ranskalaiset*) were not a large group and were seen mainly as individuals. The Finnish immigrants socialized almost exclusively with other Finns in their hall and churches. But their children, growing up in a multi-ethnic environment, had friends other than Finnish Americans and began to expand their associations even by marrying non-Finns.

The Finns in the three towns lived, for the most part, in particular areas of town that were primarily Finnish. Very few built their own houses; they bought old Yankee farms. "All those houses on_____ St. and well all around _____ that were taken over by the Finns were where the Yankees had failed to make a living. But the Finns found a place where they could live and raise crops and have animals and make a living out of it."[16] In Carver they lived mainly in the south and west sections of town. Middleborough had few Finns; they lived mainly in the section of South Middleborough between Carver and Wareham. In Wareham they lived in West and South Wareham. These sections form an almost continuous whole. For this reason and for the reason that the Finns in the three towns functioned as a single group, those who lived here will be regarded as forming one community. Only one of these sections, Soini in South Wareham, has a Finnish name; the others merely went by "Fingliska" versions of their local names (e.g., Clark's Station in West Wareham became *Laaksteisoni*). All the organizational buildings were in Wareham. The *Helluntai (Seurakunta)* church was in Soini. The *Suomalainen Evankelinen Siioni Lähetysseurakunta* was in West Wareham. The *Amerikan Suomalainen Kansanvallan Liitto* hall was in the Clark's Station section of West Wareham. My informants have estimated that in the 1920s and 1930s the permanent Finnish populations of the towns were approximately as follows: Carver—44 households, 200 persons; Middleborough—16 households, 80 persons; Wareham—29 households, 136 persons.

The Finnish community was divided into various factions. It was segregated by hall and church members. (There were two churches. The Pentecostal church was the result of a split from the Congregational church. As it was quite small it will not be considered in this discussion.) Someone who grew up in the church explains: "There was a definite distinction. A lot of Finnish church people would not set foot in the hall. . . . You were raised with this feeling—there was something very bad, very sinful about the Finnish hall in West Wareham. I mean the people might have been your neighbours and your friends and beautiful people; but to set foot in that hall was the wrong thing to do."[17] The role of the church was central to the lives of the member families. "It was very, very important, either the Finnish church or the hall. The Finnish church was very much a part of the lives of the people who were the Christian people, supposedly, of the community . . . and great respect was done for the church. . . . You had a solid sense of belonging. . . . The whole family went to church of a Sunday afternoon. . . . It was the thing to do. It was the social centre of the community."[18]

The *West Warehamin Suomalainen Evankelinen Siioni Lähetysseurakunta* was a vital centre for the maintenance of Finnish ethnic identity. It was in its Sunday School that many of the second generation learned to read and write Finnish. "I learned the language and if I hadn't had that church I don't think that I would

have learned the language. I got the taste of it in a way at home
where it was spoken there. Then I got, let's say, my Finnish *Aapinen, Raamatun historia*, and you know was confirmed with the
Finnish language, to learn to read it, write it."[19] The church was
also used by a large number of community members for significant
occasions. Children were christened and confirmed through the
church. "I think that you found among the Finnish immigrants that
even if you belonged to the hall group, they had this feeling that
their children must be confirmed, must be christened."[20] A son of a
hall member remembers: "Pa believed in baptism. Oh boy, his
children had to be baptised and his grandchildren."[21] At the end of
their lives, not only the faithful church members, but other immigrants also were buried from the church. The membership of the
church began to wane after World War Two and dropped sharply
as the immigrants began to die. Very few of the second generation
remain members. There is still a Finnish minister serving the congregation who leads a Finnish Sunday morning adult Bible class
and a monthly *ompelusseura*.

The *Amerikan Suomalainen Kansanvallan Liitto* hall had supposedly "one of the best dance floors in the country."[22] It drew
Finns from the three towns as well as the Cape and other neighbouring Finnish settlements in addition to local non-Finns. It was
begun in the 1920s. It seems that originally support for the hall
was doubtful. "It didn't even have a foundation under it. . . . There
was something about it. They didn't know if they could carry it
through anyway. But they finally paid the mortgage off anyway."[23]
Between fifty and a hundred people attended the Saturday night
dances where the schottish, polka and winderska were played. A
few times a year there would be *kappaleita*(either plays or vaudeville type shows). Traditional holidays, both Finnish and American
were celebrated. On *Juhannus* members would travel to Saima
Park in Fitchburg for the big celebration. In August there would
be a *Kolmiojuhlat* for the combined West Wareham, Norwood and
Abington halls. In the fifties the Finn Hall was sold due to lack of
support; but into the forties it was an important centre of the
community were Finnish ethnicity was promoted through dance,
drama and song as well as traditional celebrations.

The community was also divided politically. "At one time
there were a lot of people here who thought that the Communists
were the most wonderful people around. And there were those
who didn't believe in it. . . . That was the biggest argument the
Finns had as far as politics was concerned. . . . I can remember my
father's crew arguing; half of them believed in Communism, half of
them didn't."[24]

There were believed to be other feelings which kept the
Finns from promoting themselves as a group.

> Well I tell you right now they [Finns] got along in a
> way now. But a Finn is jealous of another Finn. If
> another Finn is succeeding the others would be very
> jealous of him and that's the way it is with all the Finns.
> Now if someone ran for office in town the Finns
> wouldn't vote for him, 'cause they'd be jealous of him.
> If a Cape Verdean ran for office, the other Cape Ver-
> deans wouldn't vote for him. . . . In a town like this
> where the biggest population is Cape Verdean and
> Finns . . . if they got together and would vote for one of
> their nationalities . . . they could've run the town. No,
> they were too jealous of each other so the Swamp Yan-
> kees ran the town for years.[25]

Yet on the whole the Finns were helpful to each other. "I
think there could occasionally be feuds and jealousy; but I think,
for the most part, they were very helpful and compassionate to
their neighbours in need because you called neighbour upon neighbour to help each other in time of need.[26]

Just as community life was defined by the dimensions of its
ethnicity it was also governed by the life rhythmn of the cranberry
bogs. Every season had its own demands. One 60-year-old who has
worked a lifetime on bogs explains:

> A cranberry man really has to be on the job summer
> and winter alike. In the summer you have to irrigate
> when it becomes very, very hot otherwise you lose your
> crops. You have to irrigate at the right time. It has to
> be dried up before the sun comes and burns everything
> the next day. Then again in the winter you have to
> lower your water level, because if the ice remains on
> the bog for a long period of time with all the heavy
> snows on it there becomes a lack of oxygen underneath.
> And you have to let down the water supply and then
> later on when it's been let off for a little bit, them you
> have to make sure that there's more water on there to
> cover it and so forth, you know, as you do with the
> winter flow. But there are many, many problems. Like
> in the summer you have the worms to contend with and
> the bugs. They have to be checked out every so many
> days. . . .

So it's a year round job. It is not that you just harvest
the berries in the fall. And this is what I don't think a
lot of people realize when they talk about cranberry
growing. They think, well, the cranberry man is really
getting rich. But if you figure up all the hours that he
spends on it and plus your spring and your fall frosts
and everything with sleepless nights, I think your compensation many times will not be equal to that if you
worked out for another company on another job.[27]

The Finns had the reputation of being excellent bog
workers. Most places there was more Cape Verdeans
than there was Finns. But the Finns had more, I mean
they were more in jobs like a foreman.... But most of
the Finns were steady help. The Cape Verdeans were
summer help. If there were something real important to
do in the winter, well they'd give a little work in the
winter. But mostly the Cape Verdeans only worked till
after the harvest and then they'd be off all winter right
up until the spring work began again. They'd have their
bag full of rice and a big bagful of beans and that's what
they lived on all winter.[28]

The Finns were aware of their reputation; everyone would
hire a Finn.

Oh I always felt I was much higher as far as working on
the Cranberry bog is concerned; because many of your
people that employed you, where I was employed, were
Finnish people and you were in high regard. So many of
the Cape Verdeans were not the kind of worker that a
Finn would want to have. But because they were in
need of work so badly, they would hire them. I mean,
there's always an exception to the rule; but the majority
were not pushers.[29]

Bog work was a family affair. Without the cooperation of all
the members it would be impossible to meet all the demands of the
hand labour required on the bogs in those days. "All the family had
to be involved in this kind of living especially if you had your own
cramberry bog. You *had* to be involved! There was no other way
around it. You didn't have the money to hire."[30]
The various jobs were determined by sex and age. The

women would do the weeding, hand-picking, scooping and screening. The children would also weed and pick the best they could. Men would do the heavy work such as transporting the berries, sanding and ditch cleaning. Since nearly every mother, even the more wealthy, worked, they would bring their children along to the bogs. The younger children played on the shore and the babies were placed in a carriage or even a cranberry box under the supervision of the older children. The children had to be quite well disciplined. Nevertheless it was demanding for the mothers to do their work as well as oversee the children, for families were large. One mother who had an exceptional number is described as working with "*yks niskassa, yks kantapäällä ja yks mahassa.*" Women would do this hard work despite their pregnancies. This could cause difficulties. One woman remembers how her mother spoke of having to pick during an exceptionally cold fall when the bog ditches were actually frozen. She got a bad chill which led to problems in her pregnancy and continual ill health in the child which was born.[31]

Children would help with the weeding and picking. They usually began to help when they were 10, 11, or 12 years old. "Of course you did it for your family as soon as you were old enough to carry a scoop and were able to push it.[32] On new bogs children would be able to pick by hand or with a snap machine into six-quart measures (*meissiä*). Or on their own family's or others' smaller bogs they could be allowed to scoop; but as it required a good deal of strength, it was not until they were about 14 that they were really able to work. At this age it was possible to leave school via a permit from the school committee and legally work. Most of the immigrants children did leave school after the eighth grade to help their parents by working on the bogs. Children also weeded under their mother's supervision on the family bogs.

Bogs had to be weeded to prevent the quick-growing weeds from overpowering and killing the cranberry vines. It was largely women's work. "Men never liked the weeding and it would be women more or less who would be doing it for the small growers. Of course the larger companies where they had men, employed them year round so the men would have to do it."[33] Weeding was begun in April when weather permitted and before the bog was in blossom. Later when the bog had "set" and there were small berries it was possible to resume weeding and it would be continued on and off until harvest. Crews of several women, usually numbering from two to twelve, would be formed and they would work a large part of the late spring and summer.

Weeding was demanding work. A woman who began working out as a weeder at 14 describes it as terrible. "It's hard on your hands, the strain. The muscles of your arms really take a toll and your forefingers. You know you usually use your forefinger and thumb for part of the pulling and your back is ready to break; because, especially at certain times of the year, you can't even go on your knees and you're usually in a semi-bent position, probably resting your left arm against your left upper leg. And your back is ready to break, like I say, at times by the time you're through. It's very hard work. And then when the heat gets to be ninety plus it's a little bit more than humans should endure."[34]

Today there is little demand for weeders as the use of chemicals has taken their place. But until World War Two weeders were used extensively and it was possible to hire out and earn money to supplement the family income. Pay in the 1920s and 1930s was 25 cents an hour for an eight or nine hour day. On the small bogs the owner and his wife would work along with the crew and on the larger bogs a foreman would survey the work. The Finns' skill could always get them a job weeding. "There were just so many that were good weeders and that you could trust and so forth. There would be a lot of Cape Verdean people that were able to do that and that were willing to do that. But they were not the kind of weeders the Finnish people were. You knew they'd give you a good day's work and not have all the vines in their hands."[35]

The upkeep of the bog demanded much other work. A discussion of this is beyond the scope of this paper; but some jobs can be mentioned in passing. In the winter and spring sanding was done to promote growth. In summer bog dikes had to be mowed periodically. In warmer weather ditches had to be cleaned. When there was no other pressing work equipment was repaired. There is always something to be done on a cranberry bog; but the focus of work came with the fall harvest. The traditional start of picking is on Labour Day weekend and, depending on weather conditions, it can continue into November. Whenever night frosts threatened, bogs would be flowed with water and picking was delayed until the bogs dried.

The exact manner of picking was dependent on the age and acreage of the bogs; but until the 1940s it was mainly hand work. Berries would be picked by hand literally for the first two years after a bog was "set out" (planted). Then they would be picked by a small metal-toothed utensil called a snap machine (näppi masiina). Finally they could be picked with the traditional wooden scoop (kuupa).

Scooping was tedious work. The hours were somewhat shorter (six or seven) than in weeding, because the bog had to be dry. On some days there would be no work because of rain or needed irrigation. A picker worked in a row going across the bog sections. A row could be one or two scoops wide. One scoop wide was favoured, because it made it easier to keep pace and no one did more work than another. Some pickers did pick two wide because of their skill, but they did not earn more. One smaller bogs there would be six to twelve scoopers, on the larger thirty to fifty per section. The larger company bogs paid by the box picked. This system promoted cheating as the more aggressive pickers tried to get the best picking. "If you were in a crowd that was hungry, I mean when it got to poor picking, well you'd find yourself with all kinds of acreage and if it was good picking they'd grab all ahead of you so it was really a tough racket to pick amongst the other people . . . who were really out to make the dollars. . . . You see they could make, if they had good picking, . . . probably twenty, thirty dollars a day and that was a lot in those days."[36]

One had to keep pace with the other pickers, trying to keep up with the person ahead of you and ahead of the person behind you so as not to interfere with their picking. A picker with over forty years experience explains: "You felt terrible every day. You were exhausted. Your arms would ache. Your knees would ache. Your knees would give the greatest problem and your arms. Your legs would ache. And then sometimes if it were very damp, you might have to pick standing up with your back just hunched over for a number of hours. In fact some people, a few people, prefer to pick that way if they have a strong back. It's a terribly hard job. . . . You had to be tough to survive the ordeal. No weakling could ever do it."[37] On the large bogs "you'd see a foreman standing there with his hands on his hips, with a scowl on his face there telling the men this and that, . . . get goin' there, you're slow. And you'd see a box boy running along passing boxes to a picker, you have to move those boxes . . . , and the pickers would be on their knees scooping like sons of guns."[38]

Fall weather conditions were not always pleasant. It could be mercilessly hot. "It was very hot work when the temperature rose to about ninety. You thought you'd die on the bog."[39] But the Finns stoically worked on. "People a lot of times suffered from the heat, you know. They would have to go off the bog. . . . But not so often with the Finnish people. Well the Finnish people were very tough. . . . I can't really think of a [Finnish] person going off the bog because he felt sick or badly. I think they might have felt bad or poorly, but they kept right on working."[40] In hot weather pickers wore long sleeves and pants with large hats as protection against the sun. In cold weather more layers of clothing were added.

After the berries were picked they had to be processed by screening. The bog companies and even smaller growers with sufficient acreage would hire a number of women to screen the berries. The screener sat along a conveyer belt where the berries moved away from a separator and removed the poor berries. Men had the heavier jobs of transporting the berries in and out of the separators and into storage or onto trucks for market. The screening season lasted from one to two months during September, October and November. It was a more social time as it was often possible to talk while working. But the screener had to keep up with picking the poor berries out, otherwise "you weren't needed very long."[41] It was sheltered work which was done in a screenhouse, a barn-like structure where berries were processed and stored. Although easier than weeding or picking, screening was still physically demanding, taking a toll particularly on eyes, hands and backs. The work gave a needed boost to family income. "Many of them [screeners] had done it all their lives and looked forward to it year after year. The pay was not so much. I don't know about the twenties, but in the thirties it was just a meagre 25 cents and, of course, earlier it was even cheaper than that. So it gave them a few extra dollars that would really help them a great deal getting little extra things their families needed."[42]

The small grower would process his own berries. One woman describes how she helped her mother to process the berries picked on their modest holdings. In 1930 when my father died

> [the speaker was 9 years old] and my mother had surgery and everything. And so after that I carried every full box into the car. She tried to help me pack them into the back seat of a ... Chrysler about fourteen to twenty boxes or something and a few on the [front] seat and drove the car to the shed where we kept them, what we called a *tulsusetti*, ... and packed them in there. And when we started screening somebody who came along, the buyer would come along for a certain wholesaler and he'd buy them and then we'd start dumping them into the high separator and turning the crank by hand and the berries came through and you'd lift that box and put them into a handscreen and let

them run, usually into the quarter barrel boxes that you had to pack tight and nail them. I usually nailed them, you know the cover on, and pack those again into another area so they could be picked up by a man who was trucking them....You'd only sell to certain buyers, some of them were fly-by-night, and sell only to certain Boston houses... You were paid only after the berries were sold and got minus the commissions and the truckers' salary.[43]

Prices fluctuated from year to year. Sometimes, fortunately rarely, a grower would lose money after paying the commission and trucking fees.

Originally most of the cranberry bog acreage belonged to the big and inevitably Yankee-owned companies. They would hire crews of fifty to one hundred men and even more were hired for harvest. Work on these bogs first drew Finns to the area. The Finns quickly realized that it would be profitable to build their own bogs. For example, in Carver the first record of a bog built by a Finn was in 1901. "Everyone wanted to have the bogs. That way you were able to get ahead a little bit better than you would normally."[44]The men would continue their company work while building their own bogs on the side. A child remembers a father. "He carried the sand across the two rivers and he went over there and carried the sand over to the bog and pulled the stumps out as much as he could with the horse. Just physical labour you know. It was hard for him to do it. He did it all himself. After that he got very sick and I think he got that double pneumonia again [which consequently led to his death]."[45]

Although it was possible for a man to build a bog by hand, it was tremendously difficult considering the long hours a man would have to work elsewhere. One man remembers how the immigrant men "worked like jackasses and built them in the dark."[46] Considering this and the relative cheapness of the cost of building a bog (it cost about $1,000 per acre in the 1920s and 1930s), most elected to hire a crew to do the work. People would earn the extra money by having their families go out and pick blueberries in the swamp. A few earned extra money by picking "floats" (the berries which rose to the surface when bogs were flooded after picking). A few made and sold moonshine. Some got mortgages; but it was difficult. "The banks did not lend money to foreigners very easily in those days. If you were a Yankee, you had collateral; whether you had collateral or not, they'd lend you the money. But a foreigner had a hard time going into a bank and getting money, so they had to have the downpayment on a bog."[47] One of the largest Finnish growers, after making a success of his bogs, in turn loaned money to other Finns to help them get a start.

Into the twenties and thirties bogs were made by hand. Finnish men were versed in the construction techniques, for this was the work they had first done; and some headed their own crews. One man tells of his father's early experiences.

> So he came out here in the country and started grubbing for a living for 90 cents a day, nine hours a day; and a lot of the work was building cranberry bogs. A lot of it was piecework, turfing the swamps, stumping, and clearing the land for cranberry bogs. They paid so much a rod for clearing. Turfing they probably got 10 cents a rod, if they worked hard enought they might make 90 cents a day. And there was—bog. It was a bunch of Finns worked on that. It was a leather leaf, brown brush swamp and I thing that's what they got, ten cents a rod for turfing it... Turf was about that thick [eight inches]. And they had to mow the brush off of it first. The leather leaf brush it, well, grows thick, all massed together and they *worked*! That wasn't just cutting the turf and pulling it up, they had to wheel it off the bog besides! For ten cents a rod! You had to really hoof it up to make ninety cents a day![48]

"But more or less in the early thrities they started buying into bigger bogs. A lot of Finns had built prior to that, say in the ... twenties, they's already built themselves an acre or two."[49] Initially the Finns built bogs and later many were able to purchase bogs (often failed Yankee ones) already built which showed a faster profit. Over 60 per cent of the Finns in the area built or bought their own bogs. Only about one third of the area Finns became full-time growers; others did it on the side of a regular job. Much of the acreage was relatively small. "If you had five acres you were well off... If a family owned twenty acres of bog he was rich, oh he was rich, very rich."[50]

As the family operations were often small it was important to rely on your Finnish neighbours to help out, especially at harvest. Neighbours would go from bog to bog.

> If someone in the neighbourhood was able to give a hand they did. Sometimes we gave them a hand. See we

never had, for years we didn't, have any pump to pump the water on for the fall frosts or spring frosts. So what we got happened to be by chance ... So in the fall it would be neighbour would help neighbour. We'd go over there and help; supposing they had a moment, they might help us. Generally it was us, that we did our thing first most of the time and then we went on to help the others.[51]

After the family work was done it was also possible to hire out on larger Finnish-owned bogs.

Finns were excellent cranberry growers. Even today it is a Finnish family which is said to have the largest yield per acre in Massachusetts.[52] At one time there were practically all Finnish foremen on the bogs. When they left to work on their own bogs, the success of company bogs often suffered.

But a lot of these Yankees gave up the bog business 'cause they couldn't produce ... But when the Finns got a hold of the cranberry bogs, they doubled their production. They were able to produce a lot more. It was the Finns that had the knowledge in the cranberry bogs—how to run the cranberry bogs, how to raise the cranberries. They were the ones who were able to do it. You take like_____down here ... , when they had Finn foremen over there, they got beautiful crops. Those bogs were in beautiful shape. But lately they haven't been able to produce the berries that they used to. It was the Finns who had the knowledge to raise cranberries. They worked for these big companies. They were able to produce tremendous crops and when the Finns stopped working for these companies, that's when the companies had to sell out, when they had to give up because they weren't able to produce the cranberries.[53]

The previous descriptions have made it clear that bog work was not easy. The big companies were especially hard on their employees. "They were all the same. They got cheap labour and worked the hell out of the men ... They made sure you worked."[54] The Yankee owners had little consideration for the immigrants. "They were miserable employers. Men meant nothing to them. They were just slave labour as far as they were concerned."[55] One Yankee owner will be forever famous among the Finns for a remark he made. A second generation Finn remembers. "Yeah when one of

his Cape Verdeans died—he dropped dead on the bog pushing out
a wheelbarrow— He said 'Too bad, my best horse died.' . . . Yeah
that's how they treated you, you were nothing but animals."[56]

In the early days all work was done by hand and, except for a
lunch break, everyone was expected to work unceasingly as the
following explains:

> I know one time when I was working for_____, a guy
> got a heart attack and all of a sudden, he just flopped
> on the bog over there. So they went and called a doc-
> tor, but they left him lying there when he had a heart
> attack and everyone else *worked* . . . We made him
> comfortable, but laid him on the cranberry bog in the
> hot sun . . . That's the way we had to work there.[57]

It is not surprising that the Finns were anxious to leave work
under such conditions. A man who owned his own bog had to work
hard, and perhaps even harder, but he was his own boss and he
gained the opportunity to improve his lot. He created his own job.
There were few jobs in the area other than working for the large
companies. In fact, some in the Finnish community believed this
was not accidental. "The reason they didn't have any more work
in_____was 'cause they wanted to keep the work down. The
Republicans ran this town and they wanted bog workers. So they
made sure there wasn't too much government work allowed in
town . . . Work didn't come around until after World War Two."[58]

The war marked the end of an era and life in the area
changed dramatically. Machinery and chemicals came to take the
place of human labour. With technical aids one man could do the
jobs of many and it became possible for a man to care for more
acreage. As immigrants became successful and began to retire in
the years after the war, their sons entered the cranberry business
and now their grandsons and even great-grandsons are following
suit. The time of Finnish immigration coincided with the age of
cranberry bog expansion. Finns learned from their early labouring
jobs how to grow a crop which was not cultivated in their homeland. They were apt students and became successful farmers, providing good homes in Massachusetts for their families. In the early
years the farming was of a subsistence level, but later they were
able to earn a comfortable living.

The Finns were a small group, but they have left a permanent mark on the area through their success in agriculture. But
because of the inter-ethnic character of the area many of the

second generation intermarried with members of other groups, to say nothing of the subsequent generations. The Finnish community has been overwhelmed and after the second generation goes it will cease to exist. In this paper there has not been the space to describe the community completely; much remains to be said, for example, about social customs and home life. But, hopefully, here the vital definition of the community in terms of the farming of a specialized crop and of being Finnish had been explained. The fact that the men and women of this community in Carver, Middleborough and Wareham were not only Finns, but also cranberry bog workers makes their story unique in American immigration history.

# Notes

1. Cranberries are native to the muck land of southeastern Massachusetts. Nurtured by the easy availability of water a cranberry industry grew in the nineteenth century when it was discovered that wild berries could be improved by farming. The natural resources of Plymouth County make it especially well suited for cranberry bogs and here one finds more than half of Massachusetts acreage with the most in Carver followed by Wareham, Plymouth, and Middleborough in that order (Fredrika A. Burrows, *Cannonballs and Cranberries* [Taunton: William S. Sullwold, 1976], p. 76).

2. It has been said that about 1872 some Finns settled in Barnstable Country (about thirty miles south on Cape Cod) and that some Finnish sailors had left ships in the Boston area around 1860 (Horace H. Russell, "The Finnish Farmers in America," *Agricultural History*, XI [1937], p. 74). The first Finnish bog worker supposedly was hired in 1890 near Hyannis on Cape Cod (Russell, p. 75). If the town of Carver, as the centre of the cranberry-producing area, is taken as an example to trace the influx of Finns, it is found that,according to town reports, the first Finns in the area to be noted were members of the Gusta (also Kustaf, August) and Hannah (Kankaslara) Nylund (also Nyland) family beginning in 1895. Starting in 1898 other Finnish families are mentioned. One of the greatest concentrations of Finnish names in the early years (1898-1901) is in the "Receipts and expenditures connected with the support of the poor" (primarily for burial or medical expenses). In 1898 the first Finn is listed as having worked for the town and in 1900 at least thirty-four Finnish men were paid for fighting fires. In 1901 the first Finn is listed as having "set" (planted) a bog of between one and two acres. It is quite extraordinary that a Finnish immigrant would have the capital to do this at so early a

104    M. Penti

date. By 1929 (the final year of published taxable valuation reports) there were thirteen Finnish bog owners with a total of over 85 acrea (two owned over 25 acres each, making them fairly wealthy men). By 1910, 185 identifiable Finns had been included in town reports. (It should be noted that it is difficult to make a true assessment of the Finnish population through town records; for example, Finnish names are grossly misspelled, many Finns quickly Anglicized their names making recognition difficult, and many Finns simply did not come into contact with town government so that community population estimates based on town records should be considered conservative.)

3. Väinö Välkiö, *Silta Yli Atlannin* (Hameenlinna: Kustannuskeskus Päivä, 1973), p. 210.

5. K.A., interview 1979.

6. S.T.

7. E.V., interview 1979.

8. K.A., interview 1979.

9. S.T.

10. T.K., interview 1979.

11. E.V.

12. E.V.

13. S.T.

14. T.K.

15. E.V.

16. S.T.

17. T.K.

18. T.K.

19. T.K.

20. T.K.

21. S.T.

22. S.T.

23. S.T.

24. E.V.

25. E.V.

26. T.K.

27. T.K.

28. S.T.

29. T.K.

30. T.K.

31. T.K.

32. T.K.
33. T.K.
34. T.K.
35. T.K.
36. T.K.
37. T.K.
38. E.V.
39. T.K.
40. T.K.
41. T.K.
42. T.K."
43. T.K.
44. T.K.
45. T.K.
46. E.V.
47. E.V.
48. S.T.
49. E.V.
50. E.V.
51. T.K.
52. S.T.
53. E.V.
54. E.V.
55. E.V.
56. E.V.
57. E.V.
58. E.V.

# Second Generation Finnish-American Migration from the Northwoods to Detroit, 1920-1950

*Michael M. Loukinen*

In a recent essay on the concept of community in American history, Thomas Bender shows that a misreading of Töennies' theory of social change, the reification of ideal type contrasts between *gemeinschaft* and *gesellschaft*, and the schism between sociology and history, have misdirected scholarly inquiry in both fields.[1] The process of social change has been described by various scholars as a transition from one form of social structure to another: society based upon traditional status becomes one whose foundation is the contract. Other scholars speak of it as an historical progression from *gemeinschaft* to *gesellschaft*, mechanical to organic solidarity, rural to urban, and traditional to modern.[2] Although the theoretical language is somewhat different, in all of these formulations change

Portions of this paper were presented at Finn Forum, an international conference in Toronto, Canada, November 1-3, 1979; at Michigan State University, East Lansing, Michigan, November 26, 1978; and at the Finnish Center Association, Farmington, Michigan, December 18, 1979. This research was funded by a 1979 research grant from Northern Michigan University, and by the Institute for Cultural, Environmental, and Heritage Studies at Northern Michigan University. The author is grateful for the assistance provided by Steven Blixt, Elaine Foster-Loukinen, Melvin Holli, Elvira Kanerva, Dan Maki, David Nearing, John and Debbie Nelson, Jon Saari, Thomas Sullivan, Kenrick Thompson, James Walsh and Richard Wright.

has been viewed at the societal level, as a linear progression described by a zero-sum equation, such that any growth of modern urban structures necessitates a concommitant decline of the traditional ethnic community.[3]

Beginning in the 1950s and continuing today, there has developed a vast literature documenting the shortcomings of the linear model of social change. The rural community was thought to have disintegrated with the out-migration of its youth, ethnic culture was believed to have withered away, the extended family seemed to have broken up into isolated nuclear units, and supportive neighbourly relations were thought to have been replaced by superficial nodding acquaintances. In many contexts these predictions have been shown to be false.[4]

In the early 1960s, social anthropologists found that the time-honoured tribal urban dichotomy implicit in a structural functionalist determinism failed to come to grips with the enormous rate of back-and-forth migration and the importance of individual choice in determining community attachments and ethnic identity they found in African cities.[5] As long as community was thought of in holistic terms, having an implicit territorial referent, one could not think about change without the assumption of collapse and disintegration.

If, on the other hand, community were defined in terms of communal experiences rooted in social interaction, it would be possible to search for the structural forms containing it. The concept of social network allows us to do precisely that.[6] A particular social network may be defined in terms of the specific forms of social relations connecting individuals. This flexibility allows one to analyse social change at the level of individual decision making, taking into account the particular social relations which activate the sense of community and ethnicity, and to identify the interface between them.

A network analysis of the second generation Finnish American migration is especially illuminating, because most of the group grew up in rural communities and many thereafter migrated to the cities.[7] Furthermore, this second generation has been relatively untouched by scholarly inquire. This study will explore the outmigration from a rural hamlet, and the relationship between the rural ethnic community of origin and the initial encounter with the city.

The research strategy for this study was to first develop a complete list of immigrant families that had settled in Pelkie, Michigan, a small hamlet in the northwoods region of Baraga County in Michigan's Upper Peninsula. Geographical and occupational mobility patterns of all of the second generation Finnish-American youth were recorded to determine the extent of their outmigration. Many of the second generation farm youth had already died, so efforts were made to contact all of the surviving members who had migrated to Detroit between 1920 and 1945. A total of 155 interviews were conducted. Information about the years of migration from and ages of deceased migrants was obtained and verified through more than one family member's reports. Respondents were interviewed in person, by telephone, and in a few cases, by mailed questionnaires.

# The Urban Destination: Detroit 1920-1945

By the turn of the century, Detroit's population of 285,704 began to increase at a faster rate than the other American cities, and between 1910 and 1930 it was one of the fastest growing cities in America. The automobile industry attracted immigrant labourers and by the beginning of this century about one-third of Detroit's population were immigrants.[8] Between 1910 and 1920 the foreign-born popluation doubled, and by 1925 about one out of every two Detroiters were immigrants. By 1930, when Detroit's population was 1,568,622, the largest immigrant communities were found among the Poles (66,113), Germans (32,716), Italians (28,581) and Scots (23,546).[9] By the beginning of World War One, the inflow of southern blacks was noticeably increasing; by 1920 they numbered 40,838 and in the following ten years had increased their numbers threefold. By 1940, the number of blacks reached 149,119, accounting for about 9.2 per cent of Detroit's population.[10]

Into this multi-ethnic manufacturing city came the Finnish immigrants. The limited data available suggest that most of the Finnish immigrants had lived elsewhere in the United States before migrating to Detroit. Many had first lived in the copper-mining towns of Michigan's Upper Peninsula. Table 1 shows the distribution of Finnish immigrants in the United States, Michigan, Upper Peninsula of Michigan, and in Wayne County (surrounding Detroit) from 1920 to 1950.[11]

Although the concentration of Finnish immigrants in Michigan declines slightly between 1920 and 1950, about one out of five lived in Michigan. Within the State of Michigan, the Finnish Americans were especially concentrated, with more than eight out

**Table 1: Distribution of Finnish Immigrants, 1920-1950**

|                  | 1920    | 1930    | 1940    | 1950   |
|------------------|---------|---------|---------|--------|
| United States    | 149,824 | 142,478 | 117,210 | 95,506 |
| Michigan         | 30,096  | 27,022  | 21,151  | 15,501 |
| Upper Peninsula (of Michigan) | 26,542 | 22,048 | 17,378 | 11,787 |
| Wayne County     | 2,000   | 3,218   | 2,275   | 2,241  |

of ten living in Upper Peninsula. In 1920, 6.7 per cent of the Michigan Finns lived in Wayne County; by 1930 this proportion rose to 11.9 per cent and then declined to 10.8 per cent by 1940. It is clear that the Upper Peninsula and Detroit have been the major points of Finnish immigrant settlement.[12]

Census data show the growth of the second generation Finnish-American population in the Detroit city limits (see Table 2)[13]

**Table 2: Detroit's First and Second Generation Finnish Ethnic Community 1920-1950**

|                   | 1920  | 1930  | 1940  | 1950  |
|-------------------|-------|-------|-------|-------|
| First Generation  | 1,814 | 2,811 | 1,944 | 1,869 |
| Second Generation | 1,455 | 5,185 | 5,440 | 5,236 |
| Total             | 3,269 | 7,996 | 7,384 | 7,105 |

According to the U.S. Bureau of the Census the Finnish ethnic community in Detroit more than doubled in size between 1920 and 1930. If one were to include the 432 second generation Finns living in Highland Park along with the six in Hamtramack, and the 15 domestic workers in Grosse Point, the total by 1930 is 8,449. It is clear that most of the increase between 1920 and 1930 is due to the expansion of the second generation Finnish-American population which expanded at a rate of 2.3 times the immigrant population.

A complete institutional life emerged in a zone about five miles northwest of the city's downtown financial centre. In 1906, 30 Finnish immigrant socialists founded a workers' association. By 1920, the membership had grown to 600 and four years later the membership built the Fourteenth Street Hall, which contained study rooms, a cooperative store and a main hall with a capacity of 700.[14] The next year they organized the Finnish Summer Camp Association at Loon Lake about twenty miles northwest of the downtown area. Several cooperative and private boarding-houses were operated by the immigrants. For instance, the New Hope Club, which was founded in 1919, in four years grew to member-ship of 147 males.[15] The Suomi Synod organized three congrega-tions: the Finnish Evangelical Lutheran Church (1914) which was renamed St. John's Lutheran Church in 1943; Bethlehem Lutheran (1937), and Northwest Emanual (1957). Three Apostolic congrega-tions were formed: The First Apostolic (1918), Old Apostolic (1925), and the Apostolic Lutheran Church (1928). In 1921 the Salem Lutheran Church was founded, which affiliated with the National Lutheran tradition. There also appeared societies devoted to the preservation of the ethnic culture (1917), a temperance society (late 1920s), and even a shortlived attempt to establish a Finnish-language newspaper (1926).[16]

By the end of World War One, the Finnish residential settle-ment was concentrated in the downtown area near the Michigan Central Station, and in Highland Park near the Ford Motor Com-pany.[17] By 1923-24, Finns began to concentrate in the Woodrow Wilson area, about one mile east of Highland Park.[18] Until the 1950s the Woodrow Wilson area was the urban village of the Finnish ethnic community. It was a twelve-block area of taverns, restaurants, small shops, theatres and dance halls. In the "village square" was a four-block strip containing thirty-two taverns—a record worthy to mention in *Ripley's Believe It or Not*. Ethnic foods, Finnish-language newspapers, and even four commercial saunas were established to serve the ethnic community.

# The Site of Outmigration: The Rural Hamlet

The source of outmigration in this study is a haven in the woods typical of the many northwoods hamlets established by the Finnish immigrants in the Lake Superior region. It was named Pelkie after a French Canadian who had decided to leave the lumber yards of the Thomas Nestor Sawmill in Baraga to start a homestead in the late 1890s. By that time it had become a landing site for French Canadian lumberjacks and a few Swedish homesteaders.

At the turn of the century, Finnish immigrant farmers began replacing the French Canadians, who were moving either west-ward following the logging industry, or into nearby sawmill towns.

Out of every ten immigrant families, only one had come directly from Finland. Slightly more than that had first lived in the multi-ethnic sawmill town of Baraga, and seven had come from the mining towns of the Copper Country. The vast majority arrived between 1905 and 1920.

Most of the immigrants carried with them the residue of the confrontation with corporate power in the mining towns and of the class conflict in Finland—the "Church Finn/Red Finn" schism. Factionalism based upon one's beliefs worked its way into the fabric of community life. In 1905 a Suomi Synod congregation was formed. Followers of the Laestadian movement had been meeting informally in homes and had built their own church in 1918. Fourteen years later this church experienced its own painful schism, which resulted in the building of a new church in 1932. By 1922 the leftists organized the entire community to build the Taimi Hall, which was then called the Pelkie Hall by Church Finns who liked to believe that their sons and daughters would never go to the dances it sponsored. Pelkie had its own post office (1903), farmers' cooperative store (1914), and a short-lived creamery and cheese factory. Virtually all subcultural traditions of the Finnish immigrant community were represented in Pelkie.

In 1900 the Mineral Range Railroad ran a line east and west through the centre of Pelkie, connecting the copper mines around Mass City with an ore-stamping plant in Keweenaw Bay. The early community was organized into eight distinct neighbourhoods, all but one of which had its own one-room schoolhouse, railroad spur, and athletic team among the youth. Between 1900 and 1936 informal labour exchanges, house-to-house visiting, celebrations and communal harvesting were contained within these neighbourhood units.

By the middle 1920s, the roads and bridges were improved, a new school was constructed in the central village area (1932) and the one-room neighbourhood schools closed, the railroad discontinued its line through Pelkie (1936), and the combine replaced the steam threshing machines, thus ending the communal harvesting among neighbours. In a period of just a few years all of these events broke down the tightly knit neighbourhoods, and social relationships began to spread throughout the larger community.

When they came of age between 1920 and 1950 many of the second generation Finnish American youth that had grown up on the farms and had listened in the churches and halls, decided in their words, "to make a go of it," working in the factories and homes of the wealthy in Detroit.

# Leaving the Rural Hamlet

The Finnish immigrant pioneers who married and settled in Pelkie raised an average of 6.5 children per family that survived to young adulthood.[19] Out of every four children, three left their rural community. Fifty-nine per cent of all of the second generation Finnish-American children migrated to Detroit, which, by sex, amounts to 65.5 per cent of the females and 52.2 per cent of the males. As shown in Table 3, a few had left the farm before 1920, and by the late twenties the out-migration gathered momentum.

Table 3: Second Generation Finnish-American Migration from Pelkie to Detroit by Date of Departure and Sex

| Time of Departure | Males | | Females | | Both | |
|---|---|---|---|---|---|---|
| | No. | % | No. | % | No. | % |
| Before 1920 | 4 | 2.2 | 5 | 2.7 | 9 | 2.5 |
| 1920-1924 | 8 | 4.6 | 16 | 8.7 | 24 | 7.0 |
| 1925-1929 | 20 | 11.4 | 33 | 17.9 | 53 | 14.8 |
| 1930-1934 | 25 | 14.3 | 30 | 16.3 | 55 | 15.3 |
| 1935-1939 | 57 | 32.6 | 53 | 28.8 | 110 | 30.4 |
| 1940-1944 | 33 | 18.9 | 36 | 19.6 | 69 | 19.2 |
| 1945-1949 | 14 | 8.0 | 7 | 3.8 | 21 | 5.8 |
| 1950 and after | 14 | 8.0 | 4 | 2.2 | 18 | 5.0 |
| TOTAL | 175 | 100 | 184 | 100 | 359 | 100 |

The rate of outmigration was constant even during the worst years of the Depression, when it had been estimated that over 150,000 of Detroit's workers returned to the rural communities of their origin.[20] In the first five years after the Depression, 109 of the second generation farm youth went to Detroit. A strong outflow continues from 1940 through 1944 when Detroit was working feverishly to meet the defence needs of the nation. By the end of World War Two there was a sudden decline in the outmigration as this cohort of second generation Finnish Americans in both the rural community and Detroit began to marry, settle down and raise the third generation.

Women were not only more likely to migrate than men, they were more likely to leave in the earlier years of the outmigration. Before and during the Depression years, the female migrants were more likely to have departed, and it was only after World War One that the male outmigration exceeded that of the females. The age profile of the migrants is consistent with this trend (see table 4).

114     *M. Loukinen*

Table 4:  Age and Sex Profile of Pelkie's Second Generation Finnish American-
          icans Migrating to Detroit 1920-1950

| Age Categories | Male No. | % | Female No. | % | Both No. | % |
|---|---|---|---|---|---|---|
| 0-14 | 6 | 3.4 | 3 | 1.6 | 9 | 2.5 |
| 15-20 | 50 | 28.6 | 104 | 56.5 | 154 | 42.9 |
| 21-25 | 61 | 34.9 | 48 | 26.1 | 109 | 30.4 |
| 26-30 | 31 | 17.7 | 18 | 9.8 | 49 | 13.7 |
| 31-35 | 14 | 8.0 | 4 | 2.2 | 18 | 5.0 |
| 36-40 | 8 | 4.6 | 5 | 2.7 | 13 | 3.6 |
| 41 and older | 5 | 2.8 | 2 | 1.1 | 7 | 1.9 |
| TOTAL | 175 | 100 | 184 | 100 | 359 | 100 |

Between the ages of 15 and 20, there were twice as many female as male migrants. More women migrated before age 20, whereas more men migrated after 30 when there was substantially less outmigration for both sexes.

From this profile of migrants one can easily estimate their marital status at the time of departure. By examining those migrants (N = 155) for whom we have data, 80 per cent were single at the time of departure, and one notices a tendency for female migrants to be more likely to be unmarried (83.3 per cent), as opposed to their male counterparts (75.8 per cent).

When asked to relive their decision and report their reasons for going to Detroit, 69.2 per cent of all migrants gave responses that fit into the general category of economic justifications. As one man who had gone to Detroit in 1923 explained, "There was no future up north [in the Upper Peninsula]. I could see that. I was working in the [lumber] camps and the wages were very low. You were doing good if you got $1.25 a day. But that's all there was to do. When we came down here I did carpentry work. It seemed like we were making a fortune. But then we were getting good wages for those days—85¢ an hour for building houses."[21] Another man who had left in 1936 said, "I was working for the Alston Mill for 15¢ an hour, ten hours a day. My first check in Detroit was $72 for two weeks. Earlier in the depression I was making $44 per month on WPA. I felt like a millionarie." A woman reflected: "There was no money here, but in Detroit there were pages and pages of ads for domestic workers."

Another closely related motivation seemed to be the desire to raise one's self-esteem, as indicated by the 8.2 per cent who "wanted to better myself." Even though the value system of the city had permeated the countryside and had for some become the yardstick of self-evaluation, social approval was sought within the networks of the rural hamlet. Another 11 per cent were motivated by a sense of curiosity. They wanted to see the city, to feel its excitement, and to buy its goods; however, this experience was only validated when it was revealed to those back home.

Another force prompting the outmigration was rooted deeply in the traditional social structure of the rural community—the desire of its members to associate with one another and to participate in a local trend. Thirty-two per cent of all migrants expressed a desire to remain in contact with the local network of siblings and/or friends. Twenty per cent said they had gone to the city "because my friends were there" or because "everyone was going." A woman who had left home in 1930 said, "It was time to fly the coop. All the young folks were leaving. I felt that I wanted to join the parade. I was not going to be left out. My sister had already been there for many years. She came home for a visit and wanted me to go down [to Detroit] with her." Another who left in 1939 said, "All the girls were there. So many were already down there. It seemed like the natural thing to do: as soon as you got out of high school you went to Detroit. I really didn't even think about it. I just went." A male had this revelation in 1942: "All of a sudden it hit me. When I wanted to have some fun I realized all my friends had gone to Detroit to get jobs, so I thought I'd go down and try it myself."

Another 12 per cent claimed it was "because my brother [or sister] was there." It would be a mistake to understand this response as merely an instrumental motive facilitating initial adaption. The tone in which this reason was given and in-depth probes often revealed a strong desire to remain in contact with a sibling as an end in itself. Traditional social bonds created for many the primary source of the impulse to migrate.

The sheer volume of outmigration impacting on the second generation cohort made the acts of leaving home and finding a job a rite of passage, a transition from child to adult status. One man half-jokingly said: "You weren't considered a man unless you had gone to Detroit." Even to have asked for help in finding their first job seemed to some of these migrants to have been at the cost of realizing adult status.

Sex differences are apparent in these data. Women were more than twice as likely as the men to migrate in order to maintain relationships with others. Fourteen per cent of the women but none of the men cited their desire to participate in a

community trend ("everyone is going") as the first reason mentioned; and when the men expressed this motiviation, it was always
the second or third reason reported. A similar pattern of sex differences is reflected in the desire to be with a sibling as a motive for
having migrated. Women were also more likely (7.7 per cent) to
migrate in order to be with their spouse, whereas this motive was
not reported by any male migrants. The consistent sex differences
associated with the likelihood of mentioning one's desire to be with
members of the traditional ethnic community, the order in which
this motive was cited, and the manner in which it was verbally
expressed support the claim that the traditional social network had
a greater impact on the outmigration of females.

Other evidence suggesting that leaving the community was
not merely an individual act shaped by self-interest is that the
second generation Finnish Americans' commitment to the family
members remaining on the farm was often the primary reason for
leaving. Again, the women were much more likely to have cited
this as a reason for having migrated. One who left in 1930, during
the beginning of the Depression said, "We had a big family. All I
could do was eat—just another set of feet under the table. There
were seven of us [children] and we could not all stay home. There
was simply not enough money. We needed clothes and my mother
and father could not afford to buy them for us. It hurt them so. We
did not expect them to help. We knew we had to get out and
support ourselves." Virtually all of the respondents for whom the
family was a social unit transcending their individual interests and
who left home to "ease the burden" or "to make some money to
send home" migrated during the Depression. The preponderance of
women citing their family responsibility as a reason for migrating is
a joint function of several processes. The traditional patterns of
socialization stressed the females' primary commitment to the family unit. Females in large families may have believed they were
more of a burden on the farm as compared to their brothers
because they did not perform as many of the heavy manual labour
tasks required in the labour-intensive farming and lumbering economy, yet they consumed about the same household subsistence
resources. Finally, there seems to have been a demand for female
domestic workers that continued on throughout the very worst
years of the Depression, whereas by 1931 the factories in Detroit
had laid off 42 per cent of all male employees.[22]

It should also be mentioned that women were more likely
than men to see life on the farm in negative terms and to cite this
as a reason for leaving. As one woman who had left home in 1937

said, "I did not want to stay on the farm! I wanted to get as far
away from it as I could. Milking cows, getting water, spreading hay
and straw, and shoveling cowshit . . . I did not like that at all."

# Work and Leisure in the Finnish American
# Community in Detroit

Although there were a few attempts by Detroit employers to recruit workers from the Upper Peninsula, at the time of their first
trip to Detroit only 10.6 per cent of the males and 4.6 per cent of
the female migrants had a "good lead" on a job, and only 6.1 per
cent of the males and 2.3 per cent of the females had actually
obtained a job before migrating.

Finding a job seems to have been regarded by most of the
migrants, and especially the males, as an individual challenge
through which they could attain adult status. When asked if anyone helped them find a job, respondents often proudly asserted
their independence: "I found my own job. When it came to finding
work I paddled my own canoe. I did it all myself. No one had to
help me." Most of the men said they simply walked down the
street, stepped into one of the long lines and waited their turn,
while the women responded to the newspaper ads for domestic
workers. Two weeks without finding a job was thought to have
been an exceptionally long time. They usually took the first job
that was offered, seeing it strictly as a temporary way to make
money rather than the first step on a career ladder. On weekends
when they assembled with their friends in the taverns and restaurants, they compared their wages and as soon as they had earned
enough money to meet their immediate living expenses they found
a better job. Many changed jobs within the first three months.

The migrant's second job was usually found by informed
brokers circulating in the ethnic hub—the Woodrow Wilson area.
As one male migrant who had settled in Detroit on three different
occasions said, "Pull counted a lot in those days. If you were
working someplace you could just write your name on a piece of
paper and give it to a friend. He would give it to the personnel
manager who then checked back to see if the employee making the
recommendation had been a good worker. A guy would have a
much better chance than someone coming in right off the street."

But for 17.5 per cent of the men and 33 per cent of the

women, finding their first job was a task to be solved by activating their informal social network. In such cases, males (64.7 per cent) were more likely to rely upon friends and kinsmen from their rural community than were the women (39.4 per cent). Ninety-four per cent of these informal employment brokers were Finnish ethnics, usually of the same sex as the migrant.

The first job obtained by one out of every two female migrants was that of a domestic worker; She washed the clothes, dishes, floors, windows and walls, prepared meals, made beds, carried out the trash, and ironed the handkerchiefs of the wealthier Detroit residents. Another 20 per cent worked in various clerical jobs, 11.9 per cent as factory workers, and 18.1 per cent as various service workers, such as nurse's aids, waitresses and laundresses. In the early 1920s, the average earnings for the female migrants working as domestics was $8.50 a week plus room and board, and it had increased to $9.40 by the late twenties. During the depression years wages fell to $5.30 a week and had risen to $6.80 by the late thirties. Throughout the 1940s these Finnish-American domestic workers' wages averaged $12 a week.

Immediately after the Depression the female migrants were more likely to find employment as secretaries and clerks earning about $20 per week. During the years of intense war production they began to find work in factories, averaging $45 a week.

During this same period 72 per cent of the Finnish-American male migrants worked in factories with average weekly earnings of $28 between 1930 and 1934, $33 during the late thirties, and $53 from 1940-1944. Fifteen per cent of the male migrants found employment in the skilled trades related to the home construction industry, 10 per cent worked in clerical jobs, and the same proportion worked as truck drivers and as labourers in lumberyards and warehouses.

It is a widespread belief among these second generation Finnish Americans that they were (and are) superior workers to other ethnic groups and that their employers knew it. When asked about it, 42 per cent of the men and 49 per cent of the women who had gone to Detroit said their employers had a distinct preference for Finnish workers from the Upper Peninsula.

The narratives of the migrants also support this claim. "As soon as I said I'm from up 'Nort' he told me to step off to the side." "As soon as I said my name was Maki his ears perked up. He asked if I was a Finlander from the U.P. and a couple hours later I was hanging doors on the Model T's." One migrant recalled Appalachian migrants taking informal speech lessons in the Finnish taverns in order to master the Finnish accent so that they might find work. When probed further, most conceded that it was also a regional preference—coming from the Upper Peninsula—and not simply ethnic background that appealed to employers. Since Finnish Americans were by far the numerically dominant ethnic group in the Upper Peninsula, regional origin and ethnicity had been blurred in the eyes of employees. Yet the newspaper ads, such as the one below appearing in the *Detroit News* of September 26, 1927, often cited preference for Finnish girls as domestic workers.

### A GOOD MAID

One who does not run out nights, do cooking, general housework, family of three, will pay good salary to one who can qualify. Must have the VERY BEST REFERENCES. Steady position. Unless you remain with this position a long period do not apply. No "floaters." Interview me at my office first. $18 a week. Prefer Irish or Finnish woman.

Many of the women had found a modest claim to dignity in the belief that "Finnish girls were so neat, clean, and so honest that the rich people wanted us." Yet some of the more seasoned domestic workers said that they had watched how employers took advantage of a naive girl fresh off the farm. They would be asked to do things that no experienced domestic worker would even consider. Many of these women still resent how they had been treated and claim that it was actually because the Finnish girls were "so meek" that they could easily be made to work for next to nothing and would never dare talk back to their "betters." After they had been in the city for a few weeks and had compared their situations to their girlfriends', many found another household in which to work.

Unlike ethnic groups working in single industry towns in the textile mills in New England and the North, virtually all of these Finnish Americans had been separated at work from kin and the members of their rural community, but not all had been isolated from the larger ethnic community.[23] Fifty-eight per cent of the women and 37 percent of the men said they worked in a setting without having fellow ethnics with whom to converse. The larger proportion of women who were separated from their ethnic community is undoubtedly due to the many who worked alone as domestic workers.

On the other hand, for 38 per cent of the men and 25 per cent of the women there were from one to four fellow ethnics providing a supportive cultural environment at work. In fact, one-fourth of the men and one-sixth of the women were supported by five or more fellow ethnics in their work setting.

If it is true that the presence of fellow ethnics in the daily work environment cushions the impact of the urban social order on the ethnic workers, it is clear that among Finnish Americans, the women were less protected than the men.[24] While talking about their experiences, the former domestic workers expressed having felt resentment, loneliness and confusion more so than did the other female workers. Alone in a strange house where they both worked and slept, they had no one to turn to for support. They suffered continual insults that were not always subtle. Whether it was because they had to wash and iron their master's underwear, or pound the master's pillows so his head would be comfortably positioned into the crease; or because they always ate alone in the kitchen, they were continually reminded of that difference between those who were rich and those who had come from the farm. Some sensed a sharp discontinuity between their rural work habits and the industrial time schedules imposed on them by their employers. Irritated by having to work exactly when, and for as long as an employer determined, several said they "felt like a slave" and "missed the freedom they had left back up north."

Separated at work from kin, friends from the rural hamlet, and in some cases from fellow ethnics, leisure time was spent with those from home. Since virtually all of the migrants rented small rooms or shared very small apartments, they met in public places. On Thursday nights—*Piika Päivät* (Maid's Day)—and Sunday afternoons, dances were scheduled. On Friday and Saturday nights, Woodrow Wilson Avenue came to life. The street was lined with thirty-two taverns. Just as their immigrant fathers had done after climbing out of the dusty mines or after walking the trail back from remote lumbercamps, most of these second generation factory workers sought relief in the taverns. On Saturday night, there was said to have been a two-block line waiting to get into the *Caravan Gardens*. One person reported having stopped into the *Silver Star* during the afternoon to talk with a neighbour boy from back home that he had met on the street, and soon had six bottles of beer sitting in front of him—compliments of the boys from back home who had seen him come in. Within an hour after his arrival on Woodrow Wilson another saw his cousin being forcibly escorted from a bar. The Woodrow Wilson area was a meeting place for these farm youth. Although it was also the gathering place for the entire Finnish-American community in Detroit, prior to 1950 people seemed to congregate in those places where they would expect to see friends and kin from their home community.

When asked where they went to have fun in the city, respondents recalled that three taverns that had permitted dancing were clearly the most popular: The *Silver Star*, *Caravan Gardens*, and *Monte Carlo*. Males were much more likely than females to frequent the taverns. Most women thought it improper to enter such a place without a male escort and would otherwise only go with their girlfriends, and only if there were a dancing room available. They were far more likely than the men to attend church and to enjoy themselves in friends' homes, dancing at the Greystone Ballroom and 14th Street Hall, shopping at Hudson's, dining at the Finnish Restaurant, and the Alpha Cafe.

When asked how many people from their rural community they would expect to see on Woodrow Wilson on a Saturday night, estimates ranged from twelve to fifty. Several insisted that, "You saw more Pelkie people on Woodrow Wilson than you ever saw in the village area in Pelkie."

The bonds of the rural community were reaffirmed in the taverns of the city. If a respondent indicated a specific setting as having been a gathering place for people from his/her rural community, the males were more likely to have personally gone there to have fun (98 per cent) than were the females (72 per cent). When asked which taverns he preferred, an elderly man said, "Why, the ones where you could always find a ride home."

Interviews suggest that people who had been merely nodding acquaintances or had only heard the other's name mentioned often became close friends while in the city. Some who would not have crossed the Church Finn/Red Finn boundary to socialize with one another back home in their rural community admitted one another into their circle of friends on Woodrow Wilson. A woman who had been in Detroit in the late 1930s was astonished to see church people sitting at the same table with the communists, saying "that would never have happened back home." She felt uneasy at first but said, "In a little while, it was like being a part of one big family. We felt close to one another."

Back home in the rural hamlet distinctions based upon upposing beliefs remained significant. But in the Detroit urban setting there was a blended sense of contrast between fellow ethnics and the strangers of the city; and between kin and friends from the same rural community and Finnish Americans born elsewhere.

# The Fate of the Rural Ethnic Community

During this strong outmigration to the city, was the Finnish-American rural hamlet redefined relative to the city as an undesirable place to live? Did this outmigration undermine the belief that Pelkie was a good place to live? It seems as though the outmigration precipitated several contradictory processes, having both a positive and negative impact on the perceived quality of life in the rural community. Those who remained clearly had the feeling of having been left behind. They incorporated the widely held stereotype of the backward country bumpkin into their understanding of themselves. The men who stayed seemed to have suffered a loss of self-esteem. When asked why she went to Detroit, one woman said, "Are you crazy? There was nothing in Pelkie. I wasn't going to stay home and marry a hay farmer."

As with many rural areas experiencing sustained outmigration, those men who stayed in the rural hamlet were often viewed as unattractive candidates for marriage. They were twice as likely to remain unmarried as the men who had gone to Detroit. Of the 81 per cent of all men who married, the likelihood of having to search outside the ethnic community to find a spouse was higher for those who stayed (38 per cent) than for the migrants (23 per cent). No such differences were found among the females.

Class distinction crept into the ethnic community in Detroit. Some were said to "have gotten all dressed up and then acted like they didn't know you." Others tried to hide the fact that they were from Pelkie, an unknown backwoods hamlet. One woman said that "everyone was pretending she wasn't from Pelkie. They would say they were from Houghton or Hancock as a way of making a better impression. And some even pretended that they were not of Finnish heritage and that they did not understand the Finnish language."

Those who stayed watched others return on summer vacations—an unknown experience to the farmer. They envied their shiny new cars, neckties and wrist watches and were stunned by the latest fashions. It was said by some women that you "weren't anybody unless you had gone to Detroit, danced in the Greystone Ballroom, and shopped at Hudson's." One male admitted that the reason he went to Detroit was so that he could buy a new Chevrolet to show off back home. Some were clearly "high-hatting it"—a term residents use to describe the attempts made by some to invoke a social class distinction based upon their new lifestyle. The urban brothers and sisters came home on their vacations and played, while the farm family worked. They helped themselves at meal times, and left, saying how lucky were those in dirt-stained work clothes to be living in the peaceful and beautiful countryside.

On the other hand, all who went to Detroit did not settle there permanently. Of all the migrants, 29.7 per cent returned within five years and another 11.7 per cent returned after staying away for six to ten years. Some did not want to leave the city but lay-offs, family crises and other personal experiences caused them to return to the country. Many simply rejected urban life, saying they "didn't feel free dozn there. The city was easy to figure out. It was nothing but a rat race. Sure you made good money, but whenever you took a step you had to reach for your wallet."

Rather than understand themselves in terms of the failure-to-adjust stereotypes then prevailing, those who rejected urban life encouraged the belief that the quality of life in the country and the solid morality of country people was simply superior to what was "below the bridge." "Here," said one urban exile, "there's less greed. Everyone is not all out for himself. People are still willing to lend a hand. No sir! They're not going to get me to go down there because of those big bucks."

In the late 1940s, Finnish Americans began to speak of the deterioration of the city. Several people had been brutally murdered, and the stories spread like wildfire throughout the community, enhancing racial hatred. During this period many returned to the Upper Peninsula or moved out to the suburbs northwest of the inner city. And now the native sons and daughters who are retiring are returing in droves as they leave behind the high taxes, fear and violence of the city. The return migration over the years has been continually revitalizing the agrarian ideology.

In other ways outmigration of the second generation Finnish Americans from a backwoods hamlet actually supported the communal solidarity of rural life. Money sent home made life more bearable, and in several cases actually allowed the farm to remain in the possession of the family. Years later the home farm became a place to assemble on summer vacations to reaffirm the bonds of kinship and community. Social interaction in the Woodrow Wilson area made friends out of former acquaintances and among those who might elsewhere have found one anothers' beliefs objectionable. The spreading of friendships throughout the larger social network served to integrate the rural community, because many of those friendships were sustained.

It seems as though the declining significance of the Church

Finn/Red Finn schism in the urban setting may have been a situational phenomenon. Toward the late 1940s, when the second generation began moving out of the Woodrow Wilson area, buying their own homes and raising the third generation, house-to-house visiting seems to have become the primary manner in which they related to fellow ethnics. No longer gathered around a table in the *Silver Star* in one big family, association became more selective and the barriers of belief may have reappeared.

For the Finnish Americans who had gone there, "those Woodrow Wilson Days" were a pivotal experience defining their generation. Today in the northwoods that common experience is still talked about over coffee. Even if they have not seen one another for forty years since the Woodrow Wilson days, people seem to pick up their relationship right were they had left it. When the urban exiles now living in the Upper Peninsula go to Detroit they sometimes make a pilgrimage to Woodrow Wilson. The continuous back-and-forth migration for over forty years, and now the coming home of the second generation in their twilight years, has sustained commitment to their rural community of origin.

# Notes

1. Thomas Bender, *Community and Social Change in America* (New Brunswick, N.J.: Rutgers, University Press, 1978).

2. For a discussion of the typological tradition in sociological theory see: John McKinney and Charles Loomis, "The Application of Gemeinschaft and Gesellschaft as related to other Typologies," in Ferdinand Töennies, *Community and Society* (New York: Harper Torchbooks, 1963) pp. 12-29; Also see: Bender, *op. cit.* pp. 15-44; Edward Shils, "The Contemplation of Society in America," in *Paths of American Thought*, Morton White and Arthur Schlesinger, Jr, Eds (Boston: Houghton Mifflin, 1970), pp. 397-400; and Werner Cahnman, "Työmies in America," *History and Theory.* Vol. 16, 1977, pp. 147-67.

3. Bender, *op. cit.*, p. 29.

4. On the decline of rural communities, see: Arthur Vidich and Joseph Bensman, *Small Town in Mass Society* (Princeton, N.J.: Princeton University Press, 1968); Rolland Warren, *The Community in America* Chicago: Rand McNally, 1963); Maurice Stein, *The Eclipse of Com-*

*munity* (New York: Harper, 1964); Joseph Kasarda and Morris Janow-itz, "Community Sentiment in Mass Society," *American Sociological Review*, Vol. 39, 1974, p. 329. On the predicted decline of ethnicity, see: Louis Wirth, "Urbanism as a Way of Life," *American Journal of Sociology*, Vol. 44, 1938. Space is insufficient to list the refutations but a summary is provided in Claude S. Fischer, "Toward a Subcultural Theory of Urbanism," AJS, Vol 80, 1975; and Marc Fried, *The World of the Urban Working Class* (Cambridge: Harvard University Press); Herbert Gans, *The Urban Villagers* (New York: The Free Press, 1962); Edward Lauman, *The Bonds of Pluralism* (New York: John Wiley and Sons, 1972). On the predicted decline of the extended family, see: Talcott Parsons," On the presistence of kinship interaction beyond the boundaries of the nuclear family, see: Marvin Sussman, "The Isolated Nuclear Family: Fact or Fiction?" *Social Problems*. Vol. 16, 1959; Bert N. Adams, "Isolation, Function and Beyond: American Kinship in 1960's," *Journal of Marriage and Family*, Vol. 32, 1970; Carole Stack, *All Our Kin: Strategies for Survival in a Black Community* (New York: Harper, 1974); Joyce Aschenbrenner, *Lifelines*(New York: Holt, Rine-hart and Winston, 1979). On the persistence of supportive neighbour-hoods, see: Gerald Suttles, *The Social Order of the Slum* (Chicago: University of Chicago Press, 1968) Eugene Litwack *et.al.*, "Primary Group Structures and Their Functions: Kin, Neighbors, and Friends," *American Sociological Review*, Vol. 34, 1969, pp. 461-81.

5. On the origins of network analysis, see, Alvin Wolfe, "The Rise of Network Thinking in Anthropology," *Social Networks*, Vol. 1, no. 1, (August 1978), pp. 53-64; and Clyde J. Michell, ed., *Social Networks in Urban Situations* (Manchester: Manchester University Press, 1969).

6. Bo Anderson and Manuel Carlos, "What is Social Network Theory," in *Power and Control: Social Structures in Their Transformation* (Bev-erly Hills, Cal.: Russell Sage Foundation, 1976). Norman Whitten, and Alvin Wolfe, "Network Analysis" in *Handbook of Social and Cultural Anthropology*, John Honigman, Ed. (New York: Rand McNally, 1973).

7. By 1920, 47% of the Finnish immigrants in the United States lived in rural communities and in 1940, 61% of the Finnish immigrant farmers lived in Michigan, Minnesota and Wisconsin. William Hoglund, "Flight From Industry: Finns and Farming in America," *Finnish Americana*, Vol. 1, 1978, p. 402.

8. See Melvin Holli, *Detroit* (New York: New Viewpoints, 1976), pp. 117-40; and Keijo Virtanen, "The Influence of the Automotive Industry on the Ethnic Picture of Detroit, 1900-1940," Publications of the Insti-tute of History, General History, Publication #9, (Vaasa 1977), pp. 71-88.

9. Ibid., p. 269

10. Ibid., p. 271

11. United States Census, 1920, 1930, 1940, compiled in Virtanen, *op. cit.*

12. One exception to this bi-modal pattern of settlement is the community of Kaleva in the western Lower Peninsula of Michigan.

13. United States Census, 1920, 1930, 1940.

14. Elvira Kanerva, "Growing up in the 14th Street Hall," in *Greater Detroit Finnish-American Bicentennial Record* (Detroit, Michigan, 1976).

15. Financial records of the New Hope Club in Walter Reuther Library, Wayne State University, Detroit, Michigan.

16. The paper was *Detroitin Uutiset.* It started and failed in 1926 (Virtanen, 1976).

17. Oral history interview with second generation Finnish-American real estate salesman, C.A. Rustick, Tamarack Mills, Michigan, 1978.

18. Ibid.

19. This is based upon the total number of immigrant families settling in Pelkie for whom it was possible to locate a surviving son or daughter to determine the number of siblings that survived to age 18. (N = 120 families).

20. B.J. Widick, *Detroit: City of Race and Class Violence* (Chicago: Quadrangle Books, 1977), p. 44.

21. The second generation respondents are still alive. Some of the oral history data are concerned with sensitive information, so in order to alleviate their anxieties I promised not to reveal their identities. All are second generation Finnish Americans who grew up in Pelkie. The sex of the respondent is indicated in the text.

22. Sidney Fine, *The Automobile Worker Under the Blue Eagle* (Ann Arbor, Michigan University of Michigan Press, 1963), p. 4. It should be remembered that many of the so-called employed workers were working only a few hours a day.

23. See Tamara Harevan, "The Dynamics of Kin in an Industrial Community," in *Turning Points: Historical and Sociological Essays on the Family.* (Chicago: University of Chicago Press, 1978).

24. Herbert Gutman, "Work Culture and Society in Industalizing America," *American Historical Review, 78,* 1973, pp. 541-42.

# Early Finnish-American
# Settlements in Florida

*William R. Copeland*

The establishment of the Florida Finnish-American Historical Society in January 1975 gave impetus to a long-felt need to compile a
history of the Finnish settlements in Florida.[1] It was well known
from oral accounts that the Lake Worth – Lantana Finnish settlement was not the first in this southern state. The Palm Beach
county colony, although today the most viable one in the state, was
preceded by at least three earlier attempts to found Finnish settlements in Florida. Two of the early Finnish plantations blossomed
and withered well before any Finns had settled in Lake Worth.
The third settlement, in New Port Richey, thirty-eight miles north
of Tampa, still has a sizable Finnish community today.

This paper represents a first, tentative effort to come to grips
with the general problem of the Finnish immigrants in Florida.[2] It
seeks to make some observations concerning the early, pre-World
War Two, phase of Finnish migration to Florida. The history of
Finns in Florida since 1945 will be subject of another study. The
paper endeavours to consider some problems relating to sources as
well as motivation for moving to Florida during the early period
and the evolution of the Finnish settlements.

This presentation should be regarded as a working paper in
that it is not a finished study but an early draft—a collection of
observations—about problems encountered in studying the early
history of the Finns in Florida. One of its main functions is to
inform other historians as well as the general public that such an
undertaking has taken shape in Florida. An awareness of this pro-

ject, it is hoped, will facilitate the collection of source material, both written and oral.

The study attempts to offer some hypotheses on when Finns first ventured beyond their traditional belt of settlements along the United States – Canadian border. Why they came to Florida is another important question that must be answered. Migrating to Florida was not unique to the Finns, as one quickly realizes when moving about in that state. Many other American ethnic groups established colonies in Florida. More than 200,000 Cubans have turned Miami into a "small Havana"; sponge fishing on the west coast is dominated by the Greeks; and the Germans had several halls and churches in Jacksonville. Very little serious historical research has been carried out on the ethnic pockets in Florida. Did the Finnish experience in Florida substantially differ from that of other ethnic groups and if so, why was it different and how did this difference manifest itself? It is possible to approach this subject from several directions.

## Some Observations on Sources

The picture of Finnish migration to Florida is unusually faint and fragmentary. The traditional motives of "pushing" and "pulling" are to be found almost entirely from within social and economic history. Political motives for migrating to Florida are almost non-existant.[3] There are no passport records or passenger manifests to consult. The task is compounded by the fact that a large percentage of Finns "moved to Florida gradually." meaning that they often spent the winter months there before settling permanently.[4]

Two sources of information stand out when trying to piece together the history of the early Finnish colonies in Florida. In 1912, Finnish-American newspapers began publishing local news stories from their correspondents in Florida. The earliest such columns are to be found in *Raivaaja*.[5] These columns are indispensable in charting the progress of the early Finnish pioneers in Florida. The problem is that there were not enough correspondents in Florida. There is almost no coverage of the smaller settlements such as those at Haile and Fort Lauderdale. The only published reference to perhaps the earliest Finnish agricultural group near Gainesville is in S. Ilmonen's history of the Finnish-Americans.[6]

Interviews with Florida Finns constitute another useful

source of information. However, in the case of the early years of Finnish migration to Florida (1895-1925), the collecting process was launched at least twenty years too late. Relatively few of the early immigrant pioneers were alive or in possession of a good memory when the society's interviewing project was initiated in 1966, although interviewing has been particularly useful in adding a "human element" to the history of the Finns in Florida.[7]

Unfortunately, two traditional sources of accurate data, church records and minutes of various Finnish organizations, are totally lacking for the early period. The first Finnish social organizations in Florida were not founded until 1944.[8] Although an unofficial entertainment committee had existed since at least 1937, the Finnish Tourist Club of Lake Worth was not founded until January 1944.[9] A more politically oriented organization, the Finnish Workers Educational Club of Lake Worth, was organized formally in March 1944.[10] An influx of individuals with stronger class views led to the formal parting of the ways in 1944. Socialists of various hues gravitated to the *Kenttä-haali*, while a more amorphous group supported *Turisti-haali*.

In the case of the New Port Richey colony it was not until 1949 that a Finnish American Club was officially established.[11] For more than twenty years the settlement managed without there own church and hall. Its religious needs were attended to by visiting ministers from the north until 1951 when a church was built.[12]

Generally speaking, the Finnish populations attracted little attention in the larger American communities around them. The language barrier and the modest size of the colonies, in most cases, accounted for this silence. Local media only began noticing an ethnic community when it grew large enough and constituted a potential customer in terms of circulation or advertisement. The *Palm Beach Post/Times*, as a case in point, began yielding useful information on a reasonably regular basis as soon as the Finnish community was large enough. As part of its community service, this newspaper has published more than two thousand obituaries of Finnish-Americans since 1950.[13]

Because of Florida's geographic location along the shipping routes between Europe and the new world it is almost certain that Finnish merchant marine personnel first visited Florida ports. At least Pensacola and Jacksonville were good-sized ports around the turn of the century. Ilmonen tells us that Finland maintained a sailors' home in Pensacola during the latter part of the nineteenth century and that some Finnish sailors put down roots in the area. In the main, however, the larger ports of San Francisco, New York

and Boston were usually the destinations of Finnish sailors intending to jump ship. Certainly these early visits had little or no impact
on subsequent Finnish migration to Florida.

The United States census reports, as a rule, offer a reliable
picture of any given community in terms of the composition of its
population. However, with respect to the early years of Finnish
migration to Florida the data are probably incomplete. A very
large proportion of Finns in Florida during 1910-1930 period continued to maintain a permanent residence in the north because
they only spent a part of the year in Florida.[14] Particularly during
the 1920s it would have been impossible to "credit" hundreds of
foot-loose Finnish carpenters to any particular city. They were
shifting from work site to work site while the U. S. census had
them residing up north.

In 1926 Ilmonen estimated the Finnish population of Florida
to be "about a thousand."[15] A year later he increased this estimate
to about 1,100 in twelve localities in the state.[16] Because we have
no data on how this estimate was arrived at it is difficult to
comment on them. For what they are worth, interviews suggest a
higher figure.[17]

The United States census gives the following data on Finns in
Florida for the first three decades of the twentieth century:[18]

| Year | First generation | First and Second generation |
|------|------------------|-----------------------------|
| 1900 | 42 | |
| 1910 | 89 | 137 |
| 1920 | 311 | 555 |
| 1930 | 333 | 637 |

In general the increases indicated for the second decade parallel what is known about the establishment of the Finnish settlements in Astor, Jacksonville and New Port Richey. Their failure to
blossom into northern type Finntowns is also reflected in the statistics of 1920-1930. The most puzzling numbers at this stage of
research are the forty-two first-generation Finns that were found to
be living in Florida in 1900. Although available data fail to adequately account for this group, it is probable that they were
composed of sailors and other "loners" of Finnish background who
had for diverse reasons settled in Florida.[19]

# The Pull and Push southward

Three prerequisites had to be present before significant Finnish migration southward was possible. First, Finnish immigration to the United States had to reach a certain volume before a large enough flow would even theoretically be available to be diverted southward. Independent of other factors, it is possible to suppose that when Finnish immigration to the United States passed 50,000 in 1895 the flow was strong enough. Or perhaps 1899 is more appropriate, because in that year Finnish immigration for the first time exceeded 10,000 persons per year.[20]

However, the fact of the matter was that the flow of immigration from Finland was overwhelmingly to established Finnish settlements and to localities where employment suitable for non-English-speaking immigrants was available. This left precious few Finnish immigrants to venture south.[21] This situation naturally changed somewhat once the immigrants learned the language, knew more about the country, and about employment and other opportunities in Florida. Reino Kero's study suggests that before 1895 there were no Finns in Florida to attract additional countrymen to that state.[22] The importance of this aspect of the "pull" phenomena can quite readily be understood when examining the reasons for the sharp increase in immigration from Finland to Florida in the 1960s and 1970s.[23]

The second impediment that held up the migration of European immigrants to Florida was the relative backwardness of the economy of the state. Florida did not begin to develop economically until the last two decades of the nineteenth century.

In the racially segregated South of the early years of this century blacks predominated in construction work, land clearing, farm labour and many service occupations. This labour supply was available all year round, it was satisfied with lower wages, and it could generally perform better than white labourers under near-tropical climatic conditions. Under normal circumstances there was little need for Florida to attract labourers from the north.

Florida experienced several building booms of various kinds that suddenly required vast numbers of extra workers. Flood-control projects, railroad construction, building construction, road building and defence-related needs of World War One opened up Florida to immigrant workers.[24] In normal times restrictive segregation laws prevented Blacks and Whites from working side by side. Booms tended to remove or lower racial barriers in the labour market. Interviews suggest that Finnish immigrants harboured no great reluctance to work side by side with Blacks.[25]

Booms in Florida, however, coincided usually with the business cycles of the national economy. This meant that when employment opportunities were plentiful in Florida jobs could also be had in the north. The reverse was also true: recessions quickly spread to Florida and, if anything, these economic fluctuations were felt more acutely in Florida than in the industrial centres of the north.

Florida's peculiar tourist-oriented economy must also be mentioned when discussing economic prerequisites. Until the state's economy became more diversified after World War Two, fluctuations in business activity in Florida were extremely seasonal. The four winter months provided large parts of the state with sustenance for the entire year. The system tended to perpetuate seasonal employment practices. This meant that Finnish immigrant workers usually had to contend with the slack season. Perhaps also for climatic reasons, but primarily in order to obtain work, they usually went north in March or April.[26] This meant that before settling permanently in Florida an additional element of financial security had to be present. Social security, savings and the inducements of a thriving Finntown in the late 1940s were important to a decision to settle. Miami very nearly developed into a Finntown in 1921-26 because so many Finns flocked to the area. The inability of the colony to generate immigrant institutions such as a church, a hall, or other organizations coupled with the consequences of the economic bust of the late 1920s, postponed the grounding of a Finntown until after World War Two.

# How Finnish-Americans learnt about Florida.

The question of how the Finns in the north received information about opportunities in Florida also merits some attention. When did information about Florida begin to reach the northern Finntowns and how accurate was this information? Two developments were responsible for causing the Finnish-American media to focus on Florida. The migration of Finns to Florida and their decision to settle there in 1910-1919 was the initial reason. The Finnish newspapers contained very little information about Florida before 1912.

However, once the group in Jacksonville attracted enough Finlanders and joined the Finnish Socialist Organization it was only a matter of time before local correspondents of the Finnish settlement began forwarding news of *Raivaaja*, published in Fitchburg, Massachusetts.[27]

A second development triggered off a prolonged preoccupation with Florida and involved all of the eastern and midwestern Finnish newspapers. This was the effort by the Duluth Land Company to sell agricultural land to Finnish immigrants in Astor, Florida. Because the undertaking was launched at a time of feverish ideological struggle in the Finnish-American labour movement and because one of the sponsors of the colony was a noted radical leader, Martin Hendrickson, the land-selling venture immediately took on political overtones. This meant that almost from the beginning Florida evoked controversial emotions among Finns in the north.

The spectacular building boom of the 1920s initially focused the attention of the northern press of Florida. Fortunes were made and lost on speculative land-buying. The state understandably wanted to promote economic development and large business concerns exploited this mood. Inevitably, however, this adversely affected the flow of information from Florida.[28] Land agents could not resist the temptation of making extravagant claims about the land they were selling.[29] In the minds of many northerners Florida loomed as a southern Eldorado. Inevitably more was promised than was delivered. Florida state legislation did not seek to correct these unsound business practices until the outcry from disillusioned buyers threatened the good name of the state.[30]

Both the New Port Richey and the Astor settlements were originally conceived in the minds of land developers. The land was marketed to Finns in the north through Finnish sales agents. The New Port Richey colony north of Tampa, on the west coast of Florida, was developed by H.G. Hermanson and A. Saarelma, and most of their land was sold in New York, Massachusetts and Ohio.[31] Although the claims made about this settlement were quite measured and reasonably accurate, many buyers later accused the two developers of misrepresentation. They complained in *Industrialisti*, the IWW paper, that the land they had been sold was unsuitable for the kind of cultivation to which they were used.[32] Unhappy remarks were also made about the hot summer, insects, marketing problems, etc.[33]

The effort by the Duluth Land Company to establish a Finnish agricultural settlement in Astor in 1914-1919, was by far the most controversial effort undertaken by the Finns because of the involvement of Hendrickson as a land-agent for the company and because the settlement did not flourish as a "utopian commune."[34]

When Martin Hendrickson began promoting the Astor colony in 1915 his reputation as a firebrand speaker assured "Big Martti" enthusiastic and ready audiences.[35] Having actually seen the Astor land he was selling gave his pitch an aura of respectibility. The problem was that Hendrickson was usually describing the citrus orchards of the Astor estate and these had been put into production at great expense.[36] Inexperienced immigrant pioneers did not have the resources that Astor had.

Between fifty and one hundred Finnish immigrants purchased one to ten acre plots in Astor, usually sight unseen.[37] This attests to the effectiveness of Hendrickson's sales pitch. Although many factors beyond the control of the Duluth Land Company combined to add to the woes of the Finnish farmers in Astor, the basic fact remains that the reality of the east Florida settlement did not resemble the picture that Hendrickson had painted.[38] Though fired by determination to make the land produce and finally resolved not to admit to having been hoodwinked, the Finns found that the soil refused to support the immigrant farmers. Only the hardiest and the most stubborn of the pioneers stuck it out for more than five years.[39] Some of the children of the original pioneers today live in retirement in Astor.

Both *New Yorkin Uutiset* and *Raivaaja* adopted *a priori* a rather skeptical and hostile attitude toward the Astor settlement. In this they were influenced by the fact that Martin Hendrickson, their ideological opponent, was identified with this decidedly capitalist proposition. It would have been asking too much to expect the *Raivaaja* faction and the Finnish non-socialists to adopt a benovolent attitude toward Hendrickson's business enterprice. In any case, the result was that the majority of those who purchased land in Astor were socialists, most of them Syndicalists. It is possible to conjecture that the notoriety which *Raivaaja* and *New Yorkin Uutiset* attributed to the Astor experiment dampened enthusiasm among non-Syndicalists in the east for buying land in Astor. Martin Hendrickson's own publication, *Floridan Sanomat* did not seek to play down the "class nature" of the Astor settlement but he hardly meant to convey the farm settlement as a "Bolshevist commune," the derisive label put on the settlement by the hostile media.[40]

The Astor experiment underscored some important predelictions among the Finnish Americans. The willingness of so many to buy land in Florida simply on the word of a glib land agent—albeit of a very persuasive one—underscored the fact that many Finns continued to yearn for a farm of their own. The phenomenon also suggests that Finns were prepared to strike out in a new direction in search of land. In other words, had the timing of the Astor experiment been more propitious and had the colony's lands lived up to their expectations, a Finntown of some note might indeed have evolved in Florida in 1916-1920.

The second consequence of the Astor failure, aired thoroughly by *New Yorkin Uutiset, Raivaaja* and finally even by *Industrialisti*, was the spread of a sense of disbelief and skepticism about Florida.[41] It was difficult to take news about Florida seriously. This attitude was reinforced during the 1920s by the bust of the land boom in Florida. The hurricanes of 1926 and 1928 along with periodic frosts did not help the state's image. The state continued to attract hundreds of Finnish immigrants each winter. Few, however, were prepared to put down roots in Florida. Only gradually did a number of these visitors find the resolve to establish a home in Florida. From these new Finnish settlers evolved after 1935 the nucleus of the Lake Worth – Lantana settlement, which in the late 1940s became Florida's first true Finntown.

# Early Finnish sojourners in Florida

It is premature to state categorically when and where the first Finn set foot in Florida. It is only possible to document some early Finnish sojourners to Florida. Strangely enough, the struggle of the Finns to resist Russification in 1899-1905 played a role in two of the earliest known Finnish penetrations of this southern state.

In late 1907 pro-resistance elements in the Finnish police told Lars Florell, a young Finnish architect and activist,[42] that the Russian authorities had discovered his complicity in smuggling arms into Finland in 1906.[43] Preferring exile to imminent arrest and internment in a Russian prison, Florell fled abroad. He made his way to the United States and settled in Tampa, where he received a job in an architect's office.[44]

During the years before World War One Florell travelled extensively in the Mid-West and tried his hand at citrus farming in DeLand, Florida, only a short distance from Astor. With another Finn, Oskar Kivilahti, Florell purchased ten acres of land. He became an ardent socialist and a friend of Martin Hendrickson.[45] Sometime before 1913 Florell told Hendrickson about his citrus

farm and the possibility of establishing a Finnish settlement in
Florida.[46] In 1916, but probably also earlier, Hendrickson accompanied Florell to DeLand and Astor and observed how productive
were the citrus orchards of New York millionaire T. Astor.[47]

The mechanics of how Hendrickson became a land agent for
the Duluth Land Company and whether he was instrumental in
setting up this company remain obscure. Additional research will
hopefully solve this riddle. In any case, in 1916 the company did
exist and Hendrickson began selling land owned by this company
to Finns in the north.[48] While plugging Syndicalism, he was also
talking up the farming land in Astor. His intention, he told his
listeners, was to try to establish a thriving Finnish agricultural
settlement in Astor.[49] When *Floridan Sanomat* appeared in 1919, it
caught the imagination of many immigrants in the middlewest and
fifty to one hundred plots of from one to ten acres were sold.[50] The
venture foundered on a number of miscalculations, some deliberate
and others beyond the control of the Astor settlers.

Simply clearing the bush broke the determination of many
newcomers. High humidity and continuous temperatures in the 90s
made the physical exertion required to clear the land of palmetto
roots and stumps unendurable.[51] Bruno Kallio never remembers
having seen so many stumps around cleared land in Finland as he
saw in Astor.[52] To carve out even a small farm usually meant that
the heavy clearing work had to be contracted out to Blacks. In
1918 they charge at least $75 an acre for this work.[53] This strained
the limited financial resources of the settlers. Finns were also
inexperienced in such technical matters as fertilizer, animal di-
seases, irrigation, etc. An awareness of these and other difficulties
gradually filtered up north and dampened enthusiasm among potential settlers.[54]

After 1919 most of the Astor settlers cut their losses and
made their way to Miami, New Port Richey or to other settlements.[55] Twenty-seven graves of the early pioneers today stand as
dramatic proof that some stuck it out to the end.

Several sources prove beyond a doubt that more than one
hundred Finns made up a small colony in Jacksonville, seventy
years ago.[56] Although the origins of this group are still somewhat
obscure, some evidence suggests that Russification indirectly
formed the colony.

Nicholas Bobrikov's policies in Finland led to a number of
different initiatives to resist Russification. Among the earliest to
dream of a new secure homeland in the new world was Konni
Zilliacus.[57] In May 1899 he proposed to the leadership of the

Finnish resistance movement that conscription-aged Finnish men should be sent to Finnish settlements in Canada rather than permit them to serve in the Russian army. He went so far as to actually discuss the founding of a Finnish settlement in western Canada with Canadian officials before the Finnish resistance leadership withdrew their support from the undertaking. They considered the plan too impractical.[58]

In 1903, several Finnish resistance leaders, exiled from Finland in May, arrived in New York determined to seek new ways to continue to resist Russification. This group, led by Eero Erkko, established *Amerikan Kaiku*, a Finnish newspaper, and introduced a novel idea of founding a Finnish colony in Cuba.[59] In the process of setting up this colony Jacksonville, a port-and-railroad-centre in northeast Florida, came into the picture. As the most convenient port from which to board ships bound for Havana, it became the starting-off point for the Cuban colonization effort.[60]

While Finns thus occasionally stayed in Jacksonville the city experienced a building boom. A large area of the downtown section had burned down in 1901.[61] In addition to rebuilding of the destroyed houses, the city also decided to construct a number of new port facilities.[62] Large numbers of construction workers were suddenly needed in the city and the contractors advertised for labour as far away as New York and Boston. A group of carpenters of Finnish background, aware of the demand for workers in Jacksonville, in 1904-1908 moved to that city. This was the beginning of the short-lived Jacksonville Finnish colony.[63]

By 1910 the Jacksonville colony grew to around 100 to 130 persons. The Finnish carpenters established a local of the Finnish Socialist Organization, which had thirty-seven members in 1910.[64] The settlement continued to thrive and two years later four new members joined the FSOin the city.[65] Little is known about the fortunes of the settlement after this, other than that it began to decline during World War One. One of the last "messages" from the group was a wish expressed in 1918 in *Industrialisti* for "success in the class struggle."[66]

The primary reason for the decline of the colony in Jacksonville is probably the completion of the major construction projects that had attracted the Finnish carpenters in the first place. Shipbuilding converted from wooden ships to iron ships after 1918.[67] Defence-related building projects at a nearby naval base also came to an end in 1919. With no work to be had locally, some of the Finnish carpenters returned to New York, while others moved to Astor, Jessup, Georgia, Miami or elsewhere.[68] By 1926 Ilmonen was able to find only twenty-seven Finnish families living the Jacksonville area.[69]

Once the Jacksonville settlement declined it never regained its former size. The north Florida city was not far enough south to attract passing winter tourists once such resort cities as Miami, Fort Lauderdale and Lake Worth began to compete for tourist dollars in the early 1920s. Jacksonville's chances of attracting a larger number of Finns were also limited because the Finnish community never grew large enough to justify the construction of a hall, a church, or other institutions identified with a Finntown. It is also possible to conjecture that its pronounced "class identify" prevented less committed Finns from settling there.

# Notes

1. The bylaws of the Florida Finnish-American Historical Society were approved on June 18, 1975. The founding meeting was held 21 January, 1975, and was attended by forty-one members.

2. For a brief analysis of post-World War Two Finnish migration to Florida, see Keijo Virtanen, "The Migration of Finnish-Americans to Florida after World War II," in Turun Yliopiston eripainossarja No. 30, 1976, pp. 432-45.

3. In so far as the Jacksonville colony was originally populated by Finns intending to take refuge in Cuba in order to escape the Russification of Finland, this might constitute the clearest politically motivated move to Florida.

4. According to a survey or 175 Florida Finns in August 1972 by this author, it was rare for a Finn to move permanently to Florida without having spent at least one winter there previous to moving. The average was three to four visits to Florida before permanently settling there.

5. *Raivaaja*, April 16, 1912.

6. S. Ilmonen, *Amerikan Suomalaisten Historia*, III (Hancock, Michigan, 1926), p. 293.

7. The urgency of reaching the older settlers is underscored by the fact that of the 18 persons interviewed in 1966 only three are alive today. Thus far more than 240 persons have been interviewed and more than 400 hours of taped information is available.

8. *Morketinpolttojuhlan muistoksi omistettu Historiakatsaus Turistiklubin toiminnasta vuosina 1937-1951. I. Osa.* (Fitchburg, Mass., 1959), pp. 4-5.

9. Ibid.

10. *Dedication of the New Hall, March 10-11, 1956,* (Fitchburg. Mass., 1958), p. 8.

11. Mauno E. Nikander, and Staff, *Directory of the Finnish Speaking Population in Florida* (Fitchburg, Mass., 1959), p. 21.

12. Ibid. pp. 20-21.

13. These data have permitted Lennart Borman to observe that 117 Finns passed away in 1968 in Palm Beach County—the peak year during 1950-1975.

14. Bruno Kallio interview, July 1974. Lake Worth, Florida.

15. Ilmonen, *op. cit.*, p. 292.

16. *New Yorkin Uutiset,* No. 126, p. 6.

17. Kallio interview.

18. United States census reports for 1900, 1910, 1920, and 1930, (Bureau of Census, Washington, D.C.)

19. Ilmonen, *op. sit.*, pp. 294-95.

20. William A. Hoglund, *Finnish Immigrants in America, 1880-1920,* (Madison, 1960), p. 152.

21. Reino Kero's study on the destination of Finnish immigrants in 1872-1905. The study will be published by the University of Turku.

22. Ibid.

23. The overwhelming percentage of Finns that moved directly from Finland to the Lake Worth – Lantana area after 1955 were pulled there by the existance of the Finntown in that area. This is borne out by numerous interviews among these recent arrivees.

24. Charlton W. Tebeau, *A History of Florida* (Coral Gables, Florida, 1971), pp. 382-87.

25. Kallio interview,

26. Vilho Hedman interview, June, 1966; Kallio Interview. The interview of 175 charter-flight passagers in August 1972 (West Palm Beach – Helsinki – West Palm Beach) indicated that Florida's climate became an increasingly potent magnet as *Floridan Kävijät* (visitors to Florida) got older. See the brief annlysis of data received from this group in *Suomen Silta,* 2, 1978, pp. 9-10.

27. See, e.g., *Raivaaja,* April 16, 1912.

28. Tebeau, op. cit., pp. 383-84.

29. The advertising brochure prepared by Bryant and Greenwood, a land developer from Chicago, billed Lake Worth, for instance, as "the Wonder City of the East Coast," where "words cannot picture the beautiful flowers" of the city. The brochure was published in 1914.

30. Phillip E. DeBerard, "Promoting Florida: Some Aspects of the Uses of

140    W. Copeland

Advertising and Publicity in the Development of the Sunshine State,"
Master's thesis (University of Florida, 1951) pp. 46-49.

31. *New Yorkin Uutiset,* Nos. 137 and 149, 1926.

32. *Industrialisti,* October 5, 1918, p. 3.

33. Ibid.

34. Kallio interview.

35. *Industrialisti,* May 10, 1919, p. 3.

36. Kallio Interview.

37. A. Gustafson interview, June, 1979; Kallio interview, *Industrialisti,*
August 28, 1919, p. 3.

38. *New Yorkin Uutiset,* October 28, 1919, p. 1:, Kallio interview.

39. *New Yorkin Uutiset,* October 25 and November 20, 1919.

40. *Floridan Sanomat,* No. 2, November, 1919, pp. 2-3.

41. *Industrialisti* changed its attitude when Hendrickson gravitated toward the Workers Party in 1919.

42. Lars Fiorell interview, July 1966,

43. *Suomen Kuvalehti,* No. 27, 1932, p. 9.

44. Florell interview, O. Castrén to Lars Florell, 28 January, 1908, Lars
Florell Papers, the author.

45. Florell interview, F.J. Syrjälä, ed., Kolmannen Amerikan Suomalaisen
Sosialistijärjestön edustajakokouksen Pöytäkirja. 28-80 elok., (Fitchburg, 1909), pp. 119, 195.

46. Florell interview.

47. Kallio interview.

48. *Industrialisti,* May 10, 1919, p. 3.

49. Kallio interview.

50. The first number was a seven-page weekly. In November 1919 it was
changed into a 32-page monthly. The author has been unable to find a
copy of the first number.

51. Kallio interview; *New Yorkin Uutiset,* May 6, 1920, p. 8.

52. Kallio interview.

53. Ibid.

54. See, e.g., *Industrialisti,* May 10, 1918, p. 3.

55. Kallio interview; Gustafson interview.

56. Ilmonen, *op. cit.,* pp. 292-93; Olga Florell interview, July 1966; Aku
Rissanen, ed., Suomalaisten sosialistiosastojen ja työväenyhdistysten viidennen eli Suomalaisen sosialistijärjestön kolmannen edustajakokouksen pöytäkirja (Fitchburg, 1912), p. 17.

57. The best biography of Zilliacus is Herman Gummerus, *Konni Zilliacus: Suomen itsenäisyyden esitaistelija* (JyvasKylä, 1933).

Early Finnish Settlements in Florida    141

58. Konni Zilliacus, *Från ofärdstid och orologia år, I.* (Åbo, 1919), p. 49-55, Eino I. Parmanen, *Taistelujen Kirja, III* (Porvco, 1939), pp. 106-7.

59. S. Ilmonen, *Amerikan Suomalaisten Sivistyshistoria*, I, (Hancock, 1930), p. 101; Parmanen, *op. cit.*, pp. 106-8. The Finns considered establishing colonies in Texas, Central America, Australia, Sweden and a number of South American countries. Research on these colonies has been done at the University of Turku.

60. Olga Florell interview. She actually visited the city and remainded there for more than two weeks while waiting for passage to Cuba.

61. Thomas F. Davis, *History of Jacksonville, Florida and Vicinity, 1518-1924* (St. Augustine, Florida, 1925), pp. 219-28, 235.

62. *Handbook of the Port of Jacksonville* (Jacksonville, 1916), p. 5.

63. Olga Florell interview,

64. Rissanen, *op. cit.*, p. 29.

65. *Raivaaja*, April 16, 1912, p. 3. Olga Florell has stated that most of the members of the Jacksonville group came from New York City.

66. *Industrialisti*, December 18. 1918.

67. *Handbook of the Jacksonville Port* (Jacksonville, 1916),p. 5.

68. Kallio interview; Gustafson interview.

69. Ilmonen, *op. cit.* (1926), p. 296.

# Church and Labour Conflict in Northern Michigan

*Arthur E. Puotinen*

Being a native of a farming and iron mining community in Upper Michigan, I have been interested in my assigned topic throughout my life, but it has been only during the last ten years that I have made a conscious effort to investigate it more closely. This issue served as a subject in my doctoral dissertation, and the subsequent research process involved delving into regional and Finnish immigrant literature, as well as interviewing numerous older American Finns as part of the oral history project at Suomi College in Hancock, Michigan.[1]

Earlier in this investigation of relationships between the church and the labour or working-class movement in the Finnish immigrant community, I observed certain ameliorative factors, particularly from the 1940s onward.[2] The gains for the labour movement during the Roosevelt New Deal era, the cooperative movement emphasis on non-partisanship and consumer advocacy in its later stages, and the apparent assimilation of second and third generation American Finns into local communities (for example, the influence of the public school system, intermarriage and other cultural factors) supported the viewpoint of diminishing tensions and improved relations among various factions in the Finnish-American community.

But the period between the Civil War and World War One intrigued me more. This era was the boom time in copper and iron mining in the upper Midwest. Most Finnish-American organizations were founded during those years, and the Minnesota iron miners' strike of 1908 and the Michigan copper strike of 1913 revealed the critical issues and perspectives which divided Finnish churchmen and radicals. On several occasions I have told the story of the 1913 copper strike.[3] While the tale deserves repeating because of its importance, my approach here will not be to chronicle, but to analyse certain important factors which account for the intense Christian-Marxist conflict at that time and the basis for ongoing dialogue.

On the eve of World War One many immigrant Finns in Michigan and Minnesota disagreed sharply over socialism, strikes and strategies for church unity. To account for this conflict, ethnic historians such as B.W. Rautanen, Elis Sulkanen and others have pointed out that personality clashes such as the Eloheimo-Ekman and Risto-Aaltonen disputes typified a cantankerous, independent spirit present among many immigrants. After arriving in America, freedom-loving Finns put a high premium on open expression of opinion in their ethnic organizations and periodicals.[4] Other writers such as U. Saarnivaara, J. Nopola and W. Lahtinen took seriously the fine points of church doctrine and socialist ideology, and their passionate disputation represented an earnest quest for truth. More recently, John Kolehmainen, Douglas J. Ollila Jr., and Michael Karni have examined the peculiar social conditions in Finland and America which fostered Finnish radicalism. But A. William Hoglund said it well: "If Finland prepared the immigrants for socialism, America ripened them."[5]

These various psychological, ideological and sociological factors help explain the dynamic forces at work in Finnish associational life, but the conflict motif can be defined in very personal terms in the character development of individual immigrants. In the Midwestern mine fields Finnish-American workers experienced various kinds of deprivation, brought on by factors beyond their control. These same forces encouraged a sense of self-deprecation in individual personality development. As a result, the immigrant laboured with compensatory vigour to earn his survival pay and sometimes the respect of others in more favourable positions of power in local mining towns. Or he chose to protest these conditions vigorously, recognizing that such action maintained his self-respect and contributed to changing the social environment.

As he moved into a Michigan or Minnesota mining town, an immigrant Finn generally underwent a profound crisis. Given the stake of mining companies in the local marketplace, his life amounted partly to a quest for economic survival. Having been agricultural or industrial labourers in Finland, most newcomers were accustomed to hard work. But economic worries were further compounded by a certain feeling of uprootedness from familiar surroundings and folkways. Adjustment to these circumstances was made more difficult by some mining town residents who considered immigrant Finns to be alien and inferior. Certain community leaders were less concerned with Finnish folkways than they were with Americanizing a particular "foreign element" as rapidly as possible into a stable work force.[6] A "noblesse oblige" shared by several mining managers extended beyond wages and welfare programs to public education of immigrant children. This social pressure channelled through the school system urged the coming generation to assimilate as rapidly as possible. While this educational boon offered many Finnish children the prospect of upward economic and social mobility, their parents felt sometimes that important values were being lost in the process.

In leaving the unfavourable conditions in Finland during the late 1800s and early 1900s, many emigrants found adaptation difficult in the United States.[7] Those that remained in the mining towns of Michigan and Minnesota experienced certain hardships. Because of their limited skills in the English language, lack of mining experience and late arrival in comparison to other immigrant groups, most Finnish workers in the mining industry found unskilled jobs such as tramming and timbering.

When a man applied for work, the shift boss sometimes also assigned him a new name. The task of Americanizing a Finnish family name reputedly speeded up book-keeping and other procedures; it also reminded some workers that they were unacceptable unless they adapted to new circumstances.[8] Once they went underground, many Finnish labourers allegedly experienced discrimination in the type of tasks and wages they were assigned.[9] The lack of a uniform pay scale and the discretionary power given to shift bosses led to more than usual complaints about working conditions. In addition, mining companies strongly influenced, and sometimes controlled, the outlook and practices of local businesses, newspapers and political institutions.

By way of contrast, C.H. Benedict, Timothy L. Smith and W.G. Mather argued that local mining captains were men who generally desired better conditions for their workers, as well as increased production and profits.[10] But the controversial strikes of 1907 and 1913 amply demonstrate that "benevolent paternalism" was indeed a mixed blessing in the minds of some workers.

The debatable character of mining company aims and policies also existed in its most lasting investment and contribution to local mining town life, the public school. In iron and copper districts tax revenues for public education came mainly from the mining companies. Many captains served on community school boards which hired competent teachers and planned the construction of attractive buildings. According to Timothy L. Smith, the schools on the Mesabi Range in Minnesota, whose facilities paralleled similar programs in the Michagan districts, represented certain common aspirations of mining town fold.

> Indeed, temples these buildings were, shrines to the faith in education which had captured the allegiance of both rich and poor, new and old Americans. The tiny churches scattered about the village or nestling up against the school grounds seemed by contrast with the cathedrals which dominated European towns, forlorn reminders of a past that was forever gone. Gleaming in the sunlight which bathed their hilltop campus, cleaned and polished by the loving attention of custodians to whom the superintendents had imparted their fierce zeal for cleanliness, these grand buildings worked a subtle alchemy in the minds of the newcomers.[11]

Many immigrant Finns themselves placed a high premium on education. Due in part to the Church of Finland's implementation of national statutes pertaining to public education, a high literacy rate was achieved in the nineteenth century. Between 1899 and 1910, only 1.3 per cent of the population in Finland 14 years of age and older was unable to read or write.[12] After settling in Michigan or Minnesota many immigrant workers who were married desired that their children not only acquire basic reading and writing skills, but also obtain other necessary knowledge to advance up the local economic and cultural ladder.

At the same time many school board members shared a "determination to bring the children of non-English families up to the standard of achievement being set by those from the homes of mining and professional men." Timothy L. Smith believed this philosophy was pursued with a religious zeal that eroded in the minds of youngsters the ideals being set forth by both the immigrant church and socialist movement.

> They convinced the newcomers, as they were themselves convinced, that education was the key to the good life, the gateway to health, wealth, and happiness.

The priests and prophetesses of this faith, performing their rites daily amidst the splendor of their hilltop temples, were an aristocracy whose power over the minds of the workingman proved greater than that which mining captains, merchants and bankers could muster. For this reason and not because she was a lackey of capitalism, the teacher proved an effective deterrent to political radicalism as well. Her words were law, her will a synonym for wisdom.[13]

Many teachers were recruited from major eastern and midwestern American universities, and they initiated progressive new educational programs in language instruction, vocational training, home economics, arts and sciences. In addition, kindergartens provided language instruction and cultural training for children at an early age.

More often than not, the alchemy taking place in the minds was not necessarily subtle. In Tapiola, Michigan, for example, a Finnish youngster named Toivo was informed by his teacher that thereafter he would be known as Clyde.[14] As the educational process continued, a child of immigrant Finns might hear discussed the literary values of *Beowulf* without any reference being made to such a recognized epic poem as the Finnish *Kalevala*. In addition, many young Finns were called "roundheads" or "dumb Finlanders" by children of other nationalities.[15]

While this prejudice originated partly from the existing social class structure in mining town society, immigrant Finns themselves added to their undesirable reputation in the public eye. Before 1890 drunkenness was an acute problem in the ethnic community. To cope with this trend, the Finnish temperance societies,churches and the socialist movement each taught a particular philosophy for living and provided various activities which relieved the loneliness, boredom or frustration of many workers and their families. While the church and temperance societies were generally endorsed by the general public—mining companies donated land and modest sums of cash to many of them—the Finnish Socialist movement challenged paternalism in the mining industry and traditional American ideals being taught in the public schools. According to Walfrid Jokinen, Finnish socialism in the minds of its adherents

> was looked upon as a way of life. "Bourgeoisie" [*sic*] culture was viewed as something not only corrupt but intended to keep the worker in a subjugated position.

> Therefore, it was not sufficient merely to organize polit-
> ically or industrially to end this state of affairs, but it
> was necessary to cultivate the "whole" person, to have
> a healthy socialist mind in a healthy socialist body to
> replace the decadent capitalistic arts with wholesome
> socialistic interpretation.[16]

This aim partly explains the great emphasis on athletics, music, drama and other educational programs which were incorporated into hall life. As long as these activities took place in the privacy of home or hall, most local residents tolerated the socialist movement.

For those persons interested in strict law-and-order policies, the red flag of socialism held aloft during street parades and mass meetings denoted anarchy and the violent overthrow of American institutions and values. James MacNaughton, general superintendent of Calumet and Hecla Mining Company in Michigan, claimed "the name 'red socialism' would apply to a militant socialist, a man who fights to enforce his doctrine on somebody else."[17]

The red flag, however, suggested a different symbolism for some Finnish socialists. In May of 1908 labour organizer John Valimaki reportedly told Governor Johnson of Minnesota:

> We don't want violence, we are not anarchists, we
> believe in government and we will obey the laws till we
> can get control of the government by our votes and
> make the laws we want . . . . The Finnish socialists carry
> the red flag when they parade, but it is not all red, like
> the anarchists. The flag is made red because the social-
> ists are made of all workers. They are out of every
> nation. They only know two kinds of people—the capi-
> talist class and the laboring class. They cannot take a
> white flag because all men are not white. So they take
> red because red is the color that runs in the blood of
> every man.[18]

A Finnish newspaperman further suggested that immigrant socialists shared a distinctive perspective.

> In America—the great melting pot of peoples—the
> working class movement must perforce be international.
> The immigrant is a cosmopolite in the true meaning of
> the word, he carries in the recesses of his soul two

worlds: old and new. He cannot for a moment think of freeing America from Capitalist oppression without at the same time thinking of Europe's delivery.[19]

These views seemed consistent with the ideals of the Socialist Party of America, for one of its noted leaders, Victor L. Berger, testified during the copper strike of 1913, "The red flag is the international emblem of brotherhood and fraternity ... but we also stand for our Star Spangled Banner, the emblem of the first great experiment in democracy."[20]

To some nationalistic Americans, however, international-based socialism seemed un-American, anarchical and alien. Such allegations were levelled at socialists by prosecution witnesses following the Red Flag parade in Hancock during 1907, by framers of the "Judas resolutions" during 1908, and by leaders of the Citizens Alliance and Finnish-American Anti-Socialist League during 1913-14.[21]

These developments suggest that the conflict between Finnish churchmen and socialists was further complicated by another ideological dimension. The tenets of Marxism prompted the latter group to be more ambivalent towards American institutions and laws whereas various Finnish clergymen promoted traditional American ideals. During the Mesabi Range strike of 1907, Suomi Synod historian S. Ilmonen prepared a modest tract on United States presidents and the ideals of the nation's founding fathers.[22] Suomi College and Seminary, the Synod's primary educational institution, sought and gained a reputation for instilling American ideals among its students.[23] Clemens Niemi also attested, "the action of the church has molded his [Finnish immigrant] morals, acted to check lawlessness and other un-American forces."[24]

Several factors might explain this viewpoint of various churchmen: a recognition that an alien "a wish to preserve local churches and other religious institutions in the mining districts, an approach to church-state relations based upon an old world pattern of mutual support, and a desire to improve the reputation of immigrant Finns among other ethnic groups.[25] In summary, this policy of accommodation was conceived as a pragmatic response to given economic opportunities, political conditions and public opinion which existed in the copper and iron districts.

Despite the international perspective of Finnish socialists and patriotic tendencies of churchmen, both groups nonetheless felt compelled to affirm their national origin. Local churches and socialist halls, as well as Suomi College and the Work Peoples' College, offered instruction in Finnish language, history and culture, as well as classes in either the Bible or Marxist teachings. Despite numerous differences of opinion, a shared language served as a common denominator between the Finnish factions and as a means of cultural preservation. The parental generation of Finnish immigrants grew increasingly concerned as their children were growing up under the strong influence of an educational philosophy in the public schools which emphasized the melting pot concept at the expense of certain ethnic values and folkways.

For the Finnish immigrant, the spoken and written word possessed inherent value and potential power. At organizational meetings which were sometimes heated and argumentative, debates often had a therapeutic function. Resentments surfaced, disagreements were discussed, and critical issues carefully weighed. This type of decision-making resembled a grass-roots experience in democratic debate and the art of give and take. That experience either prepared immigrants for more effective participation in the American political process or at least provided them with a catharsis before another day of work.

Besides the events of everyday life which entered into daily conversation, most Finns shared an awareness of deeper dimensions of meaning which exist in human speech. The well-conceived word could stir up or soothe one's spirit, and as he read or listened to the pronouncements of an ancient bard, inspired preacher or fiery agitator, a person might well find himself reflecting upon the ultimate questions of life.

According to Ralph Jalkanen, Finnish mythology in the *Kalevala* spoke to the plight of personal suffering.

> In Finnish life and history, suffering belongs inextricably to human existence. To be man means to have been born to suffering. The socio-political-economic history of the land tells about the anguish of wars and plagues, crop failure, and the harshness of the climate.... Suffering in its broadest sense means being acted upon. It implies an encounter with and confirmation to requirements imposed by someone or something from the outside which seeks to shape the self and the society. It is the anguish experienced, not only as pressure to change, but also as the threat to integrity, self-fulfillment and self-determination of the individual as well as the nation.[26]

In the nineteenth century, Church of Finland pastors read through the Bible, the teachings of Luther and German pietists as source materials for their sermons and instruction bases upon fundamental Lutheran beliefs. Famine, pestilence and war assuredly caused human suffering, but these external natural forces were overshadowed by the anxious realization that man himself was basically to blame for his own predicament.

The nineteenth-century revival movements subsequently broke open a new perception of guilt and grace, sometimes in very dramatic fashion. Tutored originally in the arts and natural sciences, Lars Levi Laestadius changed from a cautious cleric to convincing preacher after he openly confessed his personal sins of pride and unbelief. Believing in the atonement of Jesus Christ of human sinfulness, Laestadius mounted his pulpit to call the whisky peddlers and wayward members of his congregation in his northern parish to repentance and faith. The premise behind his preaching was simple. The spirit of God at work in the human will provide a resolution to human suffering and societal ills. An awakening to faith in Jesus Christ meant assurance of an abiding relationship with God, motivation to mend one's ways and hope for the future. Whether in this world or the after life, God would grant his children peace and justice.

For the penitent Finn both the wrath and love of God were real. This perception of the Christian faith was especially strong in those areas of Finland which eventually yielded the largest numbers of emigrants bound for America prior to 1900. J.K. Nikander, A. Heidemann and other church leaders who guided the three major Finnish Lutheran denominations in America kept these theological insights alive as they instructed future clergymen and laymen in religious matters. As various pastors subsequently considered the plight of workingmen in the mine fields, person-centred Christian principles constituted the substance of their spiritual counsel.

When the Finnish socialist movement took hold after 1900, various pastors felt compelled to formulate a Christian apologetic for the times. Reacting to the utopian idealism of Matti Kurikka, K.F. Henrikson criticized his efforts to build the community of Sointula (Harmony) in British Columbia and his optimistic view of man. In dealing with the abuses of capitalism, however, Henrikson himself appeared overly optimistic about the power of the preached word of God. He suggested holding a two-week series of revival meetings each year in addition to regular Sunday services. A special effort would be made to invite wealthy capitalists to worship; once they converted to Christianity, necessary social reforms would follow.[27]

Some Finnish pastors suggested that Christians approach the issue of socialism with an open mind. I. Katajamaa served a synod parish on the Mesabi Range during the strike in 1907 and for several years called for cooperation between the two camps. In his essay on "Temperance Work and the Working Class Question," Katajamaa first acknowledged the power struggle taking place in local temperance societies between churchmen and socialists. But he also foresaw a possible resolution in their ideological conflict. Whereas Christianity strengthened the inner man, socialism provided an economic perspective and political strategy for improving working conditions.[28] In another essay Katajamaa argued that biblical prophets (e.g., Isaiah 11 and Revelation 21) envisioned the good society where justice prevailed. In quest of that end both Christianity and socialism needed each other's corrective. Whereas socialism tended to view man as innately capable of achieving the good, the Christian faith maintained that sinful man is empowered to bear good fruit after experiencing forgiveness of sins through Jesus Christ. If socialism offered a concrete means and plan for rebuilding human society, Christianity underscored that the spirit of reconciliation and the love ethic prevail as men work for justice.[29] Cooperation, rather than class struggle, was needed.

The teachings and example of Jesus Christ offered the proper ethic to follow. The highly personal dimension of Christian faith, with its emphasis on inner freedom and forgiveness of sins, attested that Christianity can thrive in various kinds of societies, be they capitalist or socialist in nature. Jesus himself suggested this view inasmuch as he associated with all manner of men and favoured no one group or party. This principle further affirmed that the church must not identify itself wholly with a particular social order. According to J. Wargelin, the socialist criticism that the institutional church wholly endorsed capitalism in America was misleading. He compared the church to a mother who had given birth to such social movements as temperance societies, anti-slavery movements, settlement house work and other efforts which sought reform of existing conditions.[30] While the church must not endorse the political platform of a particular party (e.g., prohibition, the Socialist Party of America), the individual Christian must take a stand on specific issues. Thus he willingly supported workmen's compensation, child labour laws and other legal measures which would improve working conditions.

Wargelin's primary criticism of socialism fixed on the Marxist strategy of class struggle. He observed: "We know people who are both Christians and socialists, and they are among our finest acquaintances . . . but it is the power of the gospel, not the teachings of Marx, that make them love their fellow man."[31] The idea of class hatred existing between the bourgeoisie and proletariat seemed repugnant as well to B.W. Rautanen, the primary spokesman for organized labour in the Suomi Synod. In his observations on the copper strike of 1913 he criticized Finnish socialism for lacking the love ethic. In a sermon examining the views of American agnostic Robert Ingersoll—"how can a person love his enemies, it is good if he can get along even with his friends"—Rautanen again emphasized that Jesus showed compassion for all men, not one particular class.[32]

Regarding a God known through revelation, Christ experienced as Saviour, and an ethic based upon love, Finnish socialists largely disagreed. At their convention in Hibbing in 1906, delegates of the Finnish Socialist Federation endorsed the principle of religion as being a private matter. Olga Heinonen introduced the resolution partly for tactical reasons so that Mohammedans and Hindus would feel no discrimination should they join the Federation. Desiring a stronger statement, Moses Hahl argued that "all religions . . . that deny class struggle as a means of gaining economic equality are opposed to the social democratic party in America." Hahl's insistence that agitators speak against the church in their organizational work was finally endorsed by a vote of 19 to 17 in a resolution calling for clear exposition of the church's teachings in the light of historical and scientific evidence.[33] This position was reaffirmed in 1909 at the following Federation meeting in Hancock.[34]

The anti-church stance of the socialists stemmed partly from two intellectual trends. The writings of agnostic Robert Ingersoll were initially translated in Finland, circulated among Social Democrats and then transported to the United States by the wave of more radical emigrants who came around 1900. Wilho Leikas, for example, arrived in Calumet in 1904 and arranged with the *Worker* publishing house in Hancock to publish a series of Ingersoll's pamphlets. In such lectures as "God and Devils," "Heaven and Hell," "What is religion?" "Christmas Sermon," and others, Ingersoll criticized traditional Christianity, described various errors in the Bible, extolled human reason, made man his own saviour and fundamentally questioned the existence of God. As he put it, "I do not want to say that God does not exist, but I would say that I do not know whether or not he exists."[35] Ingersoll appealed to numerous Finnish

liberals, free-thinkers, and other persons interested in the evolution-
ary theories of Darwin.

The teachings of Karl Marx, however, dealt a more resound-
ing blow to the immigrant church. The *Worker* and other Finnish
socialist publishers made available the major works of Marx, F.
Engels, K. Kautsky, A. Bebel, A. Pannekock and others in Finnish
translation.[36] In the Michigan and Minnesota mine fields, basic
Marxist principles took on flesh and blood. Mine owners and management, as well as certain Finnish clergymen and businessmen,
were viewed by socialists as bourgeoisie who enslaved the working
class through inadequate wages, risky working conditions and an
industrial system which allowed the workers no voice over bargain-
ing of contracts and other policies.

In voicing their criticism, Finnish socialist journalists adopted
several approaches. In satirical fashion they printed cartoon carica-
tures of black-frocked pastors and corpulent capitalists. These pic-
tures easily caught the eye, but theoretical writers raised more in-
depth issues. Most Finnish clergymen agreed with socialist agitators
that workers shared a hard lot, but a basic difference in their
analysis is suggested by an interpreter of Marxist theory, M.M.
Bober: "It is not the consciousness of men that determines their
existence, but, on the contrary, their social existence determines
their consciousness."[37]

To encourage workers in meeting their daily tasks, Finnish
pastors preached faith in Jesus Christ as a means for strengthening
the human will amidst difficulties and for achieving harmonious
relationships between various classes of people. Not all clergymen
went to the extreme of saying, "God has decreed that some must
suffer here on earth and they should accept their lot and leave to
God the improvement of social conditions."[38] But in urging adaptation to existing conditions in the mining districts, many pastors
perhaps too readily pictured all manner of suffering as being ultimately redemptive in nature. In the Marxist view philosophers and
preachers have only interpreted the world and the human condition; "the point, however, is to change it."[39]

Finnish socialist agitators felt compelled to criticize the
church in order to awaken a new perception in the minds of
workers. According to Marx,

> religious distress is at the same time the expression of
> real distress and the protest against real distress. Reli-
> gion is the sigh of the oppressed creature, the heart of a
> heartless world, just as it is the spirit of a spiritless
> situation.[40]

In the Marxist view, reality consists of the material world and human hope is confined to earthly existence. Resolution of personal suffering depends more upon political action than prayer. The power for social change and achieving justice no longer originates from a transcendent God, but in the militant struggle of persons against the social forces that oppress them. Thus in the minds of some Finnish workers, the word of truth emanated from socialist agitators who, underground in the mines and on the surface, sounded the call to protest with impassioned rhetoric.

In urging unionization and political activity, the socialist movement did not, however, divorce itself completely from historical Christianity. Moreover, a socialist interpretation of the life of Christ and the early church offered a model of early aspirations among working class people. According to F. Engles:

> The history of early Christianity has notable points of resemblance with the modern working class movement. Like the latter, Christianity was originally a movement of oppressed people; it appeared first as the religion of slaves and emancipated slaves, of poor people deprived of all rights, of peoples subjugated or dispersed by Rome. Both Christianity and the workers' socialism preach forthcoming salvation from bondage and misery; Christianity places this salvation in a life beyond, after death, in heaven; socialism places it in this world, in a transformation of society.[41]

In the *Great Struggles of the Slaves* Leo Laukki examined signs of an early working-class movement in ancient Egypt, Greece and Rome. He further stated that Christianity appealed to the lower classes because of its expectation of a coming millennium to be established by Christ and such practices as helping the poor, sick, orphaned and widowed.[42] Similar themes existing in the writings of Karl Kautsky were made available in Finnish translation by the *Worker* publishing company.

Given these patterns in the early church, it seemed logical for some socialists to portray Jesus as an early proletarian. In *The Political Economy of Jesus* A.W. Ricker asserted that the Nazarene carpenter and his followers were members of primitive unions who shared the communistic lifestyle which the early church in some places adopted. Ricker further noted, however, that Jesus knew as little about true socialism as he did about the telegraph.[43] In the *Gospel of Flesh* Moses Hahl criticizes Ricker's portrayal of Jesus as a forerunner of communistic ideals. Hahl argued that it would be

as incorrect to view Jesus as a socialist agitator as it would be to
describe him as saviour of mankind. Furthermore, his teachings
such as "consider the lilies of the field . . . " was nothing more than
"stupid advice of a stupid anarchist."[44] Robert Blatchford in *God
and My Neighbor* saw nothing distinctive about Jesus. A person
might find happiness as readily from the teachings of Buddha,
socialism or determinism. In any case, "mankind's greatest curse is
ignorance. The only cure is knowledge."[45] A.B. Sarlin in *How Jesus
Died* debunked the resurrection accounts in the Gospels and
claimed that Jesus survived the crucifixion, met his disciples a few
more times and eventually died in solitude.[46]

In stripping Jesus of his divinity the Finnish socialist movement also questioned the love ethic of Christianity. On the one
hand, leaders such as Moses Hahl were drawn to the philosophy of
Friedrich Nietzche and his critique of tender-hearted, turn-the-
other-cheek views of some Christians. Other Finnish socialists such
as F. Aaltonen claimed that so-called Christians were not particularly loving. His funeral oration for the Italian Hall disaster victims
in Michigan alleged that capitalists extracted blood from the working class.[47] The copper strike of 1913 did demonstrate that law-
and-order advocates could be as prone to intimidation and violence
(e.g., the Seeberville incident, banishment of Moyer from the Copper Country, etc.) as the strikers who they deemed as anarchists. At
the height of this controversial labour dispute churchmen were
forced to take a position which socialists had held for some time,
namely, that no man, not even Jesus, could be wholly neutral and
without a party. While professing that Christ loved all manner of
man, various Finnish pastors nonetheless aligned themselves with
the mining companies to help evict the Western Federation of
Miners from the copper district and also cooperated with the
Finnish-American Anti-Socialist League to curtail the influence of
their more radical countrymen.[48]

Members of the Finnish Socialist Federation perhaps chose
up sides with less hesitancy. In the Marxist analysis of the bourgeoisie and proletariat classes, a clearly defined ethic made radical
action both necessary and desirable. Class hatred existing between
the two groups dictated that militant measures be employed by the
working class. The debates over IWW direct action measures from
1906 to 1914 in the Finnish Socialist Federation suggested that a
more radical faction led by Work Peoples' College teachers in
Smithville was moving from a hope placed in the ballot box to
strikes, sabotage and various intimidatory measures to achieve desired social goals.

While hatred towards capitalists was fostered, Finnish socialists also valued solidarity and cooperation as workers struggled in a common cause. As one leader put it, "Greater love hath no man, than that he lay down his life for his class."[49] In retrospect, the confrontation strategy of Finnish socialists amounted to a calculated risk to overthrow paternalism in the mining industry and establish a socialistic system. During the heat of strike activity, they appeared ready to settle for less than that, namely, more democratic procedures in the relations between labour and management. But this gain, too, they were largely denied until the New Deal era.

In discussing the conflict between Finnish churchmen and socialists in the mine fields of Michigan and Minnesota, I have sought to highlight several perspectives which can be overlooked in the Finnish immigrant experience up to World War One. For too long , two intellectual traditions in a particular ethnic community have been pitted against each other without an earnest analysis which permits each one to stand on its own merits. This overview may contribute to the dialogue among American and Canadian Finns and interested historians over the vital issues present in this particular episode of Christian-Marxist conflict in America. Secondly, much previous historical treatment of this particular conflict has tended to emphasize internal dynamics within the Finnish immigrant community as the chief reason for factionalism. My view is that environmental factors present in the mining town marketplace intensified, if not catalysed, the spirited competition between Finnish pastors and socialist agitators. Thirdly, spokesmen from both camps gave thoughtful consideration to basic beliefs in their respective intellectual traditions in coping with the workingman's alienation and hardship.

# Notes

1. *Finnish Radicals and Religion in Midwestern Mining Towns, 1865-1914* (Arno Press, 1979) was originally my Ph.D. thesis at the University of Chicago Divinity School in 1973. The oral history project entitled Folklore and Social Change in the Great Lakes Mining Region was made possible by a five-year grant from the National Endowment for Humanities and various friends of Suomi College.

158    A. Puotinen

2. See "Ameliorative Factors in the Conflict Between Socialism and the
    Suomi Synod," in *Faith of the Finns: Historical Perspectives on the
    Finnish Lutheran Church in America*, ed. Ralph J. Jalkanen (Last
    Lansing, Michigan State University Press, 1972), pp. 227-49.

3. see "Cooper Country Finns and the Strike of 1913," in *The Finnish
    Experience in the Western Great Lakes Region: New Perspectives*, eds.
    Michal G. Karni, Matti E. Kaups, Douglas J. Ollila Jr. (Institute for
    Migration, University of Turku and Immigration History Research
    Center, University of Minnesota, 1975), pp. 143-53. Also, "Early
    Labor Organizations in the Copper Country," in *For the Common
    Good*, ed. Michael G. Karni, Matti E. Kaups, Douglas J. Ollila Jr.
    (Superior: Työmies Society, 1977), pp. 119-66.

4. John I. Kolehmainen, "The Inimitable Marxists: The Finnish Immi-
    grant Socialists," *Michigan History*, 36 (December 1952), p. 399,
    quotes a Finnish socialist writer: "Nowhere in this world are newspa-
    per columns filled with such torrents of official, semi-official and
    unofficial resolutions, proclamations, statements, and records of the
    local chapter, committees, boards, individuals, and groups in perpet-
    ual conflict with each other, nagging, splitting hairs, bickering, argu-
    ing, and ending where they began—inextricable confusion."

5. A. William Hoglund, *Finnish Immigrants in America* (Madison: The
    University of Wisconsin Press, 1960), p. 57.

6. Timothy L. Smith, "School and Community: The Quest of Equal
    Opportunity, 1910-1921," manuscript, Minnesota State Historical Ar-
    chives (St. Paul, 1963), p. 24, observed; "the principle objective of
    both the vocational and academic courses was the promotion of per-
    sonal success. At every stage of the venture, however, the superin-
    tendents and school teachers realized that their achievements would
    be limited to the degree that social conditions outside the school
    placed a damper upon individual ambition. They set out, therefore, to
    educate the whole population of their towns."

7. Walfrid J. Jokinen, "The Finns in the United States: A Sociological
    Interpretation," Ph.D. thesis, Louisiana State University, estimates
    that upwards of 40 to 50 per cent of the immigrant Finns returned to
    Finland.

8. See references to this practice in the interviews of this writer with
    Nick Hendrickson, William Mattila and James O'Meara in the Suomi
    College Folklore Oral History Project.

9. Such charges were made by various Finnish workers in *Conditions in
    the Copper Mines of Michigan. Hearings Before a Subcommittee of the
    Committee on Mines and Mining. House of Representatives, 63rd Con-
    gress, Second Session. Pursuant to H. Res. 387.* (Washington: Govern-
    ment Printing Office, 1914).

10. See C.H. Benedict, *Red Metal: The Calumet and Hecla Story* (Calu-
    met: Roy W. Drier, 1968); Timothy L. Smith, "Factors Affecting the

Social Development of Iron Range Communities," manuscript, St. Paul, State of Minnesota Historical Archives, 1963. Walter Havighurst, *Vein of Iron: The Pickands Mather Story* (Cleveland: The World Publishing Company, 1958).

11. Timothy L. Smith, "School and Community: The Quest of Equal Opportunity, 1910-1921," manuscript, St. Paul, State of Minnesota Historical Archives, 1963.

12. Jokinen, "Finns in the United States," p. 137.

13. Smith, "School and Community," p. 41.

14. This incident was mentioned to the writer during a course on Oral History and Folklore in Upper Michigan which he taught at Suomi College during the summer of 1973. Mrs. Viola Brown recalled this happening from her school days.

15. In upwards of two hundred oral history interviews, as well as numerous responses to a written questionnaire, many Finnish Americans mentioned being called "roundhead" or "Dumb Finlander." Their recollections were in response to a question, "How did Finns get along with other ethnic groups?"

16. Jokinen, "Finns in the United States," p. 150.

17. *Congressional Hearings on the Copper Strike*, p. 1484.

18. Rudolph Pinola, "Labor and Politics on the Iron Range of Northern Minnesota," (Ph.D. thesis, University of Wisconsin, 1957), p. 26.

19. Kolehmainen, "Inimitable Marxists," p. 398.

20. *Congressional Hearings on the Copper Strike*, p. 679.

21. see *Amerikan Suometar*, January 19; March 4, 11, 18, 25; April 1, 8, 14, 15; June 24 in 1908 for reports on the resolution meetings. On Citizens Alliance activity, see their publication *Truth* published in Hancock in 1913. Also see, "Pöytäkirja tehty Hancocking suomalaisen anti-sosialistisen liiton," (manuscript, Hancock, Finnish-American Historical Archives).

22. Salomon Ilmonen, *Abraham Lincoln rattiusmiehenä ja lyhyitä piirteitä hänen elämän kerrastaan* (Pori, 1909) depicts Abraham Lincoln as a model of temperance. S. Ilmomen, *Piirteitä yhdysvaltain presidenttien uskonnollisesta elämästä* (Hämeenlinna, 1908) examines the religious beliefs of such men as George Washington, J.Q. Adams, and others.

23. The Oliver Mining Company files in the State of Minnesota Historical Archives include the following letters: F.E. Keese to J. H. McLean, October 4, 1919, writes that James MacNaughton informed him that Suomi College "is run strictly along American educational lines and that the pupils attending this school are taught the proper American spirit." J. Wargelin, President of Suomi College, to W.J. Olcott, President of Oliver Mining Company, January 6, 1921; "We are engaged in a great work for the uplift of American youth of Finnish extraction

160    A. Puotinen

to clean, moral and righteous life. . . . The social, political and religious
customs are being threatened by ultra-liberal propaganda. We need to
preach again the fundamentals of civilization, viz. respect for persons
and property rights."

24. Clemens Niemi, *Americanization of the Finnish People in Houghton
County, Michigan* (Duluth: Finnish Daily Publishing Company, 1921),
p. 25.

25. See *How To Become an American* (Duluth: Americanization Committee of the City of Duluth, 1919), p. 13. Also, Henry R. Kangas,
"Blades, Ears and Corn (Suomi Synod, 1890-1962)," manuscript, Hancock, Finnish-American Historical Archives, 1962, p. 162. See *Amerikan Suometar* numbers for March and April, 1908. which pertain to
anti-socialist resolutions.

26. Ralph J. Jalkanen, "Certain Characteristics of the Faith of the Finns,"
*Faith of the Finns*, p. 45.

27. K. F. Henrikson, *Sosialismi ja Matti Kurikan teoria* (Fitchbury: Totuus
lehden kirjapainossa, 1902), pp. 27 and 33.

28. Iisakki Katajamaa, "Raittiustyö ja työväenkysymys," *Raittius kalenteri,*
*1904.*

29. Katajamaa, "Sananen sosialismista ja sen suhteesta uskontoon," *Raittius kalenteri 1907*, pp. 129-48.

30. John Wargelin, "Aikamme yhteiskunnalliset parannukset ja kirkko,"
*Raittius kalenteri 1913*, pp. 51-58. See J. Wargelin, *Kristillinen hyvän-
tekeväisyys* (Porvoo; Werner Soderstrom Osakeyhtiö, 1927), for further
development of this view. On pp. 78-85 he discusses Inner Mission
efforts in German, social service work of W.A. Passavant in America,
Walter Rauschenbusch and the social gospel, and other social movements fostered by the church.

31. J. Wargelin, "Kirkko ja sosialismi," *Amerikan Suometar*, June 7 and
14, 1911, The quote is from the latter number.

32. On the love ethic, see V. Rautanen, *Kirkko ja sosiaaliset kysymykset*
(Hancock: suomalais-luteerilainen kustannusliike, 1913), p. 12. For the
sermon, see *Kylvömailta: Suomi-Synodin entisten ja nykyisten pappien
saarnoja* (Hancock: Book Concern, 1928), p. 201.

33. *Pöytäkirja amerikan suomalaisten sosialistiosastojen edustajako-
kousesta, Hibbingissa, Minne. elo. 1-7, 1906* (Hancock, 1907), p. 42,
for the Heinonen resolution; p. 47 and *passim* for extended debate on
the Hahl proposal; p. 134 for the final issue.

34. *Kolmannen amerikan suomalaisen sosialistijärjestön edustajakokouksen
pöytäkirjakokous pidetty Hancockissa, Michigan, 23-30, p. elok., 1909,*
F.J. Syrjala, sec'y (Fitchburg, 1909), pp. 10-11.

35. Robert G. Ingersoll, *Miten ihmiskunta on parannettava* (Hancock:
Työmiehen kirjapaino, 1907), p. 41. See also *Complete Lectures of Col.
R.G. Ingersoll* (Chicago: J. Regend and Company, n.d.), p. 89, "Man

must learn to rely upon himself." Note *Ingersoll's Greatest Lectures* (Hackensack, New Jersey: Wehman Brothers, 1964), p. 349, "Science is the real redeemer . . . It will put thoughtful doubt above thoughtless faith." For a churchman's critique based upon traditional biblical exegesis, see L. A. Lambert, *Huomautuksia Ingersollille*, trans. J. Hirvi (Ironwood: Suomalaisen kirjapaino-yhtiön kirjapainossa, 1908).

36. Karl Marx ja Friedrich Engels, *Kommunistinen manifesti* (Hancock: Työmies, 1914), p. 40, analyses differences between the bourgeoisie and proletariat; Anton Pannekoek, *Marxilaisuus ja darwinismi*, trans. J. Kari (Superior: Socialist Publishing Co., 1914), p. 21, examines Christianity in light of Darwinian thought; Karl Kautsky, *Kristinuskon alkuperä historiallinen tutkimus*, trans. J. Kari (Superior: Työmies Publishing Company, 1918), pp. 369-74, discusses primitive communism to be found in the New Testament.

37. M. M. Bober, *Karl Marx's Interpretation of History* (New York: W.W. Norton and Company, Inc., 1965), p. 5.

38. John I. Kolehmainen and George W. Hill, *Haven in the Woods: The Story of the Finns in Wisconsin* (Madison: The State Historical Society of Wisconsin, 1951), p. 119.

39. Karl Marx and Friedrich Engels, *On Religion* (New York: Schocken Books, 1964), p. 72.

40. Ibid., p. 42

41. Ibid., p. 316.

42. Leo Laukki, *Suuret orjataistelut, piirteitä vanhanaja työväenliikkeestä* (Fitchburg: Raivaaja Publishing Company, 1909), pp. 130-33. In a later work, *Teolliseen yhteiskuntaan*, Laukki discussed the role of Martin Luther and Thomas Muentzer and the Peasants' Revolt in Germany. On pp. 512-60 Laukki spelled out his vision of the ideal industrial society.

43. A.W. Ricker, *Jeesuksen taloudellinen politiikka*, trans. A. Ollikkala (Fitchbury: Suomal Sos. kustannusyhtion kustannuksella, 1905), pp. 16-21. For a view of Jesus as a tragic proletarian figure, see Bouck White, *Natsaretin Kirvesmies*, trans. Kalle Tahtela (Superior: Tyomies, 1916), p. 373.

44. Moses Hahl, *Lihan evankeliumi* (Fitchburg: Raivaajan kirjapaino, n.d.), p. 44.

45. Robert Blatchford, *Jumala ja lähimmäiseni*, trans, Kaapo Murros (Tampere: M V. Vuolukan Kustannuksella, 1907), p. 255.

46. A. B. Sarlin, *Miten Jesus kuoli* (Superior: Tyomies, 1915), p. 46.

47. *Amerikan Suometar*, December 30, 1913.

48. See "Pöytäkirja tehty suomalaisen antisosialistisen liiton, Hancockissa, huhtik: 19 p:nä, 1914," pp. 6-7.

49. *Ahjo* (The Forge), September 1920, p. 239.

# Finnish Temperance and its Clash with Emerging Socialism in Minnesota

*Michael Karni*

In February 1886, the Finnish temperance society *Pohjan Leimu* (Northern Light), began operations in Soudan, Minnesota, the first mining community developed in the northeastern section of the state after the discovery of iron ore in the area two years previously. *Pohjan Leimu* was originated at the behest of one Herman Helander, an organizer for the Good Templars Society of Republic, Michigan, which sought in temperance the means for alleviating the effects of Demon Rum in America. Members of *Pohjan Leimu* solemnly agreed to do their part in reducing consumption of alcohol, establishing a mutual benefit fund to aid members with needed cash during sickness or death, and to promote a friendly haven for lonely immigrants.[1] Later in the same year *Toivon Tähti* (Star of Hope) or Duluth and *Kilpi* (Shield) of New York Mills, Minnesota, were established. Three years later *Vesi* (Water) was established in Ely. Soon, in fact, the northern third of Minnesota was dotted with halls that bore idealistic names such as *Valon Tuote* (Reward of Light) in Virginia, *Totuuden Etsijä* (Seeker of Truth), Hibbing, *Rauhan Koti* (Home of Peace), Mountain Iron, *Valon Lähde* (Wellspring of Light), Eveleth, and *Järven Kukka* (Lake Flower), Sparta.[2] Between 1886 and 1900, by which time temperance development had nearly run its course, some forty societies were founded in communities ranging from Brainerd in the west to Winton in the northeast, and including such strongly Finnish communities as Palo, Pike River, Suomi and Toivola.[3] By 1940, fifty societies had been launched.

When the Finnish temperance movement ceased to function

eighty-five years later,[4] it had undergone many changes caused by often violent disruptions within the Finnish-American subculture, changes within the larger American community and the simple ravages of time. But the Finnish temperance movement is important because as the predecessor to the establishment of Finnish-American churches, it served as both a place to meet and socialize with other immigrants from Finland and as a strong parental influence on Finns half a world away from home. Demands of the church, once it was established, and later demands of the socialist movement among Finns in the United States, caused severe disruptions in temperance ranks, disruptions which were intensified by a new generation of young immigrants who believed American society needed more than an organization against drinking, dancing and card playing.

Organized Finnish temperance activity got under way in northern Michigan in association with the Scandinavian lodges of the Good Templars. Finnish interest in temperance was based squarely on the Finns' experience in America. By the 1880s Finns in America clearly perceived that many of their countrymen were locked in a damaging cycle of working and drinking that had turned the immigration experience sour, and organized temperance seemed to provide the answer. While there was a temperance movement in Scandinavia and Finland, it is generally accepted that Finnish immigrant involvement in temperance came as a response to American conditions.[5]

In 1883 a number of Finns joined the Norwegian *Tornea* chapter of Good Templars in the mining town of Allouez, Michigan, in the copper country. Soon more Finns joined the Norwegian *Nora* lodge in nearby Calumet; others joined with local Swedes. A year later so many Finns belonged to the Norwegian lodge in Hancock that they were urged to form their own society, which they did at a meeting in a Norwegian church on Washington's birthday in 1885.[6] Throughout the Upper Peninsula similar lodges flowered between 1880 and 1890, as well as in Ohio, New York and other places where Finns were establishing themselves. Some were purely Finnish groups; others were mixed Scandinavian alliances between Finns and Norwegians. All were a part of the Independent Order of Good Templars in the Midwest.

A misunderstanding between the Finns and the New York office of Good Templars over the sale of handbooks led to a rupture in the Scandinavian temperance alliance. The Finns began to speak of forming their own independent league more in line with what they perceived the needs of Finnish immigrants to be. Simultaneously a Finnish newspaper, *Uusi Kotimaa* (New Homeland) of New York Mills, Minnesota, began to agitate for a purely Finnish movement. And, finally, word had reached the immigrants of the establishment in Finland of a national brotherhood called the Friends of Temperance. Thus in 1888, five Finnish lodges separated from the Good Templars and formed *Suomalainen Kansallis Raittius Weljeysseura Pohjois Amerikassa* (The National Finnish Temperance Brotherhood in North America) totally free from association with Norwegians and Swedes.[7]

Among the reasons for the split was the continued language problem and the friction between Finns and the Templars national office. But a more significant reason was to be found in the basic perception regarding the role of temperance among immigrants. The Norwegians and Swedes, already relatively well-established in America, apparently saw temperance more as a social movement, and probably sought in the Good Templars a pleasant fraternity enhanced by the colourful ritual and secret ceremonies, which must have made life seem less drab on the Midwestern frontier.[8] The Finns, on the other hand, only recently arrived, saw in temperance a means by which to help members make the necessary adjustment from a pre-industrial society to a highly advanced technological society.[9] In other words, they thought temperance provided the means by which to divert the youthful and largely masculine energies away from the uproarious drunkenness that they seemed so prone to. They also found in temperance a means by which to help the group advance.

The main objection by the Finns to the Good Templars was its secrecy and exclusiveness. Rather than offer temperance to a select few and keep its precepts behind closed doors, the Finns wanted a virtual temperance crusade. They wished to involve every Finn in North America. Thus when they formed their independent brotherhood they borrowed certain trappings from the Templars—procedures, hierarchy of officers and the like—but dropped secrecy and invited all comers to join. The idealistic spirit with which temperance meetings were conducted is evident in the opening remarks made at each meeting. "There is no nobler work than the cause of temperance," intoned the presiding officer. "May all intoxicating liquors be banished from our otherwise fair land."[10] New members were asked to pledge abstinence and older members took their turns reading frightening passages regarding the evils of drink.

Once these formalities were concluded, however, members turned to less sombre matters. Kolehmainen has characterized them:

> An erring member asked forgiveness for his use of alcohol to fight a cold, and it was granted; a debate was held: "who suffers more from drunkenness, a man or woman?" Somebody played a five-stringed *Kantele*. Two or three poems were read.... Dolls, corsages, and needlework were auctioned, letters exchanged, and the society's handwritten newspaper read by its editor. An innocent game or two, perhaps a playlet, a closing benediction, and the festivities were over. Youthful Finnish immigrants hurried home to their rooms and boarding houses, happy, released from the tensions of life in a strange land.[11]

The temperance movement was ideally suited to Finnish immigrants in northeastern Minnesota. In 1884, when the first load of iron ore was shipped from Soudan, until the 1930s, the area was a virtual frontier with attendant male dominance in numbers, large numbers of bars, and extremely difficult working conditions. Northeastern Minnesota must have seemed like Babel to the Finns when they first arrived. At least half of the population was foreign-born. Over forty different ethnic groups sent young, strong men to mine in the Mesabi and Vermilion pits. They laboured side by side under dangerous working conditions for very low pay, with extremely limited chances for advancement. A mining company official frankly admitted discriminatory practices against the foreign-born when deciding on employee advancement. "We move men," he said, "along faster than in other companies, but we don't push any but the American-born on to the [steam] shovels or other machines."[12]

The worker had other serious problems to contend with. Danger was one. During 1905-1906, the death rate on the Mesabi was approximately 7.5 workers per thousand employed. Between 1905 and 1909, 277 workers were killed in St. Louis County alone.[13] If a worker in northeast Minnesota sought relief from mining, he could only choose a lumber camp. Such was the paradise Finns found when they arrived in Minnesota.

But come they did, along with thousands of other nationalities who arrived yearly to work in the mines. By 1905, 19,847 Finns lived in Minnesota with over 95 per cent residing in five northeastern counties. By 1920, their peak year, 29,108 Finns lived in the state.[14] They were the largest foreign-born group in northeast Minnesota and the first to arrive.

The most active decade for temperance organization was the 1890s. As near as can be determined, some twenty-one societies were established, including large ones in Hibbing, Virginia, Mountain Iron, Sparta/Gilbert, Biwabik and Eveleth during the decade. Finnish population is difficult to determine accurately, but an idea of the extent of Finnish population in certain localities can be determined by the totals Finns themselves arrived at. They counted in 1903, for example, 1,705 Finns living in the city of Virginia. Of that total, 835 were men, 342 were women and 528 were children. The *Valon Tuote* temperance society in Virginia had 372 members, or nearly 40 per cent of the Finnish adults living in the city at the time.[15] If the same approximate percentage holds true in other Range communites, the temperance movement, at its peak, was indeed a large and influential organization among Finns.

The 1890s saw three distinct periodicals emerge, each different but each designed to bring the message of abstinence to members and those who would be. The earliest was *Raittiuslehti* (Temperance News), established in 1892 and devoted to printing theoretical treatises on temperance, chapter news and what could best be described as allegorical stories on the evils of drinking. *Raittiuslehti* suffered some difficulties in finding a permanent home and editorial staff—it was located in its first years in New York Mills, Minnesota; Superior, Wisconsin; New York City; Calmet and Kaleva, Michigan, before settling in Hancock—but there was no doubt about its editorial impact. Titles such as "Temperance and Religion" and "Alcohol and Unemployment" are found regularly between chapter news and idealistic poetry. A typical example of a news story concerns a happily married young man with a beautiful daughter who decides to take in a boarder. Eventually, his wife and daughter run off with the boarder. Since the man doesn't have strong relgous principles, he gives himself to drink. After two months of continuous imbibing, the man, in despair, poisons himself with strychnine. The news article goes into great detail describing his convulsions and last cries. Finally, he curses the man who ran off with his wife and daughter, and then succumbs. He was a good man, but weak, the article implies. The message is clear: always stay away from the bottle, if you wish to avoid a similar fate.[16]

A different publication, begun in 1896, was *Raittiuskalenteri*, a yearly almanac given to enlightening articles, obituaries, news of chapters in SKRV, as well as name days, calendars and factual data carried by similar yearly volumes. Minnesota and other temperance groups often rendered brief accounts of annual meetings in *Raittiuskalenteri*'s pages also. Of the two Journals, the latter seemed to meet personal preference better. It survived until the early 1970s.[17] In Addition to these two purely temperance journals, a good number of conservative and religous Finnish-American newspapers carried temperance news. Most important among them was *Päivälehti* (Daily News), published in Duluth. Originally published as a temperance newspaper, *Päivälehti*'s circulation climbed to nearly 15,000 in the early years of the present century when it expanded to carry church news as well as covering the national and international scene (with emphasis on news from Finland) and printing accounts of activity among temperance chapters.

Perhaps the most interesting "publication" fostered by the Finnish temperance movement was the *nyrkkilehti* (literally "fist paper"), a handwritten newsletter containing heavy doses of inspirational poetry and prose. The only surviving issues in Minnesota are eight copies of *Erämaan Tähti* (Wilderness Star) written in Hibbing during the summer and fall of 1904.[18] This particular *nyrkkilehti* contains little in the way of chapter news. Instead it is full of idealistic essays, lofty poems and translations of inspiring Finnish literature. A *nyrkkilehti* was designed to be prepared weekly or monthly and read aloud at temperance meetings. After being read, it was posted conspicuously for individual perusal until the next issue was prepared.

In addition to publications, Finnish temperance societies built libraries of popular and inspirational literature which was lent both to members and the general public. The *Valon Tuote* society in Virginia held a library containing over 800 volumes as late as 1940. At its peak, the Virginia society made over 685 loans in one year. About one-half the loans were made to non-members.[19]

Another important aspect of the temperance movement was its service as an aid society to members who were ill and to families of members who died. Nearly every society in Minnesota had such services at one level or another. *Valon Tuote* paid out $415 in 1900 to members who were too ill to work, and over $900 to relatives of deceased members between 1893 and 1930.[20]

The *Sovinto* (Understanding) society of Hibbing declared temperance was, indeed, "more than the banishment of the wine glass. ..."[21] A major factor in temperance was to hold people together, to help them advance by removing Demon Rum and preventing its return. But when a member did fall, societies were generally quick to forgive after a few harsh words, a stern rebuke and a solemn promise by the fallen never to let it happen again. Expulsion, then, was often "more symbolic than real."[22] The *Totuuden Etsijä* society of Hibbing, for example, placed members on probation only after a pledge had been broken three times within three months. The weak, another society declared, would be forgiven "not seven times, but seventy times seven."[23] The *Vesi* society of Ely, Minnesota, had 862 violators among its 2,104 members in a twenty-five-year period. Expulsions ranged from a few weeks to forever, with the former the most likely penalty.[24]

The Finnish temperance movement, therefore, was a fraternal, social, cultural and educational movement was well as a crusader against the evils of strong drink—the perfect means, it seems, to help a group instill in itself enough self-discipline to advance in a highly technological society. Until the early years of the twentieth century it was, in fact, extremely successful in doing just that, especially given the fact that it had such a strong religious base. But first in the mid-1890s and later shortly after the turn of the century, divisive issues occurred that stopped the growth of temperance in a world that had suddenly become too complex to let the banishment of liquor be the simple solution to every man's problems.

In the 1890s and the first decades of the twentieth century, the changing character of immigrants from Finland began to force differences in temperance ranks in all parts of America, and particularly in Minnesota. Many more immigrants from southern Finland began to arrive who, influenced as they were by the growing number of clashes with Czarist oppression in Finland, were less likely to be swayed by the religious doctrines as they were practised in the temperance movement—doctrines which the temperance movement adhered to because of its close affiliation with Finnish Lutheranism as it was practised in America. In fact, from the turn of century onward, liberals and even radicals began to organize in the United States and cause problems for both the church and the temperance movement.

The first trouble occurred in 1895 over the issue of dancing and card playing. Solomon Ilmonen, a young minister, published the answers he received from prominent ministers and temperance advocates in the United States on the question of dancing as a legitimate activity for societies to allow. The resultant castigation of such worldly pleasures by those questioned caused a major break in several Minnesota societies as well as in dozens more throughout the United States. *Pohjan Leimu* of Soudan went on record forbidding dancing, card playing and gambling of any variety. *Valon Tuote* of Virginia confessed it had allowed "secret" dances and card games. Such practices, however, were now banned. Undesirable members of the society were kicked out and even the poetry readings of Kalle Koski, the society's poet, were forbidden. *Valon Lähde* of Eveleth withdrew from the league in anger. Eventually, however, more conservative members gained control, booted the "flippant" members out and rejoined the *Veljeysseura*.[25] In Hibbing the *Tapio* society disengaged itself from the movement over similar issues in protest. Shortly "reliable" members split with the modernists and formed a new society called *Totuuden Etsijä*. The two societies never rejoined.[26] In Mountain Iron a *hajannus*, or split, also occurred between older, more conservative members and younger members who broke away and formed a "free" society. It lasted until 1905.

As the new century dawned, the troubles grew more serious. The controversy over dancing and card playing had been mild compared to what eventually happened over the issue of socialism. In Minnesota, as elsewhere, those Finns recently arrived from the old country believed that the cause of intemperance and various other social ills was not personal failures. Rather, they believed drunkenness to be only one result of a harmful social and economic environment.[27] This message was hammered home by men such as Dr. Antero F. Tanner and Martin Hendrickson, the first two "apostles" of socialism. The charm and energy of these two men is worth noting. Tanner held audiences literally spellbound with his seemingly profound knowledge and his ability to perform "miracles"—in the middle of his talk on science and socialism he would make water "burn" by igniting potassium in it. He was even more spellbinding when he blasted capitalism, praised socialism, and declared that man had indeed evolved from the apes.[28] After several years of "preaching" as an "apostle" of socialism, Tanner settled down in Ely, Minnesota, where he built a large hospital and organized the Ely chapter of the Imatra society, a pre-socialist workers' organization, which later became a branch of the Western Federation of Miners and finally a socialist chapter.[29]

Martin Hendrickson, receiving his rebirth as a socialist after hearing Dr. Tanner speak, became a tireless agitator. In one nine-month period, he claimed to have travelled 13,000 miles through twenty-eight states. In 122 Finnish communities he gave 190 speeches on socialism to a total of 45,000 Finns.[30] By the early years of the century, men such as these two had launched a blistering attack on conservatives and clergy, an attack which in northern

Minnesota was particularly heated. In 1906, declaring that the Mesabi Range was where Finnish and other workers were most oppressed, Finnish socialists formally organized into the *Suomalainen Sosialistijärjestö* (Finnish Socialist Federation) and declared war on capitalist employers. Within ten years the Federation grew to nearly 17,000 members in individual chapters and became the largest foreign-language federation of the American Socialist Party.[31] During the same period, socialists wreaked havoc on Finnish churchmen and temperance groups as many Finns responded to the urgings of agitators.

A Finnish Lutheran minister perhaps summed up the situation best when he declared that socialism had literally engulfed the Finns; it had spread among them, he said, "like dry skin absorbs hot fat."[32] Some temperance societies seemed to exist beside socialist locals with no apparent sense of disharmony. The *Järven Kukka* society of Gilbert, for example, reported in its 1907 minutes that it rented its meeting hall to socialists. No apparent animosity existed.[33] In Virginia, Tower-Soudan, Mountain Iron, Ely and Hibbing, however, the story was different. In Hibbing, for example, after the 1906 formation of the *Socialist Federation* when the socialists had rented the *Tapio* temperance hall for their meeting, the socialists tried to seize the temperance hall. Members of the socialist society *Hedelmä* joined the temperance society and then tried to change the society by vote to a socialist organization. *Tapio* never fell, however. The temperance people and socialists as well quickly learned the advisability of organizing holding companies to keep property out of the hands of unscrupulous members.[34] Gone were the days, indeed, when Matti Kurikka, the utopian leader from British Columbia, and Dr. Tanner, could book speeches in the Hibbing temperance hall.[35] Thus, the temperance societies which could not be converted, or controlled by socialists, ended up in the so-called right wing camp with the church people whom the socialists reviled.

Temperance, for the first twenty years of the present century, was beset by one crisis after another. The establishment of new societies stopped altogether, and a good number of liberal members were lost. This is not to say, however, that the advent of socialism spelled the demise of Finnish temperance. Temperance, rather, had reached a point where it no longer served as the only secular organization available to Finnish immigrants. Many potential members chose either to become socialists or simply to stay away from temperance because it seemed to be an old-fashioned answer to modern questions. The socialists made this clear in their preach-ments about temperance, but they nevertheless pointed to temperance as one of many important planks in their platform.

Finnish temperance enjoyed a brief revitalization with the advent of prohibition, but sank even deeper after its repeal in 1933. In 1936, the newspaper *Päivälehti* paid editorial tribute to the fifty years of Finnish temperance in America.[36] But, by then, young members were next to impossible to recruit. While temperance held on until the 1960s, in name at least, its major efforts and accomplishments had occurred at the turn of the century and before, when it served as an agency which forced members to stay away from strong drink, and, more importantly, when it served as a fraternal, social, cultural and educational agency designed to help Finns better adjust to life in America.

# Notes

1. Minutes, *Pohjan Leimu* temperance society, April 30, 1886, Immigration History Research Center (IHRC), University of Minnesota, St. Paul. The minutes of temperance societies on microfilm cited in this article were obtained by the IHRC from the Emigration History Research Center, Turku University, Turku, Finland who, in turn, microfilmed them at Suomi College, Hancock, Michigan. I am greatly indebted to the Iron Range Historical Society, Gilbert, Minnesota for permission to use portions of two articles I did for its journal *Range History* on Finnish temperance in December 1977 and March 1978.

2. After Sparta was moved to make way for the opening of a new mine, the society's quarters were transferred to the village of Gilbert in 1910; see *Järven Kukka* Collection, 1910, IHRC.

3. John I. Kolehmainen, "Finnish Temperance Societies in Minnesota," *Minnesota History*, 22, (1941), pp. 391-92.

4. I arbitrarily call the date which the IHRC was given the records of *Valon Tuote* of Virginia in 1971 as the end of organized temperance activity in Minnesota. Shortly after the local body of Knights and Ladies of Kaleva took possession of *Valon Tuote* hall, also.

5. Kolehmainen, "Temperance," p. 393; Michael G. Karni, "Norwegian Influence on Finnish Church and Temperance Groups in America," in *Norwegian Influence on the Upper Midwest*, Harold S. Naess, ed. (Duluth, 1976), p. 38.

6. Armas K.E. Holmio, *Michiganin Sumalaisten Historia* (Hancock, 1967), p. 329. For earlier important works on Finnish temperance, see

J.W. Lilius,ed., *Rauhankokous ja Pääpiirteitä Amerikan Suomalaisten Raittiustyön Historiasta* (Hancock, 1908), and S. Ilmonen, *Juhlajulkaisu, Suomalaisen Kansallis-Raittius-Veljeysseuran 25-Vuotisen Toiminnan Muistoksi* (Ishpeming, Michigan, 1912).

7. Holmio, pp. 335-36.

8. I realize that this is an indefensible way to write off the Swedish and, especially, the Norwegian temperance movement and leaders. But the only help I have been able to get on the subject in the English language has been Kenneth Smemo's paper read at the Organization of American Historians' 1974 annual meeting titled "The Immigrant as Reformer: the Case of the Norwegian American."

9. Herbert G. Gutman,[11] Work, Culture, and Society in Industrializing America, 1815-1919," *American Historical Review*, 78 (1973), pp. 543-50.

10. John I. Kolehmainen and George Hill, *Haven in the Woods: the Story of the Finns in Wisconsin* (Madison, 1951), p. 114.

11. Ibid., p. 115.

12. Neil Betten, "The Origins of Ethnic Radicalism in Northern Minnesota," *International Migration Review*, 4 (Spring, 1970), p. 51.

13. Hyman Berman, "Education for Work and Labor Solidarity: the Immigrant Miners and Labor Radicalism on the Mesabi Range," manuscript, University of Minnesota, 1964, p. 6.

14. *Fifth Decennial Census of Minnesota, 1905*, pp. 193-95; *Fourteenth Census of the United States*, III, p. 521.

15. *Valon Tuote Raittiusseuran 60-Vuotisjulkaisu, 1953*, pp. 14-15.

16. "Hänen Viimeinen Ryyppynsä", *Raittiuslehti*, June 20, 1893, pp. 81-82.

17. The 1971 issue, at least, is the last issue available for study at the IHRC.

18. These valuable editions are a part of the Edith Koivisto Collection, IHRC, University of Minnesota.

19. Kolehmainen, "Temperance in Minnesota," p. 398.

20. Ibid., p. 397.

21. Ibid.

22. Ibid., p. 395.

23. Ibid., p. 396.

24. John I. Kolehmainen, *The Finns in America* (New York, 1968), pp. 20-21; see also the *Vesi* Collection, IHRC, University of Minnesota.

25. S. Ilmonen, *Juhlajulkaisu*, pp. 75-76.

26. Edith Koivisto, *"Lupaus, Hibbingin Suomalaisen Raittiusliikkeen Historia,"* vv. 1895-1957, manuscript in Koivisto Collection, IHRC, pp. 85-100.

174    M. Karni

27. Carl Ross, *The Finn Factor in American Labor, Culture and Society* (New York Mills, Minnesota, 1977), p. 27.

28. *Lehtipaja: Työmiehen Neljännes Vuosisata Julkaisu* (Superior, 1928), pp. 169-74.

29. See *Imatra Society Pöytäkirja*, Ely, Minnesota; IHRC, University of Minnesota (microfilm).

30. Martin Hendrickson, *Muistelmia Kymmenvuotisesta Raivaustyöstäni* (Fitchburg, Mass., 1909), pp. 106-109.

31. see *Yhdysvaltain Suomalaisen Sosialistijärjestöjen Neljännen Edustajakokouksen Pöytäkirja* (Astoria, Oregon, 1915), p. 34.

32. Kolehmainen, *The Finns in America*, p.21.

33. *Järven Kukka* Collection, July to September, 1907, IHRC; University of Minnesota.

34. Edith Koivisto Collection, Notes, IHRC, University of Minnesota.

35. Edith Koivisto, "Lupaus", p. 29.

36. *Päivälehti*, June 8, 1936, p. 2.

# Working-Class *Herrat*: The Role of Leadership in Finnish-American Socialist Movements in the Pacific Northwest

*P. George Hummasti*

John Higham, introducing a recent investigation into the nature of ethnic leadership, argues that "ethnic groups in an open society are, in some degree yet to be specified, the creation of their leaders."[1] While this statement may place too much emphasis on leaders, it does seem clear that the role of leadership was more crucial than usual within ethnic communities, where one primary concern is to define relationships of the group with an alien society unfamiliar to most of its members. It likewise appears evident that among immigrant radicals, such as the Finnish socialists, whose major concern was not the furthering of old-country causes but the development of ties with American working-class movements, leadership is of even more central importance. Of course, the importance of leaders in explaining radicalism among Finnish-Americans has received frequent comment. There can be little doubt that one of the major reasons for the strength of radicalism among Finnish immigrants in America was the availability of talented radical leaders who were forced to file the oppressive policies of Finland's Russian governors.[2]

But if radical leaders were an important factor in the size of radical organizations among Finnish-Americans, and if leaders played a crucial role in such ethnic radical organizations, a great deal can be learned about the *nature* of these organizations by studying their leaders and the relationships that existed between these leaders, and the rank and file. In the case of the Finnish Socialist Federation (*Suomalainen Sosialistijärjestö* (SSJ)), the Pacific

Northwest provides an excellent field of examination of the role of leadership in the organization and of the relationships between leaders and followers. The region was the site of enough Finnish settlements of moderate size to make it an important area of Finnish ethnic activity, at the same time that it was isolated from the centres of control of the SSJ and of the socialist and communist parties to which it was affiliated, providing opportunity for thought and actions that diverged from the official position of the Federation. This is an area, therefore, where the role of leadership in the organization can be fruitfully examined. Of course, because of the unique conditions in the Pacific Northwest, conclusions based on the actions of Finnish radicals there may not always be applicable to other parts of the country.

In the SSJ, as in any organization in human society, there are leaders and followers. By the very nature of their position, the leaders possess an extraordinary amount of authority and influence in directing the affairs of the organization. By the nature of their position, the followers, to a given extent, submit to the will of their leaders when issues of importance are decided. Simply stated, this means that leaders lead and followers follow. However, in any human grouping, survival of the organization, and of the leaders' positions within it, depends to a greater or lesser degree on the ability of that organization to meet the needs of its members.[3] Therefore, all leaders of all organizations must to some extent harken to the desires of their followers.

Since influence flows both ways in the relationship between leaders and followers, it is often difficult to determine exactly who the leaders were.[4] For example, for almost all the time it existed, Toveri (Comrade), the official organ of the Western District of the SSJ published in Astoria, Oregon, manifested an editorial policy identical to the positions taken by the Finnish socialist local of Astoria. It is impossible, however, to determine from the available sources exactly to what extent the Astoria local maintained an influence over the editorial policies of Toveri and to what extent the editors of the paper had special influence within the local.[5] Thus it must be recognized that it is not completely possible to determine exactly the role of leadership among Finnish socialists in the Pacific Northwest, because it is improbable that the exact combination of factors that influenced any given decision will ever be known.

Nonetheless, it is worthwhile to analyse the role of these leaders in the organization, and to do so it is useful to divide them into three categories: national, regional and local leaders. National leaders might include members of the executive committee of the SSJ and of its central office, as well as those whose reputations or positions gave them a national influence among Finnish socialists. Regional leaders included some members of the editorial staffs of district newspapers, some district organizers and speakers, and again those whose reputations or positions gave them less formal influence in one of the three districts into which the SSJ was divided. Local leaders—those with authority in the affairs of a particular Finnish community—were closest to the rank and file of the organization and, in most cases, probably rose to their positions from the rank and file. Of course, this division of leaders into three categories is simply a useful logical tool of analysis and therefore somewhat artificial and imperfectly correspondent with reality.

It is not always clear how specific leaders of the Finnish-American socialist movement fit into these categories. Some individuals can be counted as both national and regional leaders, especially in the Eastern and Central districts that were close to the sources of national power. In some cases, in the Western District at least, district organizers or editors of the district newspaper can be seen as national, but not as regional leaders. Some local leaders, especially in the larger local organizations, were regional and/or national leaders, who also exercised local authority in the communities where they lived. Nonetheless, the SSJ was so structured that each of these categories of leaders had distinct functions within the organization, so this division makes sense.

The national leaders of the SSJ were, among other things, the direct link between the Finnish movement and the American socialistic parties with which it was affiliated. Thus the national leaders were extremely important in the accomplishment of the major *formal* objective of the SSJ—the forging of lasting ties with the American working-class movement and the furthering of its goals. Given this position, they were of crucial importance in defining the *official* program of the SSJ and the place of the Finnish socialists in American radicalism. The regional leaders functioned in part as lines of communication between national leaders and local organs of the Federation, and thus were a part of the link between the membership of the SSJ and the organizations of the American working class. But they were also leaders of their own districts and as such had much to do with determining the special character of each district, which in turn had some influence on the nature of the Federation nationally. Indeed, a fruitful area of research that would explain much about why the three districts of the SSJ were so different in their approaches to socialism would be to determine whether the differences in style and doctrine that existed between leaders of the different districts were caused primarily by their awareness of special conditions within their separate districts, or by other elements in their backgrounds, including their experiences in Finland.

Because the national and regional leaders were most influential in establishing the formal policy of the Federation, their ideas dominate the publications of the SSJ and the other documents most often used by investigators who have studied the Finnish socialist movement in America. Thus, much of the information we have about the official programs of the SSJ and about which organizations or doctrines within the American radical movement it supported, is based on the opinions of and decisions made by these two groups of leaders. The role of local leaders and the rank and file in formulating these policies was confined for the most part to passive support of decisions made at higher levels.

But although the local leaders had little direct influence in general policy-making in the SSJ, they played extremely important roles within the Federation and were crucial in establishing its nature. They were the men and women who organized Finnish-American socialists at the grass-roots level and who directed the everyday affairs of local clubs with much dedication and often some sacrifice. Much of what the SSJ was at the local level depended on these presidents and treasurers, committee chairmen and secretaries, choral leaders and newspaper correspondents. The glowing description by a *Toveri* editor of local correspondents to the paper could well apply to all of them:

> The news and articles that they send are born at the end of a hard day of work. They have sat up when others have already sunk into the deepest sleep in their beds. The have believed in the victory of our great cause when many comrades have doubted. They have kept the torch lit, shown the light and pointed out the road to the wanderer. They have refreshed tired minds, inspired apathetic workers, encouraged and enjoined. Simply put, they have always been first and last in the battle field of the class struggle, striving for the common good of working people.[6]

Continuing, the editor told the correspondents of their importance in spreading the message of socialism and in doing so showed an understanding of the contributions of local leaders to the strength of the SSJ:

On your work depends the extent to which the *Toveri* draws into its circle of influence working-class elements that to this point have been beyond its reach. To a large extent, it depends on you how well our agitation among the unorganized succeeds. It depends on you how much the *Toveri* is read and subscribed to. Furthermore, it depends to a great extent on you how many unorganized workers, who have thus far been apathetic to all class-conscious activities, will adopt the *Toveri* as their own paper. Because you, living daily among them, know best what kind of language they easily understand and by what means their thoughts can best be attracted to social issues.[7]

One reason for the importance of local leaders was the tendency of most Finnish socialists to play a passive role in their organization. A problem that frequently vexed national and regional leaders of the SSJ was that of getting ordinary members to participate actively in the affairs of the Federation.[8] Because they never succeeded in solving this problem, even in regards to local activities, members who were active in the affairs of their locals often found themselves forced to take on numerous responsibilities. Thus, for example, when Enoch M. Nelson, a leader in the Fort Bragg, California, SSJ local, migrated to Soviet Karelia in 1921, members left behind despaired of finding the five men needed to fill all the positions he held. Since no one could be found who was willing to succeed Nelson as chairman of the entertainment committee, that committee decided that "Nelson will have to handle this job as long as he is 'on this side of the Russian border.'"[9] It is little wonder, therefore, that local leaders sometimes were frustrated by the situation that faced them. One of these leaders from Portland, Oregon, portrayed the importance of active local leaders very well when the fact that only about thirty-five of the ninety to one hundred members of the Portland SSJ local took any part in the activities of the club caused him to write:

Why indeed have the rest joined our local? Perhaps many of them say, what's the matter with our old officials. I can say right off that nothing is the matter with us. There are many of us who never feel tired in performing our functions in our local. At present, however, the scope of our activities is so broad that it is in no way possible to attend all the meetings even if one wanted to. In addition to the regular activities of our

local, we have the district committee, the central committee of the city, the Friends of the Soviet Union
committee and the preparation committee for the
lower-Columbia summer festival. In addition to this we
also intend to help small communities in the area with
their summer festivals. We do not, then, ask for help
from the membership without reason.... If you do not
want to take any responsibility, then at least say that
you are not willing to perform any function for the
good of your local. At this point, that is your minimum
duty.[10]

Thus, not only did local leaders have much to do in determining the nature of SSJ activities, but in many cases, by their dedication and willingness to sacrifice time and energy, they kept local
Finnish socialist organizations alive. To them as much as to talented national and regional leaders must go credit for the strength
of socialism among Finnish-Americans.

To researchers interested in examining Finnish-American socialism, local leaders are also significant because they are the leaders closest to the rank and file. It is therefore probably a safe
assumption that their opinions came nearer to expressing the attitudes of ordinary members of the Federation than any other group
of leaders. Since these ordinary members have left behind very
little historical evidence, the knowledge available about local leaders can provide revealing hints on what they thought about the
purposes and activities of their organization. As far as Finnish
socialist organizations in the pacific Northwest are concerned, the
best source of information on local leaders is contained in the
letters sent by local correspondents to the district newspaper, *Toveri*. These letters are the one place where local leaders regularly
expressed their opinions and reported on their activities.

Care must be taken in using these letters as source material,
for they were penned by diverse authors: some were elected by
their locals as official correspondents to *Toveri*, others held this
position informally, and still others wrote just out of a desire to put
their personal opinions in print. So too was the subject matter
diverse, ranging from local gossip and weather reports through
reports on the activities of a local to discourses on philosophical
topics of interest to workers. Thus there is a danger in taking these
letters individually as accurate expressions of the attitudes of the
rank and file. But analysed collectively, they can be seen as the
best available source on just what local leaders and the rank and

file thought about their organization, its programs and its leaders. They can also be used as a major source in discovering the relationships that existed between various groups within the SSJ and thus can help to reveal much about the nature of Finnish-American radicalism.

One point that is indicated by a reading of these letters is that a difference in outlook existed between the local leaders writing them and national and regional leaders whose opinions find expression in the editorials and other articles in the newspaper. Part of this difference, of course, derives from the different nature of these writings: the major task of the correspondents was to report local news, especially of the socialist organizations in the area, while the editors of the paper and writers representing the SSJ nationally had to be more concerned with general affairs of importance to the district or the Federation as a whole. Naturally, this difference in purpose would be reflected in differences in tone, style and content. Still, these differences often appear to be radical and to reflect, in addition to a divergence in purpose, also divergences in attitudes. Only rarely, for example, were issues that sparked editorial concern in *Toveri*, such as the bogus "good times" that capitalists were announcing in 1916-1917, also commented on by local correspondents.[11] More common was the situation in April 1917, when reading the letters of local correspondents gives no notion that the United States had just entered the First World War, although this action received considerable coverage and comment by the editors of the paper. Another difference is evident in the continuing interest by local correspondents in trade union affairs and news of work sites, topics that received much less coverage in other sections of *Toveri*. This indicates that there was probably some basis for criticisms of *Toveri* that the editors were not sufficiently interested in union matters and the day-to-day affairs of the working class.[12] On the other hand, the correspondents wrote almost nothing about the affairs of the Federation and the American parties to which it was affiliated, except for the frequent descriptions of the business meetings of local clubs. But the editors and other leaders writing in the paper stressed these subjects above all others. Indeed, one correspondent to the paper wrote: "If we have a mind to get readers for our paper, its treatment of party affairs and its articles of propaganda must be curtailed by a great amount, and contents that satisfy the desires of the reading public of the paper must be put in their place."[13]

On the whole, local correspondents were both more specific and more general in approach than the editors and other regional

and national leaders whose writings appeared in *Toveri*. The bulk
of their letters described precise incidents in the community or
local club, and they rarely generalized from these events to put
them in a socialist perspective. They did include socialist theory in
their letters, but usually only in the form of broad platitudes, the
most common of which were various expressions of the idea that
workers must unite and work for the good of their class.[14] By
contrast, the editors of *Toveri* were remarkably adept at using
newsworthy events to illustrate specific points of socialist doctrine.
An excellent illustration of these differences in approach can be
seen by comparing the letters written by Leo Leino, the Seattle
correspondent in 1917, with those written by other correspondents.
In addition to being a local correspondent, Leino had sufficient
influence in the West to be a regional leader and he shared the
approach of that group. While he, like other correspondents, reported on local news and on the activities of the Seattle Finnish
socialist club, he, unlike most of the others, drew socialistic lessons
from these stories and explained their significance for the SSJ.[15]

Thus it appears that different groups of leaders within the SSJ
viewed the Federation from slightly different perspectives. This
circumstance created an undercurrent of conflict beneath the many
shared goals that all groups of leaders believed in and worked for
ardently. Although differences in outlook, and thus the potential
for conflict, were greatest between local leaders on the one hand
and regional and national leaders on the other, a certain amount of
tension also existed between the latter two. This was particularly
true in regard to regional leaders in the Western District, since,
unlike the other two districts of the SSJ, the area's isolation kept
leaders of national stature away. Such leaders of national reputations among Finnish socialists that did move west, men like Aku
Rissanen, Santeri Nuorteva, John Viita, and Elias Sulkanen, were
never able to remain there very long before being drawn eastward
toward the focal points of national power.[16] Thus, in the West, it
was rare that regional and national leaders were identical, as was
often the case in the other two districts. Differences in geographical perspective were therefore added to other differences that might
have existed between these two levels of leadership.

In part, the tension between national leaders of the SSJ and
regional leaders in the Western District was the result of the minor
power struggles that occur among leaders of any organization.
Thus, the executive committee of the SSJ found it necessary from
time to time to warn leaders of the Western District against exer-
cising too much independent authority.[17] But the conflict also

involved more than this, and it appears that the needs of the Federation seemed a bit different from the perspective of the Western District than they did to the national leadership. This was particularly true after affiliation with the Community Party necessitated increasing centralization in the SSJ, so that during much of the 1920s and 1930s, the national leadership attempted unsuccessfully to divest the Western District of what it felt to be "right-wing tendencies."[18] National leaders were particularly concerned about the lack of enthusiasm in *Toveri's* support for the national policies of the SSJ, and they were able in 1931 to force closure of the paper, partly on the grounds that it had become "naive" and was no longer "in shape for combat."[19]

The basis for this type of conflict was greater, however, between local leaders and rank and file on the one hand and regional and national leaders on the other. This tension is visible in much of the day-to-day business of the Federation. It is evident, for example, in the debate over "hall socialism" that engaged Finnish socialists for as long as they belonged to formal organizations. While regional and national leaders continually urged members of the Federation to spend less time on social activities and entertainments at the socialist hall and more on political, economic and educational activities, they were for the most part ignored on the local level where social activities continued to flourish.[20] But just as SSJ members at the local level refused to reduce activities that their leaders thought unnecessary, they also refused to support activities that the leaders urged on them. In the minds of most leaders, one of the major purposes of the SSJ was the education of the Finnish working class and they frequently urged members to spend more time learning, and teaching to others, the doctrines of socialism, but never with much success.[21] Finally, in 1930, the executive committee of the Federation resorted to requiring each local to hold at least one meeting a month where issues of importance to the working class were discussed.[22] Even when members took part in such educational activities, their participation was apparently often passive, for Aare Hyrske, an organizer in the Western District in 1920, had to tell local leaders to remind their members that speeches by the organizers were not "occasions where they are merely pumped up with socialism, but rather that they have the right to address questions and criticisms to the organizer."[23]

Perhaps for most leaders, the primary purpose of the SSJ was to tie Finnish-Americans to the American working-class movement and thus to further the goals of that movement. Consequently their writings are filled with suggestions and demands that members of the Federation take active roles in the American class struggle,[24] but most of these stimulated either passive disregard or excuses such as that by a Seattle correspondent that "surely it is not proper of us Finns [of Seattle], who are only a handful, to crow that we alone could cram the people of this city of 300,000 full of the Marxist world view."[25]

A good example of the difficulty that leaders of the SSJ had in persuading members to involve themselves in the American working-class movement was the problem of getting Finnish socialists to join the International Labor Defense (ILD). When the ILD, an organization backed by American communists and dedicated to aiding prisoners in the class war, was founded in 1925, national and regional leaders of the Federation urged Finns to join. When the response of the membership to this appeal proved disappointing, some locals, such as the Astoria local in the West, decided to affiliate with the ILD themselves, automatically assessing each of their members for dues in the organization. But even this tactic proved unsuccessful in getting many Finns into the ILD, and in 1932 the executive committee decided that the Federation would join it as a whole, paying dues for each of its members and then collecting them from the locals.[26]

While this type of mild conflict was evident in much of the normal operations of the SSJ, it was intensified whenever a major crisis threatened the survival of the Federation. At such times, the basically passive posture of local leaders and the rank and file toward the policies of their leaders turned into active interest. Thus, in 1913-1914, when the Western District was split apart by disagreement over how much support to give the radical unionism of the Industrial Workers of the World (IWW, leaders whose positions differed from influential locals in the Northwest found life a bit uncomfortable as they faced opposition from an aroused membership. August Wesley, an official organizer of the SSJ, who advocated support of the IWW, found the doors of several socialist halls around the West closed to him.[27] When John Viita, chosen editor of the *Toveri* in 1913, began supporting the policies of the IWW in the newspaper, he was quickly recalled.[28] Although Viita's predecessor, Santeri Nuorteva, had the support of the majority in the Western District in his opposition to the IWW, the pressure placed on him as a leader in a crisis induced him to resign in 1913 shortly after the conflict began in earnest. As he wrote to Aku Rissanen: "I am soon leaving here for peace from the hell that I have experience here for a year and a half."[29]

During 1919-1921, the SSJ struggled through another major crisis as Finnish socialists debated, in the wake of the Russian Revolution, whether to remain in the Socialist Party of America or to join the fledgling American communist movement. Again the crisis brought the conflict between leaders and followers into the open. Organizers sent by the national organization to explain its policies in the West found that they could no longer expect to be listened to with respect at every local where they spoke. What met them at some locals was far from respect, as the tone of the comment by one local correspondent in the West on organizer Moses Hahl illustrates: "This Moses of ours seems to be more talkative than Aaron's brother, Moses, in the Old Testament, but for all his talk there is so much less socialist clarity."[30] Lauri Brusila, another SSJ organizer in the West, learned from ample experience how Finnish socialists in the Pacific Northwest responded to leaders with whom they disagreed,[31] until he was moved to write: "The concept has crystallized among the people that one can no longer be a proper socialist or a true blue class warrior unless he is capable of spitting cleanly in the eye of some party official."[32] This conflict continued through a series of crises involving tactics and ideology during the 1920s, but it was more muted, because the increasing centralization of the Federation under communist directives made open criticism of leaders more reprehensible.

During any period of conflict within the SSJ, the clearest way in which ordinary members showed their dissatisfaction with the policies of their leaders was to leave the organization altogether. This was not a small step for most of them. Even to those more or less apathetic to the goals of the SSJ, it meant dissolving friendships and foresaking a whole world of cultural activities; to dedicated socialists, leaving an organization considered to be *the* organ of the Finnish-American working class was not to be done without serious consideration. Yet during each major crisis thousands of Finnish socialists expressed their disagreement with the policies of their organization by leaving it. Largely as a result of the conflict over the IWW, SSJ membership in the Western District declined from 3,458 to 2,130 between 1912 and 1915.[33] Between April and November of 1920, during the dispute over which American party to affiliate with, membership in Oregon and Washington dropped from about 900 to 682. Between 1919 and 1921 membership in the SSJ as a whole declined from 10,884 to 6,390.[34]

Perhaps the greatest crisis to face the SSJ began in 1925 when orders from the international communist movement required a reorganization of the Federation that threatened to eliminate the open, socially oriented locals that were the heart of the organization in the minds of the rank and file. As a result, many of the local leaders and members rose up bitterly against regional and national leaders who were attempting to realize the objectives of the international movement.[35] Thousands of others left the Federation as membership dropped from 7,134 in 1924 to a low of 2,779 in August, 1927.[36]

But these periods of crisis were not only times of conflict and defection; they were also times of analysis. Something had gone wrong, and membership of the SSJ from top to bottom sought to discover what it was. In doing so, they were forced to define specifically what had for most of them been only a vague assumption—the nature and purpose of their Federation. The depth of the crisis during 1924-1927 over reorganization of the SSJ brought out an especially large amount of agonized analyses that reveal clearly the basis of conflict between local leaders and regional and national leaders. The major concern of leaders at all levels at this time was survival of the Federation, but they saw survival in different terms. To regional and national leaders, the major purpose of the SSJ was to unite Finnish-Americans with the American working-class movement, and to them survival meant a satisfactory realization of this goal. Thus, they worked hard to reconcile the demands of their leaders in the international and American communist movement with the needs and desires of Finnish-American socialists.[37]

The local leaders and the rank and file, however, saw survival of the SSJ differently. By their very positions within the Federation, their major concern was the local club, and survival to them meant the club's survival. Thus they worried about maintaining its membership at a certain level and about continuing undiminished the broad range of activities that supported this membership. To them socialism meant something very specific that involved less the affairs of the world than it did converting *individual* workers to correct social consciousness. To local leaders, the crisis was basically a moral crisis, in which declines in membership and activity led to a moral decline among Finnish-American workers in the area. A correspondent from Kent, Washington, disgusted at the lack of activity among local Finnish workers, expressed this moral indignation, writing: "We are exemplary sprouts of this rotten society and also its props. Isn't that so?"[38] A good example of the jeremiads that appeared regularly in the letters of local correspondents, especially in 1926, is the following by Kalle Kaljupää of Portland, Oregon:

Stills, beer, and debauchery are already dangers threatening the culture of the entire Finnish-American working class. Our children to a great extent have already left us and in large groups they speed to seek their pleasure in dance halls that resemble saunas used to malt barley. And we often wonder why things have turned out this way. Some find the blame here, others, there. As social democrats, we too were very handy at sticking the blame on society as a whole, and we left our educational work to be done by it also. And now, in a way, the results of this bad practice are before us. But, now that we at least see and feel where the Finns are also sinking, we must hasten to save the good. We must forget personal bickering and join all of us together to raise by our common strength the level of the spiritual and moral lives of ourselves and our children. We must begin action to increase the combat fitness of our class.[39]

The conflict of local leaders and rank and file with regional and national leaders stemmed not only from a difference in prespective on what the Federation was supposed to accomplish, but also from a general suspicion of leaders. Finns (like most other peoples, perhaps) customarily were wary of the *herrat*, the "big shots," who, full of self-importance, worked to lead their "inferiors" down the true path,[40] and something of this feeling invaded the attitudes of Finnish-American socialists toward their leaders. For example, local correspondents from time to time observed that their leaders had soft jobs and spent unnecessary time performing worthless jobs.[41]

Adding to this traditional suspicion of leaders was the fact that Finns found an unfamiliar form of leadership in America. Like most European immigrants to America, most Finns had their roots in traditional peasant societies where leader-follower relationships were usually traditional, personal and informal, and thus often muted. Indeed, when compared to the professional, bureaucratic and businesslike leadership required in the modern industrial world of America, it was possible to believe that this type of society had no real leaders at all.[42] At least this was the opinion of the correspondent to *Toveri* who wrote under the name of Asarias Vilja:

In American bourgeois society it is typical for the people to follow leaders, fawning on them, persuading themselves and their leaders how important, big and honorable they are. Political clubs, social and business life seem to depend on artificially created, ornamental leaders with supposed abilities. Any rascal whatsoever can make himself listened to and obeyed, if only he has first succeeded in manipulating, stealing and forcefully oppressing his neighbors. Then these leaders need no more than to say sarcastically "you are intelligent" and those fools say in turn that there is a wise fellow. Certainly, the fashion of following leaders has come from the general customs of American life to the workers' organizations still existing in our time. It can be often heard said, when talk turns to the real purpose of the working-class movement, that it surely is so, but we don't have the leaders. The entire spirit of the organization depends on the leaders.[43]

Amidst its bitterness, this statement by an unkown correspondent contains an important insight. For, if the modern, bureaucratic form of leadership that the Finns experienced in America was something new to them, it was one of the many new experiences forced upon them by America. Thus the forming of organizations such as the SSJ that needed this type of leader and learning to follow this leadership were significant parts of the process of Americanization for Finnish socialists. Like other aspects of Americanization, these changes were difficult and often resisted (as the letter of Asarias Vilja indicates), and thus acceptance of the new, modern leadership of the Federation took time.

Therefore, a basis for conflict between followers (local leaders and rank and file) and leaders (regional and national) existed within the SSJ in the Pacific Northwest. This being the case, we can perhaps best understand the nature of the SSJ by viewing it on two levels. The upper level was the world of regional and national leaders, where it was the tie with the American working-class movement that was important. The lower level was the local community, the world of the local leaders and the rank and file, where importance was placed on group activities among Finns and on individual commitment to socialism.

The leaders in the upper level were concerned with things such as strikes and elections and party purges—the stuff that makes history—and thus have received most attention by investigators of the SSJ. The followers in the lower level were concerned primarily with a whole cultural mileu that gave self-identity, moral direction, and proper working-class meaning to the lives of Finnish workers in a community. This is not to say that local leaders and the rank and file were not interested in strikes and elections and such; they certainly were, as leaders discovered periodically when their decisions threatened local notions of what the SSJ should be. But, except during such rather brief periods of crisis, two almost separate levels did exist within the SSJ, connected primarily by a common dedication to a socialistic world view. Within this dual structure, regional and national leaders were primarily responsible for establishing the national policies of the Federation, while local leaders decided how socialism would work in the community. Both groups were important in determining the strength and shape of socialism among Finnish immigrants in America, and thus it is necessary to know what each was doing and thinking in order to understand what Finnish-American socialism was all about.

# Notes:

1. John Higham, ed., *Ethnic Leadership in America* (Baltimore: Johns Hopkins University Press, 1978), p. ix.

2. See, for example, S. Ilmonen, *Amerikan suomalainen sivistyshistoria: Johtavia aatteita, harrastuksia, yhteispyrintöjä ja tapahtumia siirtokansan keskuudessa*, Vol. II, (Hancock: Suom.-Lut. Kustannusliike, 1931), p. 179; Reino Kero, "The Roots of Finnish-American Left-Wing Radicalism," *Publications of the Institute of General History, University of Turku, Finland*, No. 5, (1973), p. 46; Auvo Kostiainen, *The Forging of Finnish-American Communism, 1919-1924: A Study in Ethnic Radicalism* (Turku, Turun Yliopisto, 1978), pp. 32-33.

3. Cf., James V. Downton, Jr., *Rebel Leadership: Commitment and Charisma in the Revolutionary Process* (New York: Free Press, 1973), pp. 6-7.

4. Cf., Nathan Irvin Huggins, "Afro-Americans," in Higham, *op. cit.*, p. 93.

5. Auvo Kostiainen sees the same sort of ambiguous relationship in Superior, Wisconsin, between the Finnish socialist local there and the *Työmies* (Worker), the organ of the Central District of the SSJ published there. See, Kostiainen, *op. cit.*, p. 78.

6. *Toveri*, June 6, 1922, p. 2.

7. Ibid.

8. E.g., ibid., October 18, 1926, p. 2.

9. Ibid., May 17, 1921, p. 3; see also June 13, 1922, p. 3.

190    G. Hummasti

10. Ibid., June 27, 1922, p.3; see also February 15, 1917, p. 4.

11. See, for example, ibid., January 6, 1916, pp. 2 and 3; February 1, 1917, p. 4.

12. See ibid., June 28, 1917, p. 2; July 19, 1917, p. 2; *Amerikan ss. järjestön länsipiirin ensimmäisen piirikokouksen pöytäkirja, pidetty Astoriassa, Ore., huhtik. 21-23 p:nä, 1911* (Astoria: Toveri Kirjspaino, 1911), pp. 40-41, for examples of this criticism and of the reactions of *Toveri* officials to it.

13. *Toveri*, February 19, 1917, p. 3.

14. See, for example, ibid., January 6, 1916, p. 4; February 3, 1917, pp. 4-5; May 3, 1921, p. 3; August 7, 1924, p. 7; October 7, 1926, p. 3.

15. For examples of letters from Seattle written by Leion, see ibid., February 2, 1917, p. 3; February 8, 1917, p. 6; February 27, 1917, p. 5.

16. The one exception to this generalization—Eemeli Parras, who came to Astoria to serve as editor of the *Toveri* in 1922 and remained there until 1931—came West, I suspect (though without any definite evidence), to escape the factional infighting occuring at the centres of power. At least, he seems to have played little part in this conflict in his years as the editor of the *Toveri*.

17. E.g., *Toveri*, April 1, 1920, p. 2.

18. E.g., ibid., February 4, 1927, p. 4; May 2, 1928, p. 2; September 23, 1930, p. 1; *Työmies*, September 28, 1934, p. 5.

19. Astoria *Daily Messenger*, February 25, 1931, p. 1; *Työmies*, April 10, 1931, p. 1.

20. For examples of the numerous exhortations against hall socialism, see F.J. Syrjälä, *Kolmannen Amerikan suomalaisen sosialistijärjestön edustajakokouksen pöytäkirja. Kokous pidetty Hancockissa, Mich., 20-23 p. elok., 1909* (Fitchburg: Raivaaja Kirjapaino, 1909), pp. 243-45; *Toveri*, September 15, 1917, p. 4; September 9, 1921, p. 2; November 23, 1927, p. 2.

21. E.g., *Toveri*, December 2, 1920, p. 6; May 3, 1921, p. 4; October 20, 1921, p. 6; March 31, 1922, p. 6; *Työmies*, January 21, 1932, p. 5.

22. *Toveri*, July 23, 1930, p. 3; Dec. 16, 1930, p. 2.

23. Ibid., April 3, 1920, p. 2.

24. E.g., ibid., March 14, 1919, pp. 4-6; July 2, 1919, p. 2; *Industrialisti*, June 1, 1918, p. 4.

25. *Toveri*, March 9, 1918, p. 4; see also, April 13, 1921, p. 3.

26. Ibid., June 18, 1926, p. 6, February 18, 1927, p. 6; November 15, 1929, p. 6; *Työmies*, December 1, 1932, p. 5.

27. *Sosialisti*, August 8, 1914, p. 3; November 18, 1914, p. 3; May 26, 1916, p. 2.

28. *Yhdysvaltain suom. sos. järjestön länsipiirin ylimääräisen piirikokouksen pöytäkirja, pidetty Astoriassa, Ore., huhtik. 23-27 p:nä ja toukok. 2 p:nä, 1914* (Astoria: Toveri Press, 1914), pp. 20, 24.

29. *Sosialisti*, January 28, 1915, p. 2.

30. *Toveri*, April 13, 1920, p.3.

31. E.g., ibid., May 14, 1921, p. 3.

32. Ibid., April 30, 1921, p. 6. The editors of the *Toveri* also got involved in a disagreement with an SSJ organizor (Sefa Lepistö) at this time, see ibid., April 2, 1920, p. 2.

33. *Yhdysvaltain suom. sos. järjestön länsipiirin kolmannen varsinaisen piirikokouksen pöytäkirja, pidetty Astoriassa, Ore., huhtik. 13-14 ja 17-18 pp., 1916* (Astoria: Lännen Työväen Kustannusyhtiö, 1916), p. 10.

34. *Toveri*, January 21, 1920, p. 4; April 19, 1920, p. 2; December 11, 1920, p. 4; *Suomalaisen sosialistijärjestön kahdeksannen edustajakokouksen pöytäkirja laadittu Chicagossa, Ill., 28 p. tammik.—2 p. helmikuuta, 1922, pidetystä S.S. Järjestön edustajakokouksesta* (n.p., 1922), pp. 5-6.

35. E.g., *Toveri*, November 26, 1924, p. 6; January 31, 1925, p. 2; February 24, 1925, pp. 4-5; July 24, 1925, p. 2.

36. Ibid., February 3, 1925, p. 2; March 24, 1928, p. 2.

37. Almost any publication or document of the SSJ at this time, which contain basically the expressions of regional and national leaders, clearly conveys this attitude. For a nice statement of this concern in an earlier crisis, see ibid., May 12, 1921, p. 2.

38. Ibid., October 20, 1926, p. 2.

39. Ibid., October 7, 1926, p. 3; see also, October 14, 1926, p. 2; October 19, 1926, p. 2.

40. For expressions of this attitude, see ibid., February 19, 1917, p. 3; March 12, 1918, p. 3.

41. See ibid., February 6, 1919, p. 4; April 30, 1921, p. 6.

42. On the growth of a new modern leadership among other ethnic groups, see Higham, *op. cit.*, p. 11 and Josef J. Barton, "Eastern and Southern Europeans," in ibid., p. 165.

43. *Toveri*, March 2, 1918, p. 4.

# Embers of Revival: Laestadian Schisms in Northeast Minnesota, 1900-1940

## Marvin G. Lamppa

Of three Lutheran movements established by Finnish immigrants in America, only the Apostolic remains.[1] It swept through Finnish-American settlements at the turn of the century as part of the Laestadian revival, and by 1940 had splintered into five distinct factions, all calling themselves Apostolic Lutheran. It is indeed remarkable that this movement, which refused to emphasize wordly organization and church structure, should be the only one remaining independent. Walter Kukkonen of the Lutheran School of Theology in Chicago explains:

> The fact that these church bodies have maintained their independent existence suggests that in the preservation and transmission of their heritage they have adopted a conservative stance which gives priority to maintenance of a tradition over further development of their own life and active participation in the life of the larger community.[2]

Today all Apostolic churches and congregations, no matter how divided, are similar in their practice of strict fundamentalism, spontaneous sermons, unabridged reading of scripture, the singing of simple hymns, and in their strong belief in the power of the spoken word. In some the fire of earlier times seems to have cooled and there are those who say, "You don't hear the same here as in the days of Saastamoinen and Vepsäläinen."[3] But now and then in simple frame churches in Thomson, Cokato and Virginia, worshippers still arise crying, "I no longer want the pleasures of this world! I know the Lord is guiding us ... gathering us ... leading us to everlasting glory and thanksgiving!"[4]

Laestadianism was one of many revival movements born in Finland and Sweden during the nineteenth century in response to such great calamities as famines, epidemics and war. While European Laestadians retained their revival flavour safe under the umbrella of an established state church institution, the American version encountered stresses and influences arising from a rapidly evolving society intent on technological change and impatient for the gratification of wants and the indulgence of appetites. In a land of mass production, instalment buying, reckless optimism and extravagence, immigrant Laestadians were hard pressed to retain their identity and the essence of their faith: the powerful awareness of the living presence of Christ within gatherings.

Without a central church authority to mediate disputes and establish unity, it was inevitable that this movement, which relied primarily on interpretations of scripture by laymen, should encounter controversy and schism. The dichotomy resulting from attempts to preserve a heritage while at the same time spreading a spiritual awakening led to the birth in Minnesota and Wisconsin of a wing of the faith that has no counterpart in Europe. This paper seeks to inquire into basic Laestadian beliefs and to identify those events which caused its fragmentation and the development of its uniquely American "evangelical" arm.

The ecstacies of this "living faith," so often proclaimed by those of Apostolic leaning, are rooted in a tradition established in Swedish Lapland by Lars Levi Laestadius, rector of Kaaresuvanto and Pajala from 1825 to 1861. A university-trained and ordained minister of the Church of Sweden, Laestadius experienced tremendous personal tragedy and suffering before receiving a powerful awakening while listening to Maria, a simple Lapp woman, tell how she personally experienced the presence of God after a long search.[5] Herein lies the essence of Laestadian thought: a sudden feeling of awakened joy, experienced sometimes at a moment of greatest depression, through clear realization that all sins are forgiven through Christ. Describing his awakening while listening to Maria, Laestadius later wrote, "I experienced a foretaste of Heaven that evening."[6]

The element of suffering as crucial to enlightenment is now new to world religious philosophy, and the people of Lapland—and Finland for that matter—were no strangers to suffering. This may be a reason for the phenomenal appeal of the Laestadian revival in those areas. Certainly the cold bureaucracy of the Swedish Church in 1860 held little appeal for the still half-pagan Lapps. Lapland was a cruel place and "a veneer of nominal Christianity and pagan superstitution could not begin to cover the drunkenness, immorality and violence which had become a way of life for the poverty-stricken Lapps."[7]

For the next fifteen years, Laestadius invited all who would listen to "repent and receive the gift of the Holy Ghost." He preached:

> To have Christian faith, one must go through the order
> of grace in the same way as did the disciples. They had
> to weep and lament when the Savior died; they had to
> first sink into unbelief and hopelessness. Danger to the
> soul must come before one can long after, or yearn for
> salvation. One cannot be saved as easy as people think
> ... only through great tribulation must man enter into
> 'Life'.[8]

To the sinning listener, his low spiritual state made him more ready to receive salvation than the self-righteous churchgoer who condemned him. And Laestadius openly rebuked these self-righteous people. "He who has dead faith in his skull has no penitence, he ponders nothing, he never doubts his salvation!"[9]

His preaching caused much excitement. Those who listened to him experienced visions, ecstacies and trances and a lay preacher movement was born which carried news of "awakenings" and "miracles" to many parts of Norway, Sweden, Finland and Russia.[10] In some cases, extreme fanaticism resulted, illiterate men identified themselves as Christ, women left their husbands to become apostles' wives and unbelievers were molested and even murdered.[11]

The death of Laestadius in 1861 left the movement in the hands of lay preacher Juhani Raattamaa, a gloomy and often depressed man, whose early sermons inspired much guilt but little rejoicing. But in 1853, while studying Luther's third sermon on the gospel in his *Church Postil,* the "power of the keys," Raattamaa became convinced that grace and its accompanying "rejoicing" could be achieved through open confession, the laying on of hands, and congregational pronouncement of absolution. His success gave the movement its unique practice of both confession and absolution, involving, however, only "true believers in the atoning sacrifice of Christ."[12] Raattamaa's effect on the movement was perma-

nent and from 1853 on, penitent sinners could receive personal
absolution from either a believing preacher or another Laestadian
"Christian."[13] Believing this, a person receives "faith" and is accepted as a member of the "true church of Christ."

The year 1864 marked the beginning of a significant population movement to America from Norway and Sweden. By 1870, a
large number of these people, many of whom were Finns, had
arrived in Michigan's copper country. Contrary to popular belief,
there are indications that few of these early arrivals were practising
Laestadians. Although a Scandinavian Lutheran Church established
in Quincy, Michigan, in 1867 had a large percentage of Finnish
immigrants as members, the letters of its pastor, H.C. Roernas, do
not mention Laestadians until 1872. In that year, he wrote about
"an ecstatic movement that had recently swept through Finnish
communities in Calumet and Quincy which bore resemblences to
the movement begun by Laestadius which had led to the religious
fanaticism in Kautokeino."[14] Considering that the rapid spread of
the movement did not really begin until after 1869, one can assume
that early conversions in Michigan were the work of one man,
Vittikahuhta Anti, who is singled out as a ringleader of the "ecsta-
sies" in Pastor Roernas' 1872 communication.[15] American Apostolic
tradition also credits Vittikahuhta with many early conversions in
Quincy.[16]

There is evidence that Laestadian practice in the state of
Minnesota may have predated Vittikahuhta's efforts in Calumet.
Cokato reminiscences written in 1879 describe Finns gathering in
log cabins in the late 1860s to hear "the word" as preached by
Laestadians Isak Barberg and Isak Branstrom.[17] Shortly after 1876,
these same men were instrumental in building a church in Cokato,
the first Finnish church on Minnesota soil.[18] By 1880, Laestadian
congregations were active in the Minnesota communities of Frank-
lin, Cokato, Holmes City, New York Mills and Thomson.[19] Minnesota's congregations were usually led by lay preachers "who did a
busy week's work as did John P. Marttala on his farm in Frank-
lin."[20] Religious interest was spurred in that community in 1880 by
the arrival of Angelica Charlotta Jokinen, daughter of Laestadius
himself:

> With her arrival, she brought a resurgence of her fa-
> ther's credo at its purest, and she did not hesitate to
> remind the local community if they strayed from it. Her
> only child died young, and she herself died on 19 Sep-
> tember 1900; a monument erected by friends marks the

grave of this descendant of the "apostle of the North"
in the first permanent Finnish settlement in Minnesota.[21]

The fact that Isaac Raattamaa settled in Thomson, just west
of Duluth, was enough to establish that area as the first centre of
Laestadian activity in Northeast Minnesota. With help from Peter
Esko, conversions were made and an organized congregation was
established in 1877.[22] In that same year, an Apostolic Church was
built in Holmes City and ecstatic gatherings led by lay preacher
Israel Hagel were taking place in log cabins in New York Mills.
Early baptismal records for the New York Mills Church show the
name Salomon Korteniemi of Calumet, Michigan, as pastor.[23] This
indicates that Minnesota Laestadian groups considered themselves
as extensions of the Calumet congregation and the international
Laestadian community. John Takkinen's visits to Minnesota communities in the 1880s "to conduct services and check the literacy
of parish members"[24] is further evidence of early unity.

Expulsion of Calumet Laestadians from the Scandinavian
Church in 1871-72 had led in 1873 to the establishment of the
Salomon Korteniemi Lutheran Society, the first organized Finnish
Lutheran congregation in America.[25] Although the name Apostolic
Lutheran was not applied until 1879, the establishment of this
society permanently split Finnish Apostolics from the mainstream
of American Lutheranism and left for them the task of organizing a
church of their own. This made American Laestadians different
from European Laestadians. Walter Kukkonen describes this difference:

> One major fact of life set them apart from Laestadians
> in Finland: America had no state church. Unable to be
> a movement within a church, Laestadianism became a
> church in America. Men who would have functioned as
> lay preachers in Finland became ministers of congrega-
> tions, albeit elected annually with other congregational
> officers.[26]

However, continued reliance by American Laestadians on the
European movement was clearly illustrated in 1877 with the arrival of John Takkinen in Calumet to solve disagreements between
opposing groups within the congregation. It also marked the beginning of a strong organizing effort throughout Michigan, Wisconsin
and Minnesota. Rituals of standing and kneeling were abolished

and replaced with simple services, hymns and sermons, and under his leadership the first Finnish-language book printed in America, the *Aapinen,* was completed.[27] Takkinen's harsh rebukes against "believers" and "non-believers" alike caused a segment of his Calumet congregation to leave and take up residence in a nearby Finnish hall. These *Haalilaiset* Laestadians took the view that no commandments or rebukes should be preached to those who already had the faith, and preachers should be discreet in preaching to non-believers.[28] They also frowned upon Takkinen's demanding requirements for confession and absolution.

It was the Takkinen brand of Laestadianism that first spread to Minneapolis, Brainerd and the Vermilion iron mining district, where many Finns were finding employment during the 1880s.[29] The formation of the Minnesota Iron Company in 1882 heralded the greatest mining effort of the age, and within two decades a string of mining camps and towns stretched across a distance of some ninety miles in northeast Minnesota, housing thousands of immigrants, a majority of whom were Finns. It was a bleak world to which these Finns came, a land of rubble, open pits and hastily built shack towns. Mines were dangerous and accidents were daily occurrences.[30] The barrens and cold of Lapland could not have been more harsh than the stark reality Finns faced on the Vermilion and Mesabi iron ranges.

That Laestadians were among early mining crews on the Vermilion Range cannot be doubted. Miners were recruited from Michigan's copper and iron districts and recollections of early Soudan Location residents indicate that by 1907 an Apostolic Church "located not far from Soudan's post office" was already falling into disrepair.[31] Although the building has long since vanished and its records have disappeared, it is recalled that Paul and John Leinonen, Peter Pahakka of Tower, John Pöylio, Evert and Sophia Peitso, Tillie Mikkola, William Miettunen, John Huttula and Maria Sippola of Soudan were all active members of its congregation.[32] Hans Wasastjerna places the Peitsos and Leinonens on the Vermilion Range as early as 1883.[33] He also notes a purchase of Ely's Temperance Hall "in 1896 by the Laestadian sect."[34]

By this time, the evangelical zeal of men such as Arthur L. Heideman and a host of lay preacher followers, with blessings from Finland,[35] brought about many conversions and established Finnish Apostolic Lutheran congregations in Minnesota's communities of Menagha, Wolf Lake, Floodwood and Virginia.[36] Mining and lumbering brought many Finns to Virginia, Minnesota, including Laestadians John and Hilda Pertula, Isaac and Sophia Lamppa, Sam and Maria Hill, Jakko and Maria Castren, and by 1896, a Finnish Apostolic congregation was firmly established in that community.[37] Until 1903, when a church was built at 222 Second Street North, services were held in homes.[38] Travelling preachers Jacob Wuollet, Peter Raattamaa and John Pollari preached "free and full salvation in the redemptive work of Christ"[39] to excited gatherings in homes north of Virginia's Elm Street. However, these early Virginia Laestadians were not adverse to having seminary-trained and ordained minister Heikki Sarvela of the Finnish Evangelical Church perform baptisms and marriages, as the Virginia Apostolic Church records for 1896 clearly show.

It was in Virginia that Isaac Karl Lamppa, later recognized as a leading Minnesota "evangelical of the Apostolic faith,"[40] began his preaching career. Born in Kainulesjarvi in Norbottsenlund, Sweden, on February 24, 1866, he came to Michigan's copper country along with two cousins, Peter and Herman, at about the same time A.L. Heideman was making his debut in America.[41] Family tradition places his first indoctrination to Laestadian thought in Sweden, but upon his arrival in America, his interest and activity in religion grew rapidly. In 1901, he was performing baptisms in Virginia[42] and by the time he established a pioneer business and homestead in Embarrass in 1903, he was well launched into a preaching career that stressed that "the Gospel of grace, if truly believed, bears good fruits of itself, without any teachings regarding these fruits."[43] His earliest work took him from his Embarrass homestead to homes and churches in Ely, Soudan, Virginia and Hibbing to preach, officiate at baptisms and to "evangelize."[44] His early sermons contained rebukes against drinking and self-righteousness and stressed the power of faith through readings from scripture.[45] His emotional sermons brought about conversions, and as his popularity increased, he became a trusted preacher of the Heideman version of Laestadian Lutheranism.[46] After 1911, he was often called to preach in the "Big Church" in Calumet and other places in Canada and the United States.[47] Lamppa joined a long list of charismatic travelling preachers who carried the "fires of revival" to many parts of the land.

The effect of the charismatic preachers on Minnesota's Finnish communities during the first two decades of the twentieth century is notable. Apostolic churches and congregations were established in Crosby, Duluth, Chisholm, Embarrass, Cedar Valley, Finlayson, Kettle River, Topelius, Sparta, Trout Lake, Hibbing, Pike River, Automba, Wright, Cromwell, Vermillion, Cook and Eveleth.[48] Most of the congregations considered themselves as part of one large community and gatherings took place in homes and in churches with loud singing, rejoicing and stamping of feet. These activities which marked the behaviour of Minnesota congregations were strikingly similar to those common at most American frontier revivals and were called *liikutukset* in Finnish, which means emotional agitation caused by powerful experiences with sin and "grace."[49] *Liikutukset* had always been part of Laestadian credo and were particularly strong during the early "awakening" in Lapland, Preachers Lamppa, Halvari, Pollari and Heideman himself, reminded American Finns that "God has given to mankind several times of visitation, or periods when His Spirit worked powerfully among men, calling them to repentance and faith."[50] They looked upon their time, 1900-1920, as one of those times of awakening, and in those terms, many Minnesota Laestadians saw themselves as the direct recipients of the same "spiritual lightning" that was received in Jerusalem on Pentecost Day, and by Laestadius in 1848.[51] The effect was powerful, and the feeling of the community developed by shared "physical experiences with the Holy Ghost" contributed to the fact that Finnish Apostolics were able not only to persevere in Minnesota's harsh mining climate, but to play a major role in the development of surrounding rural areas.

There is evidence that Finnish Apostolics made desirable workers in the Minnesota mines. In a scene filled with labour unrest, believing Laestadians willingly took the most menial of jobs with little complaint, and Oliver Iron Mining Company readily acknowledged that "church Finns were better workers than 'Red Finns'."[52] Not only was Oliver Iron Mining Company willing to hire "Church Finns," a portion of whom were Laestadians, but it was also willing to make donations to promote religious activity. Oliver's generosity arose in part out of a desire to enlarge that degree of social stability church-going communities promise. "It seems exceptional that any lease of property or improvements was undertaken by any church without soliciting a subscription from it [Oliver]."[53] This kind of support may well be the reason why Virginia Apostolics had a church building as early as 1903. Certainly, when repairs and improvements were needed for the building twenty years later, Virginia's Apostolics were not slow to ask for assistance from a number of private sources, including the Oliver Iron Mining Company.[54] At that time, the Virginia Apostolic Church had a membership of 125, a congregation of approximately 200, and held regular monthly services, including "a summer school for religious teaching."[55] There is no doubt that Oliver officials carefully investigated the Virginia Apostolic group before deciding to help them. Fred Mott, mining superintendent, noted:

...We have made inquiries for the purpose of ascertaining if or not the proposition is meritorious. The results are favorable. Reverent Isaac Lamppa is pastor of the church. We recommend a donation of $100.[56]

Oliver Iron Mining Company interest in promoting religious activity extended at times beyond the mining towns into the outlying areas, where Laestadian activity was great. A 1920 communication acknowledged a request for assistance from Apostolics in the Pike River Settlement, and Fred Mott commented:

While this request is somewhat out of ordinary in that it is asking assistance for people not directly interested in or about the mines, Mr. West and the writer feel that some encouragement be given them along these lines, and we recommend a donation of $150 to assist them in completing their place of worship.[57]

Mining company interest in attracting church-minded Finns to the mines brought a group of "firstborn" Laestadians to Sparta, just after the ill-fated miners' strike of 1907.[58] Led by lay preacher Caleb Erickson, people such as Ed Ogren, Thomas Flom, Arvid Nelson, John Tiensuu, John Long, Aldrich Long, and Oskar Pudas[59] gathered in curtainless mining location homes and rejoiced in noisy sessions. Having no church of their own, Mesabi Range *esikoiset* gathered in the old Sparta-Genoa School to hear travelling preachers Matt Uuskoski, Henry Koller or John Pouri deliver "the Word" in straightforward language.[60] First-born Laestadians were quick to introduce the English language to interpret sermons "if there were some present who didn't understand Finnish."[61] Sparta's congregation was small and they did not hesitate to use the services of seminary-trained minister M.E. Merijarvi of the Suomi Synod to administer baptism and weddings—although in the case of a wedding in the John Tiensuu home, as soon as Merijarvi was gone, Caleb Erickson opened the Bible at random and preached a spontaneous sermon, inspiring much rejoicing.[62]

A tendency for Apostolic families to leave mining towns to settle in rural areas is apparent in local church records and family histories, but should not be looked at as a phenomenon peculiar to Laestadians. A large number of Finns, socialist, evangelical and Apostolic alike, left the mines to which they had been first attracted and settled in Sandy, Pike River, Florenton, Embarrass, Vermilion, Waasa, Palo, Makinen, Hutter, Zim and Cherry. Reasons given include "miserable working conditions," "lack of jobs," and "an opportunity to own land." At any rate, by 1925 a large Finnish Apostolic community was established in the rocky country-side between the Vermilion and Mesabi towns.

It was a difficult life for these people. Their efforts are notable: felling trees, hewing logs, blasting stumps, piling rocks, cutting wood, draining fields, making hay, milking cows, churning butter, building barns and fences and somehow finding time to construct a church in Embarrass in 1906.[63] Before the church was built, gatherings took place in log cabins under the direction of preachers Peter Raattamaa, William Alajaki, Arthur Heideman and John Pollari.[64] The land on which the church was built was do-nated by Sam Norha. The congregation elected John Pylkka as its first pastor, but he was soon replaced by Isaac Lamppa.[65]

The frontier setting, a continual struggle for existence and unending hardship among the rocks and stumps of Embarrass, Ver-milion and Pike River townships contributed to a strong sense of community among Laestadian families. The coming of a charis-matic preacher was an event that broke the drab monotony of everyday life, and people gathered from miles around to hear the "Word," socialize and "rejoice in a feeling of oneness in Christ."[66] Preachers were rated on the amount of *liikutukset* they could inspire in listeners, and some interspersed their sermons with a great amount of singing to keep feelings high.[67] The effect, many times, was devastating: " . . . chairs and windows were broken and people jumped about and embraced openly."[68] The position of the *lukkari* became increasingly important in bringing about "high spirits" in religious gatherings in Minnesota. The *lukkari* was the song leader and in the Embarrass, Pike River and other Apostolic churches "a special pew was reserved for him from which he would post the hymn number and lead the singing."[69]

The northeast Minnesota Apostolic congregations were not isolated from the American Laestadian community as a whole, and were in many ways an integral part of that greater community. The construction of a new barn could hardly take place without help from Thomson or Cokato and news of the birth of a child was joyfully shared by Laestadians from New York Mills to Calumet. The *Walvoja, Kristillinen Kuukauslehti, Päivälehti,* and *Rauhan Tervehdus,* brought devotional reading and news of the day to practically every Minnesota Laestadian family. The *Walvoja* "be-came a sort of trumpet for various Apostolic Lutheran groups in the country." However, "internal differences among Laestadians made it impossible for the *Walvoja* to serve in that capacity indefi-nitely."[70] In spite of divisions, the Embarrass church and the Lamppa homestead saw great gatherings throughout the 1920s to hear the gospel. Congregations rippled with excitement as preachers with tears streaming down their faces proclaimed "Christ's gospel of forgiveness" and described the joys of everlasting life:

> And what a marvelous blessing we have received! The mighty ocean of God's sins has been cleansed. . . . The miraculous has happened! In Christ I have become justified and thus satisfied the Father. Not only for one emotion-filled moment, but forever and forevermore. . . . [71]

A large northeast Minnesota Laestadian community built primarily under Heideman leadership during the first two decades of the twentieth century was destined to be ripped apart by sharp doctrinal differences which can be traced at least partly to influences arising from American society itself. The abundance of the 1920s played its role, as roads were improved and radios and phonographs found their way into Laestadian homes. Automobiles quickly became a necessity and a new attitude toward hardship as a thing to be avoided by "living in the here and now" was reflected in newspapers, books and educational institutions. The young, educated in this age, began to find church services dull and even "foreign" to their tastes, and it was easy to slip away from the rigid Apostolic life to movies, parties and dances. By 1930, a clear division between young and old could be observed in many of Minnesota's Finnish Apostolic churches. While Finnish-speaking parents continued to seek God and "rejoice in Christ" inside churches, their sons and daughters socialized outside in English.[72]

There had grown, beginning in 1908, a "Big Meeting" movement among Apostolic Lutherans. Conservative in nature, the Big Meeting movement from 1908-1928 drew people in great numbers to many places such as Calumet, Berkely, and Thomson, Minnesota, where old Laestadian principles were reaffirmed and solidarity achieved on doctrine.[73] Opposed by Heideman on the grounds that the Big Meetings placed man-made laws and agreements above Christian congregations and gospel, the participants formed their own church and reached an open split in what has been termed "the mournful separation of 1929."[74] Referred to as *kovanpuulaiset* (hardwoods) by some, the Finnish Apostolic Lutheran Church of America reaffirmed all of Raatamaa's principles, set itself to the task of organizing, and took a dim view of the "worldliness" of the young. Its major publication, *Walvoja*, rebuked America's worldly Finns and called them to repent.

There may have been an unconscious attempt on the part of

a certain group of preachers within the Heideman group to cope with the growing worldliness of American society and to retain strong followings. Such preachers as William Alajoki, Alex Puotinen, Isaac Lamppa and John Pollari began more and more to stress the "forgiving aspects of Christ's sacrifice" and to downplay "rebukes, instruction and confession."

On July 2, 1917, a number of preachers had gathered in Thomson, Minnesota. While Jacob Wuollet was preaching in the church, he was interrupted by an announcement that Lamppa and Halvari would preach at other services in the town hall beginning at 3 P.M.[75] *Päivälehti* described Pollari, Lamppa, Halvari and Maki as "the new group" and this gave Big Meeting preachers reason to begin criticizing them as practising "false doctrine."[76] By 1920, this criticism had grown so great that Oskari Jussila, a "staunch traditionalist" from England, was called to America by the Heideman congregation to observe Laestadian activities in Minnesota and elsewhere, and if necessary, lead straying "evangelicals" back to the fold. He was horrified at the *liikutukset* he saw, particularly among Minnesota groups which took place more often than not during the singing and "many times was so fierce that furniture and windows were broken."[77] He also noted having observed jesting, joking and buffoonery in sermons, the purpose of which could only be "to entertain people and provoke them to laughter."[78]

That Jussila was referring to preachers John Pollari, Isaac Lamppa, Sam Kovala, Alex Puotinen and Walter Isaacs is supported by the fact that these men were not called back to preach in the copper country after 1922. The fact that the Heideman Calumet congregation excluded these preachers from fellowship in 1922, and the fact that these preachers were preaching similar to Heideman himself, and no differently than they had ever preached, led Evangelical preachers to part company with the Heideman wing forever. "A.L. Heideman complied with this decision. He had never approved of some of the extremes to which some 'Evangelicals' had gone."[79] It seems, however, that Heideman himself retained his own "evangelical views," "for no real change was noticed in his preaching."[80] It was Arthur Heideman's son, Paul, who may have had great influence in the purge of evangelical preachers from the copper country. An educated and ordained minister himself, he had always held to a more traditional view, and was, in fact, horrified at the way John Pollari spoke of confession during a western preaching tour in 1917.[81]

Without the constraints of the Heideman church and its close ties to the Central Association of Finland's Associations of Peace in

Oulu, Finland,[82] evangelical preachers were free to expound on the "brighter and better gospel" that they had discovered. Confession was practically eliminated in their services and agitation against harsh sermons and the preaching of commandments to "Christians" began.[83] "There is no need to teach good works in this Church," preached Isaac Lamppa. "We will make our Faith strong, and the good works will come from this!"[84] "Let us build the barriers high between believing Christians and the followers of the black law church," shouted Walter Isaacs.[85]

> Once Isaacs lifted his Bible while preaching and said: This book does not contain a doctrine by which one could be saved! . . . Another time he said: Go on sinning; it is only a debt for which payment has been made. . . . [86]

The evangelical movement grew strong in Minnesota and Wisconsin.[87] Large "rejoicing" congregations were maintained well into the 1940s, while more conservative branches saw shrinking congregations. After the retirement of August Saarela in 1938, the Big Meeting Pike River Apostolic Lutheran Church did not have enough of a congregation to retain a regular pastor until the late 1940s when it was consolidated with other Iron Range Apostolic Lutheran churches.[88] Heideman Apostolic Church literature admits that after 1929 "there have not been any great awakenings among adult people as in former times, only a few now and then have received the grace of repentance."[89]

In Minnesota during the 1920s and 1930s, the evangelicals continued to make conversions. In spite of the many alternatives presented by "worldly influences," when John Pollari preached in the Embarrass Apostolic Church, the building was packed. "So what is wrong with wearing lipstick? Should not the brides of Christ be beautiful?"[90] Walter Isaacs once in a sermon said:

> When I was in the bondage of law-spirit, I could not sleep unless I asked for pardon from my wife if I had offended her. . . . But when the better and brighter gospel dawned on me, I have not needed to do so, I have only believed. It is said that the Holy Spirit convicts of sin, and this is true. But it is the devil who causes man to repent of his sins—Christ has made a confession of sins for us and it is unnecessary to confess to any old man or woman.[91]

That the charismatic element of earlier times was retained among Minnesota evangelical Laestadians is quite clear. *Liikutukset* continued to be the measure of the preacher and it was not unusual to see followers of this movement "marching together out of the church in a state of great ecstacy" at the end of a session.[92] A stress on spontaneity extended to a point where bibles were opened at random and sermons preached from whatever page was opened. Many from these congregations were suddenly smitten with the "Holy Spirit," and a host of lay preachers could be found at almost any evangelical gathering. There is no doubt that competition to gain and hold congregations led sometimes to outright jealousy among preachers.[93] Strains between Isaac Lamppa and Valter Isaacs erupted into a sudden break between the two in the Lamppa living room in the summer of 1929, just after church services had finished and the congregation had gathered for coffee. It seems that Valter Isaacs had in a letter criticized Isaac Lamppa as being of "black law spirit" after it was learned that he had listened to confessions and allowed certain congregation members to "repent and receive the Grace of God."[94] Isaac Lamppa had long been troubled by sermons made particularly by John Pollari in which he sometimes seemed to mock scripture while making a point and had spoken of this to both Isaacs and Pollari.[95] Uuras Saarnivaara, Apostolic Lutheran historian, describes Isaac Lamppa's withdrawal from evangelical extremism in this way:

> Isaac Lamppa followed the "Evangelicals" a long way, but when he saw the extremes to which they went, he turned back, although not all the way to Old Laestadianism. He remained somewhere between these groups, having his own followers in northern Minnesota, who were often called 'Lamppalaiset", "Lamppaisets." In the last years of his life he was rather close to the Old Laestadian conception of Christianity, although it is not known that he had publicly confessed that he had erred.
> . . . [96]

The ascendance of Matt Reed among evangelical-minded congregations was a stablizing force on this brand of Laestadians. A man of books and letters, Reed began to find scriptural support for admonishing extremist and errant "Christians" and taught the commandments to his congregation. This more conservative approach led in 1940 to a second and more widespread split in the evangelical-Apostolic ranks. John Koskela of Esko, Victor Maki of Van Buskirk, Wisconsin, John Taivalmaa of Maple, Wisconsin, and Andrew Leskinen of Point Mills, Michigan, led a "Free Grace of God" movement away from the "Reed group," maintaining that Christians did not need commandments for their conduct.[97] They further maintained that the "Grace of God" works in believers a denial of ungodliness and an immunity to worldly lusts and they rejected the modified kind of "confession" seen among Reed followers as "Roman Catholic."[98]

Matt Reed was joined by John Pollari and Sam Kovala who made it clear that their group was the only true Finnish Apostolic Church in existence, "holding to the doctrine of the Old Laestadians that there are Christians only in one congregation or group on earth," and they, of course, were it.[99]

By 1940, northeast Minnesota Laestadians had divided into five clear factions: The firstborn, the Heidemanians, the Apostolic Lutheran Church of America, the Grace of God evangelicals and the Reed evangelicals. All maintained a certain degree of exclusiveness and all were the product of revivals, conflicts, divisions, attempts at reconciliation and new conflicts. The lack of a central church authority, competition among preachers for followers, and the growing complexity of American life with all its influences, each played its part in preventing theological agreement on such matters as the meaning of God's word, use of the law and gospel and the function of the church. Walter Kukkonen comments succinctly:

> It is one of the ironies of history that these Laestadian congregations, the product of religious revival, by and large, failed to achieve their goal to transformation by their inadequate attention to the elements of personal and parish formation. Religious revivals have to do with transformation (conversion), not formation, which is the task of the church as an institution.[100]

# Notes

1. The three major Finnish-American Lutheran movements are the Suomi Synod, National Church and the Apostolic Church. The Suomi Synod was absorbed by the Lutheran Church of America on January 1, 1963, and the National Church became part of the Lutheran Church, Missouri Synod complex, on January 1, 1964.

2. Walter Kukkonen, "Process and Product: Problems Encountered by the Finnish Immigrants in the Transmission of a Spiritual Heritage," *Finnish Experience in the Western Great Lakes Region: New Perspectives*, Michael Karni, *et al.* (Turku, Finland, 1975) pp. 131-32.

3. Many older Apostolic Lutherans mention Niilo Saastamoinen from Cokato and Robert Vepsalainen from Finland as two powerful travelling preachers who caused much excitement with their sermons. A letter from Port Arthur, Canada, appearing in the *Rauhan Tervehdus*, August 22, 1922, proclaimed: "We have had some good meetings, N. Saastamoinen and I. Lamppa have preached the word. Two got converted. Heaven will be open, and is open!"

4. The quote is from *Rauhan Tervehdus*, Calumet (Michigan), April 1922.

5. Walter Kukkonen, "The Influence of the Revival Movements of Finland on the Finnish Lutheran Churches in America," *The Faith of the Finns*, Ralph J. Jalkanen (East Lansing, Michigan, 1972), p. 90.

6. Uuras Saarnivaara, *History of the Laestadian or Apostolic Movement in America* (Ironwood, Michigan, 1947), pp. 9-10.

7. Kukkonen, "Revival Movements", p. 90.

8. Lars Levi Laestadius, "Sermon No. 39, Morning Sermon 1859" as found in *The New Postilla*, Old Apostolic Lutheran Church (Ann Arbor, Michigan, 1960).

9. Ibid.

10. Aatu Laitinen, *Memoirs of Early Christianity in Northern Lapland* (Translated by Hjalmer Peterson), published by the Apostolic Lutheran Federaltion (undated). This book supposedly records the lives and works of twenty-six Laestadian preachers, including Aatu Laitinen himself. Translator Hjalmer Peterson proclaims, "We can only thank God that he laid it upon the heart of the late Aatu Laitinen to record the events of the Great Upheaval that occurred in the northern countries of Europe."

11. Kukkonen, "Revival Movements," p. 90.

12. Saarnivaara, p. 16.

13. The term "Christian" in Laestadian terms specifically means an "accepted member of the Laestadian church body." Luther's words in the *Small Catechism* are seen in a new, and certainly exclusive, light: "Justification does not take place in the Heavenly forum only, but God pronounces his merciful pardoning judgment in His Church" on earth, through the mouth of "His Children" (Saarnivaara, p. 16).

14. *Lutheraneran*, 1872, pp. 61-63.

15. Ibid.

16. Saarnivaara, p. 20; *Coming of the Lord Draweth Nigh*, Apostolic Lutheran Mission (Calumet, Michigan, 1968), pp. 8-9. This pamphlet

describes splits in the Apostolic movement from the Heideman point of view.

17. Hans R. Wasastjerna, *History of the Finns in Minnesota,* Minnesota Finnish-American Historical Society, (Duluth, Minnesota, 1957), p. 104.

18. Ibid.

19. Ibid. pp. 97, 98, 115, 144, 630

20. Ibid., p. 97.

21. Ibid.

22. Ibid., p. 632.

23. "100th Year Anniversary, Apostolic Lutheran Church" (New York Mills, Minnesota, 1977), p. 4. Also see microfilms of these records at the Immigration History Research Center, University of Minnesota, Minneapolis, Minnesota.

24. Wasastjerna, p. 97. John Takkinen's early leadership of the American Laestadian movement is acknowledge in many writings. Under his leadership, the Laestadian Church in Calumet was in 1879 renamed the Finnish Apostolic Church of Calumet. This name was immediately applied to all existing Laestadian churches and groups in America. "Apostolic Lutheran" is not used in Europe.

25. Kukkonen, "Revival Movements," p. 102.

26. Ibid., pp. 102-103.

27. Saarnivaara, p. 22.

28. Ibid., p. 23.

29. Wasastjerna, pp. 119, 138, 368.

30. *The Ely Miner, Hibbing Tribune* and *Virginia Enterprise,* 1895-1910 record frequent accidents in Vermilion and Mesabi mines.

31. Helen Sipola Lamppa, early resident of Soudan Location, (1901-1920). Interview, April 7, 1979.

32. Ibid.

33. Wasastjerna, p. 358.

34. Ibid., p. 371.

35. Kukkonen, "Revival Movements," p. 105.

36. Wasastjerna, p. 188, 195, 585, 425.

37. Church Records, 1896-1910, Apostolic Lutheran Church of Virginia, property of the 1st Apostolic Lutheran Church, 2nd Street North, Virginia, Minnesota.

38. Ibid.

39. Saarnivaara, p. 36.

40. Ibid., p. 45.

41. Isaac Lamppa, personal papers. These include communications, letters, Finnish Bible, address book, family notes and business records.

42. Church Records, 1896-1901, Apostolic Lutheran Church of Virginia.

43. Saarnivaara, p. 36.

44. Lamppa, personal papers.

45. Arthur Lamppa, son of Rev. Isaac Lamppa. Interview of March 31, 1979, Embarrass, Minnesota.

46. Saarnivaara, p. 45.

47. Ibid.

48. Wasastjerna notes the existence of either churches or congregations of Laestadian background existing in most of the places listed. Interviews with area Laestadians confirm these places and add such sites as Vermilion and Cook. Rev. Donald Salo, Apostolic Lutheran Church of America, Pike River, interview of April 5, 1979, claims that church "elders" inform him that there were once as many as sixteen or seventeen Apostolic Churches in northeast Minnesota.

49. Saarnivaara, p. 11.

50. Ibid., p. 17.

51. Apostolic Lutheran Mission (Heideman), 1968, pp. 4-5.

52. Clark A. Chambers, "Social Welfare Policies and Progress on the Minnesota Iron Range, 1880-1930," manuscript, p. 36.

53. Ibid.

54. Fred R. Mott to W.J. Olcott, "Letter dated February 19, 1923," Oliver Iron Mining Company Executive Files.

55. Ibid.

56. Ibid.

57. Fred R. Mott to W.J. Olcott, "Letter dated September 16, 1920," ibid.

58. *Polk Directories*, Sparta, Minnesota, 1903-1910. The names of most of Sparta's *esikoiset* Laestadian congregation appears suddenly in the 1908 Polk Directory. None can be found in earlier directories.

59. Helen Laukkonen, resident of Sparta, Minnesota, since 1906. Although not a practising *esikoiset* herself, she was close to all families of this brand of Laestadians. Interview of August 8, 1979.

60. Saarnivaara, p. 30.

61. Ibid., p. 85.

62. Helen Laukkonen.

63. Eino Noeha, *Embarras Townshipin Historiaa*. Embarrass, 1960, p. 12.

64. Ibid.

65. Wasastjerna, p. 543.

66. Wayne Lamppa, son of Rev. Isaac Lamppa, Duluth, Minnesota. Interview of June 3, 1979. Wayne Lamppa attended many services conducted by Jacob Halvari, Kuoppa-Valteri, John Pollari and his father, Isaac Lamppa, and witnessed much *liikutukset* during the 1920s.

67. Ibid.

68. Ibid. This description is repeated by many who witnessed services conducted in northeast Minnesota Laestadian homes and churches, 1910-1930.

69. Donald Salo, pastor of the Pike River Apostolic Lutheran Church, Apostolic Lutheran Church of America. Interview of March 6, 1979.

70. David Halkola, "Finnish Language Newspapers in the United States," *The Finns in North America,* edited by Ralph J. Jalkanen, Suomi College, Hancock, Michigan, 1969, pp. 84-85.

71. Oskari Jussila, *Rauhan Tervehdus,* Vol. 1, April 1922.

72. Leonard Lamppa, this phenomenon is echoed by every person interviewed. It was common for young people, particularly those in their teens, to remain outdoors during the services in the late 1930s and 1940s. Strangely many parents, intent on their own rejoicing, seemed either indifferent or incapable of keeping their children in the church during services. Obviously, this was not true in a minority of cases.

73. Saarnivaara, pp. 42-44.

74. Apostolic Lutheran Mission (Heideman) 1968, p. 31.

75. Saarnivaara, p. 45.

76. Ibid.

77. Ibid., p. 48.

78. Ibid.

79. Ibid.

80. Ibid.

81. Ibid., p. 49.

82. From the very first day Heideman arrived in Calumet, he always held close ties with the traditional Laestadians of Finland. For many years the only preachers the Old Laestadian movement in Finland would send to America were those called by the Heideman group. This led to many bitter controversies between the Heideman Apostolic Church and the Big Meeting groups. However, the bond between the Calumet Apostolic congregation and the Central Association of Laestadians in Finland has always been strong.

83. Saarnivaara, p. 49.

84. Wayne Lamppa.

85. Ibid.

86. Saarnivaara, pp. 49-50.

212    M. Lamppa

87.  Ibid., pp. 49-50, 87-88.
88.  Church Records, Pike River Apostolic Lutheran Church, 1920-1979.
89.  Apostolic Lutheran Mission (Heideman), p. 31.
90.  Helen Sipola Lamppa.
91.  Saarnivaara, p. 49.
92.  Wayne Lamppa.
93.  Arthur Lamppa.
94.  Wayne Lamppa. Family tradition established 1929 as the beginning of the breakup of the large Embarrass congregation.
95.  Ibid.
96.  Saarnivaara, p. 50.
97.  Ibid., pp. 87-88.
98.  Ibid., p. 88.
99.  Ibid.
100. Kukkonen, "Revival Movements," p. 105.

# A Closer Look at Finnish-American Immigrant Women's Issues, 1890-1910

*K. Marianne Wargelin-Brown*

No one has ever questioned the fact that women were an important part of the Finnish-American immigrant experience. We knew they had come in significant numbers long before we learned from Reino Kero's seminal migration study that 35.1 per cent of all emigrants leaving Finland for North America between 1869 and 1914 were women.[1] But until recently, anyone wishing to read about women's experiences in the early years of immigration has had a difficult and frustrating time, largely because materials relating to women and women's activities have been scattered and brief.[2]

In the past five years, however, Finnish-American immigrant women have received closer attention, and some idea of their experiences is beginning to emerge.[3] For example, the scattered materials relating to women have been gathered together so that we can assert that women living in mining communities raised families, tended gardens and animals, ran boarding houses, and worked as domestics in wealthy area homes, but we have yet to see any detailed studies utilizing this information.[4] In addition, from the informal histories published by local historical groups, we can

I am indebted to two people for this paper. First, Raymond W. Wargelin translated issues of *Naisten Lehti* and the *Calumetin Suomalaisen Nais-Yhdistyksen Ensimmäinen Kalenteri* as well as surveyed Ilmonen's books. Secondly, Carolyn M. Torma helped me immeasurably over a period of several months to reach the basic concepts developed in this paper.

piece together the information that Finnish-American immigrant women in the various communities shared similar experiences as they cleared and worked land, worked as midwives, masseuses and healers, ran farms, did handwork such as woven rag rugs and knitted garments, baked bread and adapted Finnish cooking methods to American foodstuffs.[5] But again, we have yet to see scholarly studies addressing these areas. And finally, from statistical data, we have become aware that while the early immigrant women were more likely to come to America in family groups, by 1900 the vast majority of women emigrating from Finland were single women who went into domestic service in major American cities as well as in service centres surrounding mining locations. This final area of reasearch is just now beginning to be explored.[6]

What the fledgling research into the history of Finnish-American immigrant women has explored thus far with some depth has been related to institutional history. (But in that regard, women's history has probably been no more remiss than most other work in Finnish-American immigration.) Perhaps the genesis of this direction of research can be traced back to Matti E. Kaups' comment that the growth of Finnish-American institutions tended to coincide with the arrival of Finnish women into the community.[7] But more likely, it originated with A. William Hoglund's comment:

> At least until they married and were tied down by family duties, thousands of former dairy maids and farm servants, who had earned little cash, if any, in Finland, became independent economically and socially in America. If they did not seek employment after marriage, women still found opportunity to leave their homes for participation in organized activities. Both secular and religious spokesmen recognized that women were able to match men in such activities. According to one speaker, since they helped create and rear future generations, women had the right to take part with men in economic and political affairs. Consequently, the view developed that harmony in both homes and organizations properly depended less upon masculine domineering and more upon feminine ability to influence people.[8]

In other words, statements such as these clearly suggested fertile and ready ground as a beginning for research on the Finnish-American immigrant woman. Thus, the primary information gathered and investigated in the past five years has told us about women's participation in the immigrant institutions. We have learned of individual women's efforts within these immigrant institutions, and we have learned of actions and ideas originating with women, singly and within groups.

Of primary interest is that women were active participants in the various immigrant institutions. No organization ever closed their door to women, and all organizations gradually loosened their restrictions on the degree to which women could participate.[9] By 1910, the churches, the workers' clubs and the temperance societies all granted voting rights to women as well as opportunities to serve in leadership capacities as board members, as speakers, as agitators, as delegates, as teachers. The following brief review of several of these institutions should help us understand more clearly what this participation involved.

From the beginning, the temperance societies included women as members. Membership rose from an initial 20 per cent to an eventual even balance or dominance in the local units. The local units encouraged women to recite and sing at the programs, to edit the *nyrkkilehti,* to teach and run temperance schools for children in the community. In the Finnish National Temperance Brotherhood, for example, women frequently won the prizes in the essay contests. The 1903 annual meeting of the Brotherhood included an official representative from the Women's Christian Temperance Union who brought greetings. Initially, this kind of participation did not include leadership responsibilities, but in 1905, unofficial restrictions ended when Hanna Siltala was appointed a member of the Brotherhood board. Now more and more women began to hold positions of authority. By 1909, the Brotherhood's national meeting not only elected Miina Perttula to a position on the national board but also elected Alma Hinkkanen secretary. These two women later represented the Brotherhood at the 1910 Anti-Saloon League convention in Chicago.[10]

More important, however, than these various forms of participation is the phenomenon of the woman speaker which developed. From the beginning, the programs in the local units and at the regional and national festivals always included speakers. Women and men both tried to develop rhetorical skill and platform manner; a number of these women became so skilful in their local units that they began to be in demand throughout their regions. Among the women who became well known as temperance speakers were Lydia Kangas, Hanna Siltala, Hilda Luoma, Linda Malmberg, Miina Perttula and Augusta Lahti, and most importantly, the Brotherhood showed in 1908 that they appreciated and valued the skills of women speakers when they called Alma Hinkkanen to come to America from Finland to spend a year travelling and speaking to all the regional associations.[11]

What we see here in the temperance movement is paralleled in the history of women in the workers' clubs as well. Right from the beginning, women were included among the membership. Women were members of the pre-socialist groups, the Imatra society of Brooklyn, New York, and the Saima Society of Fitchburg, Massachusetts. By 1912, reported membership figures for the Finnish Socialist Federation were 13,160 of which 3,790 were women. In areas like Boston, Massachusetts, and New Rochelle, New York, women even outnumbered men. As in the temperance societies, women involved themselves in similar ways: they participated in the local programs as reciters, performers, speakers; they served as teachers in youth education; they helped to organize festivals, theatricals and weekly meetings. On the national level, they served as correspondents to newspapers and other periodicals. Some women, like Hulda Anderson, Ida Pasanen, Sanna Kallio-Kannasto and Hilda Sikanen-Sandberg travelled—speaking, stirring up, and organizing men and women to socialist thinking. And finally, like temperance society women, they served as delegates to national meetings; when the Finnish Socialist Federation was organized in Hibbing, Minnesota, in 1906, three women—Hulda Anderson, Olga Heinonen and Ida Pasanen—were among the forty delegates attending; and while only one woman, Hilda Sikanen-Sandberg, was a delegate to the 1909 meeting, in 1912 over a half of dozen women came as delegates.[12]

The churches, on the other hand, were somewhat slower to utilize the abilities of women. Initially, only men had voting privileges in the national and local organizations. The Finnish National Church, for example, gave men the right to vote, but its 1901 rules said that if it seemed appropriate within the individual congregations, women should also be granted the right to vote. The Suomi Synod also did not grant women the right to vote, but within individual congregations, women frequently voted by custom. Nevertheless, the churches finally granted women full rights and privileges as members, the Suomi Synod in 1908, and the National Church in 1909. In the meantime, the women had enjoyed the rights and privileges of serving locally as Sunday school teachers, choir members, and general local board members. Most importantly, they had always enjoyed official approval for their sewing circle auxiliaries which not only met women's individual needs but which also furthered the work of the local congregation.[13]

Once this full membership privilege was granted, the women took their place within the organization as significantly as they had done within the workers' clubs and the temperance societies. For example, women were elected to the boards of the Book Concern and Suomi College soon after they gained full membership rights. Three women, Alma Haapanen, Lydia Kangas, and Miina Perttula, along with two men, authored the first *Lukukirja*, published by the Suomi Synod for use in the Sunday and summer schools. Women also began to serve as speakers and promoters for the various causes of the church and in that capacity travelled and visited numerous congregations across the country.[14]

Thus, within the three major institutions of the Finnish-American community, immigrant women were very much involved as participants and leaders on both a local and a national level. But women also enjoyed the immigrant community's cultural approval to a right to an education. Women were admitted as students and teachers into both the *Kansan Opisto* (later the *Työväen Opisto*) and the *Suomi Opisto*. In addition, the community encouraged women to attend other institutions of higher learning in such numbers that by the end of World War One, large numbers of Finnish-American women had been able to become nurses and teachers serving in the greater American society. And in 1931, Ilmonen was able to list four women principals, one associate professor at the University of California, seven medical doctors and four dentists. Women were also not afraid to enter government: two had become mayors, twenty-seven had become postmistresses.[15]

Women did indeed find socially accepted opportunities not only within the developing immigrant institutions but also within the developing Finnish-American economic structure. A good example of this is Maggie Walz who came to the United States as a young girl of 12 to work as a domestic for a Finnish family. Through her own initiative, she managed to learn English, attended Valparaiso University and entered business, ultimately owning her own building and business in Calumet. She served as an agent for young women wanting work in America as servants; she sold steamer tickets to Finns wishing to bring other loved ones to America; and after 1902, she founded a colony on Drummond Island which she served as land agent and postmistress. Maggie Walz had started the colony as a conscious means of getting people away from the evils of liquor, but when it became predominantly socialist she left it to its own devices. She devoted the rest of her life to suffrage,—gaining acceptance into American suffrage organizations; and to temperance, attending as an American delegate the world conference of the Women's Christian Temperance Union in Scotland in 1910.[16]

Yet the most interesting aspect of Finnish-American women's

involvement in institutions is that the women themselves organized
and ran several institutions, which directly affected several other
Finnish-American immigrant institutions. The story of these institutions dates from 1893 when a group of Brooklyn, N.Y., women
formed an organization for women, Pyrkijä, which served as a
benefit society and cultural and social club. This initial organization encouraged the start of a second group, the Calumet, Michigan, Finnish Women's Society, begun in 1894 by Linda Malmberg
and Maggie Walz. This ultimately became the spiritual leader of a
number of women's organizations nationally when it assumed publication of a women's newspaper, *Naisten Lehti*, begun originally in
1897 by Hanna Nyland Järnefelt in New York. For ten years the
women published this paper, at times regularly, at times sporadi-
cally, presenting women's ethnic, national and international issues
and events. Through numerous philosophical articles arguing for a
broader understanding of women's potential, the newspaper continually encouraged women to develop themselves intellectually, to
raise their aspirations, and to demand equality. Through this newspaper, as well as through the personal visits of Maggie Walz,
women in major cities such as Cleveland and Chicago, in mining
communities such as Little Falls, Montana, and Ishpeming, Michigan, and in industrial areas such as Ashtabula, Ohio, and Duluth,
Minnesota, organized themselves into Finnish Women Society units
to support women's awakening.[17]

Thus, not surprisingly, Finnish-American immigrant women
began to assert themselves. First, in New York, women by 1912
built their own home with spaces for forty workers and organized
their own employment agency,—to free themselves from exploiting
middle men and bad employers. (Other similar homes developed in
San Francisco and Los Angeles.) Secondly, in 1908, Finnish-American women began to lobby actively for the right to vote. They
joined the American suffrage movement, marched in parades, passed petitions, and promoted the cause in the Finnish-American
community. Thirdly, Finnish socialist women, finding the *Naisten
Lehti* and the Finnish Women's Society too conservative, yet agree-
ing with the concept of separate women's organizations and newspapers to awaken and develop women's potential, lobbied their
own National Finnish Socialist Federation to sanction such developments. After fiery discussions at the 1906 and 1909 conventions,
during both of which the men vehemently opposed such developments, women went ahead, without office sanction, to start a newspaper, *Toveritar*, begun in 1911 (at one point with 10,000 subscri-

bers), and to organize women's groups, often called sewing circles, which the Federation approved after the fact in 1912.[18]

What emerges from this survey of women in Finnish-American immigrant institutional history is a picture of remarkably active and assertive women. In fact, from our late twentieth-century perspective, the early Finnish-American community's attitudes toward women look remarkably liberal and progressive, especially when we compare our knowledge of women's position in the larger American society from 1890 to 1910 with our knowledge of women's position in the early Finnish-American community. We can conclude that the early Finnish-American community was very enlightened toward women and that the many women involved in pushing women's opportunities even further had to have been "dyed in the wool" feminists.[19] No dull, backward immigrant culture this, no timid, retiring women these! This was a highly modern and advanced community with women pushing hard for even further advancements.

Yet this kind of pride encourages us to overlook distortions that may occur because we look with a late twentieth-century perspective—a perspective which may impede our ability to arrive at any accurate picture of that early community's definition of women's role and opportunities. In other words, as we become further removed from that time, we are more likely to judge the activities of that community by our own standards. Using our present conception of women's issues, we may judge the early Finnish-American community as progressive and the early Finnish-American women as feminist when the community and the women themselves may have concluded otherwise. We may also try to superimpose cause-and-effect relationships between events, ideas and people which are observable only to our eyes, using our late twentieth-century vision, and not understand the dynamics of the vision of the people involved in the period.

We may be better able to appreciate how we distort an earlier age with ideas from our own if we now re-examine a few examples of what we have been labelling feminist. Because our concept of a feminist is one who uses rhetoric like "a woman should be able to decide her own destiny," we judge Linda Malmberg a feminist, even though in that same 1894 speech she says:

> You have perhaps heard something about women's emancipation, you have heard of women establishing societies and organizations, clothing themselves in the

manner of men and demanding for themselves the same
privileges that men have, or in other words, making a
man out of a woman. That, of course, is foolish to hear
and it is against the Creator's intent and the natural
laws of creation.[20]

Because today we think that advancing women's civil rights is
feminist, we find a feminist in Ida Pasanen, even though in the
article in which she outlines the civil rights denied to women, she
begins, "I am not known as a special advocate for women's questions, only as a writer for the proletariat," and proves throughout
her biography that the statement accurately assesses her position.[21]
Furthermore, because our concept of a feminist newspaper is one
which fumes at women "remaining by their pots and cradles,"
which exhorts women to "rise up from their position as wards of
men" and to "pound away at those chains which bind women into
slavery in a so-called land of liberty," we catagorize the *Naisten
Lehti* as feminist, ignoring those other articles which encourage
women to take their rightful position as their husband's "work
companion," as partners in their husband's work, which assert that
the women elected to the Finnish Parliament are devoting themselves to social issues, leaving the political issues rightfully to men,
and which advise women to settle marital quarrels with "Christ's
rule that the woman is to be obedient unto her husband . . . the
wisest rule that has ever been given."[22] And finally, because we
think that if someone brings up women's issues that person must be
a feminist, we therefore label as feminist the socialist women who
pushed for women's issues and ignore that when they finally cau-
cused as a separate group at the 1912 Federation convention, they
pushed for issues which reaffirmed their roles as wives and mothers.[23]

And if we turn form the women we have judged as feminists
to the community we have judged as progressive and enlightened
about women, we discover additional distortions we have made in
our rush to see a modern society. Concentrating on the community's generosity toward women, we have ignored the additional
qualifications women had to meet in order to be an equal part of
that community. B.V. Rautanen, the liberal minister who pushed
for women's vote in the church, supported his position with the
assertion that "women have demonstrated that they can do what
men can do."[24] In the workers' clubs, also, women soon discovered
that while all were equal under socialism, only women had to
prove that their issues were as important as the issues identified by

men; only women had to justify that their work was appropriate socialist activity.[25]

We have also ignored the slighting tones with which women's issues were discussed throughout this early period. The Finnish Socialist Federation dismissed the subject of Women's work at the 1906 convention with Martin Hendrick son's single remark: "I see no relative importance to this question because both men and women are people; therefore, there is no difference between the sexes." And the Federation continued to dismiss it at the 1909 convention even after Hilda Sikanen-Sandberg's long and heated speech on women's needs. Again characteristic of the dismissal was Martin Hendrickson's remark: "So long as women fit with men in the same bed, they better also fit into other joint activities with men."[26] And the women themselves didn't always detect the slight because they published the following letter in the *Naisten Lehti* to indicate that men too supported their goals:

> I am completely unable to understand the basis upon which these rights of women are being denied. They seem to be very childish as far as I am concerned, even laughable. . . . I certainly wouldn't go to vote unless my wife *would go along* and vote also. This is as natural as eating dinner. It *doesn't take a great deal of deep intelligence* to vote but I would like to say directly to women: Get organized . . . I do not exhort you to follow the ugly way the women in England forced themselves into Parliament. Women have within their possession better and sharper means for securing of their voting rights. Form among yourselves a league and include in it all laundries so that no woman and no laundry will assume to wash any senators' or representatives' shirts, or pajamas, until the voting right law has been granted. . . . [27]

This male writer not only dismisses the importance of the vote, he also quickly puts women in what he considered their rightful place with a behaviour code and an assumption about the type of labour the should do.

Most crucial, however, is that we have ignored that frequently the community totally misunderstood what women who spoke up about women's issues wanted and meant. S. Ilmonen's comment about the women's movement indicates this well: "Equality was understood of itself; in fact, it was even possible to observe the worship of women within the community."[28] The confusion of worship with equality indicates that men's and women's definitions of equality could indeed vary considerably. And Moses Hahl's 1904 article justifying the need for women's agitation work not only puts down women but is insensitive to the women's own arguments for agitation work amongst women:

> Judging from the commotion I have seen presently existing in the Finnish workers' clubs in this country, I could suppose that some of the awakening wind which travels from man to man has always carried some women away with it as well. Newspapers are filled with columns of controversial articles suggesting that something is afoot, although, as of yet, it isn't possible to figure out what it is. . . . But I also know that here, as in the homeland, women copy men—they have not yet understood the issues as individuals, only going along with whatever is the current claim.
>
> There are towns where the women almost outnumber the men. In those communities, women are determining which issues to push; the men, and the young people, are ordered about like servants. Wherever these places are, women's awakening is needed. . . . Take all the women who already think independently and get them to grab hold of the issues—surely that is fitting.[29]

Hahl argues here that if, when you agitate for socialism, you arouse women, that is good but not intentional. However, if the community is dominated by women, women's agitation should occur. He has mixed feelings about women's role in socialism: while women in leadership roles violate the social order, unthinking women disturb his concept of humanness. The socialist woman moves in a double bind.

Clearly, our picture of a progressive and enlightened community with hard working feminists is riddled with contradictions and variations which our twentieth-century perspective only inadequately accounts for. Too often we seem to be missing the dynamics of the vision of the people who actually lived through that period. We might better account for the cornucopia of ideas and actions with a change of approach. In the rest of this paper, therefore, we will examine the historical materials laid out above; only here, we will use a non-historical methodology to account for those contradictions and variations which still plague us.

This time, instead of historical research (studying newspapers, yearbooks, letters, first-generation histories, diaries, statistics, interviews—looking for what people have consciously said and done), we will use literary research (studing images, symbols, structural patterns, rhythms, sounds—looking for what an author has said and done consciously or subconsciously). But unlike the literary critic, we will look specifically at subconscious expressions: the formulaic and repeated motifs and structure found in traditional of folk literature. This folk literary patterning also will transmit, simultaneously, the subconscious intellectual and spiritual heritage of those who use it. Thus, looking at subconscious expression, we can discover the community's underlying assumptions, the unspoken yet deeply felt beliefs, values and attitudes, something we have not yet considered.[30]

Two narratives will help us reach some conclusions about the Finnish-American community's underlying assumptions about men and women. And curiously, instead of coming from traditional or folk collections, the narratives come from consciously written sources: two first-generation histories,—one an early Finnish-American church history, V. Rautanen's *Amerikan Suomalainen Kirkko*, and the other a local community history, Hannes Elenius' *Murunen Suomea Villikorpeen*. Although history books seem unlikely sources for the non-conscious traditional knowledge we are looking for, such unlikely sources as Rautanen's church history and a Michigan local community history become fruitful if we recognize that subconsciously expressed ideas are not limited to traditional or folk literature, any expression of words and structural patterns can reveal subconscious as well as conscious information if we have the tools with which to get to it. Here both of our authors have made our task relatively easy: Rautanen because he has included in his empirical evidence an anecdote with conspicuous traditional folk patterning, both motifs and structural patterns rooted in tradition; And Elenius because he included a traditional tale format along with traditional motifs. Both show through their traditional patternings the underlying assumptions about men's and women's roles with the Finnish-American society in the early twentieth century.

Rautanen's narrative appears midway through the book, after sections describing first when local congregations organized and secondly when the congregations organized nationally. Then in a third section, called "the period of two church bodies," he describes the National Church's start and gives a synopsis of its by-laws before proceeding as follows:

> Eloheimo now began to ordain ministers for the new church organization. Since this church body did not pay any further attention to regulations for theoretical edu-

cation for the ministry than what was required of laymen who wanted to preach the Word in Finland, he
didn't have any difficulty getting new ministers ready.
Already in 1897, he had ordained a certain woman
named Erika Rantanen as a deacon with preaching privileges. She began to travel from West Superior to the
Copper Country, to the state of Ohio and New York
City, preaching the Work of God to everyone. In New
York, she attempted to edit a newspaper in two languages, but the heavy amount of work made it die soon
after it started.

Prof. A Hjelft later drew the following portrait of
her:°

In Conneaut in the first row of the audience sat a
certain (*kummallinen ihmisolento*) peculiar human
creature, who, when you first looked, was hard to identify as either a man or a woman. She was dressed
entirely in black; high on her head was some sort of a
bishop's or priest's hat, and atop that a kind of protec-
tive covering. She wore heavy eyeglasses on her nose,
and bushy hair flowed down onto her shoulders. All she
lacked was a beard; otherwise, you would have thought
that she looked just like a Russian priest. After the
service was over, she came back into the sacristy and
introduced herself as Erika Rantanen "who also wants
to preach the Word to the people." She was that
woman who still roamed around the American Finnish
communities in order to preach and do other priestly
functions, even though it was generally known that she
needed care in a mental hospital.[31]

Following this anecdote, he proceeds to describe the first man
ordained into the Finnish National Church, a man, he notes, who
has little formal education or training.

This anecdote clearly predates the period where it is placed,
yet Rautanen puts it here (instead of into the Fenno-American
church section where it chronologically belongs) amidst National
Church history, after 1898. Clearly, Rautanen wants to connect the
National Church with this woman; he wants men ordained into the
National Church seen in juxtaposition to this mad woman; and he
is willing to sacrifice chronological accuracy to do it. The anecdote
says more than facts alone. Alone, the facts present the church's

° Teologinen aikakauslehti v. 1902

minimal standards; in juxtaposition to the anecdote, the facts reveal a church wracked by disorder and upheaval.

But why would he want to discredit the National Church? His introduction reveals that he is writing this book "so the foreigner who has an interest in these things can get his own opinion" and so "the sources can be preserved for a later date when they can be given a more exact examination."[32] Thus, he writes for two particular opinions: foreigners reading this book, namely Finns (since the book is written in Finnish) and posterity, both of whom will re-examine the materials, see the truth objectively, and judge the participants accordingly. This objective opinion is apparently so important to him that he would subconsciously present his conception of the truth in such a way that his readers would not fail to recognize the same truths he recognizes.

His conception of the truth he admits is "Evangelical Lutheran."[33] Since Rautanen is a man trained at the University of Helsinki, ordained by the Church of Finland, and at that time serving as a minister in the Suomi Synod,[34] we can surmise that his definition of "Evangelical Lutheran" is Church of Finland and Suomi Synod. Therefore, he would want his readers to perceive the Suomi Synod as the symbol of order and reason in the midst of symptoms of social upheaval, which this ordination characterizes; he would want his readers to assess the Suomi Synod, which maintains clerical standards, as the rightful daughter of the Church of Finland;[35] he would want his readers to judge the National Church, not the Suomi Synod, as the participant and agent of social upheaval.

But why would this story more than any other be the way to discredit the National Church? What special power could this story have—power so strong that his readers would understand it without any special explanation or introduction? If we look past the actual event described in the anecdote and examine instead the method of description, we will begin to appreciate what this special power is. Both the structure of the anecdote and the motifs within it indicate strong subconscious methods at work.

Structurally, the anecdote uses the traditional folk patterning of the repeated three—subconscious template shaping the entire remembrance. Three times, Professor Hjelft questions who this person is. The first time he sees only a "peculiar human creature, who, when you first looked, was hard to identify as either a man or a woman." Here he cannot identify her by sex. He turns to the markings that clothing and then hair and beard give. The second time he identifies her by occupation. Contradicting his first conclusion, he thinks he identifies her sex: "All she lacked was a beard;

otherwise, you would have thought that she looked just like a Russian priest." She is a priest, implying a man. But then he learns that she is "that woman that Bishop Eloheimo ordained"; now he reconciles this new information with his earlier conclusion. This third time he identifies her as a mad woman: "It was generally known that she needs care in a mental hospital." The piece, an anecdote of an identification process, includes three attempts before the speaker settles on the observation that she is a mad woman.

Turning from the structure to the motifs, we notice further subconscious forms of expression. Hjelft first tries to identify her by clothing—the traditional concept of you are what you wear. Then he tries to identify her by bodily markings or physical attributes—the traditional tests of looking at hair and beard. When he finally identifies her as a woman, he resolves and explains away his earlier confusion by using the traditional consequence faced when people violate the taboos of society—madness.[37]

Clearly, subconscious materials shape this anecdote. This template helps us the significance this event has for Hjelft. He is remembering a time when he could not identify a person. In her presence, he becomes disoriented, and the subconscious template becomes the mechanism to regain his composure. Apparently, he is disoriented because he cannot immediately identify her. While a person should be immediately recognizable, this person is not. So he applies the appropriate tests: clothing and physical traits. Obviously, he is very confused because the second identification contradicts his first. Then when Erika Rantanen identifies herself, we learn why he is so confused. She is not only a woman but a priest, a fact Hjelft cannot handle. A woman priest doesn't fit his definition, his schema for male and female roles. She violates his sense of the social structure. Nowhere has he learned the way to understand a woman as a priest. How could she be a priest as well as a woman? Only if she were mad. No rational or normal woman would violate her role this way. Therefore, she must be and, either that or in the act of becoming a minister, she violated a societal taboo which would be such a severe shock on the nervous system that it would make her mad. At any rate, madness is either the reason or the logical consequence for stepping over the boundaries between men and women.

What makes this anecdote so powerful then is that it portrays social disorder of a very basic kind—the distinction between the male and female roles. When Erika Rantanen becomes a minister, she challenges a basic assumption that men are the authority figures within the public society and culture. This challenge would not have been as clear had she chosen to be a carpenter, a lumberjack or a road builder. Those occupations are not clear symbols of authority; the ministry is. The role of the minister is the role of an authority figure, a soothsayer, a sanctifier of cultural behaviour. The minister has it in his power to sanction behaviour in behalf of the community. And it is this power to sanction that Erika Rantanen challenges.

Herein lies the power of the anecdote, which presents an image of social disorder which no reader could miss. Rautanen's public, fellow Finns both in North America and abroad, would pick up these subconscious cues and put the National Church within the framework of disruption and upheaval. Within that, of course, we have also been able to learn about a basic yet unspoken assumption of this community: men and women have separate roles and men hold the final authority.

As we turn now to our second narrative, we see that the boundaries separating men and women in this community were not totally rigid. Women in this early Finnish-American community could and did manage to participate in non-female roles. What made it possible was that the community found a way to reconcile its basic underlying behavioural assumptions with women's ventures beyond the boundaries.

Our second narrative comes from a local community history written in 1939 by John Rantamäki, under the pen name of Hannes Elenius. Rantamäki, an editor of the *Amerikan Suometar*, collected the history and stories of the people who settled the Otter Lake region beginning in 1890.[38] These people, one of the earlier groups to leave the Copper Country mines, settled in an area where they had to clear the land and live by their own resources until they could make their new farms productive. The initial portion of this history, therefore, describes what was done and who were the people doing it. That accomplished, Elenius begins to enrich the history with stories that make these people and this region come to life. The narrative we will examine comes in a section where a number of stories justify his claim that the region had bountiful hunting and fishing:

> Good game birds—wood ducks, partridge, and field partridge—were so frequent in this area that it swarmed with them. The younger men and boys shot these whenever they were sick of eating fish and deer. Deer meat and bird stews and pies were found in every home, so

much that they began to taste poorly to some, but certainly it remained a delicacy to the guests who came from the Copper Country to note the region's progress and to examine the crops.

The women folk, who did not think it was proper for women to go out hunting game with a gun, were getting very tired of hearing the men boast about chasing the deer in the woods until trapping them. "Surely, we can still show the men that we can't do any worse" thought the wives of Pekka Hyypiö and Aapo Kangas.

Therefore, one day, when the men, taking their guns with them, had left for their morning's work far off in the woods, Mrs. Kangas and Mrs. Hyypiö decided to leave on their own to look for a deer. It so happened that no neighbors had any deer meat in stock then.

When the sun rose, they left in a boat, taking with them a rope and a sturdy pole, rowing along the shoreline of the lake, looking to see if they could meet a deer crossing close on the lake, taking his morning swim. They didn't have long to wait because a pair of deer came to drink their "morning coffee" and left then to swim to the other shore. The women rowed very quickly toward the deer and got so close to their heads that one of the women struck the buck unconscious and the other threw the lasso around it. Oh, but there was a bustle and concern before they got the animal to shore, but they did it and were very pleased. They cut the deer open in the old fashioned way, bleeding and skinning the animal right there in the shoreline thicket. They sliced and brought home the best pieces.

The men were on their way home that evening when they caught the pleasing smells of deerstew coming through the doors of the Hyypiö and Kangas homes. They looked at the mixture cooking in the pot. They couldn't understand what was going on.

"What good neighbor has given us deer meat," wondered one of the men, little suspecting the total situation.

"Aren't we women supposed to be able to catch deer?" bragged one woman, raising her nose high in the air. "You can eat soon, you're probably very hungry."

The Hyypiö wife came along to the Kangas' after supper, where right away and very intently began the

wives' interesting report about their strange deer hunt
whose results both men had already been able to taste.
The wives, along with the help of "male visitors" who
had accidently seen the until then rare event, still assured their husbands that the story was accurate.[39]

Following this story, Elenius goes on to narrate several other stories
about the cleverness of other women in the community.

Elenius collected this story from present residents of the
community, largely second-generation people who tell the stories
about their mothers and fathers. A few, however, come from first-
generation settlers who remember the past.[40] What we have here,
therefore, is an era remembered some thirty to forty years later.
We do not know who told this story to Elenius; we only know that
Elenius included it because he thought it was appropriately representative of some aspect of that community's history. It is a story
which the community chose to remember and to tell when asked
later about what it was like in those early days.

Exactly whom Elenius is trying to reach through is history
and why becomes clear in his prefatory remarks. There Elenius
explains that he is writing because the Finnish-American community's young people need to know the rich and noble history of their
pioneer immigrant ancestors. No one needs to be ashamed of this
Finnish-American history; indeed, everyone should honour and
proudly acclaim it as part of the total United States history. To
further legitimate his book, he even quotes "Ukko Kivi" on being
proud ot the history of simple people.[41]

This emphasis on pride in simple pioneers may seem strange
until we also read the introduction by a Pastor A.V. Tuukkanen.
He states that this book commemorates the three hundredth anniversary of the Finnish Delaware settlement. Since only a defective
history of those early Finns exists, this type of local history can,
therefore, replace that early history because the heritage is the
same. Tuukkanen hopes that every Finnish home in America will
have a copy of this book.[42]

Thus, the spirit of the book is a high form of patriotic zeal
both for America and for Finnish pioneers. The book presents the
early history as those pioneers would like those times remembered.
Written during that period when Finns from many ideological
persuasions united to celebrate their common ancestral immigration, the book aims to reach the entire general Finnish-American
reading public. However, the book apparently struck a harmonious
chord with the Otter Lake residents as well, for when they cele-

brated their community's sixtieth anniversary in 1950, they republished the book in a gilt-covered anniversary edition to sell as a remembrance of their community's past.[43]

Our story narrates an elaborate trick the women pulled at their husbands' expense. The women leave home without a gun, yet beat their husbands' hunting skills with nothing more than a stick and a rope. That evening, they cook the deer meat and enjoy needling their menfolk with the details of the hunt. Through the story, we learn not only about the region's bountiful hunting but also about the pluckishness of the women pioneers who lived there. The jest is good-natured, and no one suffers permanently for it.

At first glance, the story seems a very literary piece. The language is frequently very dense and tightly structured: "Emännät vielä vakuuttivat kertomuksensa todeksi oikein "vierasten miesten" avulla, jotka olivat sattumalta nähneet tämän siihen asti harvinaisen tapauksen." Word choice is consciously varied and rich: references to the women vary from "vaimoihmiset" (the wife people) to "eukot" (the old ladies), "emännät (women of the house), and "naiset" (women). The story breathes with the close attention to language an editor could give.

However, here as in Rautanen's narrative, the story operates on more levels than just historical fact or literary skill. In the midst of this very literary prose, we discover several stylistic methods used in traditional folk story: 1/no assertive beginning or emphatic end: here, a vaguely relevant first paragraph leads into the actual story beginning in paragraph two; then after the climax, the story continues to narrate events later in the evening. 2/ A highly summarized story here, motivation for the hunt and the hunt itself are brief, and dialogue occurs only during the inciting incident, when the women decide to go hunting, and again at the climax, when the men return to find the bubbling stew. 3/ No more than two people ever active in any one scene: here, even when four people are present, only one or two say anything. 4/ No sharp characterization: here, we never get any description of the women or the men, and we never learn anything about their marital relationships.[44]

Several traditional formulaic motifs surface here as well. The common morning coffee motif (aamukahvinsa), for deer, cues us that Elenius writes for a Finnish audience that would chuckle appreciatively at this. Further, Elenius lets his story echo traditional marital jokes, particularly those about the competition when roles are temporarily reversed; he also associates this story with the tall tales told about hunting, the lucky catch in spite of seemingly impossible odds.[45]

These motifs and structure all suggest that in spite of Elenius' literary craftsmanship a subconscious template operates here, just as the traditional pattern of three operated in the first story. Here, this supposedly factual event has donned the subconscious template of the trickster story, a traditional folktale where someone plays a trick on someone else in order to poke fun and mock them, as occur here. Frequently, this trickster character pulls off the trick through pluck and wit and escapes unscathed, just as these women do.[46]

Thus, subconscious materials shape this story too. And, as in Rautanen's story, subconsciously expressed beliefs, values and assumptions surface here. The trickster template reveals why Elenius feels comfortable including a story where women move into male roles, challenge the men's exclusive control of an occupation, and prove that they can successfully engage in male behaviour. According to what we have learned from the other narrative, women do not have culturally sanctioned rights to engage in male behaviour, yet here they are not only allowed, but the story of their doing so finds its way into a book exalting the tremendous bravery and nobility of these early Finnish pioneers. Because their action comes within the framework of a trickster story, their venture into role reversals is acceptable. The women can reverse roles because the reversals are temporary; they are jokes, tricks. Short-term reversals do not conflict seriously with the societal taboos. In fact, they actually relieve a bit of the tension caused by the clearly demarcated sexual roles.[47] The trickster tale allows Elenius to include this story of women's independence to show, without any fear of reprisal, how brave and noble the women were too.

Of course, the story makes it clear that the women never seriously intend to usurp the men's roles: "The women did not think it was proper for women to go out hunting game with a gun." The language further indicates that the women are not a serious threat. They are never described negatively. In addition, they are always recognizable and identifiable. Before they go out, and after they return, they are referred to by the domestic titles quoted above. While hunting, they are called "they" or "women" (*naiset*). Thus, when at home, they are identified by their roles, and when they are hunting, they are identified independent from roles. This temporary venture into forbidden territory, instead of emphasizing the horror of role reversals, emphasizes ingenuity, wit and spunk—all characteristics that Elenius wants for his history of these people.

Thus, in this second narrative, we learn that women can engage in male roles, as long as they do not seriously threaten the basic cultural assumptions about male and female roles. In addition, we learn that the Finnish-American community sanctions and displays with pride the women's acts of independence. In fact, frequently, when the community wants to burst its buttons with ethnocentric pride, it will tell stories of Finnish-American women's pluckishness and independence.[48]

Thus, through these two narratives, we discover some of the dynamics we have previously missed about this Finnish-American community. We now see that males are the final authority in this community and that severe taboos prevent women from contesting this fact. This information makes us understand why both men and women disapprove of women's behaviour when it looks too much like a challenge to male authority: why Linda Malmberg vehemently renounces any role invasion; why Ida Pasanen denies being a women's advocate; why the *Naisten Lehti* tells its women to keep men's careers uppermost and respect men's final authority in decisions; why the *Naisten Lehti* does not hear derision in the letter they publish on the vote; why finally the socialist women devote their efforts to traditional role issues.

Furthermore, we see through these two narratives that the community tolerates temporary role reversals, particularly if they are associated with displays of independence and pluckishness. Now we can understand why women who meet these additional standards can take up higher roles of authority in the institutions; why women can be speakers, writers and voting members of the major community institutions; why women can go to school, developing advanced skills in traditional female activities; why the women can create their own organizations and newspapers.

Finally, we see that these two cultural sanctions can create disagreements about interpretation. Now we can understand why sometimes when women will do something that they do not consider a role invasion, the men would see it otherwise. We can understand why Ilmonen would misinterpret women's requests for opportunity and equality as requests for honour and respect; why the socialist women would ask the Federation for help to fulfill their traditional roles and the men would find the request an invasion of territory; why Moses Hahl could encourage the intellectual awakening of women and at the same time frown on women who may assert themselves because they have been awakened.

All this information comes because we have looked closely at two narratives. Normally no two narratives could speak so strongly for an entire community, but because the narratives display strong subconscious patterns at work, we can read them further for the subconsciously expressed community beliefs and values embedded in them, revealed through them, and occurring simultaneously in them.

Our search for Finnish-American women's issues has taken us far. We have gone from the evidence of assertiveness and independence to the community's openness to women; from the contradiction and denial of the women to the narrow vision of the men. Finally, through the subconscious materials embedded in the two narratives, we have come to understand that these people must be accepted on their own often contradictory terms.[49] To us, they contradict themselves, but to them, they present different strains of the same sanctioned vision. We cannot put labels of progressive or modern on this community, and we cannot put labels of feminist or anti-feminist on these people.

# Notes

1. Reino Kero, *Migration from Finland to North America in the Years Between the United States Civil War and the First World War* (Turku, Finland: Institute for Migration, 1974), p. 91-93.

2. For example Solomon Ilmonen's three-volume history, *Amerikan Suomalaisten Historia*, tells the story of early pioneer communities largely through the men. A person usually has to dig into the histories of individual men in order to find anything out about the women. Studies that do refer to women include: John Kolehmainen, *Haven in the Woods: The Story of the Finns in Wisconsin* (Madison, Wisconsin: State Historical Society of Wisconsin, 1951), p. 59 and A. William Hoglund, *Finnish Immigrants in America, 1880-1920* (Madison, Wisconsin: The University of Wisconsin Press, 1960), particularly p. 80-97.

3. Carl Ross' book, *The Finn Factor in American Labor, Culture and Society* (New York Mills, Minnesota: Parta Printers, Inc., 1977), discusses women within the context of various events and times, using primary source materials researched and organized by himself and me, separately and together, during 1974-75. See also my paper, "Naiset Mukaan: An Introductory Survey of Finnish American Immigrant Feminism" presented at the Midwest Women Historians' First Conference, 1975. See also Hilda Karvonen, "Three Proponents of Women's Rights in the Finnish-American Labor Movement from 1910-1930: Selma Jokela McCone, Maiju Nurmi and Helmi Mattson" in *For*

the Common Good: Finnish Immigrants and the Radical Response to Industrial America (Superior, Wisconsin: Tyomies Society, 1977), p. 195-216; and Carl Ross, "The Feminist Dilemma in the Finnish Immigrant Community," Finnish Americana, 1 (1978), p. 71-83.

4. See Armas Holmio, Michiganin Suomalaisten Historia (Hancock, Michigan: The Book Concern, 1967) as well as Matti Kaups, "The Finns in the Copper and Iron Ore Mines of the Western Great Lakes Region, 1864-1905: Some Preliminary Observations" in The Finnish Experience in the Western Great Lakes Region: New Perspectives (Turku, Finland: Institute for Migration, 1975). Matti Kaups has thus far done the most detailed recent study of these early communities and women's function in them.

5. The many local histories provide a rich source for information about the lives of Finnish-American immigrant women. Two good examples are Elsie M. Collins, From Keweenaw to Abbaye (Ishpeming, Michigan: Globe Printing, Inc., 1975) and karl Ahlbeck, Taming the Wilderness: A Short History of the Finnish Settlement of Isabella, Minnesota. Also useful are several sociological studies which use first-generation immigrant women interviews: Ralph H. Smith, "A Sociological Survey of the Finnish Settlement of New York Mills, Minnesota and Its Adjacent Territory," (thesis, University of Southern California, 1933); Gladys Pierson, "Acculturation of the Finns in Milltown, Montana," (M.A. thesis, Montana State University, 1941); Harry Richard Doby, "A Study of Social Change and Social Disorganization in a Finnish Rural Community," (Ph.D. dissertation, University of California, 1960).

6. Kero, op. cit., p. 125; Carl Ross' study of domestic workers included in this volume is the first important step in what hopefully will become a major investigation.

7. Kaups, op. cit., p. 87-88.

8. Hoglund, op. cit., p. 83.

9. The one exception is the Knights of Kaleva, which began as an all-male organization in 1989. But it quickly saw the error of its ways for in 1902, the Ladies of Kaleva organized as co-participants in this secret benefit society.

10. John Kolehmainen, "The Finnish Immigrant Nyrkkilehti," Common Ground, 4 (1943), p. 105-6; John Kolehmainen, "Finnish Temperance Societies in Minnesota," Minnesota History, 22(1941), p. 391-403; Solomon Ilmonen, Amerikan Suomalaisen Raittiusliikkeen Historia, Juhlajulkaisu Suomalaisen Kansallis Raittius Veljeysseuran 25 vuotisen toiminnan muistoksi (Ishpeming, 1912).

11. Ilmonen, op. cit..

12. Elis Sulkanen, Amerikan Suomalaisen Työväenliikkeen Historia (Fitchburg, Massachusetts: Amerikan Suomalainen Kansanvallan Liitto ja Raivaaja, 1951); Pöytäkirja-Amerikan Suomalaisten Sosialisti-Osastojen

*Edustajakokouksesta, Hibbingissä, Minnesota Elokuun 1-7 Päivänä 1906* (Hancock, Michigan: Työmieken Kirjapaino, 1907); *Pöytäkirja* Amerikan Suomalaisten Sosialistijärjestön Edustajakokouksen Hancock, Michigan 23-30 Elok. 1909 (Fitchburg, Massachusett: Raivaaja Krjapaino, no date); *Pöytäkirja 1-5, 7-10 Kesäkuuta 1912 Suomalaisten Sosialistiosastojen ja Työväenyhdistysten Viiden eli Suomalainen Sosialistijarjestön Kolmannen Edustajakokouksen* (Fitchburg, Massachusett: Suomalainen Sosialisti Kustannus Yhtiö, n.d.).

13. V. Rautanen, *Amerikan Suomalainen Kirkko* (Hancock, Michigan: Suomalais-Luteerilainen Kustannusliike, 1911).

14. Alma Haapanen, Lydia Kangas, K.H. Mannerkorpi, Miina Perttula, B.V. Rautanen, *Lukukirja: Amerikan Suomalaisille Lapsille,* I and II (Hancock, Michigan: Suomalais-Luteerilainen Kustannuslike, 1916).

15. S. Ilmonen, *Amerikan Suomalaisten Sivistyshistoria: Johtavia aatteita, Harrastuksia, Yhteisyprintö jä ja tapahtumia siirtokansan keskuudessa,* (Hancock, Michigan: Suomalias-Luteerilainen Kustannusliike, 1931), I p. 256, II, p. 158. Ilmonen states that in 1915, he had counted 75 teachers and that by 1931, in St. Louis County, Minnesota (Duluth) there were more Finnish women teachers than there were in the whole country sixteen years before. He claims in 1931 that the total number was many hundreds.

16. Holmio, *op. cit.,* p. 143 and 245 49; G.L. Price, "The Angel of the Roundheads," *World's Work,* 26, no. 3 (July 1913), p. 349-52.

17. *Calumetin Suomalaisen Nais-Yhdistyksen Ensimmäinen Kalenteri,* 1896. (no publisher, n.d.); *Naisten Lehti,* scattered issues, 1898-1909; *Naisyhdistys Pyrkijän 50:s Vuosijuhla 1893-1943* (Brooklyn, New York: Naisyhdistys Pyrkijä, 1943).

18. Pöytäkirja 1906, 1909, 1912, *op. cit.;* "Naistemme Pyrinnöistä New Yorkissa" *Tietokäsikirja Amerikan Suomalaisille* I (1912), p. 142-47; Emma Mattila, "Naisten Toiminta Amerikan Suomalainen Työväenliikkeessä," *Työmies* (September 12, 1946); *Naisten Lehti,* op. cit.

19. See my "Naiset Mukaan" paper referred to earlier. See also Ross' "The Feminist Dilemma" article which by its very title leads us to believe that we are looking at feminist activity. See also the tone and language used by Hilda Karvonen in her previously cited article.

20. Linda Malmberg, "A Program Presented at a Women's Meeting in Calumet, Michigan, November 29, 1894" in *Calumetin Suomalaisen Nais-Yhdistyksen Ensimmänen Kalenteri, op. cit.,* p. 25-31.

21. Ida Pasanen, "Hiukan Naiskysymyksen Johdosta," *Työmies* (November 27, 1909);: Wargelin-Brown, "Naiset Mukaan," *op. cit.*

22. *Naisten Lehti,* various issues, 1899-1909.

23. *Pöytäkirja* (1912), p. 111-13.

24. V. Rautanen, "Naiset Mukaan," *Amerikan Suometar* (April 29, 1908) and "Mille Pohjalle", *Naisten Lehti* (April, 1909).

236    M. Wargelin-Brown

25. See *Pöytäkirja*1906 and 1909; particularly note Hilda Sikanen-Sandberg's long speech, p. 197-200, and the men's replies, p. 201-5.

26. Ibid.

27. "Kirje-osasto," *Naisten Lehti* (December 1909), p. 3 (italics added).

28. Solomon Ilmonen, *Amerikan Suomalaisten Sivistys Historia*, I, p. 103-5. This attitude helps to explain why the Brotherhood earlier in 1907 had originally been taken aback by the thought of a woman coming from Finland to tour the country and speak on temperance for a year. They seriously questioned whether an educated and cultured woman could endure the hardships of travel. After some considerable discussion, they agreed to let Alma Hinkkanen come. See Ilmonen's *SKR Veljeyseura Juhlajulkaisu*, p. 240-41.

29. Moses Hahl, "Naisagitaattori," March 30, 1904, *Työmies*, as quoted in *Työmies Kymmenvuotias* (Hancock, Michigan: Työmies Publishing Co., 1913), p. 85.

30. Alan Dundes, "Folk Ideas as Units of Worldview," *Journal of American Folklore*, 84 (1971), p. 93-103; Henry Glassie, *Folk Housing in Middle Virginia: A Structural Analysis of Historic Artifacts* (Knoxville: University of Tennessee Press, 1976); David Pace, "Structuralism in History and the Social Sciences," *American Quarterly*, 30 (1978), p. 282-97.

31. V. Rautanen, *Amerikan Suomalainen Kirkko*, p. 161-62.

32. Ibid., p. iii-iv.

33. Ibid.

34. Werner Nikander, *Amerikan Suomalaisia: Muotokuvia ja Lyhyitä Elämäkerrallisia Tietoja* (Hancock, Michigan: Suomalais-Luteerilainen Kustannusliike, 1927), p. 236.

35. Douglas Ollila, "The Suomi Synod: 1890-1920" and "The Suomi Synod as an Ethnic Community" in *The Faith of the Finns* edited by Ralph J. Jalkanen (East Lansing, Michigan: Michigan State University Press, 1972), p. 165 and 251-56.

36. Axel Olrik, "Epic Laws of Folk Narrative" in *The Study of Folklore*, edited by Alan Dundes (Englewood Cliffs, N.J.: Prentice-Hall, 1965), p. 129-41.

37. Stith Thompson, *Motif Index of Folk Literature*, 6 vols., *ff Communications* Nos. 106-9, 116, 117. The *Motif Index* identifies these motifs as K1837, H50, H110, D11, D510, and Q555.

38. Nikander op. cit., p. 232; Hannes Elenius, *Murunen Suomea Villikorpeen* (Hancock, Michigan: Amerikan Suometar, 1939).

39. *Murunen Suomea Villikorpeen*, p. 41-42.

40. Ibid., p. 5-6.

41. Ibid., p. 5.

42. Ibid., p. 4.

43. *Murunen Suomea Villikorpeen*, reissued 1950.

44. Stith Thompson, *The Folktale* (New York: Holt, Rinehart and Winston, Inc., 1946), p. 456.

45. *Motif Index*, N620 and X1110 and X1130.

46. Thompson, *op. cit.*, p. 319.

47. William R. Bascom, "Four Functions of Folklore" in *The Study of Folklore, op. cit.*, p. 279-98.

48. Finnish-American community and institutional histories frequently include such material. A good example of this appears in *Työmies Kymmenvuotias*, p. 50: Supposedly, during the first significant labour strike in the copper country in 1872, Finnish women ambushed the sheriff who was trying to bring the strike leaders to jail. On their own, the women decided to hide in some stables between Hancock and Calumet so that when the sheriff and his prisoners arrived to exchange horses, they could capture the prisoners. Indeed, when the men arrived, the women threw some logs at the horses' legs and made their escape with the prisoners. This is not an example of role reversals; it is an illustration of how the community would include stories of women's bravery and independence when they wanted to look back to their heritage. All of these stories, however, will be told in such a way that the people and events would not threaten permanently the basic notions about male and female roles.

49. Even Maggie Walz, who seems to most of us the one genuine feminist in this period, is very concerned that she appear in the traditional role. In the interview which served as the basis for Price's article cited earlier, she asserts that while she may not be a mother, she is nevertheless godmother to literally hundreds of children. And in a very recent interview, her niece relayed a family story, to the effect that Maggie had been engaged to be married, but her fiance was killed in an accident. See Kathryne Belden Ashley, *Islands of the Manitou* (Coral Gables, Florida: Crystal Bay Publishers, 1978), p. 129.

# Finnish American Women in Transition, 1910-1920

*Carl Ross*

The employment of Finnish immigrants in domestic service and work in the mining industry constitute the most important work experiences shaping the Finnish-American community. The relationship of Finnish immigration to the mining industry has been examined extensively, but the employment of Finnish immigrant women as domestic servants had been noted only in passing, while its significance remained largely unnoticed. It has been suggested that work as domestics drew women to urban centres, influenced the rate and destination of women's emigration from Finland, produced an unequal geographic distribution of men and women and both male and female-dominated communities among the Finnish immigrants.[1]

Equal attention has not been given, however, to the position of substantial economic and social independence that Finnish immigrant women derived from employment as domestic workers. They were, as a consequence, less dependent on men and marriage for security and enjoyed greater freedom in social, sexual and marriage relations than that accorded to women within the context of old country tradition. Conditions of employment accentuating isolation from the immigrant community, the search for social life and male companionship, the exercise of social independence, and criticism of the behaviour of Finnish men, were factors that led young women into conflict with the conception of women's role in society and the family as defined by Finnish tradition. New conceptions of women's role in society and the family emerged from this conflict and probably conditioned the character of the Finnish-American family and the Finnish-American women's perception of their role in subsequent decades. The decade 1910 to 20 was crucial to this development inasmuch as the number of young immigrant women of marriageable age reached a peak in these years and the character of domestic work changed so as to facilitate marriages and separate households. Undoubtedly a process of migration and population shift among the Finnish immigrants, which yet remains to be examined, accompanied these developments. By 1920, the community of comparatively recently arrived immigrants, the bulk of them young and unmarried, had emerged into communities of Finnish-American family households whose characteristics were determined by American influences as much as by Finnish cultural and social tradition.

For purposes of this study, the most significant aspects of emigration from Finland were the following:

1/ Of the 301,767 emigrants to leave Finland between 1869 and 1914, 35.1 per cent were women, 64.7 per cent men.[2]

2/ While emigration from rural Finland was heavily male-dominated, "the number of men and women among emigrants leaving towns was approximately equal."[3]

3/ The emigrants were predominantly young men and women. Between 1900 and 1914, "fifty-three and two-tenths percent of the emigrants from the entire country were from 16 to 25 years old," the under-16 group constituted approximately 11 per cent of the total and the 26 to 30 age group approximately 17 per cent. Thus, 80 per cent were under 30 years of age.[4]

4/ Of all the emigrants from Finland between 1900 and 1914, only 23.9 per cent were married; 74.6 per cent were single unmarried persons, and 1.5 per cent were widows, widowers, divorcees or unknown.[5]

This statistical profile of Finnish emmigration to America graphically places the immigrant woman in perspective, as part of the whole. It indicates that the personal relationships among Finnish immigrant men and women and the establishment of marriages and households, which became the foundations of both Finnish-American communities and institutions, were essentially forged after emigration within American conditions.

Social historians have emphasized recently the central significance of work, particularly in industrializing America of the late nineteenth and early twentieth centuries, in the process of socialization and acculturation characteristic of both immigration to America and rural migration into urban centres.[6]

The underlying thesis of this paper is that the employment of Finnish-American women as domestics had a profound and lasting impact upon the fundamental characteristics of the Finnish-American community, and further, that it is impossible seriously to conduct studies of Finnish-American women outside the context of the whole Finnish-American community, or to consider Finnish immigrant history without the inclusion of the women and their particular experiences.

However, emigration statistics have consistently understated the proportion of women in the Finnish-American immigrant community, and thus, inadvertently contributed to the underestimation of women's roles and place in Finnish immigrant history that is characteristic of most studies of Finnish immigrant experiences in America. While Kero has noted that women were 35.1 per cent of all immigrants from Finland, he also reports that they constituted 41.5 per cent during the years from 1895 to 1899 and 39.8 per cent in the years from 1900 to 1914. Moreover, a significant variation from the average among several age groups must be noted.[7]

Women emigrated at a younger age. In the major years of immigration from 1900 to 1914, the number of females under age 16 was actually greater than the number of males in the same age group: the number of women immigrants 16 to 20 years of age was two-thirds the number of comparable men; while the number of women 21 to 25 years of age was half the number of men the same age.[8] The disproportion (fewer women to men) among immigrants was greater in older age groups. But after immigration, as the under-16 group reached marriageable age, the proportionate numbers of women available for and seeking marriage must have increased. Indications also are that more men than women returned to Finland.[9] As the immigrant community aged, death also took its toll and probably at an accelerated rate among males. The table below indicates that the actual percentage of women among the Finnish immigrants was 38.7 per cent in 1910, 43 per cent in 1920, and 45.8 per cent in 1930.[10]

## U.S. FOREIGN-BORN FINNISH-SPEAKING POPULATION

| Year | Men | Women | Total | Women as % of whole |
|------|------|--------|---------|------|
| 1910 | 73,549 | 46,399 | 119,948 | 38.7% |
| 1920 | 75,588 | 56,955 | 132,543 | 43.0% |
| 1930 | 67,796 | 57,198 | 124,994 | 45.8% |

SOURCE: Based on Report of the 15th Federal Census, 1930, Vol. II, p. 345

An examination of regional variations in the distribution of immigrant women in 1920 indicates that in every major area of Finnish settlement the proportion of women exceeded the average for Finnish emigration in earlier years. Federal census reports for 1920 indicate that women, as a percentage of the total Finnish immigrant population were, respectively: 47.0 per cent in New England; 55.3 per cent in the Middle Atlantic region; 42.7 per cent in the East North Central states; 38.7 per cent in the Mountain states; and 39.5 per cent in the Pacific Coast states. Women outnumbered men in five states: New York, Illinois, Connecticut, New Jersey and Delaware, while the number of men and women was essentially equal in Massachusetts and Rhode Island.[11] Among Finnish immigrants over 21 years of age women outnumbered men in New York City (5,551 to 4,213), Chicago (764 to 719), Boston (274 to 262), and Pittsburgh (61 to 39). In Manhattan women were 63.9 per cent (2,983 women, 1,681 men). In other major cities, numerical differences were not extreme[12]; for instance, Cleveland, with 566 men, 469 women; Minneapolis, 549 men, 513 women; Portland, 783 men, 554 women; San Francisco, 985 men, 789 women; and Detroit, 956 men, 705 women.

The figures support the conclusions that Finnish immigrant women were substantially concentrated in major urban centres; that there were both male- *and* female-dominated communities among the Finns; and that, assuming far wider disparities of distribution by sex in earlier years, the distribution of men and women was more equally balanced by the 1920s.

Affecting both the absolute number of women and the proportionate numbers of men and women within the Finnish-American community were increasing numbers of second generation persons of whom there were 76,261 born of immigrant parents by the year 1910.[13] Presumably they represented approximately equal numbers of males and females with an unknown number having reached adult status, or doing so by 1920. This suggests that, particularly with respect to persons of an age when they would be actively seeking marriages. Apparently the extreme disparity of sexes that prevailed earlier, especially in some mining and logging communities, was diminished. On the Mesabi Range, the proportion of men to women had been 4 to 1 in 1895 and extreme generally in mining states.[14] By 1920 the situation had changed drastically. Between 1910 and 1920 the mining states of Michigan and the Rocky Mountain area (which were strongly male-dominated) declined in Finnish population; the New England, Middle Atlantic, West Coast and some Midwest states gained both from new immigrants and migrants moving from other states. The impact was significant: for instance, Michigan lost 7.7 per cent while New York gained 47.4 per cent.[15] The underlying reasons for these population shifts are outside the scope of this study, but it is useful to point out that while there is considerable information concerning migrations of male workers, or migrations related to shifts in employment and other industrial conditions where it concerns men, or even of families to farms, little is known of migration among women or to what degree the concentration of Finnish women in large urban centres was relatively stable, increased or declined, during these years. It is, however, a fact that by 1920, the distribution on a state basis of Finnish immigrant women followed the same general pattern as the distribution of Finnish immigrant population: 43.5 per cent of them lived in Michigan, Minnesota and Wisconsin; 21.9 per cent in New York State and Massachusetts; 13.5 per cent in the three West Coast states.[16] A reasonable assumption is that 1920 represented a sort of watershed marking the end of an era in which Finnish immigrant women were strongly identified as domestic workers and that they had by and large assumed new roles as married women with families who, insofar as they held jobs outside the home, were engaged in a wide range of occupations.

Among the newer immigrants from eastern and southern Europe, Finnish women were the only group to show a decided propensity for domestic work. Italian women, for instance, avoided work incompatible with their family role, while Polish and Russian Jewish women's "preference for home manufacturing—piecework in the needle trades—suggests that they too sought work compatible with traditional family role."[17] Among the earlier immigrants, Irish, German and Swedish, the situation was quite different. For instance, the 1900 census showed that 61.9 per cent of Scandinavian women worked as servants or laundresses. Possibly Finnish women, like "Scandinavian women entering the United States, were participating in the traditional rural-urban migration wherein

244    C. Ross

young farm women entered town households as servants."[18] A
larger proportion of women immigrants than of men came from
urban Finland, in fact, the actual numbers of men and women
emigrants from urban areas was approximately equal.[19] Many had
acquired previous experience as servants in Finland. According to
Jarnefelt, for instance, 396 of 1,128 women immigrants arriving in
eastern United States' ports from June 1894 to May 1895, listed
their occupation as "servants." This was the single largest occupational group except labourer among men listed for Finnish immigrants during that year.[20]

Already in the 1890s, Finnish women were being drawn to
employment as domestics in larger cities throughout the country,
but especially on the eastern seaboard, while male Finnish immigrants were in demand as mine and forest labourers, largely in the
Midwest mining regions. The urban concentrations of Finnish immigrant women still evident in the 1920 census figures cited here
for cities over 100,000 were the result. Employment of foreign-born
women as domestics peaked in 1910 at 333,011 and fell to 207,811
by 1920, a drop of 37.6 per cent.[21] Thus, in a period of decline of
domestic workers among immigrants who were older and less likely
to work as domestics, the number of available Finnish women of
precisely the right age reached a peak, since 56.5 per cent of all
foreign-born servants employed in cities over 50,000 were aged 16
to 24.[22] Finnish women were in great demand as domestic servants
in such communities as Manhattan where they outnumbered Finnish men two to one, and a dozen employment agencies vied with
each other through advertisements in the *New Yorkin Uutiset* for
the profitable privilege of placing them in jobs.[23]

Work as domestics was available to recently arrived immigrants unable to speak English. It was assumed that a knowledge of
English and elementary facts of life in America would be learned
on the job. Maggie Walz, for instance, learned English in her first
job upon arriving as a young woman from Finland.[24] Domestic
service was perceived widely as an apprenticeship in household
skills, cooking and keeping house American style, even as a preparation for marriage. One writer in *Toveritar* was extremely critical
of mistresses who preferred to *"pleiata leiti"* (play the lady) rather
than to give attention to organizing and teaching household duties,
or were incompetent to give instruction in such matters.[25] Moreover, for the non-English-speaking immigrant newcomer, jobs in
offices, retail or manufacturing establishments hiring women were
not easily obtainable. As Katzman has pointed out in his study of
domestic work, *Seven Days a Week*, pay levels for domestic work

were comparable to, and frequently higher than pay levels in other employment available to women.²⁶

The unpopularity of domestic work among non-immigrant white women was largely due to the social stigma attached to the work and the restrictions of personal freedom that live-in domestic service imposed. Finnish immigrant women employed as domestics, on the other hand, enjoyed a high status in the Finnish immigrant community, as testified to in Akseli Jarnefelt-Rauonheimo's reports on Finnish-American life both in 1899 and again in the 1920s.²⁷ Their earnings (considering room and board as part of a live-in servant's pay) compared favourably with those of men in the community. In areas where women predominated both in numbers and as the major wage-earners, the development of community and institutional life among the Finns in early years was strongly dependent upon the support of the young women domestic workers, though gratitude for their generosity was often tempered by criticism of their expenditures for clothes, drinking beer, or entertainment outside the Finn centres.²⁸ Acceptable community status was accompanied by a degree of personal freedom from traditional and family restraints hitherto unknown to these young women. Economic independence was assured through earnings adequate for considerably more than bare necessities. Free time off the job, limited though it was, meant a new-found opportunity for personal enjoyment and social life beyond the confines of the immigrant community that was all the more attractive in that it represented participation in the social and cultural life common to young American women.

If expectations sometimes exceeded realities, domestic work still represented an experience in modernization, in acquiring job skills and work discipline associated with an industrial society, especially in the degree that household appliances were introduced rapidly in the years prior to 1920. Work also afforded an income, some leisure time, and role models of American women in the mistresses of the households. One young woman, discussing the advantages of cosmetics and modish dress in attracting the romantic attention of men, wrote that the "paint and powder" applied by the mistress always seemed to show her fading looks off to advantage, concluding that, though she herself did not use the cosmetics, it was quite proper to emulate this American way. Domestic service speeded the acculturation of the immigrant women through experiences women did not share with the male members of the immigrant community.²⁹

In other respects the disadvantages of domestic work were an introduction to the particular conditions of work and life for American women: the realities of the American woman's world, in which domestic work was at the bottom rung of occupational status values. In a cry from the heart, a Finnish woman from Portland wrote that in Oregon factory and retail employees worked a 54-hour week while live-in servants work 82 hours a week, she expressed the hope for the day when domestic servants might get better living conditions, be regarded as persons whose labour has value and would "no longer be held inferior and looked down upon as is done today."[30] A Seattle woman wrote, "our work day is fifteen hours and sometimes longer. When, then, is there time for enjoyment?[31] Servants "averaged about two more hours of work than othe working women, and long after the 5 1/2-day workweek had become prevalent, household workers continued to work seven days a week," and, except when sleeping, "a live-in domestic was at the beck and call of her mistress."[32]

Work was readily available, but job changes were frequent as the domestic worker sought positions with better working and living conditions commensurate with growing skills and experience, or as employers replaced them with new, less experienced and lower paid servants. One domestic wrote that in Los Angeles, "domestic workers are even more at the mercy of employment agencies," since there are fewer Finns than in any other large city and "domestic workers when changing jobs usually live in the homes of some [Finnish] workers they are acquainted with."[33] Fees charged by Los Angeles employment agencies were reported to be 70 per cent of the first month's wage.[34] Frequent job changes were costly in fees to agencies: Katzman reports that in New York City during 1906 through 1908, "the modal point was six to eleven months in a position," while an employment agency in Springfield, Massachusetts, in 1918, "placed 1,000 women in 4,000 domestic jobs during the course of the year."[35]

Efforts to cope with problems of domestic employment were a major incentive for women's organization among the Finnish immigrants. The *Pyrkijä* society of New York established in 1893, addressed itself primarily to the social contact, self-education, and mutual assistance needed by domestic workers.[36] In 1904 New York domestics established the *Naisten Osuuskoti* (Women's Cooperative Home) "for raising the economic position of working women," to provide at reasonable cost "a place for women to live in between jobs and on vacations," and to "aid in securing employment."[37] Both the New York women's home and one in San Francisco established cooperative employment agencies, probably the only two such agencies ever to operate in the United States.[38]

The most ambitious, but possibly the least successful, effort was launched by Selma Jokela-McCone through a series of articles in the *Toveritar* beginning in May of 1916 advocating the nation-wide organization of domestic workers beginning with the Finns.[39] The proposals on "How the Position of Servant Girls Can Be Improved" indicated a familiarity with the ideas of American liberal reformers relative to domestic labour. Jokela-McCone proposed to embark on a program of training young women in the essential skills for domestic service, from learning English to cooking and cleaning skills. She argued that those who were most skilled commanded the best jobs, worked most regularly and therefore, craft unions should be set up to train skilled domestic workers and control their job placement. She saw the women's cooperative homes and a similar club in Los Angeles as prototypes for such a labour union. But the times were hardly propitious; the proposals were bitterly attacked by *Toveri* editor William Reivo and became lost in a sea of controversy over the relative merits of craft and industrial unionism, causing one of "Selm Tati's" supporters to complain that the issue "receives little attention in print and even less from the men's quarter."[40] The several months'-long debate concerning domestic workers in *Toveritar* shows how essentially feminist and reformist attitudes overrode considerations of political orthodoxy and party factionalism among socialist women who were moving closer to mainstream approaches for resolving women's issues.

The Finnish immigrant community seemed to accept the economic independence of young women and expected their participation in immigrant institutions. But it could not provide satisfaction for the human needs arising from the isolation and loneliness of a domestic's life. They suffered restricted freedom and leisure time, separation from male companionship in the most drastic sense that most Finnish men were working in mining and lumbering towns, and little opportunities for relaxation, romance and enjoyment beyond the strict limits imposed by old country codes concerning the propriety of women's conduct. Finnish publishers turned out publications to fill empty hours with melodramatic tales centring on the dangers of drink, dance halls, seduction and white slavery, but it was not moral peril so much as sheer loneliness and the yearning for a solid marriage relationship that disturbed the young women who found the Finnish community too restrictive and the Finnish men too willing to exploit them.[41]

Both because it restricted opportunities to meet eligible men, and because of the virtual impossibility for live-in servants to maintain a separate household after marriage, domestic service was a practical obstacle to marriage. However, a gradual shift from live-in service to day-work was changing the character of domestic work as an occupation. Home appliances, increasingly introduced in the years prior to 1920, limited the need for servants. Simultaneously other technological changes were opening new occupations outside the home. Many women shifted to service trades (hotels, restaurants, laundries, etc.) or to the textile industry or other factory, commercial and industrial jobs. By 1920, domestic service "had changed from the major form of female employment to an occupation statistically unimportant among all but black women."[42] An awareness of these changes was apparent during the discussion among Finnish women in Toveritar in 1916, but actual patterns of change in their employment have yet to be examined. Bearing in mind that the major form of employment among Finnish immigrant women was domestic work, it is interesting to note that the number of married domestics increased steadily among foreign-born women after 1900 when it was only 4.7 per cent. By 1920 the percentage of those married was greater than for any other occupation.[43]

What was the situation for Finnish immigrants among whom the number of women of marriageable age peaked in the years between 1910 and 1920? Conditions of employment became less an obstacle to marriage, but actual geographic dispersal of men and women by their occupational status remained a major barrier.

These subjects became the centre of attention in 1912-1913 when the New Yorkin Uutiset with Matti Kurikka as editor, and a national circulation in the United States and Canada, became marriage-broker to immigrant Finns with columns of personal ads soliciting correspondence with intent to marry. Young men wrote offering to rescue "you who serve demanding mistresses" and young women replied that "we are fed up with this single life." Lead miners from Utah, silver miners from British Columbia, iron miners from Minnesota and copper miners from Michigan wrote poetic prose of how "the single life is sad and the heart pines for an affectionate friend," of longing for a woman "to bring grace and warmth to my just established home," and of hearts turning to "thoughts of love in the Spring." Yet with a touch of cruelty, almost without exception, the letters echoed the sentiments of three young men from Minnesota to whom letters "would be like a kiss from you," but warn that "old maids and grass widows needn't bother since there are such here too."[44]

Simultaneously the New Yorkin Uutiset opened its columns to free discussion by young people and suddenly courtship by corre-

spondence was submerged in scores of letters from women expressing disillusionment with romantic love, a desire to postpone marriage, to limit the size of families, and criticism of Finnish men for
their behaviour and treatment of women. "Everyone, of course,
marries with a feeling of love ... but love only lasts a short time,"
wrote one young woman. A "New York Girl" wrote, "I look at the
young men, how they appear in a drunken state, lacking everyday
manners, many in the best years of their youth with rags on their
backs, and owing even for these as well as for food and rent. Set up
house with them? No, say I." Another: "I've received better treatment from non-Finn boys than from my own people ... that complaint of a mother of ten was a plain picture to us young women of
how the 'old man' treats us women when we become wives and
mothers." An older woman summed it up this way:

> Those who dress themselves stylishly and are bold
> achieve their goal. That's the American talent ... get-
> ting married has been the only goal ... [but] ... woman
> is no longer just a plaything for a man, women have
> power if they will only use it. She doesn't have to step
> in front of a priest alongside a drunk if she doesn't want
> to.[45]

These letters, of which these excerpts represent a small fraction, are
unusual for being written by those who are usually inarticulate.
They challenged the traditional position of women in Finnish society and the definition of women's role brought to American from
Finland. Consequently, these attitudes were seen by the community leaders—both men and women—as a betrayal of the Finnish
national tradition and spirit, a crime far more serious than a departure from strict Lutheran standards of morality. Kurikka castigated
the young for an "awful violation of the national spirit—*Heimori-
kos.*"[46] Sara Röyhy, a women's rights activist, urged women to act
in keeping with her role "as procreator of children and educator of
coming generations ... so that her mate will hold her in high es-
teem, and not as a means to satisfy base lusts," and so that she can
be happy "as a woman and mother."[47]

Soon, as Röyhy put it, the only subject of conversation was
"the inevitable ruination of women." A "Seaman" wrote how in a
dance hall "I watched in amazement as young Finnish girls ...
danced some kind of wild dance with 'dagoes' and all kinds of
bearded men." A "Bachelor" commented that here "in this big
America" the young women "powder and rouge their face, wear

'rats "in their hair"...and though "such a woman dresses in silks and ribbons, outwardly appears like a lovely summer day, her underwear are as dirty as can be." An editorial notice in *New Yorkin Uutiset*, "To Women," summed it up this way:

> Last Thursday evening at the Imatra orchestra dance the cheap dancing customs of some couples made a disgusting impression...it is to be hoped that women who must assume responsibility, will strongly protest against the 'turkey trot' and 'bunny hug' dances. Especially now when women's position in society is the burning question...our women should use every possible means to elevate themselves so that we receive recognition from men that our demands are just. How they are treated depends upon women alone.[48]

It would be difficult to state more explicity the traditional conception of women's role in Finland of the nineteenth and early twentieth centuries.

This serious discussion involving scores of young people and older commentators was published continuously twice a week for some four years from January 1912 to November 1915.[49] This "Nuorten Pakinoita" (Youth Chat) was undoubtedly the most popular section of Kurikka's paper, running to two full pages a week at the time of his death in October 1915. Letter writers were from all parts of the country and were predominantly young women discussing their most intimate concerns frankly and fluently in an atmosphere of free dialogue not to be confused with an "advice to the lovelorn" column or a Finnish version of Ann Landers. Possibly only the *America Letters* can compare in giving a portrait of the personal life and experience, and the turmoil concerning cultural values and standards, permeating the Finnish-American community in these years.

Simultaneously the *New Yorkin Uutiset* published reports on all significant developments in the worldwide women's suffrage movement and urged the involvement of Finnish-American women. Paradoxically, though advocating women's rights to vote and in marriage, Kurikka wrote articles elaborating the more conservative traditionalist views of Finnish society under such captions as "Women and the Home," "Additional Thoughts on Marriage," and "Mothers' Right to Vote." From these pages also emerges an image of Matti Kurikka as a significant figure on the American scene; this is particularily notable since historians generally have consigned him to quiet retirement a year or two before his death when in actuality he was still contributing at least two articles a week to the paper he continued to serve as editor-in-chief.[50] His last article was carried in the issue reporting his death; Eva Witkala's moving tribute to Kurikka and his life, published in "Nuorten Pakinoita," painted his image as a charismatic leader whose utopian vision of a new world had remained an inspiration to many of his contemporaries.[51] Not least among these contributions was the opening of *New Yorkin Uutiset* to the uncensored expression of opinion by Finnish-American women.

Consequently we have an extraordinary abundance of evidence concerning their social behaviour and attitudes, evidence reinforcing the belief that the conditions of employment as domestic workers was a basic factor in shaping responses to the American environment. More explicit discussions of domestic workers' job-related issues in *Toveritar* obliquely reflect the same conclusion; as in *New Yorkin Uutiset*, phrases occurred such as "women no longer need be the playthings of men" and explicit criticism of men for their attitudes toward women.

Women leaders and suffrage activists among the Finns did not echo the sometime strident voices of the young women. But a new definition of women's role did begin to emerge. Without challenging the premise that women's concerns are centred in the home, a new definition of women's responsibility was formulated and given its most succinct definition by Selma Jokela-McCone in 1916:

> The retrogressively minded say that women's responsibility is to govern the home, care for the children, and to guard their own personal spiritual and physical welfare. We, the progressive minded, say the same, but we disagree as to what home means.
>
> The conservatives argue that the home is enclosed within four walls and that women must not mix into, or even know anything about matters outside them. We progressives hold that in modern times the home no longer fits within four walls, that nowadays it is an integral part of local, state, national, and ultimately, of world affairs.[52]

From this premise, Jokela-McCone argued that women ought to concern themselves with all public issues, fight for suffrage, act and organize politically. The concept is notable for going beyond the earlier Finnish American women's movements, all the more so in that it expressed clearly the interest and participation in public affairs that characterized the otherwise home-centred role of Finnish-American women of the first and second generation during the 1920s and 1930s. This, of course, is the subject of further inquiry, but it would seem appropriate to note that some 90 per cent of all the Finnish immigrant men and women intermarried. Reliable data on marriages and numbers of Finnish-American households are difficult to obtain, but the 1920 federal census provides a valuable clue in reporting that of 145,506 second generation children of Finnish stock, 10,931 were children of Finnish mothers and non-Finn fathers, 6,655 of Finnish fathers and non-Finn mothers, and all the remainder had Finnish fathers and mothers.[53] The degree to which, within these households, Finnish-American women departed from traditional roles lies beyone the scope of this study, but A. William Hoglund has argued that "because immigrant women tended to acquire a status equal to that of men, they entered marriage in America more nearly as equals of men than if they had been in Finland."[54] It was an equality gained largely through the nature of their work experiences and the impact of these upon the Finnish-American community.

# Notes

1. Reino Kero, *Migration from Finland To North America* (Turku, Finland: Institute for Migration, 1974).

2. Ibid., pp. 91-92.

2. Ibid., pp. 96-97.

4. Ibid., pp. 236-37.

5. Ibid., p. 125.

6. Herbert C. Gutman, "Work, Culture and Society in Industrializing America," *American Historical Review* 78 (June 1973), pp. 531-88; David Katzman, *Seven Days a Week* (Women and Domestic Service in Industrializing America) (New York; Oxford University Press, 1978); and Carl Ross, *The Finn Factor In American Labor, Culture and Society* (New York Mills, Minnesota: Parta Printers, 1977).

7. Kero, *op. cit.*, p. 92.

8. Ibid. p. 236.

9. Ibid., p. 209.

10. Report of the 15th Federal Census, 1930, Vol. II, p. 347.

11. Ibid., pp. 358-69.

12. Report of the 14th Federal Census, 1920, Vol. II, "Citizenship of Foreign Born in Cities over 100,000 by Sex," pp. 872-88.

13. Ibid., p. 897.

14. Matti Kaups, "The Finns in the Copper and Iron Ore Mines of the Western Great Lakes Region, 1864-1905," in *The Finnish Experience in the Western Great Lakes Region* (Vammala; Migration Institute, 1975), pp. 73, 78.

15. Report of the Federal Census, 1930, Vol. II, pp. 358-69.

16. Calculated from ibid., pp. 358-69.

17. Katzman, *op. cit.*, pp. 65-67, 69; Ross, *op. cit.*, p. 22.

18. Katzman, *op. cit.*, p. 49, pp. 65-69.

19. Kero, *op. cit.*, pp. 96-67.

20. Akeli Järnefelt-Rauanheimo, *Suomalaiset Amerikassa* (Helsinki; Otava, 1899), p. 33.

21. Joseph Hill, "Women in Gainful Occupations, 1870-1920," *Census Monograph IX, 14th Census, p. 38.*

22. Katzman, *op. cit.*, p. 295.

23. See *New Yorkin Uutiset* ad columns, 1912-13.

24. Katzman, *op. cit.*, pp. 170-73; Ross, *op. cit.*, p. 31; G.L. Price, "North Michigan's Jane Adams," *Detroit Saturday Night*, December 16, 1911.

25. Letter from J——y Maki, *Toveritar*, June 6, 1916; "Luettavaa Aviolit-teen Aikoville," *Toveritar*, June 20, 1916.

26. Katzman, *op. cit.*, pp. 303-14.

27. *Suomalaiset Amerikassa*, pp. 288-301; *Meikäläisiä Merten Takana* (Porvoo, Finland: Werner Söderström, Oy., 1921), pp. 104-10.

28. *Suomalaiset Amerikassa*, pp. 299-300.

20. Katzman, *op. cit.*, pp. 133-34, 151-57, 171; Letter from "Kallen Tytär," *New Yorkin Uutiset*, January 25, 1913.

30. Letter from Tillie Mays, *Toveritar*, May 9, 1916.

31. Letter from "Tarjoilia" (A Servant), *Toveritar*, May 21, 1916.

32. Katzman, *op. cit.*, pp. 110, 112-113.

33. Letter from "Paljon Kokenut" (Experienced), *Toveritar*, July 11, 1916.

34. Report on a Los Angeles Servants Club, *Toveritar*, May 9, 1916.

35. Katzman, *op. cit.*, p. 138.

36. Ross, *op. cit.*, pp. 31-33; *50th Anniversary Journal of the Pyrkijä Society*, 1943; Minutes of the Naisyhdistys Pyrkijä, 1923-1960, Immigration History Research Center, University of Minnesota, St. Paul, Minnesota.

254    C. Ross

37. Bylaws of the "Naisten Osuuskoti," *Toveritar*, June 20, 1916; "Naisten-osuuskodin Perustus Homma," *Viisitoista Vuotta New Yorkin Sosialis-tiosaston Historiassa* (Fitchburg, 1918).

38. Katzman, *op. cit.*, p. 235; Jokela-McCone, *Toveritar*, June 20, 1916.

39. Jokela-McCone, *Toveritar*, May 9, 1916.

40. Letter from Emma Mattila, *Toveritar*, July 11, 1916; Jokela-McCone, "Ammattilaisuus ja Työväenliike," *Toveritar*, May 23, 1916.

41. Among such books are: Eva Witkala, *Suomalainen Orjatyttö* (Duluth: Finnish Daily Publishing Co., 1917); *Tanssisallista Helvettiin* (Hancock; Suomalais-Luuterilainen Kustannusliike, 1916); *Ompelutyttö* (New York Mills: Uusi Kotimaa, 1904); Ari Emerik, *Valkoista Orjuutta Vastaan* (Fitchbury: Pohjan Tähten Kirjapaine, 1911); Fanny Heino *Siirtölaistytön Kohtelu*; andrew Langila, *Hotellintyttö* (Red Jacket, Michigan: Kaleva, 1892).

42. Katzman, *op. cit.*, p. 93, pp. 128-33.

43. Jokela-McCone, "Palvelujattarikysymyksestä," *Toveritar*, June 13 and 20, 1916; Katzman, *op. cit.*, p. 87.

44. Quotes are from ads placed by: M. Maki, Mohawk, Michigan, January 25, 1912; Ida Laine, Lempi Luoto, Fanny Saari, Brooklyn, N.Y., Feburayr 8, 1912; Mr. Leikkivä, Mr. S. Lempivä, Mr. L. Lysti, R.F.D., New York Mills, Minn., February 8, 1912 and by others during 1912-13, at a cost of $1.00 for one time and three times for $2.00.

45. Letters in *New Yorkin Uutiset* from Kallen Tytär, January 25, 1913; A New York Girl, January 29, 1913; Jenny, January 25, 1913; Muija, January 29, 1913.

46. Matti Kurikka, "Naapurin Emännän Nimipäivänä, *New Yorkin Uutiset, January 25, 1912.

47. Sara Röyhy, "Ovatko Naiset Tuomitut," *New Yorkin Uutiset*, February 12, 1913; see also, Röyhy, *Muistelmia, 1135 Vuorukauden Matkoilta* (New York: New Yorkin Uutiset, 1917), describing her coast-to-coast travels on behalf of women's rights; and Eva Witkala, "Ovatko Naiset Tuomitut," *New Yorkin Uutiset*, March 8, 1913.

48. Letter signed, "Seaman," *New Yorkin Uutiset*, February 19, 1913; "A Bachelor," January 29, 1913, and a brief notice, "Naisille," August 3, 1912.

49. Kurikka, "Havaintoja Nuorten Pakinoista," *New Yorkin Uutiset*, January 29, 1913. Files of *New Yorkin Uutiset* on microfilm are available at the Immigration History Research Center, University of Minnesota, St. Paul, Minnesota, for this period of Kurikka's editorship, January 4, 1912 to December 29, 1915, and also for years following July 25, 1917.

50. These and other articles on women's issues by Kurikka appeared from time to time throughout the period of his editorship of *New Yorkin Uutiset* which terminated with his death on October 2, 1915.

51. Eva Witkala, "Vainajaa Muistelessä," *New Yorkin Uutiset,* October 20, 1915.

52. Jokela-McCone, "Naisen Velvollisuudet," *Toveritar,* October 3, 1916.

53. Report of the Federal Census, 1920, Vol. II, pp. 900-1: a table enumerating persons of mixed foreign parentage giving the country of birth of both mother and father (incidentally, 9,706 of these enumerated were of Finnish-Swedish parentage). A decidedly stronger propensity among Finnish immigrant women than men to marry non-Finns appears to be indicated by these figures, especially since the number of women involved is considerably less than the number of men.

54. A. William Hoglund, *Finnish Immigrants in America, 1880-1920* (Madison: University of Wisconsin Press, 1960), p. 83.

# Finnish Women in the North American Labour Movement

*Riitta Stjärnstedt*

More than 100,000 women emigrated from Finland to America before 1920. The majority were unskilled, single, rural girls who went to America to search for a better living and a freer existence. The married women followed their husbands, who had moved earlier.[2]

There was not much freedom of choice for the unskilled women in America either. Most Finnish women wound up as domestics and in various household work in restaurants, hotels and boarding houses. Some worked in textile mills in the east. The married women generally kept boarders in places where there were many single men. There were Finnish women in all Finnish regions, but mostly in the large cities of the east, where it was easiest for the unmarried women to find work as domestics.[3]

The Finnish organized activities were very lively and the women took part in them from the beginning. The greatest number of women probably belonged to church organizations. The intention of this paper is to examine the role of women in the activities of the Finnish-American workers' movement, and their role in it. The main attention is directed toward the Finnish-American Socialist Federation before it split in 1920.

The workers' movement began to gain influence among the Finnish Americans in the 1890s. The earliest organizations of Finnish workmen's societies were the Imatra League, which was founded in Gardner, Massachusetts, in 1903 and the Finnish American Workmen's League, which was founded in the central states the same year. After many ideological disputes those who supported international socialism won and the Finnish-American workmen's societies joined the Socialist Party of America.[4] In 1906 the Finnish socialist movement took a new shape when the Finnish Socialist Federation was founded in Hibbing, Minnesota. The Federation joined the Socialist Party of America as a foreign-language organization, and the relations between the party and the Federation were handled by the translator's office. A general committee, where all the states with Finnish branches got a seat, was founded to supervise the translator's office and to handle the general matters of the Federation.[5] The committee was discontinued in 1909, however, and the Executive Committee emerged as the most important organ of the Federation. The same year a decision of the founding convention to divide the Federation into three districts was carried out.[6]

Most important matters were decided at the conventions, which were held in Hancock, Michigan, in 1909, in Smithville, Minnesota, in 1912, in Chicago, in 1914 and 1919 and in Waukegan, Illinois, in 1920. The districts of the Federation, the Eastern, Central and Western districts, also held conventions of their own. The districts were led by the district committees.[7]

The membership of the Socialist Federation continued to grow until by 1913, it had a membership of more than 12,000. The dispute over its attitude toward the trade unions, especially the Industrial Workers of the World (IWW) founded in 1905, which had been going on for years, culminated in the split of the Socialist Federation in 1913-1914. The IWW, which through the years had rejected political activity and adopted anarchist doctrines, won the largest support of the Finns in the central and western districts. In the split, these districts suffered the most. Altogether about 3,000 members left the Federation.[8]

The First World War made the activity of the Socialist Federation more difficult. It was already on its way toward its final split largely because of the Bolshevik revolution in Russia and the resulting split of the socialist movement all over the world. The Finnish Socialist Federation left the Socialist Party of America in 1920 and split into two wings, those supporting the Communists and those supporting the Social Democrats.[9]

# Women in the Socialist Federation

From the beginning attempts were made to get women into the workers' movement. In the Imatra Society in Brooklyn, New York, it was suggested in 1891 that every man under threat of punishment take with him at least one woman into the society.[10] In 1904 Moses Hahl called attention to the fact that it was very important to get women into the movement especially in the big cities, where there were more women than men. By virtue of their majority the women decided what activities the other Finns were interested in. Hahl proposed the acquisition of a woman representative to arouse the women.[11]

It is hard to find out how many women participated in the movement, because women were seldom mentioned separately in the statistics of the Socialist Federation, which are unreliable in any case. The earliest information about membership of this kind is from 1906,[12] which gives a total of 705 women in 53 socialist clubs. This was 28 per cent of all members. Their percentage of women was the highest in the eastern states and in some clubs they even formed the majority. This is easily understood, because there were great numbers of Finnish women in these parts of the country.

According to membership figures collected in the end of 1911 there were 4,065 women (28 per cent of all members) in the 189 socialist branches which had answered the inquiry.[13] The figures for the three districts were:

| | | |
|---|---|---|
| Eastern District | 1,400 | 35% |
| Central District | 1,661 | 25% |
| Western District | 1,004 | 28% |

As the number of women was largest in the Central District, the split in 1914 reduced considerably the number of women in the Federation.

In later years only the Eastern District reported the numbers of men and women separately in their annual reports, and it can be seen that the percentage of women increased over the years:[14]

| | | |
|---|---|---|
| 1916 | 2,024 | 43% |
| 1917 | 2,414 | 44% |
| 1919 | 2,735 | 47% |
| 1920 | 2,654 | 47% |

According to statistics in 1920 there were 3,279 women in the FSF, 41 per cent of the total membership. The real number was larger, because only 145 branches out of 205 answered the inquiry,[15] but clearly the number of women who belonged to the Federation was now small outside the Eastern District.

The number of women who belonged to the Socialist Party of America is unknown. According to an estimate by the Women's Committee, 10 per cent of the total membership of the party in 1910 were women and 15 per cent in 1912.[16] Evans estimates that even when membership was at its highest in 1912, the number of women did not exceed 15,000.[17] In view of this more than one-fourth of the women belonging to the Socialist Party at that time were Finnish.

Why was the percentage of women in the Finnish Socialist Federation relatively high? What made them into socialists? Many of these women had been active in the workers' movement back in Finland. Women had joined the Workingmen's Associations already in the 1890s and demands for universal suffrage and equality for men and women had been put on the platform of the Labor Party of Finland, founded in 1899. In 1905, 21.1 per cent of the members of the Workingmen's Associations were women.[18] The women's socialist movement in Finland was probably the third largest in Europe after those of Germany and Austria.[19]

The conditions experienced by some Finnish women when they came to America made them receptive to socialism. Even if the wages and working conditions of domestics were better in America than in Finland, the objects of comparison were different, too. The economic and social gulf between employers and servants were much bigger in America than in Finland. The unemployment of the men and the strikes and their consequences showed the married women the bad side of capitalism.

Women all over the world were drawn to the socialist movement by the socialist determination to improve the social status of women. The book *The Woman and Socialism* by the German socialist, August Bebel had a great influence.[20] Both *Työmies* and *Raivaaja*, two of the Finnish newspapers in America, included women's rights in their programs.[21] The position of women was also discussed in other publications of the FSF.

The percentage of women in the Finnish Socialist Federation was larger than in the Finnish Social Democratic Party. The difference is even greater considering that there were fewer Finnish women than Finnish men in America. In 1906 women comprised 25.5 per cent of the Social Democratic Party of Finland (versus 28.2 per cent in the Socialist Federation) and in 1911, 23.4 per cent (versus 27.8 per cent in the Socialist Federation). The highest percentage of women in the Social Democratic Party was in 1909 when it was 25.2.[22] What are the reasons for this difference? Soikkanen thinks that many women in the working-class and the landless rural population in Finland stayed outside the workers' movement even if they would have been its natural supporters, since it was considered unacceptable for women to take part in public life.[23] In America many women grew out of such restrictive views.[24] On the other hand some who belonged to the Finnish-

American Workers' Movement did not consider the doctrine of Socialism to be as important as being together with other Finns.[25] This was true especially with the women, who more than the men were isolated from other Finns in their jobs and lonely as they did not know the English language. In the socialist clubs they found both company and hobbies.

There were more women who supported the socialists than the statistics show. All members of the subordinate branches of the clubs did not belong to the club itself. The most important form of activity for the women was the sewing circle which evidently included outsiders.[26] Karni believes that all the wives of the men who belonged to the Socialist Federation did not belong to it even if they supported the socialists, on account of the membership dues, which were a burden especially for the men with families.[27] This problem was discussed at the convention of 1912, and many thought that married women should be totally exempted from membership dues.[28] The dues of the women were generally lower than those of the men.[29]

# The Activities of Women in the Finnish Socialist Federation

One socialist principle was equality between men and women. How did this principle operate among the Finnish-American socialists, and what part did the women play in their activities?

The everyday activities of the Finnish Socialist Federation took place in the locals, which in addition to the spreading of the Socialist doctrine, offered a wide range of activities, such as drama clubs, brass bands, choirs and sewing clubs. The most important organ of the local was the board of directors, which handled financial matters. Its members were elected every two - four years. The committee on entertainment took care of the entertainment program, organizing social events and dances. The agitation committee was trusted with the spreading of the doctrine and its duties included the arranging of the actual meetings, the planning of the instruction programs and the securing of speakers.[30]

I have studied the participation of women in the activities of the three locals whose archives from the whole period of time have been at my disposal. The Gardner Finnish Socialist Branch (*Gardnerin Suomalainen Sosialistiosasto*) and the Quincy Finnish Workers' Association Veli (*Quincyn Suomalainen Työväenyhdistys Veli*)

were in Massachusetts and the Superior Finnish Socialist Branch
(*Superiorin Suomalainen Sosialistiosasto*) in Wisconsin.[31] The local
with the greatest percentage of women was Quincy. According to
the statistics of 1906, it had 86 women, more than half of its
membership. In following years the number of women remained in
the vicinity of 50 per cent and according to the statistics of 1911
there were 192 women in the local, a good 40 per cent. The
percentage of women probably remained the same after this time
because according to the minutes of 1918, 38 per cent of those who
joined the local were women. In the Superior local 45 members, or
38 per cent, in 1911 were women. The percentage of women in the
Gardner local increased all the time and in 1906 some 20 per cent
of the membership were women. The percentage had grown to 30
per cent in 1915 and in the beginning of 1919 to some 40 per cent.
The absolute numbers of women grew from 16 in 1906 to 75 in
1915 and 143 in 1917.[32]

The number of women among the officers of the board of
directors was significantly smaller than their numbers would have
implied. At best there were three women on the boards, usually
less and very often no women at all. There seems to have been a
certain office in every local to which a woman was often elected
and also offices to which women were never elected. In Gardner,
for example, women were never elected to the positions of chairman, secretary etc., but only ordinary as members of the board.
The same was true in Quincy. In Superior women usually served as
additional members, but also as other officers. Women were never
elected auditors in Gardner, but in Superior it was a common
office for the women.

In addition to the fact that fewer women were elected to the
boards of directors than men, they did not serve so long. The same
men were usually officers for many periods, but the terms of office
of the women were mostly limited to one.

The members of the board of directors were also elected to
other offices of the locals. The same persons belonged often to both
the board of directors and the committee on entertainment. The
composition of these organizations differed from each other in that
there were significantly more women on the committees on entertainment. Even if the women were absent from the board of directors they were almost always elected to the committees on entertainment. The agitation committees included women, too, but they
were usually under-represented.[33]

The activities of the women in the socialist locals centred on
the social side, whereas the men handled the more important tasks.
The women were the main supports of the "Hall Socialism." The

men usually had the task of keeping relations with the outside; for instance women were seldom sent as representatives of the locals to the joint meetings of the socialists.

The number of women who were active in the locals in small and even proportionally smaller than that of the men. Did this depend on the men or the women themselves? Local correspondents in the *Raivaaja* often conplained about the lack of interest shown by the women in the work of the locals; they did not attend meetings, for example, or take part in the debates.[34] The women, on the other hand, complained that the men did not even want them in tasks involving more responsibility, but just wanted to keep them in sewing circles earning funds for the locals.[35] There were very likely faults on both parts. The women were unaccustomed to functioning in offices of trust and to expressing their views and the men did not encourage them to any great extent. Their long working hours were an obstacle for women. The freedom of a domestic was limited, for example, and married women were hindered by the children.

The most common activity for the women in the socialist locals as in other Finnish-American organizations was the sewing clubs. There was one in almost all locals and their purpose was to raise money for various purposes, most commonly for building halls. These clubs brought in a lot of money with their bazaars and without them the construction of many a hall would have been delayed.[36] The women were eagerly persuaded to do sewing work and one writer in *Raivaaja* even wrote that every stitch in the women's handwork was a step toward the socialist society.[37] Thus the women raised the money and the men decided how to spend it.

As mentioned earlier, the socialist locals very seldom sent women as their representatives outside the locals. In the conventions of the Socialist Federation there were women delegates only the first three times, in 1906, 1909 and in 1912. At the convention in Hibbing in 1906 there were three woman delegates, Olga Heinonen, Hulda Anderson and Ida Pasanen. At the convention in Hancock in 1909 Hilda Sikanen was the only delegate.[38]

Before the convention of 1912 the women started to demand a greater share of delegation seats. They maintained that they had to be admitted to make the by-laws of the Federation as long as they had to obey them. They also wanted to propose improvements concerning women to the by-laws. They were not just content to get more delegates; the women in the Workers College proposed a women's meeting to discuss topics of special concern to women and to present resolutions to the convention. The meeting was arranged by the local in Duluth, Minnesota, where the Workers'

College was situated. The Duluth local wanted all socialist locals and especially their woman members to prepare reports to the women's meeting. The aim was to have a woman from every state with Finnish locals.[39]

The initiative did not win unanimous support and some women even feared that the question of "women's rights" would come forward. Their opposition was motivated by the fact that socialists did not recognize any separate men's and women's affairs. The travel expenses of the women were also thought to be too high and some people thought it would be more useful to hire a woman speaker.[40]

The women's meeting was held, although only eight women took part. However, these were, the most influential women, who had held many offices of the Federation. The *agitation* work of women was discussed at the meeting and a resolution concerning it was left to the convention. Other topics which were discussed were the establishment of a youth league, maternity insurance and matters concerning the circulation and financing of the *Toveritar*. A proposal containing the arrangement of a women's meeting in connection with coming conventions was made. The convention passed it, but this women's meeting remained the only one. Seven of the delegates to the women's meeting also took part in the convention.[41] Later on women were never elected convention delegates.

Few women took part in district conventions. The district committee with the highest number of women was the Eastern District committee in 1913, when three of its seven members were women. After 1914 the only woman who belonged to any district committee of the Socialist Federation was Tyyni Koski-Hyrsky-murto, who in the years 1916-17 was member of the Western District committee.[42]

The more important the office was the less women were elected to it. Only two women belonged to the general committee of the Socialist Federation during its time of activity. To the most important organ of the Federation, the Executive Committee, a woman was elected only in 1913, 1917 and 1919.[43]

## Debate on the Women's Clubs

Many women who belonged to the Socialist Federation were not satisfied with their role in it. The division of work in the locals caused discontent and the women maintained that they could not improve themselves in the locals. It was believed that separate women's clubs would improve women's opportunities. The most stubborn fight concerning women in the Socialist Federation was fought over the establishment of these women's clubs.

The model for the women's clubs came from the workers' movement in Finland. Women had there belonged to the workingmen's associations by joining women's clubs which had been founded in connection with the associations.

By the 1890s there were women's clubs functioning in the largest cities and at the turn of the century their number had grown to about forty. There were two types of these clubs—local trade unions and women's clubs in the workingmen's associations. The difference between organizing in political and trade unions was not yet clear in Finland at that time. As the women were unaccustomed to club functions men were active in some women's clubs. For example, Matti Kurikka, A.B. Mäkelä and Taavi Tainio, who also acted in the Finnish-American workers' movement, went to the meetings of the women's club of the Workingmen's Association in Helsinki (*Helsingin Työväenyhdistys*). In 1900 the Working Women's League (*Työläisnaisliitto*) was founded. It functioned both as a central organization for trade unions and as an educational centre for the women in the party. Its work was hindered by lack of funds and thus its remained small. The trade unions withdrew gradually from the League and by no means all women who belonged to the party belonged to the League. In 1907, for example, when membership was at its highest, it consisted of 107 clubs and 2,724 members while the party itself had 18,873 woman members.[44]

Women's clubs were founded also in the Finnish-American workers' movement. The first one was the women's club founded in connection with Imatra in Brooklyn, New York, in 1904. Hanna Lehtinen was its delegate to the convention in Cleveland the same year.[45] There were women's clubs also in Fitchburg, Massachusetts, and Minneapolis, Minnesota.[46] The real debate over the women's clubs started when Hilda Sikanen, who had joined the workers' movement in Finland in 1896, came to America. She joined the Finnish Socialist local in Quincy, Massachusetts, in July 1905 and within a month a women's club was founded there.[47]

Hanna Lehtinen and Hilda Sikanen debated the need for women's clubs in the columns of the Raivaaja. Lehtinen, who represented the Imatra Movement, maintained that the separate activities of women were a division of forces. She also thought that renting rooms for the meetings was too expensive.[48] Sikanen believed that the purpose of the women's clubs was to make women familiar with the existing social system and the Social Democratic platform and to inspire the women to work with the men to carry out this program. On the other hand she wanted to leave the question of women's rights outside the women's clubs.[49] Both women travelled around the Finnish parts of the country as speakers.

A third woman speaker was Ida Pasanen, who had been a founder of the Finnish-American Workmen's League. Pasanen had also been active in the women's movement of the workers in Finland and been a member of the first national committee of the Working Women's League.[50] She maintained that the establishment of women's clubs was necessary only in such communities where there were many Finnish women who had come from the cities. She did not think that the women's clubs in Finland had been especially instructive with the exception of the trade unions.[51]

Hilda Sikanen travelled around the eastern states as a speaker and on her initiative a women's club was founded in connection with the socialist local in New York. It organized meetings with discussions and training in administrative skills needed to become an official of a socialist local.[52] These activities were necessary in view of how few women held positions of trust in the locals.

The question of women's clubs was on the agenda of the convention in Hibbing in 1906, with William Oksanen presenting the subject. He was in favour and accused those against it of opposing equality in the locals. The delegates were not unanimous; a woman delegate for instance, opposed the establishment of women's clubs. The delegates admitted, that the women had interests of their own to pursue, but they emphasized that the Socialist Party as a whole worked for equality. This was the most common argument for obstructing the efforts of the women in both the Socialist Federation and the Socialist Party itself. The convention viewed the establishment of women's trade unions favourably. In the final resolution it was established that special women's clubs were not necessary, but it was held to be natural that the women themselves would discuss questions pertaining to their inferior economic and social status.[53]

The question of women's organizations also came up in Socialist Party of America. The International Socialist Women's Congress held in Stuttgart, Germany, in 1907 and the development of the women's suffrage movement in the United States obviously activated the socialist women. In the national convention in 1908 the question of women's suffrage and eligiblility for office surfaced. Perhaps characteristic of the attitude of the Socialist Party on

women's rights was the fact that the topic was left to the end of
the convention to avoid unnecessary enthusiasm. The same opposing standpoints came forward at the convention as in the Finnish
Federation. Some believed that as long as the Socialist Party endorsed full equality for women alongside men all activities had to
be in common. The opinion of the majority was that special *agitation* had to be carried out among the women. Demanding women's
rights was not only as such a goal for the socialists but also a means
of getting more women into the party. A five-person National
Executive Committee was established at the convention for education among the women and the party set aside funds for a woman
organizer.[54]

In the summer of 1909 a call by the Women's National
Committee and directions for the establishment of women's committees in the locals were issued. The intention was that committees would be founded in all locals to educate the women in
Socialism and the suffrage movement.[55] Hilda Sikanen appealed to
this call in the presentation "Naisosastot eloon" (life to the wom-
en's clubs) which she had written for the convention of 1909.
Sikanan had been elected to the convention as the only woman
delegate. She defended the women's clubs as eagerly as earlier but
once again did not receive any positive response. The majority of
the convention opposed the women's clubs while part of the delegates expressed the view that the women's clubs could be established when the need arose. Sikanen was disappointed with the
result and claimed that the men wished to preserve their dominance. She wished that the women would become interested in
party work other than coffee-making and sewing. The convention
passed a resolution giving the women credit for belonging to the
Federation, but promised nothing.

The question of women's suffrage was on the agenda, too.
Here Sikanen strongly opposed cooperation with the bourgeois
women's rights movement.[56] The same year the Women's Central
Committee of the Socialist Party had decided to participate in
collecting signatures to a petition asking for a women's suffrage
amendment to the Constitution.[57]

There had also been difficulties, probably financial, in the
activities of women's committees of the Socialist party. The national organizer, Anna Mailey, had succeeded in founding 125 local
women's committees. At the convention of 1910 more attention to
the political education of the women in the party was called for.
The emphasis was still on the question of suffrage. The women
were also urged to join trade union.[58]

Women's committees as far as is known, were not established among the Finns until after the convention of 1910. At that time the activities of the women in the Finnish socialist locals clearly became more lively and women's committees were founded in many locals as attitude toward them became more positive.[59] Four women, among them Ida Pasanen and Esteri Laukki, had drawn up a presentation about *woman agitation* for the district convention of the Central District in 1910. They managed to get a resolution passed stating that women's committees should be founded in all socialist locals. The organizing of women in trade unions was also encouraged. The district committee was given the task of keeping contact between the women's committees and the Women's National Executive Committee of the Socialist Party.[60] At the convention of the Western District the next year there was also a positive stand to the founding of women's locals or women's committees.[61]

The number of women's committees remained small, however. At the end of 1911 there were only twelve committees with a total of 131 members. Four of the committees were in the Eastern District, five in the Central and three in the Western. Significant for the activities of the women in the Federation was that there were at the same time ninety-one sewing circles with a total of 1359 members.[62]

At the women's meeting held in connection with the convention of the Socialist Federation in 1912 there were demands on concentrating more on the question of the *agitation* of the Women. There was a proposal to found more women's *agitation* committees which would arrange discussion meetings, reading circles, etc. It was also considered important to obtain citizenship. This topic was not discussed at the convention itself, but the resolution drawn up by the women's meeting was passed.[63]

The enthusiasm had grown weaker, however, for in 1913 there were only two women's committees in the Central District and they had together only fourteen members. At the district convention of 1914 the district committee was accused of neglecting the *agitation work* of women. Both at this convention and at the district convention of the Western district the same year more attention to *agitation work* of women was demanded and the establishment of women's committees and the acquisition of women speakers were supported.[64]

Later on there was no discussion of women's committees, in large part because the Central District, which had paid the most attention to the question the *agitation* of women, left the Federation in the split of 1914. Especially damaging was the loss of the

Workers' College.[65] Many of the most prominent women left in the same split. On the other hand, the split of the Federation had perhaps a uniting influence on the rest of the locals, who did not want to encourage any further cleavages. The split of the Federation and the outbreak of the First World War brought along more important topics of discussion than the position of the women in the Socialist Federation. It was not possible to refer to the example of the women in Finland, either, because the women's movement among the workers had diminished in importance in that country.

# The Establishment of a Woman's Magazine

In addition to the question of women's clubs the Finnish-American socialists discussed at length the establishment of a woman's magazine. In this discussion two questions emerged. The first one was whether the women could make their voices heard in the old newspapers of the Socialist Federation and if the topics concerning women were treated adequately. The other one was how the establishment of a paper of their own could assist the political education of women and how this work could best be carried out.

There were many articles in *Raivaaja* discussing the relation of women to socialism by both men and women writers during the first year it was published. A feeling of inferiority is reflected in the women's writings; they discuss why they intellectually are not as advanced as the men.[66] This feeling of inferiority prevented women from writing in the papers because they were afraid of criticism from men. In 1907 women received their own column in *Raivaaja*, "The Women's Corner," where only articles by women were to be published. There were not enough contributions, however, so the column had to be discontinued.[67]

There had been talk of a woman's newspaper in the beginning of the Finnish-American workers' movement. It is believed that Hulda Anderson at Malcolm Island had proposed one at the beginning of the twentieth century.[68] At the convention in Hibbing in 1906 Olga Heinonen, who opposed the establishment of women's clubs, wanted a paper of their own in which women could champion the cause of equality, which had been granted them in the party platform. In spite of shouts of "Good" which the proposal had met with according to the minutes, no more attention was paid to the topic at the convention.[69]

The question of a newspaper was pushed aside, but appeared

again in March of 1909, when the Finnish Socialist women held a meeting in Duluth and decided that publication for women must be established.[70] For the convention in Hancock in 1909 a presentation was drawn up on whether to establish a women's magazine or a children's magazine.[71] Although the establishment of both papers won some support, doubts were raised on the financial problems involved in publishing the papers. There were differing views on where to place a possible magazine. Some people wanted it to be founded in connection with *Raivaaja*, others with *Työmies*. The former alternative was motivated by the fact that more Finnish women lived in the eastern states. A proposal was also made of giving the women one issue of *Raivaaja* to edit each week. Another possibility was to change *Säkeniä*, a journal which appeared in connection with *Raivaaja*, into a woman's newspaper.[72] The final conclusion reached at the Hancock convention was that the publishing companies should decide by themselves about the establishment of new publication.[73]

The example of Finland very likely played a part in this question, because the Working Women's league there published the newspaper *Työläisnainen* (Working Woman). Subscriptions on it were offered the Finnish-American Socialists and articles from that newspaper were often published in the papers of the Federation.[74]

In the spring of 1911 the establishment of a women's newspaper really got under way, although the reasons were mainly financial. Quite simply, there was not enough work in the composing room of *Toveri*.[75] A decision was made at its stockholders' meeting to establish a woman's newspaper if 3,000 subscriptions could be secured in advance. This number was reached in July and the very same month the first woman's newspaper, *Toveritar* (Woman Comrade) appeared.[76] The decision met with opposition especially in the Eastern District. Some feared that the establishment of a woman's newspaper would decrease the support of the other party papers, because it was believed that women would not subscribe to two papers. In this, as well as in other attempts of the women, it was feared that the bourgeois women's rights movement could gain influence.[77]

Maria Raunio-Aaltonen, who had been a Social Democratic member of the Finnish national Diet, came from Finland to become the first editor of *Toveritar*. It was accepted as a party paper at the convention in Smithville in 1912. The number of subscribers rose steadily in the beginning and by the summer of 1912 it had exceeded 5,000. The disputes over the direction of the Federation, however, also influenced *Toveritar* and its circulation decreased to such an extent that its continuation was in doubt by the beginning of 1915.[78] It is easy to understand the decrease in the support of the paper, because most of the subscribers had come from the Central District and when they left the Federation they very likely stopped taking the paper. *Toveritar* had won very little support in the Eastern District; in 1911 only 200 of the more than 3,000 subscribers came from that district.[79] In 1915 the circulation of *Toveritar* in the Eastern District had only reached 585 even though the membership of the district included more than 2000 women.[80]

*Toveritar* had not lived up to financial expectations; for example, in 1914 it caused the Toveri Publishing Company a lose of $1,000. In 1915 the circulation of the paper started to increase thanks to the new editor, Selma Jokela, who changed the editorial policy of the paper to interest women more. Up to this time the editors had changed all the time.[81] The fact that the paper was edited more in the fashion of the ordinary women's magazines brought more subscribers, but caused criticism from within the Federation, where the contents of the paper were thought to be too lightweight. Usually all magazines and newspapers of the Federation were reviewed at the district and national conventions of the Federation and at these occasions *Toveritar* received more thanks than criticisms.[82] Even if the contents did not always please everybody, the most important thing was its increasing circulation and the financial benefits that it brought, which had been the purpose of the newspaper in the first place. *Toveritar* also had an important role in stimulating an increased activity among socialist women in the years 1911-12.

# Conclusion

The importance of women in the Finnish-American Socialist movement was mainly financial and social. The women raised money for the locals with the bazaars of the sewing circles and arranged dances and social programs. They did not play an large part in establishing of the political directions of the movement, which is clearly shown in the few women who served in the most important organizations of the Socialist Federation. The women did however distinguish themselves in spreading the socialist doctrine among the Finnish-Americans as many women travelled across the country as speakers.

272    R. Stjärnstedt

What did the women themselves get out of their membership in the Socialist Federation? The socialists did not manage to improve the status of the women in America. The support of the Socialist Party of America was small and thus had little influence. The aims of the Finnish Socialist women to organize as trade unions were not fulfilled.

The most important thing in the beginning was being together with other Finns. The ablest women could rise to the leading positions of the Federation. This would otherwise have been impossible for immigrants with a low status in a purely American society.

As the time went by the Finnish socialists came more and more in contact with other nationalities. The struggle for suffrage, for example made the integration of the women into the American society easier and the Finnish women were in the struggle with the others.

# Notes

1. Suomen Virallinen Tilasto XXVIII. Siirtolaisuustilasto 1-16 (Helsinki, 1905-1922); Reino Kero, *Migration from Finland to North America in the years between the United States Civil War and the first World War*. Turun Yliopiston julkaisuja, Sarja B, osa 130 (Vammala, 1974), pp. 91-92.

2. See, e.g., Anna-Leena Toivonen, *Etelä-Pohjanmaan valtamerentakainen siirtolaisuus 1867-1930*, Historiallisia tutkimuksia LXVI (Seinäjoki, 1963), pp. 73, 147.

3. Akseli Järnefelt, *Suomalaiset Amerikassa* (Historical Studies) (Helsinki, 1899), pp. 160, 195, 214; Toivonen, p. 148; Kero, p. 105; Matti E. Kaups, "The Finns in the copper and iron ore mines of the Western Great Lakes region, 1864-1905: Some preliminary observations, "*The Finnish Experience in the Western Great Lakes Region: New Perspectives*. Edited by Michael G. Karni, Matti E. Kaups, Douglas J. Ollila, Jr. (Vämmala, 1975), pp. 78-86; Toivonen, p. 148.

4. Elis Sulkanen, *Amerikan Suomalaisen Työväenliikkeen Historia* (Fitchburg, Mass., 1951), pp. 53-83.

5. *Pöytäkirja Amerikan Suomalaisten Sosialistiosastojen Edustajakokouksesta Hibbingissä, Minn. Elok. 1-7 päivinä 1906* (Hancock, Mich., 1907), pp. 131-32.

6. *Kolmannen Amerikan Suomalaisen Sosialistijärjestön Edustajakokouksen Pöytäkirja. Kokous pidetty Hancockissa, Mich. 23-30 p. Elok., 1909.* ed. F.J. Syrjälä (Kokouksen siht.) (Fitchburg, Mass., n.d.), pp. 71-72.

7. Sulkanen, pp. 160-61.

8. Auvo Kostiainen, *The Forging of Finnish-American Communism. A Study in Ethnic Radicalism,* Turun Yliopiston Julkaisuja. Sarja B, osa 147 (Turku, 1978), pp. 37-42.

9. Ibid., passim.

10. Minutes of the Imatra-Society Feb.22. 1891. The Imatra-Society, Brooklyn, N.Y. papers, TYYH/s/m/8/38.

11. *Työmies,* March 30, 1904. *Työmies kymmenvuotias 1903-1913. Juhlajulkaisu.* (Hancock, Mich., 1913), p. 85.

12. Tilastollinen taulu Amerikan suomelaisista sosialistijärjestöistä," *Köyhälistön Nuija I (1907),* pp. 40-41.

13. "S.S.Järjestön sihteerin toimintakertomus yleiselle edustajakokoukselle, Smithvillessä, Minn., Kesäkuun 1. p. 1912," *Suomalaisten sosiatistiosastojen ja työväenyhdistysten viidennen eli suomalaisen sosialistijärjestön kolmannen edustajakokouksen Pöytäkirja 1-5, 7-10 p. kesäkuuta, 1912,* Ed. Aku Rissanen (Fitchburg, Mass. n.d.), pp. 29-55.

14. Numbers in the beginning of 1916, at the end of 1917, in the beginning of 1919. "Toimintakertomus Itäpiirin toiminnasta 1915," *Raivaaja* February 25, 1916. "Toimintakertomus Itäpiirin toiminnasta 1917," *Raivaaja* February 25, 1918. *Pöytäkirja Amerikan Suomalaisen Sosialistijärjestön Itäpiirin Edustajakokouksesta joka pidettiin Fitchburgissa, Mass. Suomalaisen Kustannusyhtiön (Raivaaja) talolla. Helmikuun 22, 23, 24, 25, 26 ja 27 päivinä 1919* (Fitchburg, Mass., 1919), p. 14. "Itäpiirin vuoden 1920 edustakjakokouksen pöytäkirja," Raivaaja, Feb 24, 1920.

15. "Tilastoa S.S. Järjestön osastoista," *Suomalaisen Sosialistijarjestön Seitsemännen Edustajakokouksen Pöytäkirja. Laadittu Waukegonissa, III, 25-31 p. Jouluk. Pidetystä S.S. Järjestön Edustajukokouksesta Toimittanut Aaro Huoske (Superior, WIS., 1921), p. 25.*

16. Mari jo Buhle, "Feminism and Socialism in the United States 1820-1920," (Ph.D dissertation: Wisconsin, 1974), p. 184 in Richard Evans, *The Feminists. Women's Emancipation Movements in Europe, America and Australasia 1840-1920* (London, 1977), p. 187.

17. Evans, *op. cit.,* p. 171.

18. Hannu Soikkanen, *Sosialismin tulo Suomeen. Ensimmäisiin yksikamarisen eduskunnan vaaleihin asti* (Porvoo, 1961), pp. 217-19.

19. Evans, *op. cit.,* p. 168.

20. The book appeared in Finnish in 1904, translated by Yrjö Sirola. Erkki Selomaa, *Yrjö Sirola, sosialistinen humanisti* (Kuopio, 1966), pp. 66-67.

274    R. Stjärnstedt

21. Sulkanen, *op. cit.*, p. 77; *Raivaaja* February 9, 1905.

22. Hannu Soikkanen, *Kohti kansanvaltaa I. 1889-1937. Suomen Sosialide-mokraattinen puolue 75 vuotta* (Vaasa, 1975), p. 172.

24. See e.g. A. William Hoglund, *The Finnish Immigrants in America 1880-1920* (Binghampton, N.Y., 1960), p. 83.

25. See e.g., Sulkanen, *op. cit*, pp. 110-11. Kostiainen, *op. cit.*, p. 35.

26. See e.g., Minutes of Gardner Finnish Socialist branch October 29, 1911. the Gardner, Mass., Finnish Socialist Branch Papers, TYYH/s/m/ 8/56.

27. Michael Gary Karni, "Yhteishyvä—or, for the Common Good: Finnish Radikalism in the Western Lakes Region, 1900-1940." (Ph.D. dissertation: University of Minnesota, 1975), p. 90.

28. *Pöytäkirja, Smithville 1912*, pp. 85-88.

29. See e.g., Minutes of Quincy Finnish Socialist Branch, December 14, 1913. The Quincy, Mass., Finnish Socialist Branch Papers, TYYH/s/m/ 8/81.

30. Syrjälä, *op. cit.*, pp. 92-95. Arne Halonen, "The Role of Finnish Americans in the Political Labor Movement." (M.A. thesis: University of Minnesota, 1945), pp. 120-21. Sulkanen, *op. cit.*, pp. 110-17.

31. The Gardner, Mass., Finnish Socialist Branch Papers, TYYH/s/m/8/56-57. The Quincy, Mass., Finnish Socialist Branch Papers,TYYH/s/m/8/ 81. Walter Salmi Papers, TYYH/s/a/10/IX, XIII, XV, XVI.

32. "Tilastollinen taulu 1906 . . . " *Köyhälistön Nuija I (1907)*, pp. 40-41. "S.S.Jarjestön sihteerin toimintakertomus 1912," *Pöytäkirja, Smithville 1912*, pp. 30, 43. Minutes of Quincy Finnish Socialist Branch 1918. TYYH/s/m/8/81. Annual reports of Gardner Socialist Branch 1915 and 1919. TYYH/s/m/8/56.

33. Minutes of Gardner Finnish Socialist Branch, 1905-1919, TYYH/s/m/8/ 56-57. Minutes of Quincy Finnish Socialist Branch, 1905-1919, TYYH/s/ m/8/81. Minutes of Superior Finnish Socialist Branch, 1905-1919, TYYH/s/s/10/IX, XIII, XV, XVI.

34. See e.g., *Raivaaja* April 8, 1909.

35. *Raivaaja*, December 26, 1909.

36. See e.g., Minutes of Gardner Finnish Socialist Branch, November 13, 1905, TYYH/s/m/8/56. See also *Viisitoista vuotta New Yorkin suoma-laisten sosialistien historiaa 1903-1918* (Fitchburg, Mass., n.d.), pp. 82-83.

37. *Raivaaja*, March 18, 1909.

38. *Pöytäkirja, Hibbing 1906*, pp. 4-5. *Pöytäkirja, Hancock 1909*, p. 3

39. *Raivaaja*, January 24, March 4, 1912.

40. Ibid., January 13, March 9, 1912.

41. Pöytäkirja, Smithville 1912, pp. 111-14, 333.

42. See Proceedings of the District Conventions of the FSF 1910-1919.

43. See the Proceedings of the Conventions of the Finnish Socialist Federation, 1906, 1909, 1912, 1914, 1919.

44. Sylvi-Kyllikki Kilpi, *Suomen Työläisnaisliikkeen historia* (Pori, 1953), passim. See also Martta Salmela-Järvinen, "Työläisnaiset nousevat poliitiseen toimintaan," *Työn naisen juhlavuosi. Sosiaalidemokraattinen Työläisnaisliitto* (Helsinki, 1950). pp. 38-68.

45. Minutes of the Imatra-Society, April 10, April 17, October 11, 1904. The Imatra-Society, Brooklyn, N.Y., Papers, TYYH/S/m/8/39.

46. See e.g., *Raivaaja*, May 11, November 9, December 14, 1905.

47. Minutes of Quincy Finnish Socialist Branch July 5 and August 16, 1905.

48. *Raivaaja*, August 31, October 5, 1905.

49. Ibid., September 7, 1905.

50. Sulkanen, *op. cit.*, p. 80, Kilpi, *op. cit.*, p. 45.

51. *Raivaaja*, November 9, 1905.

52. Ibid., March 1, 1906. See also *Viisitoista vuotta New Yorkin suomalaisten sosialistien historiaa*, p. 38.

53. *Pöytäkirja, Hibbing 1906*, pp. 124-28, 136.

54. *Raivaaja*, May 23, 1908. For more about women's activities in the Socialist Party of America, see James Weinstein, *The Decline of Socialism in America* (New York, 1967), pp. 58-60.

55. *Raivaaja*, June 29, 1909.

56. *Pöytäkirja, Hancock 1909*, pp. 195-205.

57. *Raivaaja*, March 27, 1909.

58. "Raportti agitaatiotoiminnasta naisten keskuudessa. (Sosialistipuolueen naisten kansalliskomitean laatima puoluekonventionia varten ja sen hyväksymä chicagossa 19.5.1910)" *Raivaaja*, June 30, 1910.

59. Women's committees were founded at least in socialist branches of Superior, Wis., Ely, Minn., Boston, Mass., and Cleveland, Ohio. *Raivaaja, September 17 and 29, 1910. Minutes of Superior Finnish Socialist Branch, December 11, 1911.* TYYH/S/a/10/XIII.

60. Keskipiirin edustajakokous, August 28, 1910, *Raivaaja*, August 30, 1910.

61. *Amerikan S.S.Järjestön Länsipiirin ensimmäisen piirikokouksen pöytäkirja. Pidetty Astoriassa, Ore. Huhtik. 21-23 p:nä 1911* (Astoria, Ora., n.d.), pp. 30-31.

62. "S.S.Järjestön sihteerin toimintakertomus 1912," *Pöytäkirja, Smithville 1912*, p. 54.

63. Pöytäkirja, Smithville 1912, pp. 112,333.

64. Pöytäkirja Suomalaisen Sosialistijärjestön Keskipiirin Edustajako-
    kuksesta. Pidetty Duluthissa, Minn., Helmikuun 21-28 p. 1914 (Han-
    cock, Mich., 1914), pp. 16,352-54. *Yhdysvaltain Suom. Sos. Järjestön
    Länsipiirin ylimääräisen piirikokouksen pöytäkirja. Pidsetty Astoriassa,
    Ore. huhtik. 23-27 p:nä ja toukok. 2 p:nä 1914* (Astoria, Ore, n.d.), pp.
    180-81.

65. Women's questions were often discussed in the Workers' College.

66. See e.g., *Raivaaja*, March 23, April 27, May 4, 1905.

67. Ibid., March 3, 1907.

68. *Toveritar kymmenvuotias 1911-1921. Muistojulkaisu* (Astoria, Ore.,
    n.d.), p. 7. For more about *Toveritar*, see Paul George Hummasti,
    "Finnish Radicals in Astoria, Oregon, 1904-1940: A Study in Immi-
    grant Socialism" (Ph.D. dissertation: Oregon, June 1975), pp. 69-76.

69. *Pöytäkirja, Hibbing 1906*, p. 127.

70. *Toveritar kymmenvuotias*, pp. 8-9.

71. See e.g., Minutes of Gardner Finnish Socialist: Branch, August 2,
    1909. TYYH/S/m/8/56.

72. *Raivaaja* April 6, May 7, August 3, 1909.

73. *Pöytäkirja, Hancock 1909*, p. 237.

74. *Raivaaja*, January 28, 1907, January 30, 1908, November 17, 1910,
    July 29, 1911.

75. Ibid., April 18, 1911.

76. *Toveritar kymmenvuotias*, p. 9.

77. *Raivaaja*, December 26, 1910, May 15, 1911.

78. *Toveritar kymmenvuotias*, pp. 29-32.

79. Ibid., p. 31.

80. *Raivaaja*, February 25, 1916.

81. *Toveritar kymmenvuotias*, pp. 10-11, 32-33.

82. See e.g., *Yhdysvaltain Suom. Sos. Järjestön Länsipiirin kolmannen
    varsinaisen piirikokouksen Pöytäkirja. Pidetty Astoriassa, Ore. huhtik.
    13-14 ja 17-18 pp. 1916* (Astoria, Ore., 1916), pp. 54-56. *Pöytäkirja
    laadittu Ameriken S.S.Järjestön Itäpiirin Edustajakokouksesta joka pi-
    dettiin Fitchburgissa, Mass. S.S.Kustannusyhtiön (Raivaaja) talolla
    helmik. 22-23-24 ja 27 pnä 1916* (Fitchburg, Mass., n.d.), p. 13.

# The Finnish Immigrant Theatre in the United States

*Timo Riippa*

The Finnish immigrant theatre in North America represented a rich theatrical heritage that extended back to a unique tradition of amateur theatre in Finland. The tradition had its roots in the Finnish National Awakening of the nineteenth century, a nationalistic and romantic movement to enlighten the populace and to effect changes in the country's social and educational structures. Organizations like young peoples' societies, workers' associations, and peoples' enlightenment societies promoted self-education and edification through their cultural and social activities. Primary among these activities was the amateur theatre. Because of its immense popularity, the theatre came to be an important vehicle in broadening the intellectual horizons of Finnish society. By the late 1890s literally hundreds of amateur theatre groups existed throughout the country's rural and urban communities.[1] It was this spirit of enthusiasm and fondness for the theatre that the Finnish immigrants to America brought with them at the turn of the century.

To understand Finnish-American theatrical activity, one must understand its relationship to Finnish-American associational life. Within any Finnish community there was no one representative community theatre in which all interested Finns participated. Rather, there were usually several organizations which represented different aspects of the ethnic community and each had its own theatre. Maynard, Massachusetts, for example, after 1910 had a temperance theatre and a socialist theatre. In the mid-1920s in Astoria, Oregon, there was a Finnish Brotherhood theatre as well as a communist theatre. Worchester, Massachusetts, during the same period had both a communist and a socialist theatre. Although ideological considerations often determined which theatre a person attended, one didn't have to be a temperance advocate or a socialist to attend plays at their halls. In fact, non-members could always be counted on to attend an especially popular play such as Teuvo Pakkala's *Tukkijoella* or Artturi Jarviluoma's *Pohjolaisia*.[2]

As Finnish-American associational life developed and organizations built their various "Finn halls" which became centres of social and cultural life, the stage came to occupy a central place among hall activities. Some halls, like the Socialist Opera in Virginia, Minnesota, were even built primarily as theatres. In addition to its popularity with audiences, the theatre served an important fund-raising function for organizations. As Eero Boman, a well-known director in the socialist theatre, once noted in an article on workers' theatres: "Our stages (here in America) have been built for the purpose of making money."[3] In the great expansion of associational life that occurred after the turn of the century, the Finnish-American stage was often the primary source of income that made possible the work of societies and organizations and which provided the funds for the construction of halls and clubs.[4]

The theatre also played a major role in the social life of the community. Performances were attended by entire families and after the play the evening would end with a dance. A close bond existed between the amateur actors and their audience, which nurtured the sense of familiarity and spontaneity that characterized performances. Audiences enjoyed the actors' abilities and versatility, and there was a spirit of tolerance toward the limitations of the production and the inevitable mistakes that occurred. Rehearsals also served an important social function as people met in the evenings several times a week.[5] As important as ideological convictions and political motivation were in constellating Finnish-American organizational life, the role of social activities such as the theatre should not be underestimated. Participant-observers like Lauri Lemberg, a noted playwright and theatre figure, have noted that hall-going Finns in general were more concerned with the social activities of the organization to which they belonged than they were with its ideology. "Temperance ideals and socialist teachings," Lemberg observed, "were never thoroughly meaningful to many Finnish Americans. . . . It was the activities and not primarily the ideologies of the organizations that brought people together."[6] The establishment of the Astoria socialist club in 1904 is an example. A socialist writer noted in a history of the club that at the founding meeting there was only a small group of the "politically enlightened." Most of the members joined because they were "tired of the monotonous and routine social activities of the churches and temperance societies."[7] Years later, a prominent figure in the Finnish Workers Federation looked back at organizational life and estimated that "eighty per cent of the membership in socialist locals were mainly active in cultural and recreational activities like theatre; twenty per cent, or less, were engaged in political and ideological matters."[8]

Finnish-American theatres were strictly amateur ventures, although activity in the larger cities often came close to a professional level. During their existence, the immigrant theatres were never professional in the sense that they utilized actors and actresses who made their livelihood by performing on the stage. With the exception of paid directors, who were hired by theatres in the larger Finnish communities, all actors, actresses and theatre crews were volunteers, who worked at their regular jobs during the day and then devoted their evenings two or three nights a week to rehearsals.[9] And yet, since many of the larger theatres had professional directors in the 1920s and performed full-length plays once or twice a month (and sometimes had enough actors for two separate acting crews), the quality of the performances often reached a very high level.[10] Over a period of time, the actors and actresses who worked together in given theatres came to form a core of seasoned and experienced veterans.

Finnish-American theatre was primarily a first-generation phenomenon. As one might expect, considering the age range of the performers from the immigrant generation, the "golden age" of the theatre lasted from shortly before World War One into the 1930s, peaking in the mid 1920s.[11] During this period, all organizations with any dramatic activity generally staged at least one full-length play and several one-act plays per year. The level of activity depended largely on the talents and the resources available. The frequency of performances ranged from one full-length play a year to full-scale activity involving over thirty large productions per theatre season. After 1930, levels of activity began to decline as the immigrants aged and there was no one to replace them. The minutes of the socialist theatre in Gardner, Massachusetts, for example, reflect a growing sense of exhaustion among the members of the drama society in the late 1920s. The older members of the group refused to accept large parts any more and people declined to go on tours to neighbouring cities as the custom had been in the past. Despite attempts throughout the 1920s to recruit new talent from among the young people, the efforts were only partially success-ful.[12] Vaudeville, the movies, and interests outside of the Finnish ethnic sphere drew many of the young away from the hall activi-ties of their elders.

The earliest theatre activity among Finnish Americans took place on temperance stages around 1900. The *Alku* society of Maynard, Massachusetts, began a drama club as early as 1895, while at the *Sovittaja* society in Worchester, Massachusetts, dra-matic activity got underway in 1897. However, not all temperance groups approved of this activity. The conservative, church-oriented temperance societies (principally in the midwest) roundly con-demned theatres as "satanic hell-holes" which taught "murder, theft, adultery and 'terrible love adventures.'" Along with card-playing and dancing, theatre-going was seen as being conducive to drinking. Yet, among the more liberal temperance societies, drama was by far the most popular form of entertainment. One temper-ance writer even called the theatre a "golden gem in Finnish American intellectual and spiritual development," which broad-ened the individual's horizons and taught the person to distinguish right from wrong.[13]

In large Finnish communities, especially on the east coast, temperance theatres were active from the turn of the century into the 1920s. Large societies in New York and Massachusetts fre-quently staged one-act and full-length plays, although elsewhere activity appears to have been more sporadic, being limited to special occasions. The existing records of a Virginia, Minnesota, temperance drama club, for example, suggest that although there was continuous activity over a long period of time, the productions were limited to special occasions such as fund-raisers and summer festivals.[14]

Drama activity was also popular among various mutual bene-fit organizations. Lodges of the Knights and Ladies of Kaleva fre-quently staged productions, especially in the larger Finnish centres of Washington, Minnesota, Michigan and New York.[15] But since very few lodges had their own theatre facilities, plays had to be performed in rented halls. Full-length plays were limited to special celebrations, fun-raising events and annual festivals. The same type of activity also characterized the Imatra mutual aid society of New York. However, a more accelerated pace of activity took place among the Finnish Brotherhood fraternal benefit associations on the west coast. The lodges in Seattle and Astoria had especially large theatre groups in the mid-1920s. The theatre groups in both cities benefitted from an influx of talent from the theatres of the

Finnish Workers Federation following the closing of the Federation's halls in 1925 during the reorganization or "bolshevization" of the Workers Party of America. Although affected by shifting membership and adverse economic conditions, the theatrical activity in both places reached a peak in the mid and late 1920s when the lodges even had the resources to hire paid directors.[16]

In rural areas it was common to find small theatre groups made up of farmers and their wives who frequently staged plays in rented grange halls, country schools or the halls of other Finnish organizations. After its establishment in 1917, the cooperative movement in the midwest sponsored dramatic activity that lasted into the 1930s. The Finnish Cooperative Wholesale in Superior, Wisconsin, produced its own drama literature in Finnish and in English of both one-act and three-act plays which entertained as well as educated audiences in cooperative themes. The Northern States Women's Coops Guild Drama Department distributed plays such as *Nurkanperän Osuuskaupan Vuosikokous* (The Back-woods Cooperative Annual Meeting) and *Liittyykö Mäenpään Isäntä Osuuskauppaan?* (Will Farmer Maenpaa Join the Cooperative?) Another source of plays was the Education Department of the Cooperative Central Wholesale, which produced well-received plays in English such as *A Gala Day in a Cooperative Store*, a musical comedy complete with vaudeville routines and chorus girls.[17]

Of all the organizations that promoted drama, the Finnish-American labour movement developed the most advanced and sustained level of theatrical activity, from both a technical and an artistic standpoint. The movement reflected its Finnish counterpart as well as the heritage of the National Awakening in that from the very beginning it had a considerable cultural and educational orientation. Already in Finland, workers' associations had been active in founding amateur theatres, many of which went on to become prominent professional institutions.[18] These theatres later provided a number of famous actors and directors for the Finnish-American socialist stage. In fact, during the 1920s all the larger theatres in places like Astoria, Detroit, Fitchburg and New York hired full-time, salaried directors, most of whom had professional training in Finland.

The ambition of most socialist, industrial unionist and communist theatres was to perform new plays as often as possible. Rather than sporadic, seasonal activity, the larger theatres of the labour movement staged a new play at least once a month for nine to ten months out of the year. Although this is the level of activity that audiences came to expect, not all theatre-goers were satisfied with the results. One director, in complaining about the poor quality of many productions, observed that the pressure to stage new plays frequently "only encourages those numb-skulled performers who aren't ashamed to step in front of an audience, although they can't get their lines straight *even* with the prompter's help." In time, however, two plays a month during the theatre season became the norm at the most active theatres that had the available talent and resources. The famous socialist theatre in Fitchburg, Massachusetts, for example, in 1923 and 1924 staged thirty-six productions a year and averaged 417 spectators per play. In each of those years it took in $6000.[19]

The workers' theatre movement was also busy in other areas. Drama was continually discussed and debated at annual conventions, in newspapers, and in theoretical journals. In 1919 the Finnish Socialist Federation established a national drama league with a central play-lending library. Individual theatres sponsored acting classes for beginners and young people under professional directors like Eero Boman and Kaarlo Nissinen.[20] In these classes not only were people instructed in the fundamentals of acting, but they were also taught correct pronunciation and "standard" Finnish. Directors often faced a problem because the actors and actresses spoke their lines with very noticeable Finnish dialects.

In a sense, the immigrant audiences that attended the theatre did not differ greatly from all theatre audiences past and present. Plays presented a means of escape from daily hum-drum life into other realms of existence and experience. The Finns enjoyed plays that transcended everyday life and idealized their thoughts and feelings about life, society and human nature. They liked visually spectacular historical dramas and melodramatic romantic tragedies. They also liked Finnish folkplays that romanticized Finland's rural life and stereotyped the regional characteristics, dialects and traditional rivalries. They enjoyed comedies and farces. Socialist audiences favoured proletarian themes that idealized and justified their struggle and cause. And everyone liked musicals, particularly gypsy musicals.[21]

While it is difficult to generalize about Finnish-American play preferences and repertoire for a period that covers three decades, nevertheless certain favourites stand out. Prominent among the plays that formed the core of Finnish-American stage repertoire from 1900 through the 1920's were Aleksis Kivi's *Nummisuutarit* (Cobblers on the Heath), *Kihlaus* (The Betrothal) and *Karkurit* (The Fugitives). All of Minna Canth's social plays and comedies were performed and of these *Murtovarkaus* (The Burglary), *Papin Perhe* (The Clergyman's Family) and *Työmiehen Vaimo* (The Worker's Wife) were especially liked. Kaarlo Halme's dramas and comedies—*Murtuneita* (The Oppressed), *Maattomat* (The Exiles) and the Pöllönkorpi series—were extremely popular. Teuvo Pakkala's *Tukkijoella* (The Lumberjacks) would probably head any list of all-time favourites, followed closely by Arturi Jarvilouma's *Pohjolaisia* (The Bothnians). Among historical plays that were often performed, especially in the period before World War One, were Topelius's *Regina von Emmeritz,* Wecksell's *Daniel Hjort,* and Gustav von Numers' *Elinan Surma* (Elina's Death). A good farce borrowed from the English theatre, *Charley's Aunt,* always drew well and could be counted on to bolster falling box office receipts. In fact, most theatres alternated comedies and dramas throughout the theatre season.

Music seemed to be the key to packing a theatre and most theatre groups sought to stage at least one big musical a year. At a time when directors could count on filling the theatre only once with any given play, *The Merry Widow* and *The Gypsy Princess* would sometimes play for three nights to a full house. By all indications, musicals were by far the best-loved and best-attended form of theatre, although they were performed less frequently than other types of plays due to their heavy demands on a theatre's resources and time. The musical took many forms. There were operettas, musical comedies, musical folkplays, musical proletarian plays and even adaptations from grand opera like *Il Trovatore,* which Fitchburg's socialist theatre staged in 1924.

Plays for the Finnish-American stage came primarily from Finland. They were either Finnish in origin or Finnish translations of foreign plays. Of 605 plays listed in a Finnish Workers Federation drama league catalogue, approximately 70 per cent were Finnish, while about 24 per cent were translations into Finnish.[22] Only 6 per cent were written by Finnish-American or Finnish-Canadian playwrights. Since the theatres were so dependent on Finland for plays, and since the pace of activity in the socialist theatres required a large number of plays, many plays which otherwise would have been disregarded as being "bourgeois" or "nationalistic" were also performed in the workers' theatres.[23] In fact, in many socialist theatres almost any play, as long as it wasn't hostile to Marxism, was acceptable. This, of course, resulted in constant criticism of the theatre and demands for more strict ideological criteria. Already in 1915 Moses Hahl and Eero Boman had disagreed over the proper function of the workers' theatre.[24] Both of them agreed that the theatre was a cultural device that should both educate and entertain, but they disagreed over which aspect was more important. Those like Moses Hahl, who emphasized ideology, saw the theatre primarily as an instructional propaganda vehicle that could also entertain. Professional theatre directors like Eero Boman saw the theatre as a source of entertainment that could simultaneously instruct people ideologically. "In addition to agitation," Boman wrote, "theatrical art has to be and must always be the creation of something envigorating and entertainig."[25] The distinction may seem academic, but it was a very real one to the theatre people who tended to resist any dogmatic views that threatened their favourite plays and roles by restricting their repertoire. Socialist theatres generally sought to keep a balance between "heavier" didactic plays and "lighter" entertainment, but in many local chapters the critea for acceptable plays was very often rather fluid and reflected the financial needs of the chapter or the personal preferences of the actors rather than ideological concerns. The complaints from year to year at the socialist conventions about the prevalence of "inappropriate" plays suggest the general unwillingness of the Federation itself and the local chapters to tamper with a lucrative enterprise.

In 1930 the situation changed for the Finnish-American communist theatres when the Komintern in a general evalution of Finnish-American workers' social activities criticized the "bourgeois trash" being shown on the workers stages.[26] What resulted in the Finnish Federation was a burst of playwriting activity which produced a large body of socio-political drama literature dealing with subjects such as the rise of the Soviet Union, the emigration to Soviet Karelia, opposition to the NRA, the Spanish Civil War and the Depression. For a time, many of the old favourites disappeared from the stages of the Finnish Federation.

These political plays from the 1930s were actually part of a long tradition of Finnish-American proletarian drama. From the earliest days of the socialist movement, the playwrights of the Finnish-American left were the most active of all Finnish immigrant playwrights. In fact, except for a handful of non-political dramatists, they were the only Finnish-American playwrights. Even the most famous of the non-political dramatists, Lauri Lemberg, began his stage career in the socialist theatre. As Reino Kero has noted, the amount of activity and energy among writers (and playwrights) of the Finnish-American left can largely be explained by the fact that there were three labour factions, each of which needed literature suited to its ideology.[27] This also explains why the majority of Finnish-American plays fall into the category of didactic political melodrama— as many of their titles suggest:

*Luokkaviha* (Class Hatred), *Hehkuva Tulivuori* (The Glowing Volcano) and *Yleislakko* (The General Strike). But whether the plays date from the early socialist period or the peak of IWW activity or from the 1930s, all of them paint vivid protraits of the social conditions of the time. If they are lacking in technique and sophistication, they certainly lack nothing in ambition and political fervour. What they may lack in artistic merit, they more than make up for in socio-political interest.

Among the playwrights of the Finnish-American left were many well-known figures: Moses Hahl, Eemeli Parras, Anna Stein, Mikael Rutanen, Helmi Mattson, Niilo Terho and Fanny Ojanpää. Yet perhaps the best-known, the best-loved and the most representative of all Finnish-American playwrights were Felix Hyrske and Lauri Lemberg. Both were leading figures of the stage, whose lives touched on all aspects of the Finnish-American theatre. Their wide experience, talent and extensive writings place them in the forefront of all Finnish-American playwrights.

Felix Hyrske was a professional actor-director-playwright who already had fourteen years of stage experience in Finland when he came to the United States in 1907. He was one of the most gifted and respected figures in Finnish-American theatre history. He excelled in classical repertoire, especially in depicting heroic figures. His Dr. Jekyll and Mr. Hyde was said to have been electrifying. In addition to acting and directing for over twenty-five years on most of the major stages of the Finnish-American labour movement, Hyrske wrote over twenty plays, both comedies and dramas, adapting and translating many of them from contemporary literature. Hyrske considered the cultural education and education of the worker to be one of the most important functions of the labour movement. This concern is reflected in many of his serious plays, but especially in *Farmikodin Vastuksia* (The Difficulties of a Farm Home), one of his better dramas from the 1930s. The plot deals with a struggling Finnish-American farm family facing foreclosure. As Hyrske examines the priority of cultural values against a backdrop of economic deprivation, he skilfully blends contemporary themes such as the united front with typically Finnish concerns such as the cultural importance of hall activity. The drama contains a strong indictment of a system that leaves people economically and culturally impoverished. Unlike many other writers, Hyrske brought a restrained, sensitive touch to proletarian plays, avoiding the heavy melodramatic treatment which generally characterized the genre.[28]

Lauri Lemberg was a talented and innovative actor-director-playwright, who got his start in acting and directing in the socialist and IWW theatres. His four earliest plays from the 1920s reflect industrial unionist themes (one of the plays, *The Plot*, was dedicated to Joe Hill) and all of them bristle with indignation at the oppressive machinations of evil factory owners and law officers. But at the same time, Lemberg was also writing romantic comedies and dramas, farces and musical folkplays. This was the creative direction to which he turned after 1924 and for which he is best remembered. In all he wrote fifteen plays and adapted nine from books and movies. *Laulu vaaleanpunaisesta silkkipaidasta* (The Song about a Pink Silk Shirt), a farce which he adapted from an obscure American movie, became one of the great favourites of the Finnish-American stage. In 1920 at a time when most plays had to be ordered from Finland, he began a successful play rental service in Duluth, Minnesota, which catered to all theatre groups in the United States and Canada. His detective comedy, *Herttaviitonen* (The Five of Hearts), was staged by the National Theatre of Finland in 1921, thereby earning him membership in the Finnish Dramatist League. He is the only Finnish-American playwright to have had a play staged in the Finnish National Theatre. There are few, if any, Finnish-American playwrights who equal Lemberg's dramatic output. Among non-socialist playwrights, there are none.[29]

What, in the final analysis, was the contribution of the Finnish-American immigrant theatre to the life of the ethnic community? What did it achieve, other than providing a major social activity at a time when the immigrants had few social outlets? In an aesthetic sense, the theatre served as a major creative outlet for actors and actresses, directors and playwrights. It acquainted many immigrants who had very little formal schooling with a large number of classics from the Finnish theatre and, to a smaller extent, from world theatre literature. Instruction in acting, speech projection, singing and poetry recitation provided a positive sense of self-esteem and self-confidence, particularly to those with a minimum of formal education. The theatre introduced contemporary social issues in the plays of Minna Canth, Kaarlo Halme and the proletarian dramas. On the other hand, historical dramas and the familiar folkplays dealing with Finland served to strengthen and preserve Finnish identity among the spectators. Thus, the theatre kept alive the sentimental bond to the homeland and the past. The legacy of the theatre, in the words of Lauri Lemberg, was that "from its many participants, it developed people with wide cultural interests —singers, musicians, speakers and poets—who, in addition to their

dramatic activities, enriched all other social and cultural activities
of the Finnish American community."[30]

# Notes

1. Ritva Heikkilä, "The Theatre," *Finlandian Introduction*, ed. Sylvie
   Nickels *et al.*, (New York. Praeger Publications,1973), pp. 261-62.

2. In his remarks to the 1919 Finnish Socialist Federation convention,
   the Drama League secretary referred to the numbers of non-members
   attending plays in various Finnish communities. *Yhdusvaltain Suomalaisen Sosialisti järjestön Viidennen Edustajakokouksen Pöytäkirja Chicagossa, Ill. Lokakuum 25 p:stä marraskuun 3:ään, 1919*, ed. J.F. Mäki
   (Superior, Wisconsin: Työmies Publishing, 1920), pp. 113-14.

3. Eero Boman, "Näyttämötaide ja työväenluokka, " *Kalenteri Amerikan
   Suomalaiselle Työväelle*, p. 84.

4. Lauri Lemberg, "Amerikan Suomalaisten Seuranäyttämö, " *Tie Va-
   pauteen*, X (April 1928), p. 15.

5. "Amateur Theatre Movement of the Finnish Immigrants," *70th Anni-
   versary Souvenir Journal 1903-1973 Työmies* (Superior, Wisconsin:
   Tyomies Publishing company, 1973), p. 35; "Drama Clubs of the
   Progressive Finns in the United States," a paper given by Sirkka
   Tuomi Lee at a symposium June 24, 1978 at Mesabi Park, Minnesota,
   contains an excellent inside picture of immigrant theatre activity.

6. Lauri Lemberg, "Amerikan Suomalaisista," *Kangassalon Sanomat*
   (Finland), March 18, 1956.

7. *Toveri kymmenenvuotias 1907-1917* (Astoria, Oregon: Toveri Press,
   1917), p. 67.

8. John Wiita [Heikki Puro], "Cultural Life of the Finnish American
   Labor Movement," manuscript in the John Wiita Collection, Immigration History Research Center, University of Minnesota.

9. Victor Rautanen, "Finnish American League for Democracy, New
   York City Branch," in *A History of Finnish American Organizations in
   Greater New York 1891-1976*, ed. Katri Ekman *et al.* (New York:
   Greater New York Finnish Bicentennial Planning Committee, Inc.,
   1976), p. 211.

10. Elis Sulkanen, *Amerikan Suomalaisen Työväenliikkeen Historia* (Fitch-
    burg, Massa: Raivaaja Publishing Company, 1951), p. 111.

11. An overview of socialist theatres done in 1910 revealed that out of
    forty actors and actresses, over 75 per cent were under the age of 30.
    "Meidän sosialistiset näyttämöt," *Raivaajan työvainiolta VI 1910*, pp.
    182-200.

288    T. Riippa

12. Minutes of the Gardner, Massachusetts Finnish Socialist Chapter Drama Society, September 12, 1920, February 11, 1923, January 26, 1925, (microfilm) Immigration History Research Center, University of Minnesota.

13. "*Alku*" *Raittiusseuran 50-vuotis Juhlajulkaisu 1895-1945* (Hancock, Michigan: Suomalainen Lutherilainen Kustannusliike, 1945), pp. 43-44; "Teatterista," *Raittiuskalenteri 1899*, pp. 107-08; A. William Hoglund, *Finnish Immigration in America 1880-1920* (Madison, Wisconsin: University of Wisconsin Press, 1960), p. 96; E.W. Karjalainen, "Muutama Sananen Näytelmätaiteesta," *Idän Suomalaisen Raittiuskansan Liiton Joulujulkaisu 1919*, p. 61.

14. Edith Koivisto, "Lupaus: Hibbingin Suomalaisen Raittiusliikkeen Historia 1895-1957," p. 19, manuscript in the Edith Koivisto Collection, Immigration History Research Center, University of Minnesota.

15. Lemberg's play rental register indicates plays being periodically sent to Kaleva lodges in these states in the 1920s from his play rental service in Duluth, Minnesota. Lauri Lemberg Papers, Minnesota Historical Society, St. Paul, Minnesota.

16. *Y.S.K.V. ja S. Liiton 50-Vuotishistoria-Muistojulkaisu* (Duluth, Minnesota: Finnish Daily Publishing Company, 1937), pp. 178-84; Walter Mattila, *The Theatre Finns* (Portland, Oregon: Finnish American Historical Society of the West, 1972), p. 53; William Mannila, "Muistelmia Astorian Näyttämöltä," *Veljeysviesti*, 44, no. 12 (December 1967), p. 43.

17. "'All the World's a Stage'—Immigrants and the Performing Arts," *Spectrum*, i, no. 1 (April 1976), p. 6.

18. Timo Tiusanen, *Teatterimme Hahmottuu* (Helsinki: Kirjayhtymä, 1969), pp. 154-61.

19. The writer of an article in 1918 about the New York socialist stage boasted: "In the past . . . we could perform five or six plays during the year, whereas now we perform one entire play almost every week around the year." "Näytelmäseura," *Viisitoista Vuotta New Yorkin Suomalaisten Sosialistien Historiaa 1903-1918* (Fitchburg, Mass.: Suomalainen Sos. Kustannusyhtio, 1918), p. 86; Vili Väre, "Näyttämötaide Amerikan Suomalaisten Kesken," *Kalevainen*, III (February 1917), pp. 51-52; Frans J. Syrjälä, *Historia-aiheita Amerikan Suomalaisten Työväenliikkeestä* (Fitchburg, Mass.: Raivaaja Publishing Co pany, 1925), p. 108.

20. Syrjälä, *Historia-aiheita*, p. 114; Rautanen, "Finnish American League for Democracy," p. 209.

21. The Finns seemed to have a particular fascination for the gypsies, judging from the popularity of operettas and gypsy musicals: *Mustalaisruhtinatar, Mustalainen, Mustalaiset, Unkarin Mustalaiset, Mustalais-Manja,* etc.; Syrjälä, p. 107.

22. *Finnish W. Federation Näyttämöliiton Näytelmä- ja Näyttämöväline-Luettelo* (Finnish Workers Federation, n.d.).

23. Jussi Latva, "Järjestömme Näyttämö- ja Kultuurityö 25-vuotistaipaleelta," *Canadan Suomalaisten Järjestö 25 Vuotta, 1919-1936* (Sudbury, 1936), p. 69. See also *Pöytäkirja Amerikan Suomalaisen Sosialisti Järjestön Itäpiirin Edustajakokouksesta joka pidettiin Fitchburgissa, Mass. Kustannusyhtiön (Raivaajan) talolla Helmikuun 22,23,24,25,26, ja 27 p:nä 1919* (Fitchburg, Mass., n.d.), p. 91.

24. Moses Hahl, "Sosialistinen teatteri ja työläisnäyttelä," *Säkeniä*, IX (September 1915), pp. 398-407; Eero Boman, "Sosialistinen teatteri," *Säkeniä*, IX (October 1915), pp. 458-59.

25. Eero Boman, "Sosialistinen teatteri" p. 458.

26. *Taistelu oikeistovaaraa vastaan. Kominternin opetuksia Amerikan suomalaiselle työväestölle* (Superior, Wisconsin, n.d.).

27. Reino Kero, "Finnish Immigrant Culture in America," in *Old Friends — Strong Ties*, ed. Vilho Niitemaa et al. (Vaasa: Institute for Migration, Turku, Finland, 1976), p. 124.

28. Syrjälä, p. 111; Kalle Rissanen, "Feidias veistää henkilökuvia, " p. 168, manuscript in Immigration History Research Center, University of Minnesota; "Meidän sosialistiset näyttämöt," p. 199.

29. Lauri Lemberg Papers, Minnesota Historical Society, St. Paul, Minnesota.

30. "Saiman näyttämö Fitchburgissa," *Siirtokansan Kalenteri*, 1948, pp. 66-67.

# Stage Recollections among the Finns

*Sirkka Tuomi-Lee*

The amateur theatre movement of the radical and progressive Finns in the United States and Canada merits serious research and study. I say "radical" and "progressive" Finns, because my experience has been with that group, having been born into it and growing up in it; but I venture to state that despite ideological differences, all the Finns in Canada and the United States who were active in theatre shared the same types of experiences, so there is a commonality here that transcends those differences.

As the old saying goes, get ten or twelve Finns together in one area and before you know it, there's a theatre group. This love of theatre and literature, including poetry, is as old as the Finnish race itself, as evidenced by the survival of the *Kalevala* tales which were handed down orally from generation to generation over hundreds of years. And, as we all know, the Finnish language has survived despite being ignored by the educated classes who spoke and read Swedish, considering it a more civilized tongue. The stubborn and tenacious nature of the Finns in clinging to their own tongue not only saved the language but reinforced a love and respect for literature and theatre among the ordinary people. Coupled with this heritage was the church's insistence that everyone should be able to read. There were schools set up every spring just to teach the youngsters how to read, *rippi kouluja*. I remember my mother saying that the *rippi koulu* whetted her appetite for learning and the rest of her life she constantly read and studied on her own, being especially fond of theatre and poetry.

Having been born into a family in which both my father and
mother were heavily involved in plays, choruses, orchestras and
bands, and having made my debut on the amateur stage of the
Socialist Opera in Virginia, Minnesota, at the tender age of three
months, I am delighted to tell you of some experiences which, I
hope, will pique you to do more research in the theatre movement.
I might add that in my debut, I lay in a cradle while the leading
lady sang to me. I've been told that I gurgled happily during her
entire song and stole the show, thus reinforcing the old show biz
warning never to play with children or dogs—they'll steal the show
every time.

What can I tell you about my stage recollections? There are
plenty of funny stories and some not so funny; but amusing stories
by themselves cannot explain the spirit of the Finnish-American
theatre movement in the United States and Canada. Funny stories
cannot explain why a man who spent ten to twelve hours a day
digging iron ore in an open pit hundreds of feet down in the earth,
arriving home afterwards so exhausted he could hardly eat his
dinner, yet wash up afterwards and walk through the cold in the
wintertime and sweltering heat in the summertime to go to a hall—
to a bare stage, and rehearse a play over and over again. He might
have been a farm hand, a *renki*, in Finland with only enough
education to be able to read a little. Perhaps his accent was that of
a Hämäläinen or an Eteläpohjanmaanlainen and his movements
were not graceful. But this man learned; he learned to overcome his
accent and make his Finnish more universal; he learned to move on
a stage and how to work with other actors; and he learned how to
take direction from a director and even how to make up his face
and help others with make up. And he still continued to dig in the
mine day after day, year after year and performed in play after
play. He even began directing plays himself. Those of us who fall
under the category of being white-collar workers or professionals
cannot understand the complete physical exhaustion that only a
manual labourer can know; it takes a strong person indeed to
overcome the exhaustion of physical labour and yet be able to cross
that great divide into the realm of the cultural world and the world
of self-expression. The women were the same. Most of them were
domestic workers and *piikoja* who worked long hours and had the
same type of background in Finland, many of them almost illiterate, coming from crofters' or sharecroppers' families. These were
the people who created the Finnish theatre movement in the
United States and Canada, and they brought great joy to thousands
of other Finns, the shyer ones who could not be persuaded to take

part in a play. They brought their children up to appreciate theatre, poetry, literature and how to speak clearly and even learn to
express their thoughts. I am doing some oral histories of the Finns
in Baltimore and have found out that many of them came from
small towns in Finland where there were amateur theatre groups,
so they brought with them this love of theatre.

How did this theatre movement evolve in the new world?
During the first sixty years of the century, the Finns established
halls and theatre groups in the United States and Canada and
frequently were involved in athletic groups and political organizations as well. For awhile they were able to bring some directors
from Finland and there were some professional companies in some
areas, depending on the size of the Finnish population. These
directors taught the immigrants acting and speech and even directing, then, when funds ran out, or the directors returned to Finland,
the students became the teachers and directors. I can recall from
my mother some of the tales of these impressarios who took
"greenhorns" from the farms of Finland—people who had, in some
instances, never been near a city or a theatre but who were eager
to learn—shaped them and made them become aware of speech, of
enunciation and of how to move on the stage. My mother said they
had a play in Worcester, Massachusetts, where the director was
tearing his hair out with frustration. The play was about one family
—the parents, the grandparents and children—and each actor came
from a different part of Finland and had a dialect which he or she
struggled to master in order to speak general Finnish. There was a
Porilainen, a Hämäläinen, a Karjalainen, an Eteläpohjanmaanlainen. Came the night of the performance and each one
clung to his native dialect. But the audience,—, those wonderful
understanding audiences—saw and listened to the play and enjoyed
it immensely, accepting this unique family with its various dialects.

Then there was the time when a particularly shy man was
asked to be in a play and only consented when he found out he had
one line. He was to make an entrance and say something like, "The
carriage is here." He studied his one line assiduously, going over
each inflection—the *carriage* is here—the carriage *is* here—the carriage is *here*. The night of the performance arrived and he stood by
the doorway, patiently waiting to go on stage, palms in a sweat,
but alert and ready. He thought it was longer than usual but
waited. Finally the curtain came down and the actors walked off
the stage. He asked one of them when he was supposed to come on
and the actor said, "Oh, we missed some lines including your cue,
but that's all right—we got the gist of the thing."

Finns did not give just two or three plays a year, but gave them once and even twice a month. Some were one-act plays and some were five acts with prologues *and* epilogues. Some were musicals and some were heavy historical dramas. Consequently, they had to rely on the most important person in the Finnish theatre, namely, the prompter or *kuiskari*, who sat in a little box under the stage covered with a rounded lid with his or her eyes level with the actors' knees or ankles. The prompter was usually one of the actors who was gifted with a loud stage whisper, clear enunciation and fortitude—who could sit scrunched up in a little hole under the stage for hours in the heat of the summer and the cold of the winter, and with the aid of a little light bulb and a quick eye, prompt the actors line by line. Since plays were held so frequently, it was impossible to memorize them because of time constraints. As I remember very clearly from both my parents, there were never enough rehearsals because of the varied shift work of the actors, so, of necessity a technique was developed where the prompter, while the actor was saying his line, would be whispering the next line. And he, while saying his line would be listening for the next. When it worked, it worked well and could be very smooth indeed. But when the actors were not attuned to the prompter, dead spaces developed with occasionally someone from the audience yelling out the line for the now panicked actor who had drawn a blank. I can recall sitting in the audience in Baltimore and watching one of the actors who had forgotten every line he ever knew. He stood there with a glassy look in his eye and in a profusion of sweat and finally leaned down to the prompter and said, "What did you say?"A man behind me yelled, "The prompter said to exit right." My father told me of the time in Virginia, Minnesota, when a prompter a stage veteran who was quick and very capable, all of a sudden discovered that the actors were saying lines not in the script. She leafed through the pages, trying to find out where they were, and then, like a light bulb going off over her head, she remembered a play given the previous week with the same dialogue. It took a great deal of desperate whispering to get the cast back on track.

In Baltimore, the prompter always took the curtain calls with the rest of the cast. The curtains would close at the end of the play, and we could hear a scrambling for position taking place behind the curtain. Then the curtain would bulge out with someone trying to keep it closed while the lid was taken off the prompter's box or *koppi*. Occasionally we would get a glimpse of a couple of the men dragging out the lady prompter who, as she got older, got stiffer, and there would be great noise and puffing and exclamations. All would settle down and the curtains would part. The audience, which had stopped applauding by now, renewed the applause and there in the middle of the stage stood the prompter, beaming happily, with the performers.

Next in importance to the prompter was the stage hand or *kulissi mies*, who frequently had an occupational hazard in his job of tippling. Perhaps it was to bolster himself for the evening's work. Who could blame him, however, for often he couldn't get to rehearsals and learn the cues of when to open and close the curtains, or role a piece of metal to make it sound like thunder. So there would be a last-minute briefing. Some were better than others and more alert, but it was not unusual to see a play end with the actors standing woodenly as a couple of them, perhaps thinking the audience couldn't see, whispering loudly from the upstage corner of their mouths, "Curtain, curtain." The stage hand had quite a job; he would have to change the heavy flats with the back metal props and also drop a corresponding scenery roller curtain in the back, or lift them—and they were heavy. He would lug furniture around and carry on make-believe rocks and even some scenes hammer a fence to the floor. One time in Warren, Ohio, the stage hand forgot to put a door in the centre at the back of the stage. The actor said his lines, turned and walked into the flat. He stood there and then, desperately seeking an exit, climbed out of a window beside where the door was supposed to be. This brought no little amusement to the audience, since just two lines previously one of the characters had looked out the window and commented on their being on the third floor.

Another time in Worcester, Massachusetts, a couple had a touching love scene on the stage, and to make it more dramatic, it was snowing. The snow came down in spurts (as it was thrown by the stage hand) but the audience was tolerant as usual and accepted it. However, they were a little startled when the entire bushel of snow together with the basket fell down on the stage beside the couple. But the actors were troopers. They continued with their touching scene, holding hands and going on with their lines. In a few moments, the stage hand came staggering out of the "woods", bent over, picked up the "snow," dumped it in the basket and staggered off stage. Then in another few moments, the clumps of snow began descending and the actors didn't even bat an eyelash. Now that's what can be called stage presence!

It was the job of the wardrobe mistress not only to costume the actors but also look after make-up and the set design as well. In some areas, three people did this one job. However, my mother did all three jobs for at least twenty years in Baltimore and I would help her with the make-up. Habit is hard to overcome. When the Finns were young, some of them were character actors and frequently played older people. They got used to the make-up artist asking them how old they were supposed to be. I can recall when I made up the face of a 65-year-old stage veteran and started to put the base on. He looked me in the eye, and seriously said he was supposed to be an older person and would need liner on his face for lines! I gently said that he wouldn't be needing it—all he would have to do is to act old.

The women who made costumes were often talented in sewing, and there was a distinct advantage to working as a domestic in a wealthy home, for when there was a play that showed rich people, the women knew what type of clothing was correct. There was one play I can recall in Baltimore when the cast from another city presented a play. This was done frequently; a group would "go on the road," visiting another Finnish community and everyone would have a wonderful time renewing old acquaintances. At any rate, in one scene, an actor came out munching on what was very obviously a baloney sandwich, and announced how good the caviar was—after all, it was *supposed* to be caviar. One could immediately tell that no woman in that cast ever worked in a *piika paikka*, a domestic job!

I can recall when we lived in Warren, Ohio, in the twenties when we went on the road with a play. One of the women had an old car with eisenglass windows, and it was a windy snowy day when we drove off to the neighbouring Finnish community of Conneaut. Actually, it turned into a blizzard but we made it to the hall, gave the show and came back that same night. But spirits were high coming back and I slept very warmly in the crush of human bodies—there must have been six or seven of us in that old car. Now when I read biographies of people in show business who talk about their times on the road, I think these brave Finns were every bit as professional in going on with the show!

Then there were the quick-thinking actors, as at the time in Lanesville, Massachusetts, when one of the actors had to stab someone in the play. He came to the moment when he was supposed to do it at the performance and he froze—he had forgotten his knife. However, being a real trooper he lunged forward and started to choke his fellow actor who, although startled, sensed that he should respond, gurgled appropriately and dramatically sank to the floor, dying beautifully. All would have been well and the audience never would have known the difference, except that the two other actors on the stage were not as imaginative and did not rise to the occasion. They were to scream, "He's been stabbed, he's been stabbed!" They could have quickly changed it to, "He's been choked, he's been choked!" But, alas, they stuck with the lines they had rehearsed.

In Baltimore, where all the men worked at the steel mill on three shifts, there were many occasions when they had to rehearse at midnight since that was the only time they could all get together. I can recall many times in the winter when members of the cast would huddle around a pot-bellied stove trying to get warm and waiting for their cue to go on the stage. During my childhood I can remember cueing my parents—kuiskaa-ing to them from the sides or roles they got from the Drama League. Very often the actors paid the rental for their roles or sides themselves when they ordered them from the League because they were trying to pay off the mortgage on the hall and felt this was one way to make a contribution. As a child, I can remember going to endless rehearsals, and when not in the show, sleeping on benches and listening to good-natured kidding of the theatrefolk. Very often, those who were most active in theatre were looked upon as bohemians by the rest of the Finns; and being show biz folk, they were more free in their speech and movement than the Finns who were never in plays. It was a miniature of the entire world where people in theatre are sometimes frowned upon because they are, to use an old-fashioned word, "loose."

The children were included in all theatrical enterprises and we had our own festivals where some of us got up on the stage, scared to death: some played the violin, or piano, some sang in quavering voices, some recited a poem, very fast, and some danced. I shall never forget in one melodrama a union leader had been murdered and his body was lying on the stage while the soloist was reciting very dramatically to the accompaniment of a piano. We got our cue and another girl and I, both of us in very healthy condition, came running out in white cheesecloth and flower bands in our hair and we skipped around the "corpse" tossing flowers on it. There wasn't a dry eye in the house, and after we got off the stage, we cried and cried, carried away with our own performance. My father then lectured to me as a fellow performer and said that no actor should ever lose control of himself—let the audience do the crying. He was a good actor, particularly at comedy, and had a real respect and love for theatre, and he was to teach me about going on with the show at a future time.

Frequently, there would be a dramatic moment when one of

the actors would whip out a gun and shoot someone, with blanks, of course. The first two or three rows were traditionally saved for the children. However, all we had to do was to see a gun and we would stampede to the back of the hall to the ladies' and gentlemen's cloakrooms where we huddled in the corners, fingers in our ears waiting for the loud shot. After the bang, we'd run back to our seats, giggling nervously and the adults would whisper loudly, "Kakarat, olkaa hiljaa", Children, be quiet. On a busy night in some of the shows, there were several stampedes and occasionally an adult would grab a child, any child as he or she flew by, and make him or her sit down. The most difficult moment for me when I was in a play was when my father was to be shot. He warned me ahead of time that I was to behave, and not panic on the stage. The actor brought out his gun and from the corner of my eye I could see all my friends scurrying to the back. Just as I was about to leap over the footlights and join the stampede, I saw my father give me a look (with his upstage eye) that reminded me of his lecture that a good actress fears nothing and the show must go on. I stood my ground and stayed on the stage acting appropriately.

As for other theatrical forms of expression, poetry was close to plays. And frequently the poems were very long indeed. As a child, I remember trying to keep a track of how many pages there were to go before the poem was concluded. There was always one of the reciters whose hands shook and this was universal in each Finnish community. Actually, in retrospect, I wish we had tapes of these artists, because most of them were remarkably good, and held their audiences spellbound. The most effective way to bring poetry as an art to the people was through group poetry presentations or *joukko runoja*. This was truly an art which, unfortunately, has not been developed in English. A group would recite in unison and have soloists, like a chorus, and could give a very effective dramatic presentation, as, for instance, the poem "Jaakko Ilkka," which may be too dramatic in today's world for some people but which, when recited, can raise the hairs of your neck and give you goose bumps if done well.

A unique form of entertainment was that of the balladeer or the *kupletti* singer, the word *kupletti* being derived from couplet. The *kupletti* singer made up dozens of humorous verses to the accompaniment of a popular song of the time, the theme based on what was going on in the Finnish community or the nation or even the world. However, there was an occupational failing tied to these singers; once they started, they were reluctant to stop. I can remember many times in Baltimore, after the *kupletti* singer had done his ballad and done it well, I would loudly applaud his performance and his creativity. One of the elder women in front of me would invariably turn around and say, "Don't applaud too loud, you'll encourage him to go on." She was right.

We had two of these singers in our community, and they were really talented. The trick for the audience was to applaud just enough to let the singer know they appreciated him but not enough to encourage him to favour us with another long presentation.

My mother had an ability to write short humorous monologues about events in the Finnish community and make some comments about the political scene. She wrote these in an Etelä-pohjanmaan accent, being inspired by the funny tales of Vaasan Jaakko. She would struggle for weeks to get a running motif for the monologues, then write them over and over and after each one read it to my father and me and we would make suggestions accordingly. And when she got up on the stage, both my father and I would sit there in a state going over each word mentally and suffering along with her.

Then there were the newspaper reviews. No matter which Finnish-American paper one subscribed to, I am sure they were all the same. After there was a play or a program at the hall, one of the people in the community would send a long review to the Finnish newspaper and all the cast members would wait anxiously to read what was said about their performances. They didn't sit up all night as they do in New York to get the *New York Times* and other newspapers' reviews, but the principle was the same. Sometimes there were hard feelings when someone was overly criticized and that would create a great deal of argument. We all had our favourite critics and tried to urge the "soft" ones to be sure to send in a review.

Each hall had its own theatre committee, and individuals would choose plays to be presented during the year and direct them. An aggressive director could persuade reluctant actors to take a part and this could be a chore, because, as with all efforts, some of the actors got just plain tired of doing nothing but attending rehearsals. Occasionally, a person who didn't know how to act at all would be drafted into a play, and at the performance, the audience would quietly mumble what a dreadful performance, but still gave the actor credit for trying. Then there were the really talented actors who, just by their presence on the stage, created an electric spark and made the evening come alive. We had a woman in Baltimore who was truly talented at both acting and directing.

Whenever she was to appear, there was bound to be a full house. She could do any type of a role and had such a magnetic personality that people couldn't take their eyes off her. She could have recited the telephone book and people would have remained under her spell.

Of course, at our hall, the plays and poetry reflected the radical perspective and the pro-union position and during the programs there were speeches which were an interesting art form. There were speakers and speakers. We children became quite adept in discerning who spoke the best. Some droned on and on, and we all quietly went to the back of the hall into the cloakrooms where we giggled and talked. Then there were some speakers who would dramatically raise their voices almost to a shout and then the next instance almost whisper so the audience had to struggle to hear every word. The techniques are universal to all speakers.

Just a brief word about music. The Finns had choruses, orchestras and bands and frequently had operettas. And often the person who was a musician was also an actor. I recall my father telling me how he studied the violin in Finland as a child and paid for his lessons by working for a shoemaker. He directed our orchestra at the hall in Warren, Ohio, and played for shows and dance music at our hall. He finally had to discontinue playing the violin when his fingers became too thick from doing manual work in the steel mill. But he was still able to conduct the chorus. He is typical of a great many of the Finns in their cultural expression, in their unbelievably hard work and sacrifice in developing their own group's culture. Each hall even had its own library with books on politics, theatre, sports, child care, art and even encyclopedias. There was a constant search to learn, and that is the essence of what I acquired from my background among the progressive and radical Finns.

And that is why I am here today, very happy that I can share some of these memories with you, some of which are mine and others of people whom I have interviewed. Mention should be made, of course, that we of the second generation, as we grew up, performed at the hall and worked with the first generation, and as our children grew, they participated at the hall as well. But it was never the same, because the interests of the second and third generation became more dispersed into the general community's activities and also the McCarthy period did real harm to some of the halls.

We have no hall left in Baltimore and the elders are dying off. But, for over sixty years, the immigrant Finns have gathered at halls and created their own culture—and a many-faceted culture at that—in addition to improving the living conditions of the working class. But this is not mentioned in any textbook; there is no comprehensive material available to the average school child, let alone the average citizen. They do not know of the wonderful theatre movement among the Finns, their poetry, their music. We in Baltimore are seeking to correct this through a slide show on the history of the Finns in Baltimore which we have developed with the aid of a local community college. Through conferences such as this I hope we may exchange information and perhaps seek a way to assure that future generations on this side of the Atlantic will have the opportunity to know of the contribution of the Finns to the cultural life.

# Finnish Dialects in America: Some Experiences and Problems

## Pertti Virtaranta

The study and recording of the Finnish language as spoken in America started somewhat later than similar studies of Norwegian or Swedish. Indeed, it was the studies among American Norwegians and American Swedes that inspired linguists to study spoken Finnish in America.[1] Of the Norwegian linguists, I would like to mention professor Einar Haugen and his classical work, *The Norwegian Language in America*, and his many papers on the subject.[2] The Swedish professor Folke Hedblom, who led three recording expeditions to study the Swedish-speaking Americans (in 1962, 1964 and 1966), has written detailed reports on the trips[3] and has published them with American Swedish texts and detailed comments.[4] Both these workers have given me much useful advice, both personally and from their publications, concerning recording and studying Finnish spoken in America.

Naturally, there have been several other contributors to this subject, some of whose work has been very useful. First, I want to mention the vocabulary of American Finnish, still unpublished, of 1,250 words assembled by V.S. Alanne, with its illustrative introduction. The following publications have also given me useful ideas: the work of Meri Lehtinen, *An Analysis of a Finnish-English Bilingual Corpus*, which is based on the language of only one informant (a third-generation American Finn); *Specimens of American Finnish. A Field Study of Linguistic Behavior*, by Siiri Sahlman-Karlsson; and some shorter papers by John Kolehmainen,[5] Lauri Karttunen,[6] Reino Virtanen[7] and Matti Kaups, whose papers deal with Finnish place names in Minnesota and Michigan,[8] among others.

There is up till now only one published work about the results of my own research concerning Finnish in America, "Finskan i Amerika," a general review of thirty pages written in Swedish.[9]

In addition, it is worth mentioning that since the end of the 1960s, the graduate theses concerning Finnish in America have been made under my supervision at the University of Helsinki. One of them is based on the students' own recordings in the United States during the years 1964-65; the others use material collected from American-Finnish newspapers, albums and other literature published in the United States. These graduate theses are kept as manuscripts at the Department of Finnish language at the University of Helsinki.

We have now about four hundred hours recorded spoken American Finnish on tape at the Archive of Recorded Spoken Finnish in Helsinki. The main part of it, two hundred and eight hours, was recorded on a two months' trip I made with my assistant Lauri Karttunen in 1965 to Ohio, Wisconsin, Minnesota and Michigan and Ontario in Canada.[10] During the same autumn, Lauri Karttunen alone recorded thirty hours of Finnish spoken by Finns living in Massachussetts.

Other recordings in the Archive include the work done by Meri Puromies in 1964-65 in New York, Massachussetts and Michigan, (32 1/2 hours), by Ritva Paavilainen, in 1972-73 in Minnesota (55 hours),[11] and by myself in the spring of 1975 in New York, Minnesota, and the region of Thunder Bay in Canada (38 hours).[12]

The work I am preparing at the moment is based on recordings kept at the Archive of Recorded Spoken Finnish (in the transcription of the tapes, I have occasionally been able to employ assistants, thanks to a grant from Suomen Tiedeseura—Societas Scientiarum Fennica). I have also used the notes I made during my trips, published papers and, particularly, the graduate theses made by my students.

This work will consist of three parts: the first part is a selection of free American Finnish speech from some one hundred interviews; the second part is an etymological dictionary of "Finglish"; the third part of the study is a survey of the characteristic features of Finglish.

I would like now to discuss some of the more interesting aspects of the Finglish dictionary. There are, at present about 4,000 words in my dictionary. The description of the word is presented as follows: first the word itself, followed by its grammatical category or part of speech, different variants of the word as they appear in Finglish, the meaning of the word, the English equivalent and finally, the most lengthy part, examples of the use of the word in spoken Finglish and in written American Finnish. At the end of each example, the person from whose speech the sentence has been recorded, or the printed reference (newspaper of album) from where the word has been taken, is mentioned in brackets.

Here is an example of such an entry: *Apar(t)mentti* s. ( = substantive, noun) ( = variants) apaatmentti - parmentti - paa(r)t-mentti - portmanti - öpaatmentti. (Finnish meaning) huoneisto 'flat'. (The American equivalent) apartment. Then several examples of which I mention one: Myytävänä viiden huoneen *portmanti* Suoma-laisessa Osuuskodissa – A five-room "portmanti" for sale in a Finnish cooperative home (Raivaaja, 1921).

The areas in which most words of English origin are found are generally those with which many of the emigrants would not have been familiar in the old country. Finns came to America from an environment with no mines and so they adopted the American mining terminology; but the words have of course been adapted to the Finnish language. For example, the English words *mine, miner, to mine* appear in American Finnish, as the forms *maini, mainari, mainata*.

A couple of examples of the last-mentioned word *mainata*: Niiltä (kaivosyhtiöiltä) loppu maa että ne ei voinu enääm mainata. – These [mining companies] worked out their land so that they could no longer continue mining (Henry Pellikka, 1964-65). Sen järven alta on mainattu oorit pois ja sitten taas täytetty vedellä. – They mined the ore from the lake bottom and then the lake filled with water again (*Amerikan Uutiset*, 1976).

There are also a number compound words, where the word *maini* is either the last or the first part. Examples of the former are: *kolimaini* 'coal mine', *kuparimaini* 'copper mine'. Examples of the latter case: *mainialue* 'mine district', *mainiengelska* 'mine English', *mainiherrat* 'the owners of the mine', *mainihomma* 'mine-work', *mainikapteeni* 'mining captain', *mainikomppania* 'mining company', *mainikontri* 'mining country', *mainikylä* 'mining village', *mainipaasi* 'mine boss', *mainirenssi* 'mine range', *mainityö* 'mine-work', *mainityöläinen* 'miner'.

To the mining vocabulary also belong the words *leveli* or *levuli* or *leveni* 'level', *pikka* 'pick', *pitti* 'pit' (Sinne saa ajaa junan sinnep *pittihin*. – You can drive the train right into the pit; Urho Lehtola, 1965), *safti* or *sahti* 'shaft' (se peipi, se oli minuv veljeni,—

kuoli, putos *safthin*. – The baby, it was my brother, died falling down the shaft; Emmi Lehtimäki, 1965), *trammata* or *rammata* 'to tram' (kuljettaa kaivosvaunua 'to drive a mine wagon')', *trifti* or *rifti* or *rihti* 'drift' (kaivoskäytävä 'mine gallery') (Meilloli semmonev vuoro että meijäm piti *rihti* puhistaaj ja sitten noustan niin toisellel levenille, rammaamaa. – We were in the shift that had to clean the drift and then climb to another level to tram; Pekka Autio, born in Kiuruvesi in Savo, 1965).

The word *oori* belongs also to the same subject and it has entirely superseded the Finnish word *malmi* (which actually is borrowed from the Swedish). The word *oori* also appears in several compound words, for example, *oorikaara* 'ore car', *oorilaiva* 'ore ship', *oorinhäntläys* 'ore handling', *ooripaatti* 'ore boat', *ooripaili* 'ore pile', *ooritokka* 'ore dock', *ooriveini* 'ore vein' (in Finnish *malmisuoni*).

The Finnish word *tehdas*, 'factory, works, mill', which incidentally is an old Scandinavian word, appears with this meaning in written Finnish as far as is known for the first time as late as 1838 in Kaarle Helenius's dictionary, and usage in this sense has developed rather slowly. Two words borrowed from Swedish, *vapriikki* (Swe. fabrik) and *ruukki* (Swe. bruk) preceded it and co-existed for a long time. The word *tehdas* does not appear at all in written American Finnish, and even in the spoken language it is rarely heard. In its place we have *mylly*—a word adopted from Swedish. See, for example, in an advertisement in a 1911 issue of *Raivaaja*: "Pumpulikankaita *myllyjen* hinnalla," meaning 'cotton fabrics for sale at factory prices'. The word appears also in many compound words, for instance: *myllykontir* 'industrial area' (as opposed to agricultural area), *kehruumylly* 'spinning mill', *kutomamylly* 'textile factory' (e.g., teimme kumpikin kovaa toyötä kutomamyllyssä. – We both worked hard at the textile Factory; *Finnish American Horizons*, p. 394), *lankamylly* 'wire mill', *paperimylly* 'papermill', *sahamylly* 'sawmill', *villamylly* 'spinning mill'.

Not until the end of the last century did the Finnish word *yhtiö* became generally accepted in its present meaning of 'company'. As its form is rather awkward compared to other Finnish words, it is not surprising that even those emigrants who were already acquainted with the word readily adopted the word *komppania* (already familiar as a military term) in place of *yhtiö*. It also appears in many compound words, e.g., *autokomppania* 'motor company', *insyyrikomppania* 'insurance company', *kämerakomppania* 'camera company', *laivakomppania* 'shipping company', *lääkekomppania* 'medical company', *mainikomppania* 'mining company', *nikkelikomppania* 'nickel company', *rautakomppania* 'ironworks', *telefoonikomppania* 'telephone company', *öljykomppania* 'oil company'.

Among words describing nationalities, the most familiar ones are the same in American Finnish as in Finnish, though in dialect form of course, so that *ruotsalainen* 'Swede, Swedish', referring to someone from the district of Etelä-Pohjanmaa, is usually *ruottalaanen* or *ruattalaanen*. But most of the names for nationalities have been adopted from English: e.g., *airis* or *aires* or *airesmanni* 'Irish'; *austrialainen* 'Austrian'; *estonialainen* 'Estonian'; *hunkerilainen, hankerilainen, unkerilainen, unkarialainen* 'Hungarian'; *intti* 'Indian'; *jukrain (i) alainen* 'Ukrainian'; *jänkki* or *jenkki* 'American, Yankee'; *kiinamanni* or *sainamanni* or *tsaini* 'Chinaman'; *kriikku* 'Greek'; *polakki* or *pulakki* 'Polack'; *slaavis* or *laavis*, Part. in.pl. *laaviksia* 'Slavic'; *talimanni* 'Italian' (Kyllä ne *talimannien* kans pärjäs paremmin, mutta *airesten* kans ne oli lujilla täällä. – It was easy to get along with the Italians, but they had difficulties with the Irish).

Some names for itinerant groups can be put in the above category: e.g., *aames* or *aamis*, usually in plural *aamekset* or *aamikset*, meaning members of a certain religious sect, Engl. Amish; *hilipilit* 'hillbillies' (mountain habitants of southern United States).

It is interesting to note that words connected with living are often borrowed from English. Even such words as *huone*(room) and *talo* (house) have had to make way for *ruuma* and *haussi*. A reason for this may be the great frequency of the words 'room' and 'house' in emigrant areas. The fact that names for individual rooms are borrowed from the English is easily explained by the fact that emigrants did not always have these rooms in their homes in Finland. Examples: *eturuuma* or *fronttiruuma* or *ronttiruuma* or *rontti* 'front room', *istumaruuma* 'sittingroom', *leporuuma* 'slumbering-room', *paatiruuma* 'bathroom', *petiruuma* 'bed room', *ruokaruuma* or *syömäruuma* or *tainiruuma* or *taininkiruuma* 'dining-room', *restiruuma* 'restroom'. Other parts of the building: *alalattia* 'ground floor', *portsi*'porch', *upstee* 'upstairs', *ätikki* or *ätikkä* 'attic'.

But why is *keittiö* 'kitchen', also *kyökki, köökki* etc. in Finnish dialects, not acceptable, but is replaced by *kitsi?* It may be because almost all other house and living terminology is borrowed. A contributing factor may have been the divergence in pronunciation of the Finnish word *keittiö* (and of the dialectal *köökki* etc.) in relation to English pronunciation.

In most cases a likely or a possible motive can be found for adopting a given loan word from English as can be seen from the examples above.

But above are also the words *haussi, ruuma, kitsi*, where the motive for borrowing is not quite clear. There are other such words whose adoption is difficult to understand, such as *elkki* 'elk', *hilli* 'hill', *huntata* (rarely *hantata*) 'to hunt', *jaarti* 'yard', *leeki* or *leiki* 'lake', *paksi* 'box', *piltata* 'to build', *ti (i) tsata* 'to teach', *äpyli* 'apple'. Why were the Finnish words *hirvi, mäki, metsästää, piha, jävi, laatikko, rakentaa, opettaa, omena* generally not used?

Each case should to be considered separately, and if one searches hard enough, an explanation will be found. For instance, why *leeki* or *leiki* and not *järvi?* Many emigrants came from Pohjanmaa, from districts where lakes are scarce. Another reason could be found in the *lake*-ending place names of the new home district: e.g., French Lake (Minnesota), Vermilion Lake (Minnesota), Beaver Lake (Ontario), Black Lake (Ontario), which for American Finns when speaking Finnish became *fransleiki* or *ransleeki, miljoonaleeki, piiverleeki, pläkleeki.*

The reason for borrowing the English verb 'to hunt' to form the American Finnish *huntata*, could lie in the fact that Finnish emigrants had many expressions for the word, in not only *metsästää*, but also *pyytää, saalistaa, käydä metsällä* or *metsää, jahdata, mennä jahtiin, olla jahdissa.* Perhaps it was a relief for the user of the language to shift from the many words of different nuances of meaning to the neutral word *huntata*, which easily adapts to the structure of the Finnish language.

When studying American Finnish loan words, attention is drawn to the fact that among them there are words which have appeared in Finnish before emigration but in a different meaning and having a different origin. Among these homonymic words there are the following: *kädi*, in Finnish 'cuckoo'—in Finglish 'keg (barrel)'; *majuri* 'major' (military rank)—'mayor'; *mestari* 'master'—'mister'; *parkata* 'to strip bark'—'to park (a car)'; *petata* 'to make the bed'—'to bet' (lyödä vetoa); *piiri* 'circle, cistrict'—'beer'; *pussata* 'to kiss'—'to push'; *raitti* 'village road'—'ride'; *ratti* 'cloth'—'rat', *siima*'fishing line',—seam' (in Finnish *kallion halkeama*).

How does language tolerate homonyms in these and other such cases? In most cases the older meaning has become obsolete, e.g., in the words *parkata,piiri, siima.*

With reference to homonyms, I would like to mention one more case, with an explanation as to its existence. The verb *kuitata* in Finglish comes from 'to quit' i.e., 'to give notice'. In Finnish *kuitata* is a word borrowed from Swedish and means "to receipt". Perhaps the meaning of this older word had so little application for the emigrants that the *kuitata* of English origin easily replaced it.

In addition to the naturalized words considered above, there are many so-called loan translations and loan shifts in American Finnish. I will mention a few examples: *alakaupunki* 'downtown' (in Finnish: *keskikaupunki, keskusta*), *alasmaksu* 'down payment' (in Finnish: *ennakko(maksu), epäummärrys* 'misunderstanding' (in Finnish: *väärinymmärrys*), *jokayksi* 'everyone' (in Finnish: *katuvaunu* 'street car' (in Finnish: *raitiovaunu*), *korkeakoulu* 'high school', *myyntivero* 'sales tax' (Tuo neljän sentin *myyntivero* kylläkin pyritään saamaan käytäntöön hyvin kierällä tavalla—They are trying to introduce this four cent sales tax in a very cunning way. *Työmies-Eteenpäin*, 1967); in Finnish: *ostoksista maksettava lisävero, liikevaihtovero, parasmies* 'best man at a wedding' (in Finnish: *sulhaspoika*), *tervatie* 'tar ad' (in Finnish: *öljysoratie*), *vanhamaa* 'old country' (Finland), *ylioikeus* 'the Supreme Court' (in Finnish: *korkein oikeus*).

Loan translations include also such loan shifts, where an already existing word is given new applications as a result of English influence. I will take as an example the word *antaa*, the application of which is greatly extended by the English 'to give':

(1) Miss Davison *antoi pianosoolon* (Työmies-Eteenpäin, 1967), English, give a piano recital; (2) "Markus-Setäkin" koettaa tehdä parhaansa, sillä sanomalehtitietojen mukaan hän on ollut *antamassa ohjelmaa* Suomen orpolapsille" (*Orvon joulu*, 1945), English, give a program; (3) Nyt ne täälläkin *antaa huomiota* kielille (Loviisa Tikkala, 1964-65), English to give attention to; (4) *antaa lunse*, English, to give a lunch; (5) *antaa juhlat*, English, to give a party; (6) Tastulan pelimannit *antavat konsertin* Saiman puistossa alkaen klo 8 ill. (Raivaaja, 1971), English, to give a concert; (7) Keijolla on neljättätoista vuotta vanha poika ja se o ahkera kalastammaaj ja se *anto* mullen *telehvoonikoulin* että "remma, hällä on kaloja sinullen" (Iida Saarela, 1965), English, to give someone a (telephone) call; (8) *syytä* tekoon *ei annettu* (Amerikan Uutiset, 1970), English, to give a reason for; (9) Foorti *antaa* hyvän *sörviisin* (Tauno Kartiala, 1964), English, to give a service; (10) *antaa ylös*, English, to give up.

In the speech and writing of American Finns there exists yet a third category of loan words, the domesticated words, i.e., words which have been taken from English without changing their pronunciation or spelling. Generally speaking, I have not included these words in my dictionary, but they are discussed in the third part of the study. Usually they are short, separate words or concise expressions, such as:

Valtaluokan mielestä avaruuden tavoittelu on suuresta merkityksestä, niinpä voi ollakin. *Who knows!* (*Industrialisti*, 1950).

Laskemattomat olivat ne ilta ateriat, joita me nälkäiset saimme nauttia niistä herkuista joita ei lähetetty dumbwaiterilla *upstairs*, mutta nautittiin siellä missä ne olivat valmistetut, *downstairs* (*Finnish American Horizons*, p. 132).

More examples: *all right, any time, excuse me, half and half, I don't know, let's see, my goodness, okay, too bad, too late, well, you know.*

The extent of borrowing of English words varies among American Finns. Loan words are used least amongst first-generation emigrants and in areas where the emigrant can easily manage speaking only Finnish, for example in small Finnish farming villages. More of these words appear in the speech of those who have worked with people of other nationalities (in other words, with the so-called *kieliset*), in the mines, in forestry, on the railroads, as cab-drivers, as housemaids, etc. To a great extent the frequency of borrowed words used depends on the spoken subject. If an old emigrant is reminiscing—as he willingly does—about his childhood and youth back in the old country, then very few loan words appear. In a speech lasting an hour, which comprises after all from 5,000 to 7,000 words, there might be only two or three borrowed words. But the number of loan words increases if the subject is changed, for example, to mining, agricultural and other machinery or politics. I have made the same observation when looking at the "peoples' letters" of American Finn newspapers: When they describe trips to Finland, borrowed words are few and far between.

A student of mine studied English word loans in the American Finnish of peoples' letters in three newspapers (*Industrialisti, Työmies-Eteenpäin* and *Vapaus*). His material consisted of about 386,000 words, and in this material there appeared only about 1,800 borrowed words (i.e., naturalized words, loan translations, and domesticated words)—in other words, only one word of English origin per about 220 words. An interesting detail found in this relatively extensive study material is the following: 1,400 naturalized cases comprised 241 different words, and over a half of the cases involve only five words, *haali* (hall) 400 times, *unio* (union) 150 times, *kaunti* (county) 100 times, *parkki* (park) 80 and *piknekki* (picnic) 40 times.

When looking at the structure of American Finnish loan words, it is important to be familiar with the phonology of the Finnish language, including Finnish dialects. When dealing with the material one should know the original dialect of the Finnish-speaking emigrant, or, if he is a second-generation emigrant, the original dialect of both parents, particularly of the mother. When dealing with written American Finnish, we naturally do not always know the author or writer, and neither do we know how much the editor of the book or newspaper has changed the language. However the old home district of the correspondent is often revealed in his text.

I would like to take one example to illustrate the importance of knowing Finnish dialects in order to understand divergences appearing within American Finnish. In the westernmost dialects of Finland there appear words beginning with *f*—as a result of Swedish influence and the use of Swedish loan words; but some are also the districts's own expressive words. Thus emigrants speaking these dialects are able to pronounce an *f* at the beginning of a word and are also able to pronounce it in English words originally beginning with *f*. But people coming from outside the *f*-district of Finland haven't generally been able to pronounce the *f*, but have replaced it with a sound phonetically close to it, namely *v*, or in the case of a group of consonants beginning with *f*, have left out the *f*.

Examples: The English word "farmer" and "farm" have been borrowed into American Finnish. People from westernmost Finland use the words in the following forms: *farmari* or *farmeri* or *farmi*, but people coming from the east of that sector use *varmari* or *värmäri*, *varmi* or *värmi*, *foni* or *fonni* or *fani* and *voni* 'funny', *foonata* and *voonata* 'phone', *fortti* or *förtti* and *vörtti* 'forty' (40 acres), *fortsulai* or *förtsylai* and *vortsulai* or *vörtsylai* (even *portsulai*) 'Fourth of July'.

A couple of examples of consonant groups with an *f*- beginning: *fluu* and *luu* (*influenza*), *frontti* and *rontti* (front). If the *f* is in the middle of the word, then people coming from westernmost Finland are able to pronounce it, but others usually cannot; for instance, in the word 'office' one hears it pronounced *ofiisi* and *offiisi*, but among emigrants from the Savo-district it is *ohviisi* and even *ovviisi*.

That area of Finnish dialects where we find certain clusters of two consonants at the beginning of a word (*kl-*, *kr-*, *pl-*, *pr-*, *tr-*) in words of Swedish origin and in expressive words, extends somewhat further inland than the *f*-district, but limits itself to the western parts of the western dialects. In other Finnish dialects we have in the place of these consonant clusters only the second consonant. In the speech of American Finns, the pronunciation of these words (and there are a lot of them) depends on the original dialect of the speaker. For instance:

to clean: *kliinata - liinata* (Ne *liinas* sen haussin tässä nyv viime viikolla. – They cleaned this house just last week; Emma Mäki).

clerk: *klärkki* or *klörkki - lärkki*
club: *klupi, klupihaussi - lupi*
Cleveland: *kliivelanti - Liivelanti*
grandmother: *krämma - remma*
creamery: *kriimeri - riimeri*
grocery store: *krosseristoori - rosseritoori*
to play: *pleijata - leijata*
blanket: *plänketti - länketti*
princilap (teacher): *prinssipooli - rinssipaali*
brandy: *pränti - ränti*
tram car: *trammakaara - rammakaara*
train: *treini - reini*
truck: *troki - roki*
trap: *träppi*, corresponding verb *träpätä, träppäillä - räppi, räpätä*
trouble: *troupuli* or *trupeli* or *trupelli - roupuli, rupeli*

Consonant components with an *s*-beginning are unknown in Finnish dialects. This shows in American Finnish loan words in that the *s*-component of the group in question is usually pronounced only by second-generation emigrants or by others with extremely good knowledge of English. For in instance:

store: *stoori - toori*
to skid: *skitata - kitata* (in Finnish *hinata*)
street: *striitti - riitti*
strike: *straikki - traikki - raikki*

To illustrate the use of vowels I will take only one example. In American Finnish there is such a duality in some words that one version is based on the English pronunciation and the other on the spelling, e.g.:

a - ä    English, accident: *aksitentti - äksitentti* (even *eksitentti*)
         English, catholic: *katolikki - kätlikki*
e - i    English, relief: *reliffi - rili (i)ffi, rili (i) hvi*
o - a    English, job: *jopi - japi*
         English, box: *poksi* (Olin työssä Anderssonin sahamyllyllä ja sitten menin Länsirannikon suurimpaan *poksitehtaaseen* työhön. – I was working in Andersson's sawmill and then I went to work in the biggest Westcoast box factory; *Finnish American Horizon*, p. 171) - *paksi*

English, solid: *solitti, soletti - saletti, saletisti* 'surely'
*u - o - a* English, bus: *pussi - possi* - usually *passi*
*aa - oo* English, hall: *haali - hooli*
English, to call: rarely *kaalata* - usually *koolata*
Concerning other changes in the adaptation process there are
two particularly interesting groups:

1. If the main stress in English is on the second syllable, in
Finglish the first syllable has generally been omitted. For example:
about; *pautti*; appraise; *preissata*; economy; *kaanami;* employment;
*loimanni*; enough; *naffiksi - nahviksi - nohviksi* (mullon täh nyj jo
*naffiksi* tropulia rintasuonis. – I have already enough trouble with
my chest, said Isidor Seppälä 1965, born in Jurva, Etelä-Pohjanmaa); example; *sämppeli;* society; *saiti.*

2. There is a group of loan words, which in English are
usually or always in the plural. Often they have been adopted to
Finglish in this s-ending form, for example: English, bean-s; *pinssi,*
*pinsi, piinssi* (in *Raivaaja*, 1941: *pinssi-illalliset syödään Allstonin*
*suomalaisella haalilla tämän viikon lauantaina.* – *Bean feast will*
*be held at Allstone Finnish Hall, Saturday of this week); carrot-s;*
*käretsi;* cookie-s; *kukes*, in plural *kukekset, kukeksit, kukessit;* grape-
s; *kreipsi;* compounds *kreipsimaa, kreipsimehu, kreipsipäsketti;*
matche-s; *mätses*, in plur. *mätsekset* or *mätsis, mätsikset;* thing-s;
*tinksi* (se (kello) oli komia *tinksi.* – *That watch was a beautiful*
*thing); tomatoe-s; tomeetus, tomeitus;* tool-s; *tulsu*, in plur. *tulsut,*
compound *tulsupaksi* 'tool box'.

In general, Finglish is a very stable form of language. Insta-
bility occurs only in words which are particularly difficult to adopt
to Finnish, because of great structural differences between Finnish
and English. For instance:

English 'furnace' (oven for central heating and smelting) has
given at least the following forms in Finglish: *föönes, fööneskä,*
*fones, fönös - vönös, fönessi, fö̈örnessi, föörnissa, foorniska, förnes,*
*förnessi, förnis, förnissa, förnissi.* For the word 'drug store' there
are in my notes, the forms *rakstoori, reksitoori, rikstoori, rukstoori,*
*rykstoori.*

The English word 'restaurant' has given at least the forms to
follow: *restorantti, restoräntti, ristiräntty, rästäräntti, rästöräntti.*

An especially awkward expression is the English 'social security'. Yet it is a necessary term for all Finnish Americans and has
therefore been adopted into Finnish. The results of this process are
as follows: *sosialikiäri, souselkieri, sosiaalisikeritti, sosiaalisikuretti,*
*sosiaalisikyrity, sosiaalisekyyri, sosiaalisikyyri* and *sosialistisikuretti.*

English phonetics has influenced Finglish generally only in
cases where the knowledge of English has been perfect. In the

speech of these people one can notice an intonation not normally found in Finnish, for example a rising tone at the end of an interrogative sentence. In the speech of these people the clusters *k*, *t*, *p* at the beginning of words can be found aspirated (*k'* ,*t'*, *p'* ) in the English loan words, for example, *k'aletsi* or *k'aaletsi* 'College', *p'ointmentti* 'appointment' and the *l*-sound can be strongly velarated (thick*r*), especially in citation loans, for example, 'well'.

The textual part of my study concerning the American Finnish language contains a selection of about a hundred specimens of Finnish American everyday speech. It should be remembered that these are not literary language but are transcribed from tapes in a manner understandable to non-specialists. The speakers' Finnish origin and domicile in America are briefly presented as well as other relevant details. Each text is accompanied by comments. The majority of these texts are spoken by first-generation emigrants. Only a small portion are derived from persons born in America of Finnish parents.

Although the texts have been gathered for research into aspects of fundamental linguistics, I should like to point out that they also throw considerable light on the life of the emigrant at this time and the way of thinking of the American Finns. The subjects discussed in depth the following themes: life in the old country before their departure for America, their reasons for leaving Finland, their voyage to America, life of the farmers, miners, forest workers, fisherman, domestic servants, etc. Other themes discussed are organizational activities, contacts with other American Finns, Finland, observations on other peoples such as Indians, relations with other migrating peoples, comparisons between American and the old country and, also, appraisal of their present conditions.

The latter part of my study is a considerably expanded version of my article "Finnish language in America" published in Swedish in 1971. It is a study of the characteristics of American Finnish language and of its phonologic and morphologic features and, indeed, of its syntactic aspects too. One of the more important considerations, as discussed by Folke Hedblom and others on American Swedish, is that, when studying American emigrant languages, the local home dialect should be taken into account. Without a knowledge of this background, many differences prevailing within American Finnish might not have been analysed.

American Finnish can also provide interesting data on Finnish dialects at the turn of the century. It is a fact that many old American Finns have kept up their original home dialect better than their contemporaries in Finland. Spoken language in Finland has, during recent decades, had what one might call a balancing effect on Finnish local dialects. I intend also to discuss such aspects as loan words and loan motivation. Some linguistic-sociological observations will also be presented.

My study of American Finnish has demanded much more effort than I anticipated when I started fifteen years ago, as is often the case in scientific studies. There are still many questions and omissions to consider. In order to further this study, I plan to make a third trip to America, to both the United States and Canada. I will be accompanied by two of my assistants, both of them gathering material for their doctor's thesis, namely Hannele Jönsson-Korhola, interested in the language of second- and third-generation Finns, and Maija Kainulainen, who is currently working on a socio-linguistic study of American Finnish. Maija Kainulainen intends to collect data from some families in which three generations still live together.

# Notes

1. See my article "Valtamerentakainen työmaa" (Search of Work across the Sea) in *Valvoja* (1964), pp. 1-5.

2. E.g. "Binlingualism in the Americas: A Bibliography and Research Guide," *Publication of the American Dialect Society*, 26 (1956); *Bilingualism, Language Contact and Immigrant Languages in the United States: A Research Report 1956-1970*, Current Trends in Linguistics, Vol. 10, 1973, pp. 505-91; "A Case of Grass-roots Historiography: Opdalslaget and its Yearbooks" in *Norwegian Influence on the Upper Midwest*, pp. 42-49, (Duluth, 1976).

3. In *Svenska Landsmål*: 1962, pp. 113-57; 1965 pp. 1-34; 1966, pp. 97-115; 1970, pp. 26-35; in *Namn och Bygd*, 1966, pp. 127-40 and in *The Swedish Pioneer Historical Quarterly* (April 1967), pp. 76-92.

4. E.g. In *Svenska Landsmål*: 1969, pp. 1-52 and 1977, pp. 7-93.

5. E.g. "Finnish Surnames in America" in *American Speech*, 2 (1939), pp. 33-38.

6. "American Finnish (Finglish)", Indiana University, Department of Linguistics (May 31, 1966), 22 pp.

7. "Finnish Language in America" in *Scandinavian Studies*, 51 (1979) pp. 146-61.

8. "Finnish Place Names in Minnesota: A Study in Cultural Transfer" in *The Geographical Review*, LVI, no 3 (1966), pp. 377-97; "Finnish Place-Names in Michigan" in *Michigan History*, (Winter 1967), pp. 335-47; "Finnish Place Names as a Form of Ethnic Expression in the Middle West, 1880-1977", *Finnish Americana*, 1 (1978), pp. 51-70.

9. *Språk i Norden* (Stockholm, 1979), pp. 79-109.

10. See my article "Suomen kieli Amerikassa" (The Finnish Language in America) in *Suomen Silta*, 2 (1966), pp. 6-9.

11. Ritva Paavilainen, "Amerikansuomea talletettu ääninauhaan" (Americanfinnish as recorded) in *Seulaset*, 4 (1973), pp. 3-4.

12. See my article "Amerikansuomea tutkimassa" (Studying American-Finnish) in *Seulaset*, 2 (1975), pp. 2-5 and *Siirtolaisuus-Migration*, 3 (1975), pp. 19-28.

# Contributors

**Robert F. Harney,** Professor of History, University of Toronto. He is the President and Academic Director of the Multicultural History Society of Ontario, and is the author of numerous works on ethnic studies, primarily on Italian emigration and settlement in North America.

**Michael Karni,** editor of *Finnish Americana,* has written and edited several works on Finnish immigration including *For the Common Good: Finnish Immigrants and the Radical Response to Industrial America.*

**John I. Kolehmainen,** Professor of History and Government, Heidelberg College, Tiffin, Ohio, can be considered the Dean of Finnish immigration history. He has published widely on the immigration of Finns to North America, has been awarded two Fulbright professorships to Finland, was decorated with the First Class Order of the Finnish Lion and was recently awarded an honorary degree by Turku University.

**A. William Hoglund,** Professor of History at the University of Connecticutt, Storrs, has written extensively on Finnish immigration to the United States, including the well known volume *Finnish Immigrants in America 1880-1920.*

**Arnold R. Alanen,** Associate Professor, Department of Landscape Architecture, University of Wisconsin, Madison, is the author of numerous works on Finnish immigration including "In Search of the Pioneer Finnish Homesteader in America" in *Finnish Americana.*

**Matti Kaups,** Professor of Geography and Ethnohistory at the University of Minnesota, Duluth, has published widely on Finnish, Swedish and Norwegian immigration to the western Great Lakes region. He is the recipient of the Personal Medal of King Carl XVI of Sweden for his contribution to Swedish-American studies and relations.

**Marsha Penti,** a Ph.D. candidate in Folklore at Indiana University in Bloomington, is the author of "The America Letters: Immigrant Accounts of Life Overseas" published in *Finnish Americana.*

**Michael M. Loukinen,** Associate Professor of Sociology, Northern Michigan University, Marquette, is the director of a documentary film titled *Finnish Immigrant Lives* and has published articles on immigrants in Michigan including "Social Relations and the Maintenance of Ethnic Culture in Finnish American Rural Communities" in *Finnish Americana.*

**William R. Copeland,** Docent of Political History, University of Helsinki, is the author of *The Uneasy Alliance: Collaboration between the Finnish Opposition and the Russian Underground, 1899-1902.*

**Arthur E. Puotinen,** Dean of Academic Affairs, Lenoir-Rhyne College, Hickory, North Carolina, is the author of *Finnish Radicals and Religion in Midwestern Mining Towns.* He was formerly Dean of Faculty, Suomi College, Hancock, Michigan.

**George Hummasti,** Assistant Professor of History at the University of California, San Diego, at La Jolla, is the author of *Finnish Radicals in Astoria, Oregon, 1904-1940.*

**Marvin G. Lamppa,** Director of the Iron Range Interpretive Program, State of Minnesota, has published and lectured widely on the history of northeastern Minnesota. He is the author of "Ghost Towns of the Vermilion and East Mesabi Iron Districts."

**Marianne Wargelin Brown,** Ph.D. candidate in American Studies, University of Minnesota, is the author of "*Naiset Mukaan*: An Introductory Survey of Finnish American Immigrant Feminism, 1893-1921."

**Carl Ross,** Research and Resource Consultant, Immigration History Research Center, University of Minnesota, is the author of *The Finn Factor in American Labor, Culture and Society.*

**Riitta Stjärnstedt,** MA candidate, Turku University, is writing her thesis on women in the Finnish American labor movement.

**Timo Riippa,** Teaching Associate in Finnish, Scandinavian Department, University of Minnesota, has worked at the Immigration History Research Center, served as translator and as associate editor of *Finnish Americana.*

**Sirkka Tuomi Lee,** member of the Baltimore Neighborhood Heritage Advisory Committee, has in recent years been engaged in gathering oral histories in the city of Baltimore. She has extensive experience on the Finnish American stage.

**Pertti Virtaranta,** Professor of the Finnish Language, Helsinki University, has studied Finnish dialects in different parts of the world including the Soviet Union. He has written widely on various aspects of linguistics and has served for twenty-five years as the editor-in-chief of the Karelian language dictionary. Since 1969 he has also served as the chairman of the Council for Instruction of Finnish for Foreigners.